Real Estate Investment Analysis and Taxation

Second Edition

PAUL F. WENDT

Professor, College of Business,
University of Georgia, Athens

ALAN R. CERF

Professor, School of Business
Administration, University of California, Berkeley

McGraw-Hill Book Company

New York   St. Louis   San Francisco   Auckland
Bogotá   Düsseldorf   Johannesburg   London
Madrid   Mexico   Montreal   New Delhi
Panama   Paris   São Paulo   Tokyo
Singapore   Sydney   Toronto

Library of Congress Cataloging in Publication Data

Wendt, Paul Francis, date.
    Real estate investment analysis and taxation.

    Includes bibliographical references and index.
    1. Real estate investment—United States.   2. Real
property and taxation—United States.   I. Cerf, Alan
Robert, joint author.   II. Title.
HD1375.W37   1979   332.6'324'0973   78-8928
ISBN 0-07-069281-5

The editors for this book were W. Hodson Mogan and Esther Gelatt,
the designer was Naomi Auerbach, and the production supervisor
was Thomas Kowalczyk. It was set in Optima
by The Kingsport Press.

Printed and bound by The Kingsport Press

Contents

Preface

The present volume is addressed to both the professional and academic real estate community concerned with the theory and practice of real estate investment. The warning about "get-rich-quick" ideas for the real estate investor expressed in the preface to the 1969 edition proved more than justified during the catastrophic years from 1973 to 1976. Meanwhile, the persistent inflationary trends in the world economy continue to attract investment capital to real estate assets.

The discounted-cash-flow framework set forth in the first edition has been widely accepted in the current literature of real estate investment. Early computer programs for estimating the internal rate of return on real estate investment have been supplanted by more sophisticated programs permitting calculation of overall capitalization rates, Ellwood rates, percent cash on cash, internal rates of return, and adjusted internal rates of return allowing for "safe" reinvestment rates. Some of the computer programs illustrated in this edition also permit sensitivity analysis of the influence upon estimated investment values of changes in target rates of return, financing terms, residual sale prices, and investors' ordinary tax rates.

These techniques have sharpened analytical procedures but have not eliminated the all-important elements of judgment involved in forecasting the uncertain future of gross operating income, expenses, interest rates, taxes, and other important determinants of investment returns.

The general organization of the book is similar to that of the first edition. The discussion of tax considerations has been condensed to two chapters, which include a discussion of the 1976 Tax Reform Act. A case study exploring the effects of recent and probable future changes in real estate tax-shelter legislation emphasizes the key importance of federal tax laws upon real estate investment.

A new chapter added on land development and investment, including a case study on planned unit development, reviews the recent trends in land values. The chapter on real estate investment and portfolio strategy has been expanded to include case material on REITs and other institutional portfolios and outlines a framework for developing a balanced portfolio including real estate and other investments.

Based upon long-term projections in the President's budget summary for 1977 and 1978 and national econometric forecasts, the final chapter proposes a diversified real estate portfolio for a hypothetical investor and analyzes the projected returns and risks. Estimated after-tax yields on diversified portfolios including municipal bonds, common stocks, and real estate investments are also examined in the final chapter.

Adequate acknowledgment of the assistance of the many individuals and institutions providing statistical data, market summaries, and case studies is difficult. Robert Ellis, Vice President of Coldwell Banker Company, very generously permitted the use of selected tables and figures from the publication "Real Estate Investment Analysis." The editors of *Fortune* Magazine granted permission for use of excerpts from Eleanore Carruth, "The Skyscraping Losses in Manhattan Office Buildings" in the February 1975 issue. Professors Keith V. Smith and David Shulman agreed to our use of portions of their valuable article "The Impact of Tax Reform on Apartment House Investments," published in the *Real Estate Review* for Spring 1974. William Applebaum permitted use of research material related to the Del Monte Center project from his work "Shopping Center Strategy." The National Association of Real Estate Investment Trusts, Building Owners and Managers Association, International, Michael Sumicrast of The National Association of Homebuilders, and Thomas R. J. Bracken, Manager, Real Estate Investment Department of the Prudential Insurance Corporation of Newark cooperated in providing guidance and material. The cooperation of the Institute of Real Estate Management; The American Institute of Real Estate Appraisers; Richard W. Seeler, President, Cross and Brown Company; and the Editors of the *Real Estate Review* is acknowledged. The Landmarks Group, Inc., of Atlanta, Georgia, provided material for the case problem in planned unit development in Chap. 9. Special acknowledgment is made to Bruce Feldman and Herbert Herman of Decisionex for permission to reproduce a case study illustrating the QUICK DCF program. Steven E. Novick, Editor, *Income Property Finance Report,* granted permission to reproduce a sample copy of the Report.

Dr. Paul F. Wendt assumed responsibility for Chaps. 1 to 3, 7, 9, and 10, and Professor Alan R. Cerf wrote the final draft of Chaps. 4 to 6 and 8. Susan Foley and Beatrice London were of immeasurable assistance in typing several drafts of the manuscript. Elizabeth P. Richardson assumed the always difficult task of final editing.

Real estate investment is one of the most diverse, dynamic, and challenging areas of investment, impinged upon by a host of international, national, regional, and local developments. It is hoped that the authors' efforts will provide some useful guidelines and analytical insights for institutional and individual investors and for the student.

Paul F. Wendt
Alan R. Cerf

ONE

Introduction to Real Estate Investment

An old axiom states that it is easier to *make* money than to *keep* it. Real estate investment can be characterized as the art of preserving capital, as distinguished from real estate development or speculation, which are generally viewed as avenues to rapid capital appreciation.

Inevitably, the distinctions between real estate investment and speculation are blurred, as high-risk investments at time A become recognized at time B as speculations. Similarly, disappointed real estate developers or speculators may unwittingly find themselves committed to long-run holding for investment returns of property originally bought for short-run profits.

What special information and capabilities do investors in real estate need?

First, they should know something about the historical background of real estate investment, its special characteristics, and its relationships to other classes of investment. This overview of the place of real estate investment in the economy should be supplemented by comparison between long-run trends in returns from real estate investment and other investments. With this background, the investor can approach specific problems of real estate investment policy and analysis.

The following questions provide the framework for the chapters to follow:

1. What is the present and possible future importance of land use, taxation, economic growth, and other public policies to the real estate investor?

2. What is meant by real estate investment value, and how should it be determined? How is it related to market value and other value concepts?

3. How should investors measure yield on real estate, and what is the historical record of real estate investment yields?

4. What is the present and future significance of federal income tax provisions affecting the income from real estate?

5. What special investment analysis techniques are most suitable for analyzing major classes of real estate investments?

6. What portion of portfolio assets should be held in various classes of real estate investments by different classes of investors?

The historical background of real estate investment, its special characteristics, relationship to the public sector, and trends in issuance of real estate debt and equity securities will be reviewed in this chapter.

Concepts and measurement of real estate investment value and yields and historical yield trends will be discussed in Chap. 2. Chapter 3 will explore in more detail the applications of present value theory and cash-flow analysis in real estate investment decisions. A general model for determining after-tax cash-flow yields and calculating investment yields on real estate will be presented.

Succeeding chapters will deal with the special tax aspects of real estate investment and with the analytical techniques applicable to special classes of real estate investments. The final chapter will deal with real estate portfolio construction and analysis.

HISTORICAL BACKGROUND

"Under all is the Land," the preamble to the code of ethics of the National Association of Realtors, reflects the historic foundation for real estate investment. Records of real estate transactions are as ancient as written history. Jeremiah described the injunction of the Lord to invest in land at Anathoth near Jerusalem in 500 B.C., when the city was about to be destroyed.

> Jeremiah said, "The word of the Lord came to me: Behold, Hanamel the son of Shallum your uncle will come to you and say, 'Buy my field which is at Anathoth, for the right of redemption by purchase is yours' . . . , And I bought the field at Anathoth from Hanamel my cousin, and weighed out the money to him, seventeen shekels of silver. . . .
>
> After I had given the deed of purchase to Baruch, the son of Neriah, I prayed to the Lord saying: "Ah, Lord God! . . . Behold, the seige mounds have come up to the city to take it, . . . and the city is given to the Chaldeans who are fighting against it . . . Yet Thou, O Lord God, hast said to me, 'Buy the field for money and get witnesses' — though the city is given into the hands of the Chaldeans. . . .
>
> The word of the Lord came to Jeremiah. Just as I have brought all this great evil upon this people, so I will bring upon them all the good that I promise them. . . . Fields shall be bought for money, and deeds shall be signed and witnessed . . . for I will restore their fortunes, says the Lord."
>
> JEREMIAH 32.

Millions of immigrants came to the United States with the hope and expectation of owning land, a privilege traditionally reserved to only a few in Europe but protected by the Fifth Amendment to the Constitution.

A real estate analyst recently quoted George Washington on the advantages of land ownership during periods of inflation.

> A moment's reflection must convince you of two things: first, that lands are of permanent value, that there is scarce a possibility of their falling in price, but almost a moral certainty of their rising exceedingly in value; and secondly, that our paper currency is fluctuating, that it has depreciated considerably, and that no human foresight can, with precision, tell how low it may get as the rise or fall of it depends on contingencies which the utmost stretch of human sagacity can neither foresee nor prevent.[1]

He went on to echo Washington's philosophy in his 1975 prediction that underlying economic forces of inflation and related capital shortages would result in an increase in the investment value and a strong market for high-quality, well-designed, and well-constructed properties in desirable locations.[2]

INVESTMENT CHARACTERISTICS
OF REAL ESTATE

The investment characteristics of real estate flow directly from its physical characteristics, which are peculiar to its resource, land. These can be identified as follows:

1. The uniqueness of each parcel of real estate
2. The immobility of real property
3. The large size and bulk of typical real properties
4. The very long or permanent life of improvements to the land

Stemming from these physical characteristics of real property, certain economic, financial, and legal characteristics of real estate tend to influence the marketability of real estate, among them

1. High valuation of real properties requiring sizable dollar investment
2. Different financial goals of the parties to a real estate investment
3. High level of leverage (debt-to-equity ratio) in real estate
4. Volatility of demand for real estate because of the fixed supply
5. Public policy impact on real estate

[1] Stephen E. Roulac, "New Economic Conditions Create New Investment Opportunities," *The Appraisal Journal,* July 1975, pp. 337–354.
[2] Ibid., p. 347.

Many people who purchase real property for occupancy view housing as a consumer-durable-goods transaction rather than as an investment.[1] The dollar amount of the transaction is not only much greater than the typical consumer-durable-goods transaction, but the legal complexities are such that a person would hesitate to purchase real property without having the benefit of financial and legal advice and of the skills of an escrow officer or a real estate broker. The large dollar value associated with real estate investments has imparted an additional characteristic to real estate investment, namely, a high degree of leverage. The immobility of real estate makes it an ideal medium for the mortgage lender, and the high value of real estate investments induces the investor to make extensive use of borrowed funds.

Real estate is the most varied and versatile investment medium of all. Individuals may purchase real estate for short-term profit, tax savings, or long-term investment. Investors may purchase multifamily dwellings, office buildings, stores, and specialty-type properties such as shopping centers, factories, and theaters, and may even view the purchase of raw land or acreage as an investment. To complicate matters further, each of these classes of property may be held in a number of types of ownership (fee simple, lease, or leasehold) or the fee may be acquired under a wide range of financing arrangements. Investors may alternatively confine their interest to that of a fee owner or a mortgagee and may hold title individually or through corporations, partnerships, or syndications. Many alternative combinations of types of property, methods of holding, and financing forms and techniques are available to investors. They may hold the property with a substantial equity interest or with a very small ownership interest and a high debt ratio.

IMPACT OF TAXATION

One of the most undesirable investment characteristics of real estate also flows directly from its physical characteristics. The immobility and high value of real estate make it an ideal medium for the tax gatherer. Unlike the owner of personal property, the owner of real property may not be privileged to hide his ownership from tax authorities. Consequently, over the history of many nations, land has been particularly vulnerable to taxation. Herein lies the Achilles' heel of the argument frequently enunciated—that land

---

[1] See, for example, A. E. Coons and B. T. Glaze, *Housing Market Analysis and the Growth of Home Ownership,* Ohio State University, Bureau of Business Research Monograph 115, Columbus, 1963, p. 133: "the housing product is a consumer durable good to the home owners in the sample. Therefore, the model of consumer behavior . . . appears to be a more appropriate tool for describing the home owners' behavior than the conventional investment analysis and its variants."

values will inevitably rise. It may be true, as some have argued, that the supply of land is limited, and it may even be true that over long periods of time the dollar value of the gross returns to land may be expected to rise with the general price level, but it is quite another thing to argue that the net returns to the owner will necessarily rise.[1] The relationship between inflation and real estate investment will be explored in Chap. 2.

The public importance of maintaining high levels of investment in real property for housing and other purposes has resulted in the enactment of various legislative tax inducements to encourage such investment, commonly referred to as *tax shelter*. The political risk associated with the modification or elimination of these investment incentives adds greatly to the uncertainties of predicting future real estate investment and returns. Recent changes in federal tax laws and their impact on real estate tax shelter will be explored in Chap. 4.

The uncontrolled development and use of land in the United States in the nineteenth and most of the twentieth century may now be a phenomenon of the past. Changes in land-use controls on real estate investment may be drastic during the remainder of the twentieth century. Land-use-control concepts, such as floodplain zoning, preservation of natural features (marshlands, wetlands, waterways), preservation of historic districts, open-space requirements of new residential developments, and zoning ordinances curtailing land development in high-growth areas, have an immediate impact on property ownership and real estate markets. The enactment of federal and state legislation to protect the air, water, and land resources will have a significant impact on future land development and investment.[2]

The high degree of leverage associated with real estate investment is evident in the continuous growth and volume of mortgage debt outstanding in the United States. Over $700 billion in mortgage debt on residential, commercial and farm property in the United States was held in mid-1975 by financial institutions, federal agencies, and individuals, as shown in Fig. 1-1.

Loans on one- to four-family homes and farm mortgages together account for two-thirds of the total mortgage debt. Loans on multifamily and commercial income properties exceeded $230 billion in 1975. A conservative estimate of an average debt ratio of 50 percent would indicate a market value of approximately $460 billion for multifamily and commercial income property held for investment subject to mortgage indebtedness. This esti-

---

[1] Compare R. Bruce Ricks and J. Fred Weston, "Land as a Growth Investment," *Financial Analyst Journal,* July–August 1966, pp. 69–78; see p. 71. Also see James D. Landauer, "Real Estate as an Investment," *The Appraisal Journal,* October 1960, pp. 426–434.

[2] For a review of federal legislation see Harold A. Lubell, "Environmental Legislation and Real Estate," *Real Estate Review,* Spring 1974, vol. 4, no. 1, pp. 94–101. *Search/A Report from the Urban Institute,* Summer 1976, vol. 6, nos. 3 and 4, contains a summary of state land-use legislation.

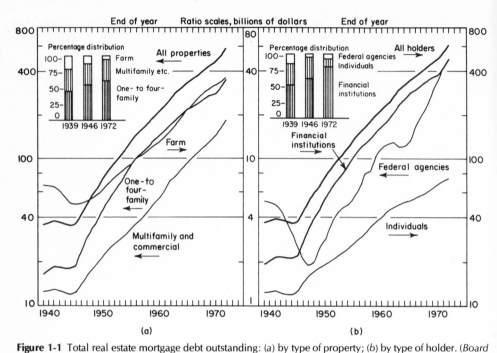

Figure 1-1 Total real estate mortgage debt outstanding: (a) by type of property; (b) by type of holder. (*Board of Governors, Federal Reserve System, Historical Chart Book, 1973, p. 52.*)

mate excludes properties owned free and clear or subject to other forms of indebtedness.

The rapid increase since 1939 in the percentage of mortgage debt held by financial institutions and federal agencies reflects the following basic trends in the economy:

1. High rates of capital investment in land and improvements
2. Continuously increasing building costs
3. Rising market values of existing building and land
4. An increasing flow of investment funds into capital markets through financial intermediaries
5. A growing preference for equity investment by individuals and financial institutions

EQUITY INVESTMENT TRENDS

The estimate that commercial and multifamily income properties had a 1975 value of approximately $460 billion, subject to indebtedness of $230 billion, suggests an equity interest of $230 billion, excluding properties held free of mortgage debt. Who owns these properties?

The most recent estimates of national wealth indicate that nonfarm house-

TABLE 1-1   Securities Offerings in the United States: A Comparison of Real Estate
Offerings to Total Offerings, 1966–1976 (Millions of Dollars)

	Real estate*		Total		Real estate bonds as	Real estate stocks as
Year	Bonds	Stocks	Bonds	Stocks*	% of total	% of total
1966	$1,120	$ 144	$13,124	$ 1,901	8.6%	7.6%
1967	821	126	16,797	1,927	4.9	6.5
1968	942	551	13,794	3,884	6.8	14.2
1969	950	1,519	13,739	7,640	6.9	19.9
1970	1,901	1,492	26,471	7,037	7.2	21.2
1971	3,017	2,516	26,357	9,502	11.4	26.5
1972	4,976	3,197	23,436	10,707	21.2	29.9
1973	3,986	2,669	20,134	7,643	19.8	34.9
1974	4,833	554	31,015	3,976	15.6	13.9
1975	4,884	361	40,328	7,413	12.1	4.9
1976†	6,184	546	38,514	8,478	16.1	6.4

* Includes real estate and financial (other than sales and consumer finance).
† Twelve months ended September 1976.
Source: U.S. Securities and Exchange Commission, Statistical Bulletin, December 1976.

holds increased their holdings of tangible financial assets from approximately $53.5 billion in 1946 to $578.7 billion in 1974, a compound annual rate of increase of over 14 percent per year. During the same period it was estimated that nonfarm households increased holdings of residential structures from $23.1 billion to $306.1 billion, an annual rate of increase of approximately 15.5 percent. Nonfarm households doubled holdings of land from $5.1 billion in 1946 to an estimated $67.2 billion at the end of 1974, approximately the same annual rate of increase.[1] Expanding investor interest in real estate in the late 1960s and early 1970s is further evidenced by the dramatic rise of real estate syndication and Real Estate Investment Trust (REIT) offerings. Table 1-1 shows the trend in real estate security offerings as a percentage of total offerings of securities from 1965 to 1975. REIT issues accounted for $7 billion of total real estate stock offerings from 1969 to 1973. Financial reverses experienced by REITs in recent years cannot obscure their emergence as a significant institutional factor in real estate investment.

Reliable data on the total national volume of real estate syndication offerings during the decade of 1965 to 1975 are not available. The attorney general of New York State reported that real estate syndication offerings in New York State alone had a value of $6.3 billion in 1971.[2]

[1] Board of Governors, Federal Reserve System, Flow of Funds and Savings Section, Division of Research and Statistics, Preliminary Estimates, January 1976.
[2] Paul F. Wendt, "New Techniques of Financing Real Estate," American Real Estate & Urban Economics Association Journal, June 1973, pp. 140–154.

TABLE 1-2   Real Estate Investment for Selected Financial Institutions, 1966 and 1977

	1966		Equities as % of total assets	1977		Real estate equities as % of total assets
	Millions of dollars			Billions of dollars		
	Mortgages	Equities		Mortgages	Equities	
Life insurance companies	$ 64,609	$ 3,351	2.2%	$ 91,552	$10,500*	3.3%
Private noninsured pension funds†	3,810	2,744	4.2	2,485	7,810	4.3
Trust department of insured commercial banks‡	6,355	7,172	1.8	7,187	14,599	3.0
Insured commercial banks§	54,099	283	0.1	169,978	3,120	0.3
REITs¶	N.A.	N.A.		7,198	9,126	60.0
Total	$128,873	$13,550		$269,411	$45,205	

* Institute of Life Insurance, *Life Insurance Fact Book, 1977*, Institute of Life Insurance, New York, 1977, data for year end 1966 and 1976.

† U.S. Securities and Exchange Commission, *Assets of Private Non-insured Pension Funds*, market value. Real estate equities not reported separately but included in "other assets." Real estate assets estimated by the author to represent 80% of other assets reported as of September 1977 and December 1966.

‡ U.S. Federal Deposit Insurance Corporation, *Trust Assets of Insured Commercial Banks*, 1968 and 1977 as of Dec. 31, 1966 and 1977.

§ Federal Deposit Insurance Corporation, *Assets and Liabilities of Commercial and Mutual Savings Banks*, Dec. 31, 1967 and 1977. Mortgages includes all real estate loans as of Dec. 31, 1967 and Sept. 30, 1977.

¶ National Association of Real Estate Investment Trusts, *REIT Statistics*, second quarter, 1977, Washington, 1978, as of June 30, 1977.

It is significant to observe that commercial banks and other savings and mortgage lending institutions, which traditionally and legally limit real estate investment to debt securities, have become unintentional equity investors in recent years through foreclosure and "swapping" of real estate equities for mortgages held in portfolios.[1]

A comparison of real estate equity investments held by selected types of institutions, shown in Table 1-2, reveals a growing dollar volume and percentage of real estate assets held in institutional portfolios over the past decade. These estimates do not include real estate holdings of industrial and commercial corporations or insured pension funds. Through its Prudential Property Investment Separate Account, the Prudential Insurance Company was the largest holder of real estate equities, with $640 million equity invested in properties in 1975.[2] Equitable Life was reported to be the next largest holder with $105 million.

Determination of real estate portfolio policies of institutions and individuals requires an appraisal of the uncertain political and economic future

[1] Burt Schorr and Priscilla S. Meyers, "Realty Trusts Raise Cash, Repay Bankers by Giving Up Assets," *The Wall Street Journal,* Jan. 5, 1975, p. 1.

[2] Prudential Property Investment Separate Account, *Annual Report for the Year Ended Sept. 30, 1975.*

as well as analysis of individual properties and their operating characteristics and comparison with alternative investment oppc. tunities. Chapter 10 will attempt an assessment of the present and future role of real estate in investment portfolios.

SUMMARY

Real estate, long a dominant element in mortgage finance in the United States, has emerged as an important and growing avenue for individual and institutional equity investment in recent decades. The sensitivity of real estate values to changes in general economic conditions, interest rates, and other financing terms has added to the uncertainties and risk traditionally associated with real estate investment. High debt ratios associated with real estate investment have magnified the returns and the risks associated with mortgage and equity investment. Further uncertainties are associated with the increasing exercise of the police power, eminent domain, and taxation by government bodies, imposing further limits upon the exercise of private property rights in land and real estate. Recent legislation imposing severe environmental constraints has added to costs and risks in real estate investment.

The foregoing review of the characteristics and background of real estate investment suggests that the following criteria are essential to maintain the historic attractiveness of real estate equity investment.

1. A stable flow of mortgage funds on favorable interest rate and other loan terms

2. Continuance of federal income tax incentives to real estate investment

3. Reform of local government tax structures to reduce the unfavorable impact of accelerating real property taxes

4. A slowdown in the public erosion of private property rights

Ideally, these criteria should be associated with continued population and economic growth, moderation of inflation, and a political climate designed to foster investor confidence.

This review of the historical background, development, levels, and trends of real estate investment focuses upon the importance of assessing the long-term future of real estate as a portfolio investment in the United States. The prospects for continued inflation suggest that tangible assets will continue to increase in value, although specific real estate investments may fare differently.

Chapter 2 reviews various concepts of investment yield and historical rates of return on real estate investment and the varied impact of inflation upon real estate investment yields.

TWO

The Rate of Return
on Real Estate Investment

(resource base)

computer

The rate of return provides the principal criterion for most investment decisions. Investment returns can be regarded as a continuum of rates reflecting the relative degrees of risk, management skill, and other criteria of attractiveness associated with investments in bonds, stocks, ships, real estate, or other productive assets.

Babcock provided a valuable discussion of the factors contributing to the rate of return for various classes of real estate and a review of rates of return for various classes of property in his monumental *The Valuation of Real Estate*.[1] Table 2-1 summarizes the factors Babcock identified as influencing the return on real estate. He measured the rate of return as the ratio between total net income before taxes, depreciation, or financing charges as a percentage of the total value of the property. It can be seen that he first identified certain general factors reflecting the level of the entire range of returns on real estate, followed by a consideration of the certainty, stability, and composition of future returns and by specific aspects of the property itself. Babcock's insights into relative rates of return provide a useful historical perspective for the present discussion.

Babcock observed that the rates of return applicable to given classes of property were generally lower in the East and Old South than in the middle Mississippi states or the West.

He also observed that rates of return applicable in larger cities were slightly lower than those applicable in smaller cities, while older cities,

[1] Frederick M. Babcock, *The Valuation of Real Estate*, McGraw-Hill, New York, 1932, p. 440.

TABLE 2-1 The Valuation of Real Estate

I. General factors affecting level of entire range of rates
   A. Availability of comparable investments
      1. General location factors
         a. Territorial location
         b. Size of population center
         c. Age of population center
      2. Marketability of property
         a. Degree to which use may be considered as typical, or familiarity of market with type of investment represented
         b. Salability in current market
         c. Availability of mortgage money
II. Degree of certainty with which prediction of future returns can be made
   A. Predictability of future returns
      1. Stability of use for which property is suited
      2. Quality and reliability of appraisal data used
III. Stability of future returns
   A. Kind and stability of immediate location
      1. Kind of district and location
   B. Characteristic yearly fluctuation
      1. Normal fluctuation of gross revenue in comparable properties
      2. Expense ratio in prediction
      3. Percentage of space under lease
      4. Diversification of tenantry
      5. Average remaining terms of leases in force, weighted by important leases and for uncertainty of renewals
   C. Importance of property
      1. Absolute size of yearly revenue
   D. Competitive factors
      1. Extent to which market contains comparable buildings in retail or sales competition; over- or underbuilt condition of market
      2. Supply of competitive land
IV. Composition of future returns
   A. Investment quality of fractions involved
      1. Ratio of land (or other fraction) to total value of property
      2. Position of fraction involved (distance out limb)
   B. Duration of return flow
      1. Remaining life of building
      2. Remaining term of ground lease
   C. Presence or absence of speculative features
      1. Future trend of values of entire properties in district
      2. Future trend of land values
V. Functional aspects of property
   A. Physical condition of building
      1. Past maintenance; present condition
      2. Probable level of yearly expense for replacements, decorations, and continued maintenance and repair
   B. Kind and quality of building
      1. Type of construction
      2. Quality of materials and workmanship
   C. Architectural quality of building
      1. Architectural beauty

TABLE 2-1   The Valuation of Real Estate   (Continued)

    2. Period of architectural advancement represented
    3. Appropriateness and permanence of architectural style
  D. Functional capacity of property
    1. Quality of the building design from functional standpoint
    2. Possibility and probable cost of remodeling or converting building
    3. Provisions in lease clauses

Source: Frederick M. Babcock, *The Valuation of Real Estate,* McGraw-Hill, New York, 1932, p. 440.

he said, "usually produce lower rates of return than newer ones." Babcock drew attention to the very important factor influencing the choice of the level of investment returns on real property, namely, the degree of management skill associated with the investment. He accounts for the prevailing high rates of capitalization for theater properties and other properties requiring intensive and skillful management on this basis. Conversely, he pointed out that office buildings and stores, which are frequently occupied under long-term leases, exempting the owner from the responsibilities of management, carry the lowest rates of return.

Capital-market theory emphasizes the close relationships between different segments of capital markets, the competition between these markets, and the factors accounting for differences in investment yields between alternative instruments. The extensive use of both debt and equity instruments in real estate investment emphasizes the interdependence of mortgage and equity investment yields.

Investment yields are generally regarded as composed of a *pure* interest

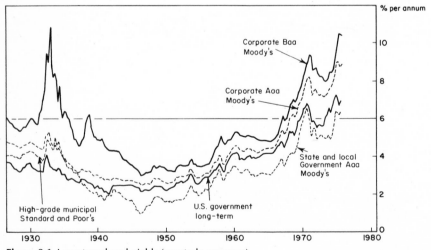

Figure 2-1 Long-term bond yields (quarterly averages).

rate, plus some variable return assignable to the risk on an investment. Figure 2-1, showing long-term bond yields, confirms the notion that yields on debt securities tend to vary directly with the relative risk associated with the receipt of returns from such investments.

The historical yield data shown reveal significant long-run secular movements in debt investment yields. Mortgage yields tend to move in close relationship with bond yields since they represent substitutes in individual and institutional portfolio decisions. Equity yields to corporate stockholders and owners of real estate equities tend to be more volatile than long-term bond or mortgage yields. Because equity interests bear the residual risk in a legal and financial sense, they are regarded as more "risky" than bonds and mortgages.

SOURCE OF INVESTMENT RISK

Investment literature identifies various classes of risk, including:
1. Business risk
2. Market risk
3. Interest-rate risk
4. Purchasing-power risk
5. Political risk

It is evident from the discussion of the physical, legal, and market characteristics of real estate in Chap. 1 that the real estate investor is exposed to all these types of investment risk. The sheer complexity of decision making in real estate investment implies a high chance for error, and, all too frequently, investment decisions are unplanned, short-sighted, and based on poor information.

Estimation of business and political risk are critical influences upon the prospective income stream anticipated by the investor. Interest-rate risk reflects the influence of unexpected changes in interest rates. These, of course, affect the cost of debt capital to the real estate investor and future resale prices of an investment. Purchasing-power risk alters the expectations of real estate lenders and equity investors and the target rates of return they view as acceptable. This element of purchasing power or inflationary risk to the debtor may be viewed as a future capital-gain opportunity or as a hedge against inflation by the equity investor concerned with maintaining the purchasing power of his investment.

All the foregoing elements of risk come to be reflected in the market for real estate investments, and the imperfections and uncertainties in that market are reflected in the concept of market risk.

The trends and volatility of bond investment yields portrayed in Fig. 2-1 have special significance in the analysis of real estate equity investment yields for two reasons: (1) bond and other money-market yields represent alternative investment-opportunity yields for present or prospective real estate equity investors; and (2) mortgage yields measure the constantly changing cost of financing real estate investments and thus affect equity investment yields.

Figure 2-2 shows the general relationships between risks and rewards in real estate investment. It is not surprising that, as in the securities markets, a high correlation can be observed between risks and returns in real estate investment. It can also be seen in Fig. 2-2 that the levels of risk and return for all classes of real estate investment vary not only with the class of property but also with the degree of financial leverage associated with the particular investment.

This consideration makes it exceedingly difficult to generalize about real estate investment returns. The importance of tax shelter to the real estate investor and its direct association with leverage is a further complicating factor. A more detailed discussion of the concepts and techniques for measuring real estate investment yields is included in Chap. 3.

COMPARING INVESTMENT YIELDS

The elements of yield in any investment over a specified holding period can be represented as the sum of the current return over the holding period plus a residual amount receivable at the end of the period. Thus, for a single payment bond or mortgage investment, the value of the investment and the return to the investor can be represented as

$$V_B = \sum_{t=1}^{n} \frac{\text{interest payments}}{(1 + r)^t} + \frac{\text{principal payment}}{(1 + r)^n} \tag{2-1}$$

and for a stock investment

$$V_S = \sum_{t=1}^{n} \frac{\text{dividend payments}}{(1 + r)^t} + \frac{\text{selling price}}{(1 + r)^n} \tag{2-2}$$

and for a real estate investment

$$V_{RE} = \sum_{t=1}^{n} \frac{\text{annual returns}}{(1 + r)^t} + \frac{\text{residual selling price}}{(1 + r)^n} \tag{2-3}$$
$$+ \text{ original debt}$$

Theoretically and, as will be argued, actually, investors alter the prices offered in the market for various classes of investments in response to observed and expected changes in the periodic income and future selling prices of investments as well as in the value of r, referred to as the *internal rate of return* (IRR) or the *discount rate,* in the above equations. The returns to a real estate equity investor are affected by the changing costs of debt

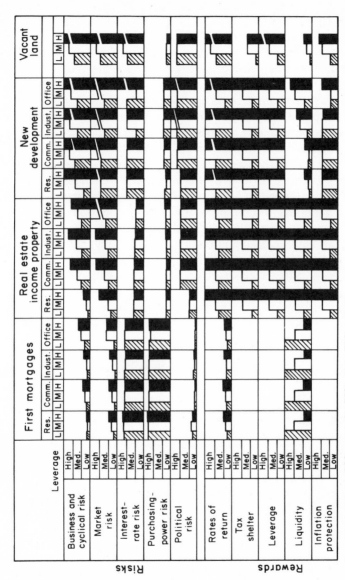

Leverage: Low = up to 60%; med. = 61-75%; high = 76% and above.

Figure 2-2 Risks and rewards in real estate investment.

15

financing in the same manner as a common-stock margin investor is affected by changes in Wall Street *call money,* or short-term interest rates. The equity real estate investor who already had debt-financing commitments will find that changes in current mortgage lending terms will be reflected in the values of all real estate investments. The prospective investor seeking new financing will find that his expected after-tax cash flows will be altered by any changes in required mortgage payments resulting from interest-rate movements.

Although the elementary constructs of yield and value represented by formulas (2-1) to (2-3) have been refined and elaborated upon in investment literature, most formulations are based upon the elements of (1) original cost or price, (2) annual income or returns, and (3) selling price or residual payments in the future. The calculation of equity yields, unlike that for bonds or mortgages, is made difficult by the fact that (1) changes in the selling prices of stocks or real estate are often relatively large in proportion to original investment outlays and (2) the volatility of income from specific equity investments may be substantial over long and short periods.

These factors tend to make future *estimation* of equity returns difficult due to market uncertainties. The wide differences in performance between individual equity investments also make the representation of comparative historical yields or the projection of future yields exceedingly difficult.

An additional consideration is that equity investments may be held in outright ownership or subject to prior debt. This complicates yield computations since the equity yield on single property investment may range within wide limits, depending upon the degree of leverage. This is true for stock investment as well, when we consider that stocks may be held on margin.

The diversity and individuality of real estate investments and the lack of reliable historical data on returns from real estate investment make generalizations concerning comparative rates of return on real estate investment difficult.

For the purposes of this volume, we will concentrate attention upon investors for income and long-run capital preservation and appreciation. The investment experience of homeowners will be viewed as a consumer investment decision. Investment for short-term appreciation can be relegated to the domain of the speculator and trader, whose time horizon is relatively near, as distinct from the investor for income, who seeks to maximize his wealth over the long run.

CONCEPT OF REAL ESTATE
INVESTMENT VALUE

The outline of the appraisal process shown in Fig. 2-3 is based upon the assumption that *investment value* is a specialized concept of value relevant

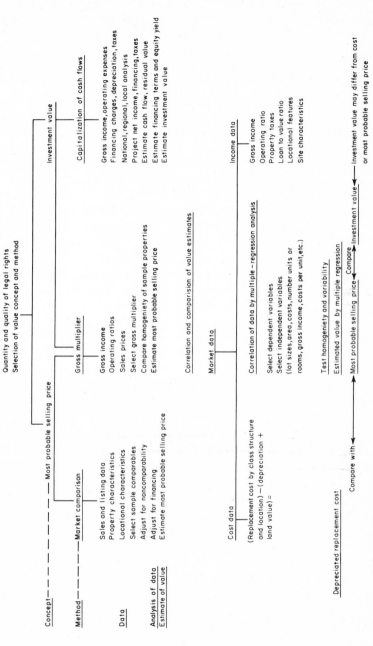

Figure 2-3 The appraisal process.

to an investor and that the method most applicable in its determination employs the discounted after-tax cash-flow techniques. Arguments in support of this view, set forth elsewhere in more detail, can be summarized as follows:

1. Investors are primarily concerned with the after-tax dollars they receive.

2. The tax positions of individual investors vary widely, often resulting in individual properties having a higher value to one individual than to another.

3. The individual physical and financial characteristics of real estate investment may result in highly imperfect market data and limit the use of the market-comparison approach.

4. The all-important forecasts which underlie pro forma real estate investment returns may vary widely between individual investors.

5. The gross income and its related gross multiplier provide the key links between the capitalization of after-tax cash-flow technique and the market-comparison method.

For these and other reasons cited below, the following reviews of historical equity yields and analytical techniques lean heavily upon the discounted-cash-flow (DCF) technique.[1]

HISTORICAL REAL ESTATE INVESTMENT YIELDS

Lorie and Fisher and others have shown that after-tax investment yields on stocks have ranged between 7 and 15 percent over the past 50 years, depending upon the holding period assumed and the tax position of the investor. Previous studies have shown that equity yields on real estate investment during the early 1950s and 1960s exceeded comparable returns on common-stock portfolios. Table 2-2 summarizes the results of a study of comparative investor experience based upon a sample of apartment properties in the San Francisco Bay Area and a randomly selected sample of common-stock investments from 1952 to 1962.

The higher investor returns on equity investments in apartment properties were primarily attributable to the higher leverage of typical real estate investments and to the associated tax shelter, as can be noted by observing that returns on total capital were slightly higher for the sample of common stocks studied during most of the period. The large margin of difference in

[1] For a further discussion of investment value, see Paul F. Wendt, *Real Estate Appraisal: Review and Outlook,* University of Georgia Press, Athens, 1974, chap. 9. McCloud B. Hodges, Jr. presented a paper entitled "All Marketable Investment Properties Have More than One Value" before the AIREA Seminar in Washington, Nov. 10, 1973, which supported the use of cash-flow analysis in real estate investment.

TABLE 2-2 After-Tax Rates of Return between Sample Apartment House
Properties and Common Stocks

	Investment period		
	1958–1962	1953–1962	1952–1962
Apartment houses:			
Equity capital, %	15.6	9.4	12.1
Total capital, %	5.6	5.3	6.0
Common stocks:			
Equity capital, %	7.9	6.5	5.7
Total capital, %	7.9	6.5	5.7

Source: Paul F. Wendt and Sui N. Wong, "Investment Performance: Common Stocks versus Apartment Houses," Journal of Finance, vol. 20, no. 4, p. 644, December 1965.

the returns on equity capital, however, reflects the benefits to real estate investors of substantial debt leverage, depreciation, and capital-gains tax shelter during a favorable economic period. The importance of these key elements in real estate investment returns will be explored in more detail below.

A study of comparative after-tax yields on various classes of investments published by Coldwell Banker Company in 1976 showed that projected real estate investment returns after taxes varied widely with leverage and assumed price appreciation or depreciation and were substantially higher than for corporate or municipal bonds or common stocks.[1]

Projected annual discounted yields on major tenant net leased investments for individuals in a 50 percent tax bracket, exclusive of price appreciation were projected in a range of 5 to 6 percent, assuming 10-year holding. Net leased investments have some of the investment qualities of a bond, since they are secured by the full faith and credit of the lessee. It is not surprising that pretax yields on leased investments follow the general trend in bond yields. Each individual net leased investment has its own special characteristics, including the credit rating of the tenant, the location and value of the property, length of lease, owner's expense obligations, cost-of-living adjustments to lease rentals, renewal options, and the terms of disposition of the improvements at the end of the lease.

Projections of investors' annual discounted yields on a sample of shopping-center equity investments in various tax brackets for 10-year holding from the Coldwell Banker 1976 analysis are shown in Fig. 2–4. Differences in the yields reflect the financial terms, lease terms, depreciation method used, and other special factors. It can be observed that projected annual after-tax yields for individuals in a 50 percent tax bracket increase from a

[1] Robert M. Ellis, Real Estate Investment Analysis, Coldwell Banker Company, Los Angeles, 1976, pp. 40–41.

DATE	LOCATION	GROSS LEASABLE AREA (SQ. FT.)	AGE (note 1)	% OF MIN. RENT FROM MAJOR TNTS. (note 2)	% OF ANN. EXPENSES & DEBT SER. COV. BY MIN. RENTS FM. MAJOR TENANTS	ANNUAL AVERAGE MINIMUM RENT PER SQ. FT. FROM OTHER TENANTS	%OF GLA ON NNN LEASES	ANN. EXP. PER SQ. FT. OF NON-NNN GLA AFTER REIMBURSEMENT (NOT INCLUDING GRD. RENT)	TYPE OF OWNERSHIP (note 3)	PRICE	PRICE PER SQ. FT. OF GLA (GROSS LEASABLE AREA)	LOAN INFORMATION	DOWN-PAYMENT	DEPRECIATION -% depreciable - method - useful life	CAP. RENTAL INCOME	CAP. OVERAGE INCOME	CAP. TOTAL	PRETAX CASH FLOW RETURN
9/70	Newhall, Cal.	164,419	3	81%	107%	3.62	24%	.46	F	3,020,000	18.36	1,950,000 — 8.5% of overage rent over 25,000/yr.)	1,070,000	71.69%, S/L, 27 years	9.1	17	9.5	8.8
10/70	San Diego, Cal.	100,609	7	35%	54%	2.83	32%	.50	F	1,950,000	19.38	418,373 — 6% 18+ yrs. 739,559 — 8% 19+ yrs.	792,068	61%, S/L, 25 years	9.5	—	9.5	9.2
12/70	Tustin, Cal.	56,672	1	62%	85%	3.32	61%	.80	F	1,400,000	24.70	900,000 — 9.75%, 27+ yrs.	500,000	73.2%, S/L, 30 years	9.6	—	9.6	8.0
5/71	El Cajon, Cal.	61,950	6	61%	77%	3.13	41%	.77	L	975,000	15.75	380,328 — 5.75%, 17 yrs. 105,380 — 5.5%, 15 yrs. 159,149 —8.625%, 22 yrs.	330,143	100%, S/L, 25 yrs.	9.3	15	9.8	11.3
8/71	Laguna Niguel, Cal.	44,420	1	37%	63%	4.34	52%	.54	F	1,275,000	28.70	700,000 — 9.5%, 25 yrs.	575,000	74%, 150% DB 35 years	10.4	—	10.4	10.2
10/71	Granada Hills, Cal.	40,020	7	0	0	3.85	58%	.74	F	1,000,000	24.98	750,000 — 8.875% 28 years	250,000	61.6%, S/L, 30 years	10.5	—	10.5	13.2
12/71	Pasadena, Cal.	122,195	13	32%	24%	2.06	0	.54	F	1,700,000	13.91	1,275,000 — 8.75%, 18+ years	425,000	60%, S/L, 20 years	11.3	15	11.6	13.6
5/72	Los Angeles, Cal.	220,000	0	0	0	7.35	0	.67	F	15,390,000	69.95	CASH	15,390,000	75%, S/L, 35 years	9.0	—	9.0	9.0
6/72	Los Angeles, Cal.	306,850	0	0	0	6.20	0	.62	F	17,490,000	56.95	13,600,000 — 8.25% 35 years plus 10% of Gross Rentals over 100% Occupancy as of Jan. 1, 1975	3,890,000	62.55%, 150% DB, 35 years	9.6	—	9.6	12.9
8/72	San Juan Capistrano, Cal.	60,930	1	45%	58%	4.80	84%	.64	F	1,910,000	31.95	1,200,000 — 8.5%, 30 yrs. 310,000 — 7% int. only, due in 10 yrs.	400,000	77%, 150% DB 30 years	8.7	—	8.7	8.7
11/72	Sylmar, Cal.	146,400	1	50%	68%	4.91	100%	.25	L	4,090,205	27.93	3,525,000 — 8.5%, 30 years	565,205 prin. 459,795 PPI 1,025,000	100%, 150% DB, 25 yrs.	10.1	—	10.1	8.8
3/73	Las Vegas, Nev.	89,088	1	70%	84%	4.92	81%	.96	F	2,757,000	30.95	2,250,000 — 8.75%, 25 yrs.	507,000	32%, S/L, 30 years	9.6	—	9.6	8.5
5/73	Hemet, Cal.	102,229	5	61%	71%	2.89	66%	.53	F	2,329,700	22.78	1,747,275 — 8.375%, 25 yrs. due in 15	582,425	66%, S/L, 25 years	9.1	12.5	9.4	9.0
8/73	Coachella, Cal.	84,435	1	53%	67%	4.16	71%	1.04	F	2,000,000	23.68	1,542,000 — 8.75%, 30 yrs., due in 12 yrs.	458,000	85%, S/L, 30 years	9.3	—	9.3	9.0
10/73	Cathedral City, Cal.	86,770	1	49%	77%	4.35	73%	.87	L	2,230,000	25.70	1,300,000 — 8.75%, 24 years	930,000	100%, S/L, 30 years	9.5	20	9.7	9.5

(a)

Figure 2-4 (a) Supporting data and (b) projected annual discounted yields on shopping-center investments. General assumptions: 10-year hold; net income assumed to remain constant; and a 39.875 percent federal capital-gains tax paid by investors in the 50 and 70 percent tax brackets. (*From Robert M. Ellis, Real Estate Investment Analysis, Coldwell Banker Company, Los Angeles, 1976, p. 63.*)

% OF MIN. RENT FROM MAJOR TENANTS	% OF ANNUAL EXPENSES & DEBT SERVICE COVERED BY MIN. RENTS FROM MAJOR TENANTS	0% TAX BRACKET RESALE AS A % OF ORIGINAL PRICE			50% TAX BRACKET RESALE AS A % OF ORIGINAL PRICE			70% TAX BRACKET RESALE AS A % OF ORIGINAL PRICE		
		80%	100%	120%	80%	100%	120%	80%	100%	120%
81%	107%	7.77	11.27	13.91	4.31	7.02	9.19	3.11	5.99	8.26
35%	54%	9.41	12.17	14.37	4.97	7.14	8.95	3.27	5.61	7.55
62%	85%	5.38	9.44	12.38	2.96	5.98	8.32	2.15	5.30	7.72
61%	77%	11.98	14.82	17.08	7.29	9.68	11.63	5.94	8.49	10.55
37%	63%	8.56	11.38	13.60	4.58	6.81	8.65	2.89	5.35	7.34
0%	0	10.47	14.95	18.09	5.47	9.22	11.97	3.40	7.55	10.51
32%	24%	14.81	18.03	20.52	8.44	11.30	13.56	6.11	9.29	11.76
0%	0	7.59	9.00	10.24	3.85	4.89	5.84	2.35	3.47	4.48
0%	0	8.77	14.33	17.94	4.80	9.40	12.60	3.00	7.98	11.45
45%	58%	3.52	10.80	15.10	2.65	8.56	12.23	2.86	8.94	12.65
50%	68%	0.54	8.50	12.92	3.66	11.42	15.45	10.89	16.92	20.45
70%	84%	6.27	12.83	16.92	4.05	9.26	12.74	3.71	9.06	12.59
61%	71%	7.33	12.19	15.55	4.26	8.09	10.90	3.33	7.35	10.26
53%	67%	5.07	11.24	15.13	3.34	8.11	11.35	3.25	8.07	11.33
49%	77%	7.96	11.04	13.43	4.68	7.09	9.04	3.75	6.27	8.30

(b)

range of 7 to 11 percent assuming no increase in sale prices to a range of approximately 9 to 13 percent assuming that the resale price in 10 years will be 120 percent of the original price.

The Coldwell Banker Company 1976 projections of annual discounted yields on a sample of western apartment investments for individuals in various tax brackets are shown in Fig. 2-5. The supporting data for Fig. 2-5 show that the projected yields vary with the loan terms and with the break-even ratios, which reflect the percentage of scheduled gross income required to meet operating expenses and loan payments. In general the higher break-even ratios reflect higher risk and higher projected yields. The range of projected yields in Fig. 2-5 is substantially higher than for shopping centers in Fig. 2-4, reflecting the generally higher risk associated with apartment investments and the attraction for investors of possible overage income for shopping center investments during a period of inflation. The Coldwell Banker analysis observed that residential income investments provide greater amounts of tax savings because of a higher loan-to-value ratio and larger depreciation. Larger percentages of personal property permit faster write-offs, and a higher building-to-value ratio further increases depreciation charges.[1] More detailed analysis of equity investment yields in apartments, shopping centers, office buildings and vacant land will be included in Chaps. 6 to 9.

A summary of a study by the American Life Insurance Association of loan commitments on multifamily and nonresidential mortgages made by 15 life insurance companies from 1966 to 1975 was published in *The Appraiser*.[2] Table 2-3 shows that the interest rates charged by insurance lenders rose sharply and almost continuously for all classes of loans between 1966 and 1975. Accompanying this, the capitalization or overall rate, derived by dividing the estimated stabilized earnings by the *total property value*, rose gradually over the decade from average levels of 8.5 percent in 1966 to rates of 10.5 percent and higher in 1975. The interest rates and capitalization rates shown in Table 2-3 represent current rates for the years shown rather than historical returns over a holding period. Had the stabilized income expectancy remained the same from 1966 to 1975, it can be hypothesized that estimated values would have fallen with higher capitalization rates. There is no way of knowing in how many cases realized income exceeded or was less than the net stabilized earnings used in the calculations.

However, the data in Table 2-3 confirm the earlier observation that investors' real estate target yields can be expected to follow the course of mortgage yields and interest rates generally. It is also evident that interest rates and yields are higher for higher-risk loans and investments. Average

[1] Ibid., p. 109.
[2] American Institute of Real Estate Appraisers, *The Appraiser*, vol. 32, no. 7, pp. 4–5, September 1976.

DATE	LOCATION	# OF UNITS	AVG. GROSS RENT PER UNIT PER MONTH (NOT INCLUDING FURN. OR MISC. INCOME)	UNIT TYPE	AGE OF BLDG. (note 1)	# OF FURNISHED UNITS	EXPENSES AS A % OF SCHED. GROSS INCOME (NOT INCLUDING VACANCY) (note 2)	EXPENSES PER YEAR	TYPE OF OWNER (note 3)	PRICE	PRICE/UNIT	LOAN INFORMATION	DOWNPAYMENT	DEPRECIATION — % depreciable — Method — Useful Life	BREAK-EVEN % (note 4)	CAPITAL-IZATION RATE	PRETAX CASH FLOW RETURN
10/70	La Habra, Cal.	84	156	68-1BR 16-2BR	1	34	34	681	F	975,000	11,600	700,000, 9.75%, 25 Yrs.	275,000	83%, 125%DB 30 yrs. 6.3%, S/L 5 yrs.	78.0	10.5	10.1
12/70	Tustin, Cal.	44	145	32-1BR 12-2BR	1	24	33	645	F	560,000	12,727	310,000, 8%, 24 Yrs. 95,000, 9%, 21 + Yrs.	155,000	78%, 125%DB 30 Yrs. 4.4%, S/L 5 yrs.	79.3	9.5	8.6
4/71	Torrance, Cal.	40	139	9 Bach 24-1BR 7-2BR	8	12	37	650	F	450,000	11,250	220,000, 8%, 25+ Yrs. 180,000, 7.5% Int. only, due in 10 yrs.	50,000	80%, 125%DB 20 Yrs. 1.3%, S/L 5 yrs.	86.3	8.8	12.0
6/71	San Diego, Cal.	94	205	28-1BR 53-2BR 13-2BR	0	36	36	937	F	1,384,424	14,727	1,000,000, 8.75%, 30 Yrs. 210,686, 8.5%, 23+ Yrs. due in 10 yrs.	135,576-PPI 173,759 PRIN. 309,335	76% SYD, 30 Yrs. 8.6%, S/L, 10 yrs.	83.3	10.3	9.1
7/71	Sherman Oaks, Cal.	51	130	13 Bach 32-1BR 6-2BR	12	32	36	613	F	490,000	9,607	350,000, 8.5%, 35 Yrs. 89,000, 8%, 20 Yrs. due in 11 yrs.	50,500	70%, 125% DB 20 Yrs. 4.1%, S/L, 5 yrs.	87.1	10.1	13.3
11/71	Newport Beach, Cal.	18	362	17-4BR 1-5BR	5	0	38	1661	F	450,000	25,000	335,000, 8%, 24 Yrs. 15,000, 8% Int. only due in 7 yrs.	100,000	85%, 125%DB 25 yrs.	79.9	9.8	11.8
12/71	Los Angeles, Cal.	126	120	98-1BR 28-2BR	20	88	38	590	F	1,200,000	9,523	860,000, 8.5%, 25 Yrs. 190,000, 7%, Int. only due in 10 yrs.	150,000	40%, S/L, 15 Yrs. 10%, S/L, 5 yrs.	87.2	9.3	10.1
6/72	Palos Verdes, Cal.	53	270	29-1 BR 23-2 BR 2-3 BR	0	0	33	1071	F	1,088,000	20,528	810,000, 9%, 30 Yrs.	278,000	90%, 200% DB 30 yrs.	78.4	9.8	10.2
8/72	Inglewood, Cal.	47	170	45-2BR 2-3BR	11	0	38	784	F	592,000	12,595	444,000, 8%, 30 Yrs. 68,000, 7% Int. only due in 8 yrs.	80,000	85%, 125% DB 20 yrs.	84.1	9.1	13.0
10/72	Los Angeles, Cal.	60	183	60-2BR	11	0	37	814	F	820,000	13,666	615,000, 8%, 30 Yrs. 105,000, 7% Int. only due in 8 yrs.	100,000	64%, 125% DB 20 yrs.	83.7	9.3	14.7
12/72	Fullerton, Cal.	40	208	28-1BR 12-2BR	0	16	33	892	F	639,250	15,981	520,000, 8.5%, 27 Yrs. 145,000, 8% Int. only due in 10 yrs.	55,750-PPI 54,250 PRIN. 110,000	83%, 200% DB 30 yrs. 5.6%, S/L, 10 yrs.	84.5	10.3	10.0
2/73	Los Angeles, Cal.	69	163	28 Bach 29-1BR 12-2BR	7	41	36	771	F	975,000	14,130	730,000, 8%, 25 Yrs. 145,000, 8% Int. only 1 yr. (50,000 due) Balance 95,000, 8% 25 yrs., due in 10 yrs.	100,000	79%, 125% DB 20 yrs.	88.6	8.7	9.2
6/73	Dallas, Texas	99	215	99-2BR	5	0	38	1012	F	1,476,486	14,914	1,088,486, 6.875%, 20+ Yrs.	378,000	90%, 125% DB 30 yrs.	77.5	9.8	11.9
7/73	Tustin, Cal.	27	191	4-3BR 23-2BR	10	0	35	808	F	404,833	14,993	320,000, 6.5%, 30 Yrs. 37,833, 7.5% Int. only due in 7 yrs.	47,000	80%, 125%, 25 Yrs.	88.6	9.1	8.4
10/73	San Diego, Cal.	112	162	80-2BR 32-1BR	0	0	35	766	F	1,520,000	13,571	1,125,000, 8.5%, 25 Yrs. 120,000, 8%, 20+ Yrs. due in 5 yrs.	275,000	85%, 200% DB 30 yrs.	84.2	9.6	9.6

(a)

Figure 2-5 (a) Supporting data and (b) projected annual discounted yields on apartment investments. General assumptions: 10-year hold; net income assumed to remain constant; and a 39.875 capital-gains tax paid by investors in the 50 and 70 percent tax brackets. (From Robert M. Ellis, Real Estate Investment, Coldwell Banker Company, Los Angeles, 1976, p. 109.)

Figure 2-5 shows resale value as a percentage of original price under different tax brackets.

# OF UNITS	AVG. GROSS RENT PER UNIT PER MONTH	0% TAX BRACKET RESALE AS A % OF ORIGINAL PRICE			50% TAX BRACKET RESALE AS A % OF ORIGINAL PRICE			70% TAX BRACKET RESALE AS A % OF ORIGINAL PRICE		
		80%	100%	120%	80%	100%	120%	80%	100%	120%
84	156	8.03	12.39	15.48	5.45	9.05	11.71	4.98	8.76	11.51
44	145	8.25	12.37	15.37	5.22	8.59	11.14	4.38	7.96	10.64
40	139	4.14	16.00	21.50	11.03	19.54	23.81	18.85	24.57	28.05
94	205	0.92	9.39	13.98	4.74	13.10	17.23	13.19	19.26	22.77
51	130	12.65	20.23	24.74	14.12	20.53	24.40	17.36	23.18	26.81
18	362	10.59	15.12	18.33	7.12	10.98	13.81	6.34	10.43	13.37
126	120	5.98	15.26	20.24	8.12	5.84	20.05	12.30	18.83	22.65
53	270	6.78	12.00	15.49	5.70	10.22	13.27	6.16	10.87	13.97
47	170	7.30	15.55	20.29	9.23	16.15	20.18	13.39	19.29	22.93
60	183	8.67	17.14	21.97	7.53	14.92	19.22	8.52	15.92	20.18
40	208	1.47	11.50	16.51	9.64	18.53	22.76	23.47	28.37	31.49
69	163	4.15	12.87	17.89	5.34	12.79	17.16	8.80	15.54	19.64
99	215	12.86	16.32	18.95	7.27	10.26	12.60	5.13	8.45	11.01
27	191	0.94	12.14	17.87	2.50	11.98	16.95	6.13	14.67	19.31
112	182	7.98	13.51	17.26	6.52	11.44	14.80	6.66	11.97	15.47

(b)

Figure 2-5 (Continued)

24

TABLE 2-3 Commitments of $100,000 and Over on Multifamily and Nonresidential Mortgages Made by 15 Life Insurance Companies, 1966–1975

	1975	1974	1973	1972	1971	1970	1969	1968	1967	1966
Apartments, conventional										
Average interest rate, %	10.15	9.54	8.78	8.56	9.01	9.76	8.27	7.80	7.06	6.65
Average capitalization rate, %	10.7	10.0	9.4	9.4	9.7	10.4	9.5	8.9	8.6	8.4
Average percent constant, %	10.9	10.5	9.6	9.6	10.1	10.6	9.8	9.3	8.9	9.8
Average term (years/months)	25/5	21/5	24/6	23/0	22/8	23/5	21/5	23/4*	+	+
National Housing Act apartments										
Average interest rate, %	11.08	+	+	8.12	8.81	8.93	7.90	7.01	6.00*	5.62
Average capitalization rate, %	10.9	+	+	8.9	9.1	9.9	7.0	8.2	7.2*	6.8*
Average percent constant, %	11.3	+	+	8.5	8.6	9.1	8.3	7.5	6.6*	6.4*
Average term (years/months)	31/8	+	+	30/1	36/6	36/9	38/5	38/2*	+	+
Commercial retail										
Average interest rate, %	10.10	9.57	8.66	8.46	9.09	10.19	8.82	7.67	6.90	6.43
Average capitalization rate, %	10.6	10.1	9.4	9.4	10.0	10.9	9.7	8.8	8.6	8.4
Average percent constant, %	11.0	10.7	10.0	9.7	10.4	11.2	10.3	9.6	9.2	9.1
Average term (years/months)	23/11	23/7	23/3	24/3	24/0	23/7	23/0	21/8*	+	+
Office buildings										
Average interest rate, %	10.19	9.53	8.71	8.53	9.08	9.98	8.75	7.65	6.88	6.43
Average capitalization rate, %	10.5	9.9	9.3	9.4	9.8	10.6	9.5	8.8	8.4	8.3
Average percent constant, %	11.0	10.5	9.8	9.7	10.2	11.1	10.2	9.5	9.1	8.9
Average term (years/months)	22/8	20/8	24/0	24/3	23/0	20/0	22/5	23/1*	+	+

TABLE 2-3 (Continued)

Commercial services

Average interest rate, %	10.15	9.66	8.81	8.69	9.26	10.15	8.96	7.60	6.85	6.40
Average capitalization rate, %	11.0	10.4	9.3	9.5	10.0	11.0	9.7	8.6	8.2	8.0
Average percent constant, %	11.2	10.9	10.1	10.1	10.6	11.6	11.0	9.9	9.6	8.0
Average term (years/months)	19/11	19/3	22/8	22/6	21/4	18/6	18/8	20/5*	†	†

Institutional and recreational

Average interest rate, %	10.6	9.64	9.19	8.85	9.18	9.8	8.78	7.58	6.96	6.48
Average capitalization rate, %	7.7	13.1	12.1	12.3	11.6	12.6	13.0	12.1	9.9	9.6
Average percent constant, %	12.3	11.0	10.8	10.4	11.2	12.1	11.3	9.9	9.6	9.3
Average term (years/months)	18/6	19/5	20/3	20/5	18/7	18/3	17/6	18/11*	†	†

Industrial

Average interest rate, %	10.29	9.66	8.76	8.57	9.21	10.26	8.82	7.69	6.89	6.47
Average capitalization rate, %	10.6	9.9	9.6	9.7	10.1	11.0	9.5	8.9	8.6	8.4
Average percent constant, %	11.5	11.0	10.5	10.3	10.9	12.0	10.5	10.2	9.7	9.5
Average term (years/months)	18/3	19/5	20/0	10/0	19/4	20/4	21/3	19.6*	†	†

Hotels and motels

Average interest rate, %	10.34	9.65	9.10	8.92	9.70	9.78	8.92	7.90	7.22	6.73
Average capitalization rate, %	13.6	12.8	11.1	12.3	12.6	13.9	11.9	11.5	11.1	11.0
Average percent constant, %	11.4	11.0	10.6	10.5	11.1	11.2	10.8	10.3	10.0	10.0
Average term (years/months)	21/6	20/8	22/2	21/4	22/1	24/8	20/5	19/9*	†	†

Source: The Appraiser, September 1976, vol. 32, no. 7, pp. 4 and 5, based on data from the American Life Insurance Association, Washington.
*Fourth quarter only; other quarters not available.
† Not available.

TABLE 2-4 Internal Rates of Return for Standard and Poor's 500 Stocks
and Multiple-Tenant Real Estate

Period for which investment is held	Rate of return, %	
	Standard and Poor's 500 stocks	Multiple-tenant real estate
1960–1966:*		
Jan. 1960–Dec. 1960	0.3	11.4
Jan. 1960–Dec. 1961	12.5	15.6
Jan. 1960–Dec. 1962	5.1	12.6
Jan. 1960–Dec. 1963	9.0	12.5
Jan. 1960–Dec. 1964	10.4	14.3
Jan. 1960–Dec. 1965	10.7	13.9
Jan. 1960–Dec. 1966	7.8	13.5
1967–1973:*		
Jan. 1967–Dec. 1967	23.6	8.5
Jan. 1967–Dec. 1968	17.2	8.0
Jan. 1967–Dec. 1969	8.3	8.8
Jan. 1967–Dec. 1970	7.1	8.5
Jan. 1967–Dec. 1971	8.4	10.2
Jan. 1967–Dec. 1972	9.9	11.9
Jan. 1967–Dec. 1973	6.4	12.5
Summary*		
Jan. 1960–Dec. 1973	7.2	13.2

* Assume single investment on Jan. 1, 1960.
    Source: Dennis G. Kelleher, "How Real Estate Stacks Up to the S&P 500," Real Estate Review, p. 63, Summer 1976, vol. 6, no. 2.

overall capitalization rates (which are reciprocals of net income multipliers) rose from the low levels of the 1960s as higher interest rates were charged by mortgage lenders.

A performance index for multiple-tenant real estate, developed by the Dain Corporation, showed that the annual net income as a percentage of selling price for a sample of residential properties rose from 8.4 percent during 1963 to 1966 to approximately 10 percent from 1971 to 1973.[1] The rising net income yields observed of course reflect lower price net-income multipliers. The author concluded that, assuming a single investment was made annually in the Standard and Poor's 500-stock average and in multiple-tenant real estate from January 1960 to December 1973, the before-tax yield to an investor would have been 7.2 percent for the Standard and Poor's averages and 12.5 percent for multiple-tenant real estate. It was assumed that all cash dividends on stock and net operating income from real estate were paid out to the investor on Dec. 31 of each year and that all assets were sold on Dec. 31 of the terminal year. Table 2-4 summarizes

[1] Dennis G. Kelleher, "How Real Estate Stacks Up to the S&P 500," Real Estate Review, vol. 6, no. 2, pp. 60–65, Summer 1976.

the comparative rates of return calculated assuming sale at the end of the years 1960 to 1966 and 1967 to 1973. The very high volatility of stock yields relative to yields on real estate reflects the greater price volatility characteristic of the stock market.

The estimated pretax real estate investment returns summarized in Tables 2-3 and 2-4 are generally consistent with Coldwell Banker's 1976 estimated capitalization rates and pretax cash-flow returns for net leased property referred to in Fig. 2-4. Rates of return for real estate investment property are observed in these and other studies to be sensitive to interest-rate changes, investor tax brackets, and to all-important leverage and resale-price assumptions.

TAX SHELTER AND AFTER-TAX RATES OF RETURN

It can be observed in Fig. 2-4 that projected after-tax equity yields on real estate investments are in many cases higher than the indicated capitalization or overall rates and are also higher than the pretax cash-flow returns as a percentage of the equity investment. Explanation for this apparent anomaly is found in the common expression *tax shelter.*

Tax shelter in real estate investment, which will be discussed in more detail in Chap. 4, arises from the fact that interest and depreciation charges are deducted before taxable income is determined. Although interest charges represent actual outlays, depreciation charges result in the retention of a portion of net income which is added to after-tax cash flows. Further, to the extent that a real estate investment results in a reported net taxable *loss,* investors are permitted to offset portions of such losses against other taxable income. Investors in high tax brackets are also special beneficiaries of tax shelter because of the difference between capital gains and ordinary income tax rates.

It can be observed in Fig. 2-4 that projected after-tax yields on shopping-center properties exclusive of potential price appreciation are low for investors in tax brackets of 50 percent and above. However, Fig. 2-5 shows that projected after-tax yields for these investors increase substantially for new residential income properties. This type of investment proves especially attractive to investors with high incomes for two reasons: (1) high debt ratios and relatively low-interest-rate loans are frequently available through government-insured loans; and (2) federal tax regulations permit the use of double-declining-balance depreciation on new multifamily residential buildings.[1]

The significant improvement in projected after-tax rates of return resulting

---

[1] Some of these advantages are offset by Internal Revenue Service regulations requiring depreciation recapture on sale of property, as discussed in more detail in Chap. 4.

from an assumed resale at 120 percent of the original purchase price after 10-year holding can also be observed in Fig. 2-4. One of the major factors influencing future resale prices of used properties is the cost of a new replacement. The Department of Commerce composite construction-cost index increased at an annual compound rate of approximately 7 percent from 1966 to 1976, while consumer prices rose at an annual compound rate of approximately 5.50 percent. During this same decade the median price of new one-family homes sold rose from $21,400 to $42,400.

INFLATION AND THE REAL ESTATE INVESTOR

The United States appears to be geared to persistent inflationary forces which have the effect of offsetting normal forces of physical and functional depreciation. It is not surprising, therefore, that real estate investors often build inflationary expectations into projections of future selling prices. A review of the impact of inflation upon real estate in the United States from 1967 to 1976 underlines the important effects of inflation upon real estate investments.[1]

The effects of inflation upon real estate investment and investors are more complex and varied than commonly assumed. More detailed consideration of its effects requires a distinction between inflationary impacts upon *existing* real estate investments and upon *new* development as well as between different types of investors and properties.

Effects of Inflation on Existing Properties

Existing real estate investment properties built and financed in the past involve limited uncertainty concerning future construction or financing costs. Barring the unusual circumstance of prior long-term leases in effect with constant rent payments, it can be anticipated that rental incomes for most existing properties will increase during any extended inflationary period. The relationship between increases in rental income and operating expenses is of course critical. However, since operating expenses are usually only a fraction of gross income, varying from 35 to 45 percent, the same *percentage* increase in rental income and operating expenses would result in an upward trend in net operating income:

	Present	Inflation, %*	
Gross rental income	$10,000	+10	$11,000
Operating expenses	4,000	+10	4,400
Net operating income	$ 6,000	+10	$ 6,600

* Assumes 10% increase in rental income *and* operating expenses.

[1] The following review draws upon an article entitled "Inflation and the Real Estate Investor," by Paul F. Wendt, published in the *Appraisal Journal* in July 1977, vol. XLV, no. 3, pp. 343–355.

Assuming that rental income and expense rose at the same percentage rates during inflation and that financing charges remained constant, the before-tax cash flow to the equity holder of this hypothetical investment would increase by approximately 10 percent. Conceivably, an increase in net income might continue over a long period of inflation even though the percentage increase in expenses was *greater* than that in rental income. The rate of increase in expenses has been so rapid in recent years that net operating incomes for many existing properties have declined. Economic analysis suggests that over the long run rental incomes should rise to offset inflationary increases in operating expenses. This is the basis for the current widespread predictions of rent increases nationally in 1978 and 1979.

Effects of Inflation on New Properties

The impact of inflation upon *new* real estate investments is quite different from that on existing properties. The developer or investor is often faced simultaneously with increasing construction costs *and* rising interest charges.

Rising construction costs often necessitate a larger mortgage loan. Higher interest rates on larger loans add to the woes of the investor in a newly developed property during inflation. Further, rising interest rates available in competitive investment opportunities during inflation cause investors' target rates of return and capitalization rates to increase, lowering market values.

The upward drift in capitalization rates for investment properties during inflation also affects *existing* real estate investments, offsetting to a degree any favorable effects of rising net incomes, as portrayed in *The Appraiser*[1] for September 1976. Marshall[2] pointed out the drastic effect of rising interest rates from 1964 to 1975 upon new risk positions in real estate and equity valuations.

Effects of Inflation on Unimproved Land

Unimproved land values are subject to adverse short-run and positive long-run influences during inflation. Increases in construction costs and interest rates are quickly reflected in lower residual returns to land investment and in lower land prices. The effect of increasing construction costs and interest rates on new real estate investments and land prices is illustrated in Table 2-5 by reference to a hypothetical investment, designed to emphasize the potential unfavorable effects of inflation upon unimproved land.

The combined inflationary effect of the assumed rise in construction costs, interest costs, and investor target rates of return offset rising potential rental

[1] American Institute of Real Estate Appraisers, loc. cit.
[2] Richard D. Marshall, "Inflation Partially Negates Risk Position Yields," *Mortgage Banker*, December, 1975.

TABLE 2-5   Inflation, Investment, and Land Values: A Hypothetical Illustration

	Before inflation	After inflation	Net change
Construction costs	$60,000	$70,000	+$10,000
Gross rental income	14,000	15,000	+1,000
Operating expenses	4,000	4,400	+400
Net operating income before financing charges	10,000	10,600	+600
30-year mortgage loan 60% value, interest rate 7% before inflation, 9% after inflation, annual payment of interest and amortization	2,901	4,088	+1,187
Net before-tax cash flow available for equity investor	7,099	6,512	−587
Target return on building investment	9%	12%	+3%
Required return on building investment, 30 years	5,840	8,690	+2,850
Residual returns to land investment	1,259	−2,178	−3,437

income in this illustration. Pro forma before-tax returns imputable to land investment decline from $1,259 to −$2,178. It is conceivable, of course, that rental income might rise sufficiently to offset rising costs with a different result, and long-run rental increases could restore the profitability of development and land values.

Although potential tax shelter might induce an investor to go forward with the project, he would most certainly offer a lower price for the land if he anticipated these short-run developments during inflation. Were the investor to capitalize these hypothetical land returns at 8 percent before inflation, the land required for the development might have had a before-inflation value of $15,737. According to the inflationary forecast and assuming a 12 percent target return, the land would have an indicated negative value *for this project under these specific assumptions*. Increased construction and interest costs and rising target rates of return may fall with heavy impact on vacant land and make many investments unattractive.

Previous studies underscore the fact that land prices must increase at annual rates of 10 percent or more to provide attractive long-term investment returns. Interest costs, taxes, high sales commissions, rising construction costs, and the absence of depreciation tax shelter limit the attractiveness of land investment during inflation.[1] Lindeman has emphasized the role of land speculators and their expectations during inflation.[2]

[1] For cash-flow analysis of land investment, see chap. 9 and also Chris Mader, *The Dow Jones-Irwin Guide to Real Estate Investing*, Homewood, Ill., 1975, pt. III, Irwin, chap. 10, and Robert M. Ellis, *Real Estate Investment Analysis*, Coldwell Banker Company, Los Angeles, 1976, pp. 38–39.

[2] J. Bruce Lindeman, "Is the Land Boom Coming to an End?" *Real Estate Review*, Fall 1974.

Agricultural and forest land represent special classes of investment in vacant land, traditionally providing an excellent hedge against inflation. The prices of agricultural products and lumber usually rise during periods of inflation, providing increased income to holders of land with long-term financing. The Department of Agriculture recently confirmed favorable farmland-value trends. According to *The Appraiser* for September 1976, values of farmland across the United States have doubled over the last 5 years and were reported to have increased by 17 percent during 1976 by the Department of Agriculture.

The unfavorable consequences of inflation for investment in *new* developments and unimproved urban land may contribute indirectly to the favorable results of inflation upon investments in *existing* properties. Declining construction of new competitive facilities during inflation strengthens the market for space in existing properties by limiting increases in the supply of such properties available for investment. Prices of unimproved land may decline during inflation with reduced new construction while prices of existing properties may be increasing, as noted in many areas during 1975 and 1976.

Further consideration of the impact of inflation upon individual properties and investors leads to the conclusion that the effects of inflation vary between new and old properties and between different property types. Shopping-center, other commercial, or industrial properties with escalation clauses in leases often provide excellent inflation hedges.[1] Long-term leased-fee properties with no escalation clauses would be affected adversely. Investors in residential properties subject to rent controls, as documented in New York and other cities, are the most adversely affected by inflation since maintenance, other operating costs, and taxes rise while rent increases usually lag behind. These observations emphasize the diversity of inflationary impacts upon different investor and property types.

THE ROLE OF EXPECTATIONS

Coming events cast their shadows before, as economic and business history has demonstrated. The nature and timing of real estate market responses to inflation depend upon the degree of inflation and upon concurrent developments in the mortgage and other investment markets.

There is no such thing as "normal inflation." A study of world purchasing power among industrialized and less developed countries, indicated an overall depreciation in the value of the dollar in the United States of 41

---

[1] *Ibid.;* Mader, op. cit., pt. III, presents an interesting series of pro forma cash-flow statements for various classes of income property under different assumed rates of inflation.

percent over the decade 1965 to 1975. The average annual rate of inflation rose from 4.1 percent for 1965 to 1970 to 6.3 percent from 1970 to 1975. This was equivalent to a compound rate of inflation of 5.5 percent per annum over the decade from 1967 to 1976.

The Citibank study observed that double-digit inflation was experienced in almost half of the industrialized countries in 1976. Differences in the rates of inflation between nations and for individual nations over the decade were substantial, although, from that study, a clear pattern emerges in Table 2-6.

Long-term interest rates rose almost continuously in the United States from 1965 to 1970. Following a sharp decline in 1971 and 1972, long-term

TABLE 2-6   World Purchasing Power

| | Industrialized countries and other Europe | | | | |
| | Indexes of value of money (1965 = 100) | | Annual rate of depreciation of money, % | | |
	1970	1975	1965–1970	1970–1975	1976*
Switzerland	85	58	3.3%	7.1%	2.2%
West Germany	88	65	2.8	5.8	4.9
United States	81	59	4.1	6.3	5.8
Denmark	73	47	6.2	8.5	6.5
Austria	85	60	3.2	6.8	7.0
Canada	83	58	3.7	6.8	7.9
Netherlands	79	52	4.6	7.9	8.4
France	81	53	4.2	8.1	8.7
Japan	77	45	5.2	10.2	8.7
Norway	79	53	4.7	7.7	9.0
Belgium *	84	56	3.4	7.7	9.0
Luxembourg	86	61	3.0	6.7	9.6
Sweden	80	55	4.4	7.3	9.9
South Africa	85	55	3.2	8.5	10.2
Australia	86	53	3.0	9.3	11.8
Greece	88	49	2.4	11.0	12.2
Yugoslavia	59	24	10.0	16.1	12.4
Italy	86	50	2.9	10.2	12.7
Spain	78	44	4.8	10.8	13.0
Finland	64	37	8.5	10.4	13.8
Ireland	77	41	5.0	11.7	13.9
Turkey	67	29	7.6	15.7	14.3
New Zealand	79	48	4.7	9.3	14.7
Britain	80	43	4.4	11.5	15.3
Portugal	74	36	6.0	13.1	17.4
Median rates			4.4	8.5	9.9

* Based on average monthly data available for 1976 compared with corresponding period of 1975.
Source: Citibank, Monthly Economic Letter, September 1976.

rates reached their highest levels in the fall of 1975 and declined sharply during the last quarter of 1976. Figure 2-6 shows that the average effective conventional mortgage rate charged by savings and loan associations for purchase of newly built houses rose from 6.46 percent in 1967 to 8.45 percent in 1970. Following a modest decline in 1971 and 1972, mortgage interest rates resumed the upward trend since 1973 to an average level of 9.06 percent in January 1976, continued at that level through the fall, and declined moderately in late 1976. It is significant that mortgage interest rates continued at high levels until November 1976, even though short- and long-term bond yields declined earlier and savings flows to financial intermediaries were at record levels. Mortgage interest rates rose rapidly in response to the inflationary trends evident in the United States economy in the mid-1960s. Conversely, downward adjustments in rates during the months of declining inflation during 1976 and 1977 were sluggish and rates rose in early 1978.

As shown in Fig. 2-6, housing rents rose gradually from a base level of 100 in 1967 to 145 in July 1976, an average annual rate of about 3.75 percent. Meanwhile, the Department of Commerce composite construction-cost index rose at a compound annual rate of almost 7 percent, from a base level of 100 in 1967 to 198.8 in mid-1976. The characteristic strong upward bias of construction costs during inflation is clearly evident, and its effect on new housing starts was dramatic.

The average purchase price of new homes financed through savings and loan institutions rose from $25,400 in 1967 to over $50,000 by September

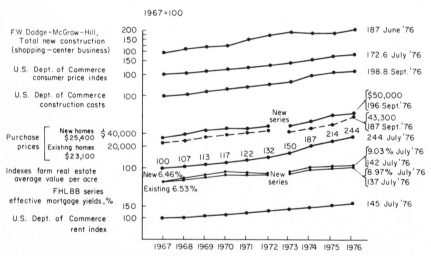

Figure 2-6 Inflation and real estate.

1976. During this same period the average price of existing homes financed through these institutions rose from $23,100 to a record high of $43,300. The indicated increase in prices of new houses represents an average price rise of approximately 7 percent per annum during a decade in which the consumer price index recorded an average inflation in living costs of approximately 5½ percent per year.

Effective interest rates on new and existing homes financed through savings and loan associations rose at annual rates of approximately 3.25 and 3.50 percent annually. During the decade total disposable personal income rose at a compound annual rate of 8 percent per annum.

The data in Fig. 2-6 support the general conclusion that house prices more than kept pace with inflation during the decade 1967 to 1976. The lag in rents compared with other indexes of inflation is particularly apparent. The consistent rise in farm real estate values over the decade is also notable. More detailed examination of real estate investment returns over the past decade reveals the pervasiveness and complexity of inflationary influences in the real estate economy.

INFLATION AND THE HOME OWNER

We can distinguish between the impact of inflation upon the typical home buyer and its impact upon the real estate investor. The potential benefits from home ownership during the decade 1967 to 1976 can be illustrated by an example. A new home purchased in 1967, with a 25-year loan, at 75 percent of value in the amount of $19,080 (0.75 × $25,400), would have required monthly payments of approximately $128.62 over the 10-year period. At the end of the decade the remaining principal balance on the loan would be $14,766. Assuming sale of the home at year end 1976 at $50,000, the owner's profit before capital-gains taxes would equal $50,000 − $25,400 = $24,600. Assuming capital gains tax liability of 25 percent, the remaining profit would be 0.75 × $24,600 = $18,450.

The homeowner would have also benefitted by tax shelter on the total of interest payments of approximately $10,102 over the 10 years. Assuming the homeowner was in a 40 percent tax bracket, this interest tax shelter would have resulted in retention of other income in the amount of $4,040 (0.40 × $10,102) over the 10-year period, which as a renter she would have been required to pay the Internal Revenue Service (IRS).

A comprehensive analysis of the relative advantages of home ownership or renting during this period would also have to include allowances for the interest foregone by the homeowner on her assumed equity investment of $6,350 over the holding period. Assuming no home purchase and monthly compounding at an average savings interest rate of 5½ percent, the homeowner's 1967 equity of $6,350 would have accumulated to a value of

TABLE 2-7 Pro Forma Cash-Flow Analysis, Home Ownership, 1967–1976*

Cash-flow schedules

Year	Effective gross income (1)	Operating expenses (2)	Net income (3)	Depreciation (4)	Interest (5)	Principal amortization (6)	Before-tax cash flow (7)	Before-tax cash on cash, % (8)	Taxable income (9)	Taxes (10)	After-tax cash flow (11)	After-tax cash on cash, % (12)
1	$3,600	$2,000	$1,600	0	$1,229	$315	$ 56	0.89%	$ 371	$111	$ −55	−0.86%
2	3,735	2,180	1,555	0	1,208	336	11	0.18	347	104	−93	−1.46
3	3,875	2,376	1,499	0	1,185	358	−45	−0.70	313	94	−139	−2.19
4	4,020	2,590	1,430	0	1,162	382	−113	−1.78	269	81	−194	−3.05
5	4,171	2,823	1,348	0	1,136	408	−196	−3.08	212	64	−259	−4.08
6	4,328	3,077	1,250	0	1,109	435	−293	−4.62	142	43	−336	−5.29
7	4,490	3,354	1,136	0	1,079	464	−408	−6.42	56	17	−425	−6.69
8	4,658	3,656	1,002	0	1,048	495	−541	−8.53	−46	−14	−528	−8.31
9	4,833	3,985	848	0	1,015	528	−696	−10.96	−167	−50	−646	−10.17
10	5,014	4,344	670	0	980	564	−873	−13.75	−310	−93	−780	−12.29

Sale schedules

Year	Selling price (1)	Selling expenses (2)	Prepayment penalty (3)	Amount realized (4)	Unpaid mortgage (5)	Before-tax residual (6)	Adjusted basis (7)	Gain (8)	Depreciation recapture (9)	Capital gain (10)	Taxes (11)	After-tax residual (12)
1	$27,178	$1,631	0	$25,547	$18,735	$ 6,812	$25,400	$ 147	0	$ 147	$ 22	$ 6,790
2	29,080	1,745	0	27,336	18,400	8,936	25,400	1,936	0	1,936	290	8,645
3	31,116	1,867	0	29,249	18,042	11,207	25,400	3,849	0	3,849	577	10,630
4	33,294	1,998	0	31,297	17,660	13,637	25,400	5,897	0	5,897	884	12,752
5	35,625	2,137	0	33,487	17,252	16,235	25,400	8,087	0	8,087	1,213	15,022
6	38,118	2,287	0	35,831	16,817	19,014	25,400	10,431	0	10,431	1,565	17,450

7	40,787	2,447	0	38,340	25,400	21,987	16,353	12,940	0	12,940	1,941	20,046
8	43,642	2,619	0	41,023	25,400	25,166	15,858	15,623	0	15,623	2,343	22,822
9	46,697	2,802	0	48,895	25,400	28,566	15,329	18,495	0	18,495	2,774	25,791
10	49,965	2,998	0	46,968	25,400	32,202	14,766	21,568	0	21,568	3,235	28,967

Rates of return

Year	Equity (1)	Before-tax cash flow (2)	Before-tax residual (3)	Rate of return, % (4)	After-tax cash flow (5)	After-tax residual (6)	Rate of return, % (7)
1	$6,350	$ 56	$ 6,812	8.19%	$ −55	$ 6,790	6.04%
2	0	11	8,936	19.19	−93	8,645	15.55
3	0	−45	11,207	21.05	−139	10,630	17.43
4	0	−113	13,637	20.93	−194	12,752	17.57
5	0	−196	16,235	20.23	−259	15,022	17.17
6	0	−293	19,014	19.36	−336	17,450	16.57
7	0	−408	21,987	18.45	−425	20,046	15.92
8	0	−541	25,166	17.56	−528	22,822	15.26
9	0	−696	28,566	16.71	−646	25,791	14.62
10	0	−873	32,202	15.90	−780	28,967	14.00

Source: Real III computer program, University of Georgia, calculations by the author.
* Assumptions: Purchase price, 1967 = $25,400; selling price increases annually by 7%, 10-year holding; mortgage 6.5%, 25 years, 75%, monthly payment; imputed rental income $3,600 per year, increasing by 3.75% per year; operating expenses $2,000 per year increasing by 9% per year increasing $2,000 per year; outside taxable income $25,000 increasing by 5% per year; 30% tax bracket; no depreciation, owner-occupied.

$10,992 (1.731076 × $6,350) by 1976. The estimated amount of interest on her equity capital lost over the period, $4,642 ($10,992 − $6,350), after allowance for taxes at 40 percent, would have equaled approximately $2,785. The net amount of interest tax shelter for the homeowner on her mortgage indebtedness would have therefore been reduced to approximately $1,255 ($4,040 − $2,785).

This amount should be added to the earlier estimated after-tax capital gain of $18,450, to result in a net after-tax gain to the homeowner of approximately $19,705 ($18,450 + $1,255). This amount represents an adjusted average annual return of approximately 12.00 percent per annum on her original equity of $6,350, about twice the indicated average rate of inflation over the decade.

No allowance was made for the imputed rental value of the home to the owner or for the offsetting costs of ownership, in the form of monthly mortgage payments, property taxes, and maintenance costs in the above example. A cash-flow analysis including specific allowances for these elements was shown in Table 2-7.

The homeowner's cash-flow calculation in Table 2-7 assumes the following:

Original cost, 1967	$25,400
Original equity, 1967	$ 6,350
Loan 25 years 6½%	$19,050
Selling price increases annually by	7%
Imputed rental income, first year	$ 3,600
Increasing annually by	3.75%
Operating expenses, first year	$ 2,000
Increasing by	9%
Outside taxable income	$25,000
Increasing annually by	5%

The rates of return in Table 2-7 show that the indicated rate of return to the homeowner on her equity under the above assumptions would have been 14 percent for 10-year holding, with higher indicated returns for shorter holding periods. Negative annual after-tax cash flows are offset by the substantial after-tax residual returns. As noted below, after-tax returns to homeowners in the Los Angeles area appear to confirm these findings.

Ricks[1] concluded that a typical Los Angeles homeowner would have realized a rate of return of 18.5 percent per annum on an original equity investment of $6,000 over a 10-year holding period on a $26,500 home purchased in 1965. He estimated that monthly carrying costs rose from $217 per month in 1965 to $332 in 1975, adjusting for tax shelter at 25 percent of mortgage interest and property tax payments and allowing for an imputed

---

[1] R. Bruce Ricks, "Managing the Best Financial Asset," *California Management Review,* University of California, Spring 1976.

occupancy value equal to 0.7 percent of the value of his owner-occupied home per month and 8 percent transaction costs. He projected that family incomes and house prices would rise at 5 percent annually and operating expenses at about 4½ percent annually for the decade from 1975 to 1985 and that a home could be purchased at $45,000 in 1975 with a 95 percent loan at 10 percent interest for 30 years. From these assumptions, Ricks projected a potential increase in the homeowner's equity from $2,250 in 1975 to $34,440 in 1985, with a possible rate of return on equity of 12.6 percent, after allowing for transaction costs.[1]

Support for the view that home ownership provided a "superhedge" against the inflation from 1967 to 1976 and a potential hedge in the next decade lies in the observation that the cost of renting, an alternative to home ownership, rose by almost 50 percent from 1967 to 1976 and promises to rise further in the coming years.

INFLATION AND MULTIFAMILY RESIDENTIAL REAL ESTATE

The typical real estate investor would have benefitted by additional tax shelter over the past decade resulting from permitted depreciation deductions in calculating net taxable income. Coldwell Banker[2] projected *after-tax returns* on residential income property of 10 to 15 percent for taxpayers in a 50 percent tax bracket, without assuming any appreciation or depreciation in selling prices. Projected yields, shown in Fig. 2-5, were higher for properties with favorable long-term loans and with "first-owner" depreciation. Assuming a 20 percent increase in selling price over a 10-year holding period raises the Coldwell Banker projected yields to a range of 12.5 to 20 percent. Construction-cost indexes have increased at a compound rate of over 7.0 percent per annum over the past decade, while home prices have also approximately doubled in value. An assumed 20 percent rise in selling prices, which represents an average compound rate of increase of less than 2 percent per annum, appears to represent a very conservative inflation projection, based on the record for 1967 to 1976.

It was assumed in the Coldwell Banker projections that net incomes would remain constant over the 10-year holding period. Annual reports prepared by the Institute of Real Estate Management indicate that net operating income for typical low-rise apartment buildings in Los Angeles rose from $284.22 per room in 1971 to $324.28 per room in 1975. Operating expenses, which have been increasing at a higher percentage rate than gross income, equaled $276.91 per room in 1975, or 44.1 percent of total

---

[1] Ibid., tables 3 and 4.
[2] Coldwell Banker and Company, *Using the Discounted Yield to Compare Real Estate Alternatives,* Los Angeles 1974.

collections of $601.22 per room. Operating expenses per room in 1971 for the same class of building were $225.37, or 40.7 percent of total collections of $509.29 per room.[1]

It can be concluded from examination of these trends that the assumption of a level net income for apartment investments during the inflationary decade from 1967 to 1976 probably represents an underestimation of average apartment investment experience. This suggests that the after-tax returns on equity investment in apartment buildings constructed at the historically favorable construction-cost levels of the mid- and late 1960s in most large metropolitan areas have probably averaged annual returns of 15 percent or better. Meanwhile, in many market areas, rising construction costs and interest rates have deterred construction of new competitive apartment buildings since 1973, and apartment vacancies have declined.[2]

Kelleher,[3] as noted earlier, reported that investors in a sample of multi-tenant real estate achieved rates of return of 13.5 percent for holding from 1960 to 1966 and of 12.5 percent for holding from 1967 to 1973. He estimated that average returns for holding from January 1960 to December 1973 were 13.2 percent and that these returns were approximately double those for holding a hypothetical portfolio of the Standard and Poor's 500-stock average. His results were summarized in Table 2-6.

Mader estimated rates of return on new residential investment property in 1975, assuming varying degrees of leverage, inflation, and ratios of net income to total capital invested. He assumed a 5 percent annual inflationary increase in sale prices and expenses, a 60 percent loan for 25 years at 8 percent, with a 40 percent ordinary and a 20 percent capital-gains tax rate. He estimated that an investor in new residential income property using 200 percent of straight-line appreciation might earn a return of 14.7 percent for 10-year holding. An increase in the debt ratio to 75 percent raised his estimated rate of return to 18.6 percent.[4] These projected rates of return are higher than the Coldwell Banker projections cited above because of the lower assumed tax liabilities and his assumption of increasing net income and sale prices over the 10-year period.

INFLATION AND SHOPPING-CENTER INVESTMENT

Shopping-center investments are generally regarded as excellent hedges against inflation. Financing and lease terms and the all-important factor

---

[1] Institute of Real Estate Management, The 1976 Income/Expenses Analysis, Chicago, 1976.

[2] The Bureau of the Census estimated that overall rental vacancy rates for the United States declined from an average level of 6.2 percent in 1974 to 5.8 percent in the second quarter of 1976 (Federal Home Loan Bank Journal, September 1976, table S6.3).

[3] Op. cit.

[4] Mader, op. cit., tables 13-1 and 13-3.

of location are of course key determinants of equity yields on shopping centers. Nevertheless, rising volume of gross sales during inflation generally contributes to increased gross incomes and higher residual sales prices for most shopping centers during inflation.

Mader estimated investor returns on a "base case" shopping-center investment for 5- to 10-year holding at 18 percent per annum assuming a 50 percent income tax rate and annual increases of 5 percent per annum in gross income and selling price and a 3 percent annual rise in operating expenses.[1]

Coldwell Banker Company in 1974 projected after-tax yields on shopping center properties in a range of 9 to 11½ percent for investors in a 50 percent tax bracket, assuming net income would be constant over a 10-year holding period and that resale prices would equal 120 percent of original cost.

The author[2] estimated returns during expected inflation for a specific shopping-center investment in a range of 13 to 18 percent, depending on financing terms. The dramatic influence of inflationary expectations upon gross income, investment values, and pro forma cash flows to the equity investor was illustrated in a cash-flow analysis. It was concluded in that study cited in Chap. 6, that while *inflationary expectations, if realized,* may result in high equity yields for shopping-center investments, a downward shift in expectations can cause a dramatic downward adjustment in sale prices, cash flows, and equity yields.

This and other analyses emphasize the role of expectations and the importance of timing in real estate investment. From admittedly inadequate factual evidence for a single decade, it would appear that well-located and well-financed residential income and shopping-center investment properties have provided after-tax rates of return high enough to offset inflation rates experienced recently in the United States.

The influence of inflation upon real estate investment is pervasive and varied. The owner of existing properties with favorable permanent financing and depreciation tax shelter is in an excellent position to profit from a general inflation, like that experienced in the United States from 1967 to 1976.

The effects of inflation upon new real estate development and upon the developer or investor may often be the reverse. High and rising construction and interest costs may interact with lagging occupancy rates and rents to result in negative cash flows, with related risks of foreclosure on new developments.

The unfavorable impact of inflation upon new construction and development may react with magnified intensity in the short run upon salability

---

[1] *Ibid.,* table 9-2, p. 136.
[2] Paul F. Wendt, "Cash Flow Analysis By Computer," *Real Estate Review,* vol. 2, no. 3, pp. 63–68, Fall 1972.

and prices of unimproved land ripe for development. It was observed that farmland and timberland represent exceptions because of rising potential incomes during inflation and generally low capital requirements and interest-rate effects.

Lease and financing terms have a critical role in influencing inflationary impacts. Percentage and other escalation-type leases and favorable tax clauses and renewal terms can obviously benefit the investor during inflation. Particular risks attach to certain classes of residential rental property exposed to possible rent control. Increasing legal protection to tenants in residential properties represents a further trend, adding to investment risks in such properties.

Rising long-term interest rates dampen increases in investment values during inflation, as a general rise in overall capitalization rates and in mortgage interest rates results in lowering of equity cash flows and the capitalized value of many income investments. The real estate investor must rely upon the offsetting longer-term influences of rising rents and increases in selling price based upon higher replacement costs.

Differences were observed in the impact of inflation upon homeowners and income-property investors, reflecting primarily the tax-shelter benefits arising from depreciation charges. From cash-flow analyses for typical new-home purchasers in 1965 and 1967, it was estimated that a typical new-home purchaser in those years might have achieved an after-tax yield on a typical original equity investment in a range between 12 and 18 percent, varying with the assumptions concerning imputed rental income from the homeowner, financing terms, and the rate of price increase of the home over the decade. Home ownership was a prime investment in the decade of 1967 to 1976.

Investors in new residential income property in 1967 probably achieved after-tax yields in a similar range for the decade from 1967 to 1976. Again, yields varied considerably with local market conditions, financing terms, and availability of first-owner depreciation. Resale prices probably rose by 20 percent or more over the decade, barring extraordinary increases in operating expenses relative to income and special local market conditions.

After-tax investment yields on shopping-center investments during the past decade were probably in an average range between 10 and 18 percent. This reflects the generally favorable lease terms in shopping-center investment and accounts for the popularity of shopping-center investments as hedges against inflation.

This review of estimated real estate investor experience over the past decade justifies the conclusion that home ownership and selected other types of real estate investment have provided a satisfactory hedge against inflation over the past decade.

The significant role of expectations in money and capital markets emphasizes the importance of timing in real estate investment decisions. If, for example, present house prices and interest rates already reflect inflationary expectations by lenders and investors, any future shortfall in their realization could result in capital losses rather than gains. It would seem to follow that successful investor experience in real estate, as in the stock market, requires anticipation of future inflation by the investor *before* it is fully discounted in the market place.

SUMMARY

Reliable historical series on real estate investment returns are not available. Capital-market theory, which holds that investment yields in various media will tend to vary with risk, appears to be generally supported by data available. Real estate equity yields were found to be somewhat higher than for mortgages, bonds, and common stocks. The tax advantages of real estate investment, particularly for high-income investors, appear to account in major degree for higher yields in real estate than in stock investment.

The measurement of real estate returns is complicated by a variety of measures and by important assumptions concerning the tax position of the investor and the degree of leverage employed.

A review of projected and annual returns on real estate investment over the decade from 1967 to 1976 revealed that after-tax discounted yields on real estate, assuming typical financing terms, averaged between 10 and 15 percent per annum for the decade. Returns from real estate were observed to vary substantially with lease terms, age, location, and type of property, financing terms, tax positions of the investors, and the timing of investment decisions. It was concluded that certain classes of real estate investment provided an excellent inflation hedge during the inflationary period of the last decade.

Chapter 3 reviews techniques for real estate investment analysis, with emphasis upon the use of the computer in after-tax cash-flow analyses.

THREE

Real Estate Valuation and Investment Analysis

The adage "chickens for their eggs and stocks for their dividends, by heck" provided the foundation for Williams' classic, *Theory of Investment Value*.[1] The well-known formula for calculating the present value of a perpetuity illustrates the interrelationship between the income from an investment *I*, its value or cost *V*, and the rate of return *R*:

$$V = \frac{I}{R} \qquad (3\text{-}1)$$

It is apparent that the above formula can also be used to represent the value of an investment as a multiple of its income by using the reciprocal of the rate *R* as a multiplier.

$$V = \frac{1}{R} \times I \qquad (3\text{-}2)$$

If any two elements in Eq. (3-1) are known, the third can be determined. For example, if the cost and income for an investment are known, we can calculate the rate of return. Lest this appear to make the valuation process too simple, it should be emphasized that inaccurate estimate of either the expected incomes *I* or the target rate of return *R* severely limits the usefulness of this formulation and forces reliance upon the market comparison or cost approaches to value.[2]

The calculation of values and rates of return by use of these simple formulations becomes more difficult, however, when

---

[1] John Burr Williams, *Theory of Investment Value*, Harvard University Press, Cambridge, Mass., 1938.

[2] For a discussion of these problems, see Paul F. Wendt, *Real Estate Appraisal: Review and Outlook*, University of Georgia Press, Athens, 1974, chap. 6.

1. Alternative measures of income and its estimation are available.
2. Incomes are not constant and vary from one period to the next.
3. Returns are expected or received for different holding periods.
4. Fractions of ownership are divided between debtor and equity holder.
5. Residual values or selling prices at the end of a holding period are unknown.
6. Rates of return are required on an after-tax basis.

The income from a real estate investment can be viewed as the potential or scheduled gross income, the effective gross income, operating income, cash throw-off, after-tax cash flows, or as the total cash generated after taxes, as shown in Table 3-1. The relationships between these different measurements and concepts are highly important but often misunderstood. A brief description of the concepts in Table 3-1 and their use in valuation follows.

The gross income or gross rent multiplier (GIM) is used in real estate appraisal to translate an estimate of gross income to value, where the multiplier is represented as $1/R$ in Eq. (3-2) and I represents the effective gross income.

Net operating income (NOI), also referred to as net income before financial charges, depreciation, and income taxes, provides another income concept used in determining the value of investment real estate. This measure of income, referred to as the annual dividend, or d in the Ellwood appraisal jargon, can also be used as the numerator in Eq. (3-1). Needless to say, the capitalization rate R or multiplier $1/R$ to be used in capitalizing the net operating income differs from the rate used for capitalizing gross income. An investor would be foolish indeed to pay the same multiplier for a dollar of *gross* income as he might be willing to pay for a dollar of *net* income.

The rate used for capitalizing net operating income is referred to as an *overall rate* (OAR) since it is applied to the income available to both the debt and equity returns before taxes. The Ellwood rate is a special type of overall rate representing a weighted band-of-investment return to the debt and equity interest, adjusted for expected appreciation or depreciation over the holding period.[1]

The term *equity dividend* is used in appraisal literature to describe before-tax cash flow to the equity investor after deducting annual debt service from net operating income. This concept of a real estate investment return R (equity dividend/equity) is sometimes referred to as *cash on cash*. Equity dividend is the income assumed to accrue to the equity investor; hence, the R used in Eq. (3-1) would represent an equity yield rate, and the V in the

---

[1] For a more detailed discussion of this and other capitalization rates, see ibid., chaps. 6 and 7.

TABLE 3-1   Measuring Cash Flows from Operations and Resale Proceeds for Investment Properties

I. Measuring cash flows from operations to the investor
  A. Estimate potential gross income from rentals
  B. Deduct from potential gross income
    1. Allowance for vacancy
    2. Bad-debt expenses
  C. Add income from other sources, such as concessions
  D. *Derive effective gross income*
    1. Calculate *gross income multiplier* (GIM) as selling price per effective gross
  E. Deduct operating expenses
    1. Fixed expenses such as real property taxes and insurance premiums
    2. Variable expenses dependent on occupancy
    3. Repairs and maintenance
    4. Replacements (carpeting, appliances, curtains, other short-lived items)
  F. *Derive net operating income* (NOI) (annual dividend)
    1. Calculate *overall capitalization rate* (OAR) as NOI per selling price (NOTE: The stabilized NOI equals *d* in the Ellwood valuation method)
  G. Deduct annual debt service
    1. Less contract interest amount
    2. Equals principal amortization
  H. *Derive cash throw-off* to equity (before-tax cash flow) (equity dividend)
    1. Calculate the cash-on-cash or *equity dividend rate* (EDR)
  I. Add back the principal amortization and replacement reserves
  J. Subtract the annual depreciation allowance equals
  K. *Taxable income from operations* × marginal tax rate equals
  L. Federal tax liability
  M. Before-tax cash flow less tax liability equals *after-tax cash flow* from operations
    1. Calculate the payback period original equity per after-tax cash flow
    2. Calculate the after-tax cash-on-cash after-tax cash flow per original equity
  N. If taxable income is negative, add tax savings on outside adjusted gross income
  O. Derive *net spendable annual after-tax cash flow* to the investor
II. Resale proceeds to the investor
  A. Estimate selling price at end of the holding period
  B. Less selling expenses and prepayment penalties equals
  C. Amount realized on resale (used in calculating tax liability) less
  D. Mortgage loan balances equals
  E. Net cash proceeds on resale (before-tax equity reversion)
    1. Calculate cash-on-equity-reversion ratio (before tax)
    2. Calculate *before-tax* equity yield from cash flows and equity reversion
  F. Deduct taxes due on resale
    1. Capital-gains tax
    2. Depreciation recapture
    3. Surtax on tax preference income
  G. Derive after-tax cash proceeds to the investor
    1. Calculate *cash-on-equity-reversion ratio* (after tax)
  H. Add after-tax cash flow from operations
  I. *Derive total after-tax cash generated to the investor*
    1. Calculate after-tax equity yield or IRR
    2. Calculate net present value

formula would represent the capitalized value of the equity interest. The value of the property is estimated by adding the dollar amount of the debt to the capitalized value of the equity interest.

THE INTERNAL RATE OF RETURN

The internal rate of return (IRR) is defined[1] as:

> The annualized rate of return on capital which is generated or is capable of being generated within an investment during the period of ownership. It may be the effective mortgage interest rate on a mortgage loan; it may be the Discount Rate on total property investment; or it may be the Equity Yield Rate on an equity investment. It is that rate which discounts all returns to equal the original investment. The IRR is generally considered to be the result of calculation rather than a specified or desired (given) rate of return.

The IRR is historically associated with the "Table for the Purchasing of Estates and for the Renewal of Leases Held under Corporate Bodies," published in 1811 by William Inwood.[2] The Ellwood rates and Inwood factors are merely different ways of expressing the before-tax internal rate of return on a level annuity.[3]

Financial analysts have long recognized the relative advantages and disadvantages of the IRR and net present value (NPV) methods for evaluating investment proposals.[4] The same basic equation is used in both these techniques:

$$\text{NPV} = \frac{R_1}{(1+r)^1} + \frac{R_2}{(1+r)_2} + \cdots + \frac{R_n}{(1+r)^n} - C = \sum_{t=1}^{n} \frac{R_t}{1+r} - C \quad (3\text{-}3)$$

$$\text{IRR Cost} = \frac{R_1}{(1+r)^1} + \frac{R_2}{(1+r)^2} + \cdots + \frac{R_n}{(1+r)^n} = \sum_{t=1}^{n} \frac{R_t}{(1+r)^t} \quad (3\text{-}4)$$

where R_t = net operating income

C = cost or value of property

r = cost of capital or IRR

The distinction between the two methods is that (1) the discount rate r is specified and the NPV found in the NPV method and (2) in the IRR method, the NPV is specified to equal zero. The value of r that forces the NPV to equal zero is identified as the IRR.

These techniques can be used to determine the value of the entire property or the value of the equity interest. When the value of the initial equity

[1] Byrl N. Boyce (ed.), *Real Estate Appraisal Terminology*, sponsored jointly by The American Institute of Real Estate Appraisers and The Society of Real Estate Appraisers, Ballinger, Cambridge, Mass., 1975, p. 117.

[2] Ibid., p. 119.

[3] Paul F. Wendt, "Ellwood, Inwood, and the Internal Rate of Return," *The Appraisal Journal*, October 1967.

[4] J. Fred Weston and Eugene F. Brigham, *Managerial Finance*, 3d ed., Holt, New York, 1969, chap. 7.

is specified in place of C, the R_t values represent the before-tax cash flows to the equity holder after financing charges, or they may be calculated as the net cash flows after income taxes. Thus we can calculate the IRR before and after taxes.

Generally, the NPV method is considered more useful when:

1. Cost of capital or target rates of return are known.

2. Projects with significantly different expected lives are being compared.

3. Frequent changes from positive to negative cash flows occur over the expected holding period of the investment.

However, the IRR method in evaluation has two advantages in real estate analysis, namely, computational ease and wide comprehension and use.

Proponents of the IRR in real estate investment recognize its shortcomings. In a research monograph on the use of the IRR in real estate investments Akerson says:

> There is no question that the IRR is a highly significant measure of investment performance. The IRR is widely used and its popularity is well-deserved.
>
> It is a mistake, however, to view the IRR as a good and sufficient measure for all investments. An appreciation of some of the limitations and possible pitfalls is necessary in order to avoid wasted effort and false conclusions. The search for a single IRR, within a plausible range is not always fruitful. Unusual combinations of cash flows can produce strange results. There may be more than one IRR, or no IRR.[1]

Messner and Findlay[2] suggest the following modifications of the IRR calculation designed to overcome shortcomings in the IRR method:

1. Eliminate negative outflows in future years, a cause of multiple solution IRR rates, by discounting them to year 1 of the holding period, at some assumed "safe" rate i_e or by utilizing prior inflows, where possible.

2. Use run-of-the-mill after-tax risk rates i_R as reinvestment rates for cash inflows; for compounding positive cash flows forward to the terminal year of holding.

3. Solve for the compound annual rate (FMRR) which equates year 1 investment and terminal compounded inflows.

The resulting FMRR derived by the authors is a weighted average of the IRR, an assumed safe rate I_L, and a reinvestment rate I_R. The theory and technique recommended are reminiscent of the arguments in support of the

[1] Charles B. Akerson, *The Internal Rate of Return in Real Estate Investments,* American Society of Real Estate Counselors and American Institute of Real Estate Appraisers, Chicago, 1976, p. 12.

[2] Stephen D. Messner and M. Chapman Findlay, III, "Real Estate Investment Analysis: IRR versus FMRR," *The Real Estate Appraiser,* vol. 41, no. 4, July–August, 1975, pp. 4–18. See also, Stephen D. Messner, Irving Schreiber, and Victor L. Lyon, *Marketing Investment Real Estate,* Realtors National Marketing Institute, Chicago, 1976, chap. 4. The initials FMRR stand for Findlay-Messner.

Hoskold sinking-fund method, which was widely discussed in appraisal literature of the early 1930s.[1]

Doenges, in a review and discussion of the reinvestment problem, concluded that "Even though the reinvestment assumption is significant in theory, the 'reinvestment problem' and its consequences for the use of IRR methodology may have much less significance in reality."[2]

The following simple examples,[3] illustrate the logic and possible remedies for the reinvestment problem.

INVESTMENT A			INVESTMENT B	
INVESTMENT: $50,000			INVESTMENT:$50,000	
End of year	Net cash flow		End of year	Net cash flow
1	0		1	0
2	0		2	0
3	0		3	0
4	0		4	0
5	$62,208		5	0
6	0		6	0
7	0	at 20%	7	0
8	0		8	0
9	0		9	0
10	$154,793 + $154,793		10	$309,587

$$\frac{\$309,587}{\$50,000} = 6.191736^* \qquad\qquad \frac{\$309,587}{\$50,000} = 6.191736^*$$

Internal rate of return   Internal rate of return

IRR = 20%   IRR = 20%

* Amount of $1 at compound interest at 20% for 10 years.

The formulas for proving the solution rate are

Investment A: $\quad \$50,000 = \dfrac{\$62,208}{(1 + 0.20)^5} + \dfrac{\$154,793}{(1 + 0.20)^{10}} = \$50,000$

Investment B: $\quad \$50,000 = \dfrac{\$309,587}{6.191736} = \$50,000$

Since the indicated IRRs for the two investments are equal, they should have an equal value to an investor, $50,000. However, it can be noted that for this to be the case, an investor would need assurance that the $62,208 received in the fifth year from investment A could be reinvested at the 20 percent IRR rate. It can be seen below that the effect of reinvesting this amount at 9 percent for the last 5 years is to reduce the discounted yield to approximately 17.5 percent.

[1] Stanley L. McMichael, McMichael's Appraising Manual, Prentice-Hall, Englewood Cliffs, N.J., 1974, chap. 15.

[2] C. Conrad Doenges, "The Reinvestment Problem, Practical Perspective," Financial Management, Spring 1972, pp. 85–91.

[3] Suggested in Nelson J. Kramer, "Utilizing the After Tax Discounted Yield for Investment Analysis," Atlanta Real Estate Journal, January 1977.

INVESTMENT A,
REINVESTMENT AT 9%
INVESTMENT $50,000

End of year	Net cash flow
1	0
2	0
3	0
4	0
5	$62,208
6	0
7	0 09%
8	0
9	0
10	$154,793 + $95,714

$$= \frac{\$250,507}{\$50,000} = 5.01^*$$

Internal rate of return

IRR = 17.5%

* Amount (approximate) of $1 at compound interest for 10 years at 17.5%.

It is apparent that investment B offers the best overall return (20 percent) when the reinvestment of the $62,208 from investment A at 9 percent is assumed.

Treatment of negative cash flows   The assumption of intermediate negative cash flows presents a problem of further difficulty, as shown by the following example.

INVESTMENT C

Investment: $50,000 + $23,199
Reinvestment at IRR rate

End of year	Net cash flow
1	0
2	0
3	0 at 16.6%
4	0
5	($50,000)
6	0
7	0
8	0
9	0
10	$339,450

$$\frac{\$339,450}{\$73,199} = 4.637^*$$

Internal rate of return

IRR = 16.6%

INVESTMENT C

Investment: $50,000 + $33,252
Reinvestment at 8.5%

End of year	Net cash flow
1	0
2	0
3	0 at 8.5%
4	0
5	($50,000)
6	0
7	0
8	0
9	0
10	$339,450

$$\frac{\$339,450}{\$83,252} = 4.077\dagger$$

Internal rate of return

IRR = 15.1%

* Approximate amount of $1 at compound interest for 10 years at 16.6% discounted yield.
† Approximate amount of $1 at compound interest for 10 years at 15.1% discounted yield.

It can be seen that when the intermediate negative cash flow is assumed to be discounted to year 1 at a rate of 16.6 percent, it is assumed that the investor would need to set aside only $23,199 in year 1 to accumulate to $50,000 at the end of year 5. If, on the other hand, it is assumed that the investor would be able to earn only 8.5 percent interest, the additional initial investment required would amount to $33,252. This additional capital investment requirement in year 1 has the effect of reducing the IRR to 15.1 percent.

The adjusted IRR, based on the assumption of a "safe" investment yield at 8.5 percent, may represent a more realistic assumption than the calculation based upon reinvestment at the 16.6 percent yield. The difficulties of accurate estimation of cash flows and residual sales prices and the resulting possibilities of substantial error in calculating IRRs suggest that refined adjustments for reinvestment rates may be of lesser significance.

NEGATIVE CASH FLOWS

Negative cash flows can present another problem since, in some circumstances, calculations can produce more than one mathematically correct IRR. In these circumstances, it is usually recommended that the real estate analyst calculate the present value of the investment by selecting a target rate of return based upon other investment yields.

The problem with the use of the FMRR, in the view of this author, is that it assumes that investors establish separate discount rates to be applied to portions of cash flows. The IRR or equity yield rate, before or after taxes, is widely recognized and comprehended by most investors. "Safe" rates are understood but considered irrelevant by most equity investors, who experience irregular cash flows over time. Reinvestment rates are difficult to assess and subject to wide variance. Although the FMRR appears to meet the tests of logic, it will once more "throw up for grabs" the ever-elusive and all-important discount rate in project evaluation.

For this reason, most analysts and investors are prepared to live with the implicit assumption in the use of the IRR that dollars withdrawn from a project may be reinvested at the IRR rate. The technique recommended by Messner and Findlay for eliminating multiple IRRs by discounting future negative cash flows to year 1 is an acceptable and widely used method. The reinvestment problem has caused the IRR to be scrutinized carefully and tested against variations of the FMRR and NPV calculations and more traditional methods of developing capitalization rates described below.

THE USE OF DISCOUNTED-CASH-FLOW
MODELS IN REAL ESTATE INVESTMENT

Professionals in the real estate industry have developed various rules of thumb for defining the *rate of return* on real-property investment. The rate of return is often defined as the relationship between *net operating income* (NOI) before taxes, depreciation, and financing charges and the *total value or selling price* of the property. Other traditional decision models still in common use for determining project desirability shown in Table 3-1 are:

1. Gross income multiplier (the ratio of the sales price to annual potential or effective gross income)

2. Payback period (the number of years to recover original equity investment)

3. Cash-on-cash or equity dividend rate (the ratio of the annual cash throw-off to the equity investment)

4. After-tax discounted cash flows, calculated as net present value or as the internal rate of return.

Decision making in real estate investment demands a computational model that will enable the investor to determine whether a specific investment opportunity will achieve his optimal investment goal within the constraints imposed by the real estate process and its environment. Such a model must also be capable of dealing with future events. The primary concerns in income-property investment lie in future changes in net income from rental space, the effects of inflation on operating expenses, the potential market value at the end of the holding period, the effects of refinancing the mortgage loan, and the future tax liability, both annually and upon resale. The computational model should have sufficient built-in flexibility to be useful to all participants in the investment process—the developer, the lender, and the investor. A generalized real estate investment-analysis model incorporating these requirements is presented in Eq. (3-5).

DISCOUNTED CASH FLOW:
THE PREFERRED TECHNIQUE

Real estate investment is essentially a capital-budgeting decision. The methodology for discounted-cash-flow (DCF) analysis has evolved from the theory and procedures developed in financial analysis and capital budgeting. The basic capital-budgeting decision model computes the internal rate of return or net present value for each investment and then ranks projects according to one or both of these criteria.

Two sources of spendable income generated by a real estate investment described in Table 3-1 are (1) the cash flow from operations (or net spendable income) and (2) the cash reversion upon future resale of the property. The after-tax cash flows are those dollars received annually by the investor after payment of all prior claims on effective gross income, including operating expenses, financing charges (interest and principal amortization), and income taxes. The cash reversion upon resale is the net proceeds received at a future date after deducting from the selling price all costs of the sale, income taxes due on the capital gain, and depreciation recapture.

Most authors argue that the after-tax rate of return on equity is the most significant measure of real estate investment return. The after-tax internal rate of return on income-producing real property can be defined as that rate which discounts over time the annual after-tax cash flows from operation including tax savings and the future after-tax cash reversion so that the sum of the cash flows and the reversion are equal to the original equity investment plus the present value of any future cash outlays. The DCF formula cited below is a modified Inwood model which determines the after-tax rate of return on *equity,* often referred to as the *after-tax discounted yield* (ATDY).

The ATDY generated for each assumed holding period is the discount rate identified in eq. (3-5) as *r* which results in an equality between the equity investment, assuming an investment in year 0, and the sum of the cash flows including tax savings and the cash reversion after taxes:

$$V - D = E = \sum_{t-1}^{n} \frac{R_t - I_t - A_t - T_t}{(1 + r)^t} + \frac{P_n - GT - UM}{(1 + r)^n} \tag{3-5}$$

where V = total cost or value
D = debt
E = equity
R_t = annual net income in period t
I_t = interest paid on mortgage in period t
A_t = mortgage amortization in period t
T_t = income tax allowance in period t
P_n = sales price or residual in period $t = n$
GT = capital-gains tax
UM = unpaid mortgage
r = rate of return (IRR)

The internal rate of return as a measure of a real estate investment's potential overcomes the major deficiency of most of the traditional investment indexes, ignoring the time value of money. The DCF models are quite versatile and usually emphasize the *after-tax* dollars received over any relevant holding period chosen for analysis. Some DCF models also permit calculation of the present value of an investment by discounting after-tax cash flows to the investor at some *target* rate or rates of equity return and adding to this figure the amount of assumed debt to derive an *investment value*.

The *solution* IRR in Eq. (3-5) is not predetermined but is implicit in the cash outlays, cash flows, and cash reversion generated by the model. The IRR is calculated by a trial-and-error algorithm. In contrast, the algorithm for determining the present value (NPV) of a real estate investment discounts all cash flows and the cash reversion at some assumed *target* rate of return. In capital budgeting, this preselected discount rate is defined as the cost of capital. Frequently, the discount rate used in valuation of a real estate project is a capitalization rate (OAR) which is based on the relationship between some estimate of net income and cost or market sale prices.

Whether it uses the IRR or NPV algorithm, the DCF decision model in real estate investment analysis provides a link between the classical income approach for the valuation of income-producing property and the real estate analysts' decision models for determining a rate of return on investment in real estate.

COMPUTERIZING THE DCF MODEL

Computational difficulties in using a DCF model for investment analysis arise from the sheer number of input variables, the numerous steps necessary to calculate the annual cash flows and the cash reversion, and the time-consuming iterations needed to arrive at the solution internal rate of return. Numerous computer applications of the DCF model for real estate investment analysis have become available since the mid-1960s to eliminate the arduous manual calculations. They vary from relatively simple teaching models to highly sophisticated versions for real estate investment analysis used by real estate professionals.

The output for typical DCF computer programs includes the following:

1. Annual cash flow from operations statements, showing before-tax and after-tax returns from operations, usually including tax savings
2. Schedules showing the net proceeds of sale before and after capital-gains taxes and depreciation recapture
3. Depreciation schedules over the estimated economic life or holding period of an investment
4. Loan-amortization schedules
5. Cash-on-cash, or so-called equity dividend, rates calculated annually before and after taxes
6. Before- and after-tax equity yields for any holding periods
7. The indicated present value of the investment assuming various target rates of return desired by an equity investor

8. Auxiliary measures of investment return, including:
   a. The gross rent multiplier (first year's income)
   b. Net-income multiplier (first year's income)
   c. Cash spendable rate (first year's net income after financing charges but before income taxes as a percentage of initial equity)
   d. Payback periods (before tax and after tax)
   e. Alternative yields or values assuming capital withdrawals are reinvested over the life of the project at different rates

DCF models can be powerful analytical tools for evaluating a buy-hold-sell situation or for ranking alternate investment proposals based upon net present values. However, certain caveats should be remembered when employing a DCF model. First, the user must accept or explicitly modify the underlying assumption of IRR analysis, namely, that returns of capital are reinvested at the IRR rate. Equally important, the user must realize that the credibility of DCF models for real estate investment analysis rests entirely on realistic estimates of the key input variables: effective gross income, operating expenses, tax liability, and the future selling price. No DCF model, however complex, will generate reliable estimates of the internal rate of return or the net present value if the most likely values of these critical input variables are not reasonable.

The program and output for a computer model developed by the author is included as Appendix 3A. A recent review of eight widely used DCF computer models concluded that except for minor differences in input assumptions and output detail, the models provided essentially similar results.[1]

Program	Source
RE 003 a. 100 Simulation Runs	Stephen A. Pyhrr, University of Texas
REAL III	Paul F. Wendt, University of Georgia
IMV	Thomas A. Prince (available on the EDUCARE Computer Network)
MRCAP	University of Wisconsin School of Business (Michael Robbins)
AIP	EDUCARE, University of Wisconsin (developed by John H. Nabors, Dallas Tex.)
RETURNRATE	Robert R. Trippi, San Diego State University
QUICK	Decisionex, Inc., Wilton, Conn.
ILLINI-COOPER	University of Illinois (developed by H. J. Olivieri, Jr.)

[1] Paul F. Wendt and Janet Tandy, "Evaluation of DCF Computer Models in Real Estate Investment Analysis," paper presented at annual meeting of the American Real Estate and Urban Economics Association, Dallas, Tex., December 1975. The DCF computer programs tested are shown above.

The principal cause of variations in calculated rates of return among the eight DCF models tested was found to result from variations in the methods of calculating federal income tax liabilities. For this reason some of the model output statements carry a footnote explaining that because of multiple variations in computing income taxes, results should be viewed as approximations only.

The input data for the test runs are shown in Table 3-2. There were only minor differences in the calculated before-tax internal rates of return and after-tax cash reversions between the eight models tested, as shown in Tables 3-3 and 3-4. The differences in after-tax cash flows, shown in Table 3-5, were explained by differences in the computation of tax liabilities by the computer programs tested.

Table 3-6, summarizing the estimated after-tax internal rate of return for the models tested, reveals a close similarity in results. The significantly lower indicated rate of return for the MRCAP model was found to result from the assumption in that program that the annual after-tax cash flows were reinvested at a "safe" rate of 7 percent rather than at the IRR, as in the other models. Although the FMRR program was not included in the eight models tested, it can be assumed that its solution rate would be lower because of the lower reinvestment rates used in FMRR as in the MRCAP model.

A 1976 colloquium focused upon the similarities and possible variations in rate-of-return computations for several widely used DCF programs. The results of this comparative analysis revealed that although individual programs differed substantially in details like output format, tax-computation, and reinvestment-rate assumptions, solution rates of return for 7-year holding were markedly similar.[1] The output of the Decisionex model, which provides additional detail and flexibility in use, is shown in Appendix 7A.

Friedman[2] has recently advocated use of what he calls the *pull factor,* a variation of the marginal-return concept, as an aid to the investor in deciding whether to hold or sell a property. The pull factor is calculated by adding the cash flow for the next year to the forecast change in the proceeds of sale at the end of the next year. The total is then divided by the current value of the current equity to result in a marginal rate of return for holding the property one more year. This rate can then be compared with alternative investment opportunities to help decide whether to hold or sell an investment.

---

[1] Colloquium on Computers in Real Estate, Georgia State University, Oct. 14–15, 1976.

[2] Jack P. Friedman, "The Internal Rate of Return Plus the Pull Factor," *The Real Estate Appraiser,* March–April 1976, pp. 29–32. The technique used in the REAL III program for calculation of reinvestment rates is outlined in Appendix 3C.

TABLE 3-2 Input Data for Example Case Study: 23-Unit Apartment Project

Purchase:

Date	Jan. 1975
Price	$448,500
Land at 0.1265 of cost	$56,735
Building (depreciable amount)	$391,765
Cash equity at 0.149 of cost	$66,827
Mortgage loan amount	$381,673

Investor:

Type	Individual
Marginal income tax rate	50%
Capital-gains tax rate	25%
Rate of return required on owner's equity (after tax)	15%
Cost of capital (opportunity cost rate)	7%

Project description:

Total number of rental units	23
Square footage per unit	1,000
Monthly rent per unit	$260.05
Square-foot cost of project	$19.50

Cash flow from reversion:

Holding period	10 years
Selling price at end of holding period (selling price increasing from purchase price at 3.1% per annum)	$609,790
Gross income multiplier	6.8

Mortgage terms:

Type	Fully amortized
Starting date	Jan. 1975
Dollar amount	85.1% of purchase price
Length of loan term	20.5 years (246 months)
Interest rate	6%
Payment period	Monthly

Depreciation:

Type	Real property, residential
Starting date	Jan. 1975
Dollar amount	87.35% of purchase price
Method	Straight-line
Salvage value	0
Remaining economic life	40 years

Cash flow from operations

	First year	Annual-growth-rate increase, %
Gross rental income	$71,774	2.5%
Less vacancy factor, %	0	
Effective gross income	71,774	
Less operating expenses*	30,863	4.2

* Equal 43% of effective gross income; this percentage increases by 1.69% yearly.

TABLE 3-3 Estimated Before-Tax Internal Rate of Return for a 23-Unit Apartment Project, Output of Eight Discounted-Cash-Flow Computer Programs[a] (Percent)

	Model										
	REAL III, based on		RE 003[c]	IMV[d]	MRCAP	AIP	RETURNRATE[e]	QUICK, based on			ILLINI-COOPER
Year	change[b]	GIM						GIM[f]	Amount[d]	change[e]	
1	50.90	91.26			[g]	[g]	51.9	86.6	48.3	51.5	[g]
2	45.09	57.92			[g]	[g]	46.7	55.2	43.0	45.1	[g]
3	40.91	46.82			[g]	[g]	43.4	44.7	39.1	40.5	[g]
4	37.73	40.87			[g]	[g]	41.0	39.0	36.1	37.1	[g]
5	35.22	37.00			[g]	[g]	39.2	35.3	33.8	34.5	[g]
6	33.19	34.21			[g]	[g]	37.9	32.6	31.9	32.3	[g]
7	31.50	32.07			[g]	[g]	36.9	30.6	30.3	30.6	[g]
8	30.07	30.06			[g]	[g]	36.2	28.9	28.9	29.1	[g]
9	28.84	28.95			[g]	[g]	35.6	27.6	27.8	27.8	[g]
10	27.78	27.77	[g]	24.93	[g]	[g]	35.1	26.5	26.8	26.8	[g]
10-yr holding period, annual average	36.12	42.69	[g]	[g]	[g]	[g]	40.4	40.7	34.6	35.5	

[a] See text for description of computer programs.
[b] Selling prices based on annual increase of 3.1%.
[c] Mean of 100 runs.
[d] Selling prices based on present dollar amounts in tenth years.
[e] Selling prices based on an annual increase of 3.6%.
[f] Selling prices based on GIM of 6.8.
[g] Not available on computer printout.

TABLE 3-4 Estimated After-Tax Cash Reversion for a 23-Unit Apartment Project, Output of Eight Discounted-Cash-Flow Computer Models[a]

	Model								
	REAL III, based on							QUICK, based on % change[e]	ILLINI-COOPER
Year	% change[b]	GIM	RE 003[c]	IMV[d]	MRCAP	AIP	RETURNRATE[e]		
1	$ 84,571	$103,816			ƒ	ƒ	ƒ	$ 86,253	$ 86,423
2	103,242	120,906			ƒ		ƒ	106,281	106,617
3	122,885	138,863			ƒ		ƒ	126,948	127,443
4	143,550	157,735			ƒ		ƒ	148,295	148,940
5	165,290	177,569			ƒ	ƒ	ƒ	170,362	171,147
6	188,152	198,062			ƒ		ƒ	193,194	194,109
7	211,612	219,445			ƒ		ƒ	216,839	217,869
8	236,311	241,944			ƒ		ƒ	241,346	242,475
9	262,315	265,618			ƒ	ƒ	ƒ	266,769	267,980
10	289,691	290,530	ƒ	$290,520	ƒ	ƒ	ƒ	293,164	294,435
10-yr holding period, annual average	180,761.9	191,448.8	ƒ	ƒ	ƒ	ƒ	ƒ	184,945.1	185,743.8

[a] See text for description of computer programs.
[b] Selling prices based on an annual increase of 3.1%.
[c] Mean of 100 runs.
[d] Selling prices based on present dollar amounts in tenth years.
[e] Selling prices based on an annual increase of 3.6%.
[f] Not available on computer printout.

TABLE 3-5 Estimated After-Tax Cash Flow from Operations for a 23-Unit Apartment Project, Output of Eight Discounted-Cash-Flow Computer Programs[a]

		Model							
		RE 003[b]							
Year	REAL III	Mean	Standard deviation	IMV	MRCAP	AIP	RETURNRATE	QUICK	ILLINI-COOPER
1	$ 4,268	$ 3,956	$1,674	$ 4,271	$ 4,655	$ 4,270	$ 4,413	$ 4,270	$ 3,954
2	4,212	4,162	1,721	4,214	4,615		4,359	4,218	3,902
3	4,132	4,365	1,804	4,134	4,553		4,281	4,148	3,826
4	4,026	4,565	1,922	4,027	4,466		4,178	4,057	3,726
5	3,893	4,760	2,075	3,893	4,353	3,915	4,048	3,946	3,599
6	3,730	4,951	2,259	3,730	4,213		3,889	3,812	3,444
7	3,536	5,137	2,474	3,536	4,042		3,698	3,655	3,259
8	3,308	5,316	2,717	3,307	3,839		3,474	3,473	3,041
9	3,044	5,488	2,987	3,043	3,602		3,214	3,264	2,788
10	2,742	5,652	3,281	2,740	3,328	2,801	2,916	3,027	2,497
10-yr holding period:									
Cumulative cash flows	36,891	48,352		36,895	41,666	37,164	38,470	37,870	34,036
Annual average	3,689.1	4,835.2	2,291.5	3,689.5	4,166.6	3,716.4	3,847.0	3,787.0	3,403.6

[a] See text for description of computer programs.
[b] 100 simulation runs.

TABLE 3-6 Estimated After-Tax Internal Rate of Return for 23-Unit Apartment Project, Output of Eight Discounted-Cash-Flow Computer Programs[a] (Percent)

	REAL III, based on		RE 003						QUICK, based on				ILLINI-COOPER
Year	change[b]	GIM[c]	Mean[d]	Standard deviation	IMV[e]	MRCAP[b]	AIP[f]	RETURNRATE[f]	GIM[c]	Amount[e]	change[f]	Amount[e]	
1	33.88	63.43				32.93[g]		35.6	71.3	33.0	35.5	33.0[g]	35.23
2	30.82	41.05				29.29	h	31.8	39.6	30.1	31.8	29.6	31.58
3	28.43	33.43				25.90		29.2	32.4	27.8	29.1	26.9	28.82
4	26.49	29.28				23.54	h	27.3	28.4	26.0	26.9	24.9	26.62
5	24.89	26.53				21.77		25.8	25.7	24.4	25.1	23.2	24.83
6	23.53	24.48				20.37		24.7	23.7	23.1	23.6	21.8	23.33
7	22.32	22.87				19.20		23.7	22.2	22.0	22.3	20.6	22.05
8	21.27	21.57				18.22		23.0	21.0	21.0	21.2	19.6	20.94
9	20.35	20.48				17.37		22.4	19.9	20.2	20.2	18.7	19.97
10	19.54	19.55	19.729	3.597	18.04	16.62	h	21.8	19.1	19.4	19.4	17.9	19.11
10-yr holding period, annual average	25.15	30.27	h		h	22.52	h	26.5	30.3	24.7	25.5	23.6	25.25

[a] See text for description of computer programs.
[b] Selling prices based on an annual increase of 3.1%.
[c] Selling prices based on GIM of 6.8.
[d] Mean of 100 runs.
[e] Selling prices based on present dollar amount in tenth years.
[f] Selling prices based on an annual increase of 3.6%.
[g] Return on equity with cost of capital equal to 7%.
[h] Not available on computer printout.

SUMMARY AND CONCLUSION

This review of techniques for the valuation of investment real estate reveals close similarities to those employed in capital budgeting and security valuation. The relatively large number of techniques reviewed for measuring real estate investment returns, including many rules of thumb and other widely used methods of approximation, precludes a simplified exposition.

Primary emphasis was placed upon cash flows to the investor and the related concepts of IRR and after-tax discounted yield. Various modifications to the IRR to adjust for the reinvestment problem were reviewed. In the light of this and other problems of interpretation of the IRR, it was concluded that the use of the IRR should be supplemented by other conventional techniques, including the overall rate of return, gross income multiplier, net income multipliers, and the payback period.

The computer is widely recognized as an essential tool for real estate investment analysis. A review of eight DCF computer models available for comparison revealed that when sources of input errors, differing assumptions about the input variables, and the different internal assumptions of each computer program are taken into account, the DCF computer programs surveyed provided essentially similar results for the case-study problems analyzed.

The user should select a DCF model that best suits his particular needs in terms of cost, availability, and amount of output detail. However, the models selected should not exclude essential details such as *annual* computation of the cash reversion to equity during the holding period or the determination of the before-tax IRR. Adequate and clearly understandable documentation would seem to be a sine qua non for the operational use of any DCF program. DCF models that permit use of alternative reinvestment rates and NPV calculations have substantial advantages in flexibility of use. Accessibility of DCF programs on time-share and complete documentation are critical to the investor user.

Real estate investment analysis is still an art, and DCF models are merely computational aids for estimating the IRR and/or the net present value. All models are *abstractions* of reality, and as such they can be useful and powerful tools for decision making. The appraiser or investor seeking to determine investment value and compare it with market sales prices will find DCF models a valuable analytical tool. But in the uncertain environment of the real estate process, computer models *do not* make decisions: developers, lenders, and investors *do*.

Unfortunately, there is no simple answer to the problem of measuring the rate of return on real estate investment, nor is there any way of predetermining the criteria individual investors will use in making investment decisions. The problem is not unlike that in the securities markets, where some investors use dividend yields, while others use price-to-earnings ratios or variations of these. Generally speaking, the more sophisticated the investor, the more sophisticated the process of yield estimation and calculation.

To the investor who asks which method is the best, one can only answer that it depends on the preferences, objectives, and sophistication of the individual. Some investors have built enviable performance records by purchasing neighborhood shopping centers at 10 times gross income. By the same token, some investors using highly sophisticated cash-flow models have gone bankrupt by using inaccurate input data for gross income and/or operating expenses.

Case examples showing the sensitivity of investment values to some of the critical input assumptions are included in the chapters that follow.

Appendix 3A includes a detailed description, operating instructions and output description for the REAL III cash-flow computer model, which is programmed for the CDC 6400 and for the IBM 360. Appendix 3B provides an explanation of compound-interest tables, which are essential tools for real estate investment analysis. Appendix 3C outlines a technique for calculating reinvestment rates. The use of probability theory in real estate investment analysis is illustrated in Appendix 3D.

APPENDIX 3A: Introduction to Real III[1]

3A-1 GENERAL DESCRIPTION OF THE REAL III COMPUTER MODEL

The REAL III computer program is a deterministic model in a batch-processing mode which has been designed for the analysis of rates of return from real estate investments. The logic of the model is illustrated in Table 3-1. Equation (3-5) calculates the present value of the two sources of profit to the investor, namely, cash flows from operations and the equity reversion upon resale, to determine the investment value of the property under analysis.

The REAL III computer program requires explicit assumptions in its input data for such variables as costs of the project, holding periods, future selling prices, gross income and operating expenses, tax rates applicable to project income, financing terms, depreciation allowances, and target rates of return on the equity investment. The model is designed to handle a number of alternative input assumptions and to compute the IRR, a modified IRR, and the investment value of the property.

The REAL III computer program is capable of:

1. Calculating rates of return and reinvestment rates for a project even when the project requires a series of project costs (cash outlays) over the holding period of the project

2. Generating up to six income streams, ten operating expense streams, eight

[1] Prepared by Janet K. Tandy, Associate Director, Center for Real Estate and Land Use Analysis, University of Kentucky.

depreciation schedules, and eight loan schedules for financing and/or refinancing the project

3. Calculating the federal income tax liability incurred by the project using current IRS tax schedules for both individual and corporate taxpayers

4. Performing sensitivity analysis of the rates of return by varying input-data assumptions

5. Determining the investment value of income property given the target rate of return of the investor, on either a before- or after-tax basis

The scope of the REAL III computer program is described in the following sections:

Input description and data format, Sec. 3A-2

Output description and details, Sec. 3A-3

Secondary data sets, alternative uses, and computer simulation and sensitivity analysis, Sec. 3A-4

3A-2 INPUT DESCRIPTION AND DATA FORMAT

The input variables discussed in this section constitute all possible *inputs* to the REAL III computer program when using the *Namelist* method for data input. The Namelist format described is for a card deck. The complete data deck consists of one or more data sets in succession. The primary data set is described in this section; the characteristics of the secondary data sets are discussed in Sec. 3A-4.

Primary Data Set

A data set consists of *two* or more of the following data cards:
1. Options and heading card
2. Namelist VALUEL cards (or formatted VALUE card)
3. Namelist REALL cards (or formatted REAL cards)
4. Namelist LOANL card(s) (or formatted LOAN cards)
5. Namelist DEPL card(s) (or formatted DEP cards)

The options and heading card *must* be included in every data set (primary and secondary). The Namelist cards (or formatted data cards) *must* appear in the data set in the above sequence.

At present, the computerized investment analysis model REAL III is written in Fortran IV to be used with a Watfiv compiler. Data may be entered by using either the Namelist input format or by using formatted data cards. The Namelist input format for reading in the program's input variables is recommended, as it has several advantages over using the formatted READ statement in Fortran.

Namelist input format shows at a glance the variables and their associated values without a check or column positions or the card sequence. More important, any variable not specified on a secondary data-set Namelist card will retain the value it had after execution of the primary data set. Therefore, one may include in the secondary data set *only* changes in the input assumptions one wants for a complete printout based on the new assumptions. When using formatted data, a value *must* be specified for each entry on the portion of the input form unless the form input states that the entry may be left blank.

Namelist cards The first card in a Namelist group must have a blank in column 1 and an ampersand (&) in column 2, followed immediately by the namelist symbol (VALUEL, REALL, LOANL, or DEPL) starting in column 3; there must be at least one blank before the variable-data items are keypunched, and an &END sign must end the Namelist group card(s). If more than one card is needed to list the input variables, the following rules must be followed:

1. The data must start in column 2 of the next card.
2. Each card must end in column 80 or before, and each card must break with a data item followed by a *comma.*

The format for each data item is as follows:

1. Symbolic name, which may be a variable name or an array-element name
2. An equals sign (=)
3. A constant, which may be an integer, a dollar amount with no embedded commas, or a percentage expressed in decimal form (7% written as 0.07)
4. A *Comma* (each data item must be followed by a comma, but the comma after the last data item in a Namelist group is optional)

A data item may be one of three types; array name refers to a subscripted symbolic name:

1. Variable name [or array name (n)] = constant
2. Array name (n) = constant 1, constant 2, . . . , constant m, where the constants are separated by commas and the number of constants must be less than or equal to the number of elements in the array
3. Array name $(n) = k^*$ constant, where k must be less than or equal to number of array elements

where variable name = symbolic name not requiring subscript

        constant = value associated with variable name

     array name = symbolic name requiring subscript

              n = subscript number, which *must* be enclosed in parentheses with no blanks between variable name and left parenthesis

              k = nonzero integer constant specifying the number of times *constant* is to be entered in array

When using the type 2 or type 3 format for data items, the subscript *number* is for the first schedule for that array name; the program then loads the first value, followed by the next values in the next schedules. For example, if there are three gross-income schedules with initial values of $45,000, $50,000, and $55,000, the variable name INCAMT may be coded as INCAMT(1) − 45000,50000,55000, instead of INCAMT(1) = 45000, INCAMT(2) = 50000, INCAMT(3) = 55000.

Blanks may appear within (or between) data items with the following exceptions:

1. Within symbolic names
2. Within array names and their subscripts, for example, COST(1) = 45000
3. Within constants
4. Within the format for repeated values, for example, BADEBT(1) = 2*0.02

In the following data descriptions, all subscripted variables (arrays) are shown followed by the subscript type (i or j) in parentheses. The input-variable names used in the REAL III program are written in capital letters in the left-hand column.

The numbers that appear in the second column in *brackets* are the values of certain variables that are *preset* in the computer program. These preset values are those which occur most frequently in typical real estate investment projects. Preset values are termed *automatic defaults;* if the preset value satisfies the project's parameters, the variable name does not have to appear on the Namelist cards. It should be noted that variable names not preset to a specific default value have an initial value of zero before the input data are read, either from the Namelist cards or the formatted data cards.

The subscripts associated with certain variable names refer either to a specific year (j) or to the *number* of the schedule (j); subscripts must be integer constants. The number appearing in parentheses after the data description indicates the maximum number of subscripts permitted for that array name in the computer program.

Options and heading card This card must be present at the beginning of every data set, primary and secondary, Namelist or formatted.

COLUMN 1: Options

  1 = run normal program sequence without valuation (output is Secs. 3A-3.2 to 3A-3.7)

  2 = run normal program sequence with valuation (output is Secs. 3A-3.1 to 3A-3.7)

  3 = run depreciation schedules only (output is Sec. 3A-3.6 only)

  4 = run loan schedules only (output is Sec. 3A-3.7 only)

  5 = run valuation only (output is Sec. 3A-3.7 only)

  6 = run short program sequence without valuation (output is Secs. 3A-3.2 to 3A-3.5)

COLUMN 2: Type of data

  1 = data are formatted input

  2 = data are Namelist input

COLUMN 3: to read VALUEL data, enter a 1; otherwise enter a 0

COLUMN 4: to read REALL data, enter a 1; otherwise enter a 0

COLUMN 5: to read LOANL data, enter a 1; otherwise enter a 0

COLUMN 6: to read DEPL data, enter a 1; otherwise enter a 0

COLUMNS 7-80: heading to be printed at the top of every output page to identify the project; a maximum of 74 characters, including spaces, is available, for example, LOS COLINDAS APARTMENTS - J. JONES, ANALYST).

Namelist VALUEL cards The property-valuation subroutine VALUE allows the user to specify a target rate of return within a time period for the real estate investment to determine the net present value (actual cost) of the project.

It is recommended that the user select option 1; then select either option 2 or option 5 in a secondary data set (see Sec. 3A-3.4 for a full discussion).

The subroutine adjusts a cost of the project through a series of iterations either until the investor's required rate of return is achieved or the limit of 10 iterations is reached. The variable CY indicates the year in which the cost will be varied to achieve the target rate of return; the input variable COST (i) must contain a value for the project cost in year CY. Other cost estimates may be present in the input assumptions and remain unaltered by the subroutine VALUE.

Variable name	Default	Code	Data description
XRETUR			Investor's desired rate of return on equity expressed as a percentage, example, XRETUR = 0.11 (11%)
J		1	Before-tax equity yield rate
		2	After-tax equity yield rate
CY	[1]		Year in which cost of project is to be varied until desired rate of return is achieved
RY			Year in which required rate of return is to be achieved; must not be greater than value for variable LP

Namelist REALL cards The input variables for the subroutine REAL consist of five sets of parameters: general, future selling price, gross income, operating expenses, and federal income taxes. In the general parameters, the variables COST(*i*) and EQCOST determine the type and the time period of project cost(s), or cash outlays. For a simple project, only the initial cost in the first year probably will be entered; however, for a more complex project with several development phases, cash outlays may be specified for any year of the holding period. The holding period in whole years is entered in the variable LP and may be up to a maximum of 30 years. A reinvestment rate for the cash flows may be indicated; the program then will calculate a modified IRR.

Sale of the property is considered at the *end* of each year from 1 to the final year of the holding period. The annual selling price is determined by one of five methods:

1. Effective gross income multiplier
2. Change (percent or dollar) from COST(*i*)
3. Arbitrary selling price for each year
4. Overall capitalization rate
5. Final year's cash reversion

Selling expenses are expressed as a percentage of the yearly selling price.

Up to six separate income streams may be used to specify the potential gross income from rentals generated by the project. For each income schedule, variables for vacancy rates and bad-debt allowances may be entered. The program uses these input variables to calculate *effective* gross income. Each income schedule requires the specification of:

1. Year in which the income stream will start (from 1 to LP)
2. Dollar amount of potential gross income in the starting year
3. Annual rate of change in potential gross income, expressed as either a percentage change or a constant-dollar amount

Alternatively, arbitrary estimates of *effective* gross income from pro forma statements may be entered, a dollar amount for each year. If indicated by INARB, both calculated-income streams and arbitrary effective gross income may be used for the same project analysis.

Up to 10 separate operating-expense schedules may be used to calculate the total annual operating expenses for the project. Each operating-expense schedule requires the user to specify:

1. Year in which operating-expense stream will start (from 1 to LP)
2. Dollar amount of operating expenses in starting year
3. Annual rate of change, expressed as either a percentage change or a constant-dollar amount

On the other hand, arbitrary estimates of annual operating expenses from pro forma statements may be entered, a dollar amount for each year. If indicated by KEXP, both calculated operating-expense streams and arbitrary operating expenses may be entered for the same project. It is recommended that operating expenses be separated into a minimum of three schedules, fixed expenses, variable expenses, and repairs and maintenance.

Federal income taxes are calculated using actual IRS methods for both personal and corporate taxpayers and according to the provisions of the Tax Reform Law of 1976. The taxes are calculated based on the outside taxable income and the tax rates (derived or specified) of the property owner.

GENERAL PARAMETERS: If *not* specified, the default value is preset to zero.

Variable name	Default	Code	Data description
LP	[1]		Holding period for project in years ranging from year 1 to maximum of 30 years, LP must be integer; example: LP = 10
COST(i)			Project costs (cash outlays) may be specified for any year (from 1 to LP) and are assumed to be incurred at beginning of that year; if EQCOST(i) = 0, COST(i) is total purchase price plus any buying expenses paid by investor at closing; program will calculate equity investment; if EQCOST(i) = 1, COST(i) is *only* equity investment; program will calculate the purchase price (30); example: COST(1) = 1500000 ($1,500,000)
EQCOST(i)		0	COST(i) is interpreted as total purchase price, and equity investment equals COST(i) minus its corresponding loan amount, AMOUNT(j) in Namelist LOANL cards
		1	COST(i) is interpreted as being the equity investment; project costs are calculated as sum of COST(i) plus its corresponding loan amount, AMOUNT(j); this option can be used *only* when loan amount is specified in dollars in Namelist LOANL cards, (i.e., AMTKEY = 0
REINTR			A reinvestment rate for annual *after-tax* cash flows from operations may be specified; this reinvestment rate may be either a "safe" or

<table>
<tr><td>INCUE</td><td>1</td><td>"opportunity-cost" rate of return; program will calculate *modified* after-tax JRR when REINTR is an input variable; example: REINTR = 0.08 (8%)

Detailed income streams and operating-expense streams will be *printed;* (do not include this variable in Namelist REALL cards if there is only one income stream and one operating-expense stream *or* if these details are not needed for analysis)</td></tr>
</table>

FUTURE-SELLING-PRICE PARAMETERS: If *not* specified, the default value is present to zero.

Variable name	Default	Code	Data description
METHSE	[1]		Sale of the property is considered at *end* of each year from year 1 to LP; estimated selling price is determined as indicated by one of following options:
		1	Effective GIM: where selling price = effective gross income (EGI) times SELRAT; in this option, SELRAT is interpreted as EGI multiplier.
		2	Cost basis: where selling price = COST(1) increased by SELRAT; in this option, SELRAT is interpreted as an annual rate of change, either percentage figure or constant-dollar amount
		3	Predetermined annual selling price: where selling price = ARBSEL(*i*); an arbitrary dollar amount must be specified for each year of holding period (1 to LP)
		4	Capitalization of income: where selling price = net operating income divided by CAPRAT
		5	Cash reversion: where selling price at end of final year (LP) is entered as dollar amount
SELRAT			When METHSE = 1, SELRAT is effective GIM expressed as rate (SELRAT = 7.54); if SELRAT = 0, first year's EGI multiplier as calculated by program is used to determine selling price When METHSE = 2, SELRAT is interpreted as annual rate of change from project cost in year 1 where: SELRAT = percentage change applied to COST(1), type indicated by SELCR [SELRAT = 0.055 (5.5%)] SELRAT = constant-dollar amount by which COST(1) is incremented [SELRAT = 40000 ($40,000)]

Variable name	Default	Code	Data description
SELCR			When METHSE = 2 and SELRAT is expressed as percentage change from COST(1), this figure is either:
		0	Compound growth rate (cumulative)
		1	Simple growth rate (incremental)
ARBSEL(*i*)			When METHSE = 3, arbitrary selling prices must be specified for each year from 1 to LP (30)
CAPRAT			When METHSE = 4, CAPRAT is specified market-capitalization rate, entered as percentage [CAPRAT − 0.0953 (9.53)]; if CAPRAT = 0, first year's overall capitalization rate as calculated by program is used to determine selling prices
ENDSEL			When METHSE = 5, this is a predetermined dollar-amount selling price at end of final year of holding period; selling prices for interim years are calculated by program, using compound growth rate applied to COST(1); therefore, this method should be used only when total project costs are incurred in year 1; example: ENDSEL = 1900000 ($1,900,000)
SELLEX			Selling expenses incurred, expressed as percentage of the selling price; example: SELLEX = 0.06 (6%)

GROSS-INCOME PARAMETERS: If *not* specified, the default value is preset to zero.

Variable name	Default	Code	Data description
NI	[1]		Number of potential gross-income schedules (*j*); maximum number of 6 schedules; if yearly arbitrary *effective* gross income (ARBINC) are the *only* entries and there are no calculated-income streams, NI must be set to zero (NI = 0)
INARB		0	Only calculated-income streams will be used to determine effective gross income
		1	Both calculated gross-income streams and arbitrary effective gross income per year will be used to determine *total* effective gross income
INCYR(*j*)	[1]		Year in which income schedule *j* will start, from 1 to LP (6)
INCAMT(*j*)			Dollar amount of potential gross income in *starting* year for schedule *j* (6); example: INCAMT(1) = 300000 ($300,000)

INCRAT(j)		Annual rate of change in potential gross income of schedule j, expressed as either:
		INCRAT(j) is percentage change applied to INCAMT(j), type indicated by INCR (j); example: INCRAT(1) = 0.0133 (1.33%)
		INCRAT(j) is constant-dollar amount by which INCAMT(j) is incremented annually; example: INCRAT(1) = 4000 ($4,000) (6)
INCR(j)		When INCRAT(j) is expressed as a percentage change from INCAMT(j), this figure is either:
	0	Compound growth rate (cumulative)
	1	Simple growth rate (incremental) (6)
BADEBT(j)		Expenses incurred for bad debt (collection losses) are expressed as a percentage of potential gross income (INCAMT); example: BADEBT(1) = 0.02 (2%)
VACKEY(j)		Vacancy rates, one schedule for each income stream, are determined by either:
	0	Array ARBVAC(j,i) calculated from VACANT(j), which may be changed by a percentage compound growth rate, DELVAC(j) (6)
	1	Array ARBVAC(j,i) read in from the Namelist REALL cards (6,30)
VACANT(j)		Vacancy rate for income schedule j in *starting* year, expressed as percentage of potential gross income (INCAMT) (6); example: VACANT(1) = 0.05 (5%)
DELVAC(j)		Percentage change in VACANT(j) which is compound growth rate; if DELVAC(j) = 0, vacancy factor VACANT(j) becomes constant for entire holding period
ARBVAC(j,i)		Arbitrary vacancy rates for each of the 6 income schedules for each year of holding period (up to 30 years) may be specified; vacancy rate, expressed as percentage of potential gross income, is entered for each year of income stream (6,30); example: ARBVAC (1,1) = 0.20, 0.10, 8*0.05; i.e., holding period is 10 years, vacancy factor in year 1 is 20%; year 2, 10%; remaining 8 years, 5%
ARBINC(i)		If NI = 0, an arbitrary effective gross-income dollar amount must be specified for each year from 1 to LP; if INARB = 1, ARBINC(i) may be entered for any year from 1 to LP; effective gross income = potential gross income minus allowances for vacancy and bad debt (30)

OPERATING-EXPENSE PARAMETERS : If *not* specified, the default value is preset to zero.

Variable name	Default	Code	Data description
NE	[1]		Number of operating expenses schedules; maximum number of 10; if only arbitrary operating expenses (ARBEXP) are entered and there are no calculated operating expenses streams, NE must be set to zero (NE = 0)
KEXP		0	Only calculated operating expenses streams will be used to determine *total* operating expenses
		1	Both calculated operating expenses streams and arbitrary operating expenses per year will be used to determine *total* operating expenses
EXPYR(j)	[1]		Year in which the operating-expense schedule will start, from 1 to LP (10)
EXPAMT(j)			Dollar amount of the operating expenses for schedule j in *starting* year (10); example: EXPAMT(1) = 120000 ($120,000)
EXPRAT(j)			Annual rate of change in operating expenses of schedule j, expressed as either: EXPRAT(j) = percentage change applied to EXPAMT(j), type indicated by EXCR(j); example: EXPRAT(1) = 0.025 (2.5%) EXPRAT(j) = constant-dollar amount by which EXPAMT(j) is incremented annually; example: EXPRAT(1) = 2800 ($2,800) (10)
EXCR(j)			When EXPRAT(j) is expressed as percentage change from EXPAMT(j), this figure is either:
		0	Compound growth rate (cumulative)
		1	Simple growth rate (incremental) (10)
ARBEXP(i)			If NE = 0, arbitrary operating expenses in dollars must be specified for each year of holding period, from 1 to LP; if KEXP = 1, ARBEXP(i) may be entered for any year from 1 to LP (30)

FEDERAL INCOME TAX PARAMETERS : If *not* specified, the default value is preset to zero.

Variable name	Default	Code	Data description
ISCHED	[5]		Method used for calculating the federal income tax liability; see note below for discussion of certain income tax law provisions

	1	Individual income tax, single taxpayer
	2	Individual income tax, married couple filing jointly
	3	Individual income tax, head of household
	4	Corporate taxpayer
	5	Tax liability calculated on basis of income tax rate (effective or marginal) of investor
OUTAMT		For all five methods, dollar amount of the taxpayer's "adjusted" gross income from sources outside of project must be specified for year 1
OUTRAT		Estimate of annual percentage change (compounded growth rate) in adjusted outside gross income
TAXRAT		Tax rate (effective or marginal) expressed as percentage; used as an input variable *only* when ISCHED = 5

NOTE ON TAX PARAMETERS: The subroutine TAXES calculates the federal income tax liability from the annual cash flow from operations, the outside taxable income, and, given the assumption of selling the property each year, the depreciation recapture and the capital-gains tax. For ISCHED = 1, 2, or 3, the personal income tax liability is derived from the IRS tax-rate schedules. For ISCHED = 4, the tax liability is calculated using the current corporate tax rate. For long-term capital gains, 50 percent of net long-term capital gains is excluded from ordinary income, and the alternative capital gain rate is 25 percent for individuals (up to $50,000 of gains) and 30 percent for corporations.

The outside taxable income OUTAMT is the taxpayer's "adjusted" gross income (after all allowable deductions and exemptions) from sources of income *other* than the subject property. For ISCHED = 1, 2, or 3, the outside taxable income is used to find the appropriate tax rate. If ISCHED = 5, the only use of the outside taxable income is to determine the total amount of regular income for calculation of the minimum tax on tax-preference income.

Tax-preference items consist of accelerated depreciation on real property in excess of straight-line method plus, given the sale of the property, the excluded fraction of the net long-term capital gain (for individual taxpayers, 50 percent; for corporate taxpayers, 37.5 percent). In all cases, the minimum tax is calculated as 15 percent of the tax-preference items minus $10,000 or one-half the ordinary income tax liability, whichever is greater.

Namelist LOANL cards The subroutine LOAN computes the financing schedules (and/or refinancing) for the subject property. One to eight separate loans may be in effect at various times over the life of the project from year 1 to LP. The number of parameters that can be specified for each loan is an indication of the versatility of the LOAN subroutine.

Specification of several parameters is required to determine the dollar *amount* of the loan; the loan is assumed to be funded at the *beginning* of the year. These parameters are the year in which the loan starts (FIRST), and a constant specified in

AMOUNT, which is interpreted by the keyword AMTKEY to arrive at the dollar amount of the loan.

Five methods for repayment of the loan(s) are available; under any of these methods, either the term of the loan in years (TERM) or the amount of the payment per period (PAYMEN) is specified and the other variable is calculated by the program.

A loan terminates under two conditions: (1) the end of the term is reached (TERM) or (2) the specified terminal year is reached (LAST); termination occurs at the *beginning* of the year if the term is an integral number of years. Termination of a loan may cause the refinancing of the unpaid loan balance; in this case, the funding year of the refinancing loan should be the same as the terminal year of the original loan. If the AMOUNT of the refinancing loan is specified as zero, the dollar amount of the refinancing loan will equal the unpaid balance of the terminating loan.

The annual contract interest rate of the loan (RATE) and the number of payment (and/or compounding) periods per year (PERIOD) must be specified for each loan schedule.

LOAN PARAMETERS: If *not* specified, default value is preset to zero.

Variable name	Default	Code	Data description
NL	[1]		Number of loan schedules (maximum of 8); in unusual case (no loans), NL is set to zero; program calculates total equity investment as sum of total project costs
FIRST(j)	[1]		Year in which loan funds (starts); funding assumed to be at beginning of year
LAST(j)	[99]		Year in which loan terminates; used where loan actually terminates *before* end of contract loan term
METHOD(j)	[1]		Methods for repayment of loan; all methods require either term in years or dollar amount of periodic payment to be specified:
		1	Fully amortized; TERM specified, amount of periodic payment calculated
		2	Fully amortized; constant PAYMEN specified, loan term calculated
		3	Equal principal payments; TERM specified, amount of principal payment calculated
		4	Equal principal payments; amount of principal PAYMEN specified, loan term calculated
		5	Interest only; TERM specified, periodic interest payment calculated with a balloon payment of principal in last year
TERM(j)			Term of loan in years [does not have to be integer; i.e., TERM(j) can be specified as decimal number such as 10.5]; if METHOD (j) = 1, 3, or 5, TERM(j) must be specified
PAYMEN(j)			Dollar amount of the payment per period;

PERIOD(j)   [12]

RATE(j)

AMOUNT(j)

AMTKEY(j)

REFINC(j)

period is interpreted by PERIOD(j), which is preset for 12 monthly payments; if METHOD (j) = 2 or 4, PAYMEN(j) must be specified Payment frequency of loan j, preset for 12 monthly payments, but quarterly, semiannual, or annual payment periods may be specified

Annual contract interest rate for loan j

Initial loan balance specified as either dollar amount or percentage of project cost; this value is interpreted by AMTKEY(j) to calculate dollar amount of loan; if EQCOST(i) = 1, dollar amount of loan *must* be entered

Interpretation of AMOUNT(j) is one of five alternatives:

0   AMOUNT(j) is actual dollar amount of loan j; when EQCOST(i) = 1, AMTKEY(j) must be set to zero (do not set AMTKEY at 0 when options 2 or 5 have been selected for subroutine VALUE)

1   AMOUNT(j) is a percentage of project cost incurred in year loan j funds, i.e., loan-to-value ratio

2   Loan j brings total loan balance on project's cost incurred in funding year of loan j up to percentage of COST(i) specified by AMOUNT(j); for example, if junior mortgage funds in year 1 and AMOUNT(j) = 0.15, dollar amount of this loan is 15 percent of COST(1) *less* total dollar amount of all other loans funding in year 1; in this case, all other loans funding in year 1 must have subscript numbers less than loan j

3   AMOUNT(j) is a *percentage* of total (cumulative) project costs incurred through year in which loan j funds

4   Loan j brings total loan balance on total (cumulative) costs incurred through year loan j funds up to *percentage* specified by AMOUNT(j); for example, if loan j funds in year 3 and AMOUNT(j) = 0.15, dollar amount of loan j is 15% of COST(1) + COST(2) + COST(3) *less* total unpaid balance on all other loans active at beginning of year 3; in this case, all other loans active during year 3 should have subscript numbers less than loan j

Specifies schedule number of that loan which will assume unpaid balance of terminating loan; schedule number of the *refinancing* loan must be greater than number of terminating loan

LOAN PARAMETERS (*Continued*)

Variable name	Default	Code	Data description
PRERAT(*j*)			Prepayment penalty, expressed as percentage, which is applied to unpaid loan balance minus that portion of original loan amount which is not subject to prepayment penalty; example: PRERAT = 0.02 (2%)
PREAMT(*j*)			Percentage of original loan amount to which prepayment penalty does *not* apply; example: PREAMT(1) = 0.20 (20%)
IEND(*j*)			Determines method used to calculate dollar amount of prepayment penalty in *terminating* year of loan
		0	No prepayment penalty; loan is terminating according to provisions of original loan agreement
		1	Prepayment penalty will be incurred if property is sold in year loan terminates
		2	Prepayment penalty will be incurred because loan is terminating *outside* provisions of original loan agreement; prepayment penalty is incurred whether or not property is sold in terminating year; if property is sold in terminal year, dollar amount of prepayment penalty is added to that year's interest payments and is not shown separately on printed output

Namelist DEPL cards The subroutine DEP calculates the book depreciation, adjusted basis, excess accelerated depreciation over straight-line, and the amount of depreciation recaptured for both real and personal property. Up to eight separate depreciation schedules can be used. For each schedule, the following data must be specified: the initial year in which depreciation is to be taken, the depreciable amount, the type of property, the depreciable life of the property, and the depreciation method. The salvage value, if any, should be entered when appropriate.

For all declining-balance methods, a switch to the straight-line method is programmed to occur in the optimum year. IRS guidelines and regulations should be checked for (1) the maximum estimated building life allowed for specific types of improvements and (2) the methods of depreciation allowed for the type of property (personal, real residential, real nonresidential).

DEPRECIATION PARAMETERS: If *not* specified, the default value is preset to zero.

Variable name	Default	Code	Data description
ND	[1]		Number of depreciation schedules; maximum of 8; if ND is set to zero, program calculates adjusted basis as sum of project costs

FIRST(j)	[1]		First year in which depreciation schedule j starts
LIFE(j)			Depreciable life of property in years; must be an integer; may be greater than LP maximum of 30 years
METHOD(j)	[1]		Depreciation method used according to the type of property and as allowed by IRS regulations:
		1	Straight-line
		2	125% declining-balance
		3	150% declining-balance
		4	200% declining-balance
		5	Sum-of-the-years-digits
KIND(j)	[3]		Type of property being depreciated:
		1	Personal property
		2	Low-income rental housing
		3	All other real property (residential and nonresidential)
AMOUNT(j)			Depreciable amount (project costs less land value) expressed as dollar amount or as percentage of cost incurred in year schedule starts (use percentage figure when option 2 or 5 has been selected); example: AMOUNT (1) = 1200000 ($1,200,000) or AMOUNT (1) = 0.87 (87%)
SALVAG(j)			Salvage value of depreciable property at end of its depreciable life expressed as dollar amount or as percentage of *depreciable amount* [AMOUNT(j)]; example: SALVAG (1) = 120000 ($120,000) or SALVAG(1) = 0.10 (10%)

3A-3 OUTPUT DESCRIPTION AND DETAILS

The printed output of the REAL III computer model is described in this section. Before printing Sec. 3A-3.1 to 3A-3.7, the program lists a summary of the input variables for VALUE, REAL, LOAN, and DEP. This listing shows the *initial* value of each variable for the project under analysis. The user can quickly check to determine whether the input entries are correct.

If INCUE = 1, detailed gross-income streams and operating-expense streams will be printed next. For each gross-income stream, the details shown are:

YEAR............................From year 1 to LP
PGI...............................Maximum rental income from 100% occupancy of all rental space, i.e., potential gross income
VAC..............................Dollar amount of PGI not realized because a percentage of the rental space is *not* occupied

BAD DEBT .... Dollar amount of PGI not realized because of collection losses
EGI .... Actual rental income realized, i.e., effective gross income

Up to 10 separate operating-expense streams will be printed when INCUE is set to 1.

3A-3.1 Valuation

Given a target equity yield rate (XRETUR), the program automatically varies COST(CY) of the project until the internal rate of return calculated is within 0.01 percent of XRETUR; then it prints the following:

$_____ COST ESTIMATE (YEAR _____)
Project cost, COST(i), of property which is initial value for COST(CY) in first iteration (YEAR = CY)

_____ PCT RATE OF RETURN REQUESTED (YEAR _____, COLUMN _____)
Target equity yield rate requested by investor; YEAR equals RY, and COLUMN refers to either before-tax rate of return (1) or after-tax rate of return (2)

$_____ ACTUAL COST (YEAR _____)
Net present value (or investment value) of property after 3 or more iterations for COST(CY); YEAR equals CY

_____ PCT RATE OF RETURN ACHIEVED (YEAR _____, COLUMN _____)
YEAR = RY; COLUMN indicates before- or after-tax rate of return

_____ ITERATIONS REQUIRED
Number of iterations required to find ACTUAL COST; a minimum of 3 iterations is performed; this number is usually satisfactory, but the number of iterations may be as many as the program limit of 10

Two error messages are printed by the REAL III program if the subroutine VALUE encounters certain difficulties:

1. If the iteration limit of 10 is reached and the rate of return achieved is *not* within 0.01 percent of the *target* rate, the iteration process is stopped and the following message is printed: "SUBROUTINE VALUE UNABLE TO FIND COST IN 10 ITERATIONS."

2. If the subroutine RATES calculates rates of return that are unusually large (positive return greater than 150 percent or a negative return of more than 50 percent), the iteration process is stopped and the following message is printed: "SUBROUTINE RATES FINDS VERY LARGE RATES OF RETURN. VALUATION STOPPED."

3A-3.2 General Input Data

A summary of certain input variables and the calculations for the traditional first-year indicators appear in this section.

TRADITIONAL FIRST-YEAR INDICATORS:
POTENTIAL GROSS MULTIPLIER _____
Year 1 project cost divided by total potential gross income (PGI)

NET INCOME MULTIPLIER _____
    End-of-year selling price divided by net operating income (NOI)
BEFORE-TAX PAYBACK PERIOD _____ YEARS
    If printed with asterisks, payback period is greater than holding period for the project (LP)
AFTER-TAX PAYBACK PERIOD _____ YEARS
    (See note above)
MORTGAGE CONSTANT _____
    Annual debt service divided by total mortgage loan amount
OVERALL CAP RATE _____ %
    Net operating income divided by year-1 project cost
BEFORE-TAX CASH ON CASH _____ %
    Before-tax cash flow from operations divided by total equity
AFTER-TAX CASH ON CASH _____ %
    After-tax cash flow from operations divided by total equity
LOAN-TO-VALUE RATIO _____
    Total mortgage loan amount divided by year-1 project cost
COST
(Year) $_____
        Project costs incurred over holding period of project as defined by input variables
        [COST(i) and EQCOST(i)]; if EQCOST(i) = 1, COST(i) is calculated as sum of equity
        investment plus total loan proceeds available in that year (if options 2 or 5 are selected,
        this figure is ACTUAL COST for year CY as calculated by subroutine VALUE)
EQUITY
(Year) $_____
        If EQCOST(i) = 0, equity amount in each year equals project costs less total loan pro-
        ceeds available in that year; if EQCOST(i) = 1, equity amount equals COST(i)*
SELLING PRICE (when METHSE = 1)

EFFECTIVE GROSS MULTIPLIER = __(1)__
    1. Input variable SELRAT; if SELRAT = 0, EGI multiplier as calculated by program for first
    year is used
SELLING PRICE (when METHSE = 2)

PRICE INCREASES FROM COST BY __(1)__% [or $__(2)__] ANNUALLY
    1. Input variable SELRAT, expressed as a percentage change
    2. Input variable SELRAT, expressed as constant-dollar amount
SELLING PRICE (when METHSE = 3)
(Year) $_____
        Arbitrary selling prices as indicated by input variable ARBSELL(i), where i = 1 to LP
SELLING PRICE (when METHSE = 4)

CAPITALIZATION RATE = __(1)__
    1. Input variable CAPRAT; if CAPRAT = 0, overall capitalization rate as calculated by
    program for year 1 is used
SELLING PRICE SPECIFIED (when METHSE = 5)

PRICE INCREASES FROM COST BY __(1)__% ANNUALLY
    1. Compound growth rate as calculated by the program from COST(1) and ENDSEL
For all selling-price methods:
    __(1)__ PCT SELLING EXPENSES
    1. Input variable SELLEX

REINVESTMENT RATE IS __(1)__ %, MODIFIED RATE OF RETURN WILL BE CALCULATED
    1. Input variable REINTR

GROSS INCOME

   (schedule number) $___(1)___ INCREASING BY ___(2)___ % [or $___(3)___] ANNUALLY, START-
   ING YEAR ___(4)___
   1. Input variable INCAMT(j)
   2. Input variable INCRAT(j), expressed as percentage
   3. Input variable INCRAT(j), expressed as constant-dollar amount
   4. Input variable INCYR(j)

ARBITRARY INCOME

   (year) $_____
        Arbitrary effective gross income as indicated by input variable ARBINC(i)†

VACANCY RATE

   (schedule number) ___(1)___ % CHANGING BY ___(2)___ % PER YEAR
   1. Input variable VACANT(j)
   2. Input variable DELVAC(j)

VACANCY RATE

   (schedule number) (year) _____
        The array ARBVAC(j,i) for arbitrary vacancy rates, where $j = 1$ to NI and $i = 1$ to LP

OPERATING EXPENSES

   (schedule number) $___(1)___ INCREASING BY ___(2)___ % [or $___(3)___] ANNUALLY, START-
   ING YEAR ___(4)___
   1. Input variable EXPAMT(j)
   2. Input variable EXPRAT(j), expressed as percentage
   3. Input variable EXPRAT(j), expressed as constant-dollar amount
   4. Input variable EXPYR(j)

ARBITRARY EXPENSES

   (year) $_____

OUTSIDE TAXABLE INCOME

        Arbitrary operating expenses as indicated by input variable ARBEXP(i)‡
   $___(1)___ INCREASING BY ___(2)___ PCT ANNUALLY, TAX RATE SCHEDULE ___(3)___, [___(4)___
   TAX RATE]
   1. Input variable OUTAMT
   2. Input variable OUTRAT
   3. Input variable ISCHED
   4. Only when ISCHED = 5 is input variable TAXRAT printed

---

* Equity investment may occur in years where *no* project costs are incurred because of loan refinancing or balloon payments. If the loan proceeds are greater than project cost for any year, the equity investment is negative, indicating that equity is being withdrawn from the project.

† If NI = 0 and there is only an arbitrary effective gross income schedule, the label GROSS INCOME is omitted.

‡ If NE = 0 and there is only an arbitrary operating-expense schedule, the label OPERATING EXPENSES is omitted.

3A-3.3 Cash-flow Schedules

In this section of the printout, those dollar amounts which reduce potential gross income to effective gross income and then effective gross income to the before- and after-tax cash flow from operations are shown.

1. POTENTIAL GROSS INCOME	Annual total of 100% occupancy rental income from all income schedules
2. VACANCY & BAD DEBTS	Total amount of allowance for vacancy and bad debt expense from all income schedules
3. EFFECTIVE GROSS INCOME	Equals POTENTIAL GROSS INCOME minus VACANCY & BAD DEBTS
4. OPERATING EXPENSES	Annual total for all operating-expense schedules
5. NET OPERATING INCOME	Equals EFFECTIVE GROSS INCOME minus OPERATING EXPENSES
6. ANNUAL DEBT SERVICE	Sum of INTEREST and PRINCIPAL AMORTIZATION
7. INTEREST	Annual total interest payments for all loans active in indicated year (see Sec. 3A-3.7 for detailed loan schedules)
8. PRINCIPAL AMORTIZATION	Annual total principal payments for all active loans
9. CASH THROW-OFF	Before-tax cash flow, which equals NET OPERATING INCOME minus ANNUAL DEBT SERVICE
10. BOOK DEPRECIATION	Annual total depreciation allowances from all depreciation schedules. (see Sec. 3A-3.6 for detailed depreciation schedules)
11. TAX SHELTER	Equals BOOK DEPRECIATION minus PRINCIPAL AMORTIZATION
12. TAXABLE INCOME	Equals NET OPERATING INCOME minus (BOOK DEPRECIATION plus INTEREST); if positive, a tax liability is incurred; if negative, project is producing a taxable loss; this taxable loss is *not* a cash loss but a book loss in that depreciation allowances require no cash outlays
13. INCOME TAXES	TAXABLE INCOME is multiplied by appropriate tax rate, which is either derived by program or is explicit TAXRAT specified when ISCHED = 5; negative amount indicates tax credit
14. AFTER-TAX CASH FLOWS (FROM OPERATIONS)	Equals CASH THROW-OFF minus INCOME TAXES; it is net spendable income received by investor each year
15. CUMULATIVE AFTER-TAX CASH FLOWS	Net spendable income received over holding period of project

The following subsection on RATES AND RATIOS shows five indicators of the property's attractiveness as an investment.

1. OPERATING-EXPENSE RATIO	Equals OPERATING EXPENSES divided by EFFECTIVE GROSS INCOME

2. DEBT-COVERAGE RATIO	Equals NET OPERATING INCOME divided by ANNUAL DEBT SERVICE
3. DEFAULT RATIO	Equals (ANNUAL DEBT SERVICE plus OPERATING EXPENSES) divided by EFFECTIVE GROSS INCOME; is also called the break-even cash throw-off
4. BEFORE-TAX CASH ON CASH	Equals CASH THROW-OFF divided by total equity investments through current year
5. AFTER-TAX CASH ON CASH	Equals AFTER-TAX CASH FLOWS divided by total equity investments through current year

3A-3.4 Sale Schedules

This section shows those dollar amounts which reduce the estimated selling price to the before- and after-tax net cash proceeds (or equity reversion), assuming resale of the property at the end of each year of the holding period.

1. SELLING PRICE	Assuming resale at end of each year from 1 to LP, estimated selling price is determined; method used to calculate selling price is indicated by input variable METHSE
2. SELLING EXPENSES	Calculated from percentage of selling price expressed by input variable SELLEX
3. PREPAYMENT PENALTY	Total dollar amount of prepayment penalties for all active loans in current year; prepayment penalties may be calculated for any loan at end of each year
4. AMOUNT REALIZED	Equals SELLING PRICE minus (SELLING EXPENSES plus PREPAYMENT PENALTY)
5. UNPAID MORTGAGE	Total of unpaid loan balances for all active loans in current year
6. BEFORE-TAX NET CASH PROCEEDS	Equals AMOUNT REALIZED less UNPAID MORTGAGE
7. ADJUSTED BASIS	Annual depreciation allowances accumulated for the adjustment to the basis of project; adjusted basis for individual depreciation schedules equals original depreciable amount less *cumulative* depreciation allowances taken over life of project; total adjusted basis for each year includes any undepreciated amount, e.g., land value
8. GAIN ON RESALE	Equals AMOUNT REALIZED minus ADJUSTED BASIS
9. DEPRECIATION RECAPTURE	Cumulative excess depreciation from all depreciation schedules which is total recapturable amount of excess depreciation to extent of the GAIN ON RESALE; under Tax Reform Law of 1976, all accelerated depreciation over straight-line for real property is subject to recapture except for low-

<table>
<tr><td></td><td>income rental housing; in this case, if property is held for 100 months (8 years, 4 months) or less, excess depreciation taken is fully recaptured; for holding period greater than 100 months, the 100% recapture rate decreases by 1% each month; thus, property held for 16 years, 8 months would have no excess depreciation recaptured; for personal property, it is assumed that selling price equals straight-line adjusted basis; therefore, excess depreciation recapture for personal property is limited to accelerated depreciation over straight-line</td></tr>
<tr><td>10. CAPITAL GAIN</td><td>Equals GAIN ON RESALE minus DEPRECIATION RECAPTURE; program uses IRS regulations for determining dollar amount of capital gain on resale of property, for either corporate or individual taxpayer</td></tr>
<tr><td>11. TAX-PREFERENCE INCOME</td><td>Dollar amount of tax-preference items, accelerated depreciation, and excluded fraction of long-term capital gain, which is subject to minimum tax</td></tr>
<tr><td>12. TAXES DUE ON RESALE</td><td>Total federal tax liability resulting from the resale of property</td></tr>
<tr><td>13. AFTER-TAX NET CASH PROCEEDS</td><td>Equals BEFORE-TAX NET CASH PROCEEDS minus TAXES DUE ON RESALE</td></tr>
</table>

3A-3.5 Rates of Return

Calculation of the rates of return from the project is based on standard methodology for determining the present value of an income stream over time. Equities are discounted to the beginning of the year in which the cash outlay is made; equity reversions from the resale of the property are discounted to the end of the indicated year; and cash flows from operations are treated as though they were spread over 12 equal installments and are discounted at the end of each month.

Reinvestment rates are calculated assuming that after-tax cash flows are invested in an alternative investment at the reinvestment rate, that interest payments are received annually at the end of the year, and that the reinvestment rates are calculated against the rate of return achieved by the project in the year LP (which best represents an overall expected return from the project). Equity investments, cash flows from operations, and equity reversions are repeated for reference.

<table>
<tr><td>1. EQUITY</td><td>Sec. 3A-3.2, general input data</td></tr>
<tr><td>2. BEFORE-TAX CASH FLOW</td><td>Sec. 3A-3.3, item 9, CASH THROW-OFF</td></tr>
<tr><td>3. BEFORE-TAX EQUITY REVERSION</td><td>Sec. 3A-3.4, item 6, BEFORE-TAX NET CASH PROCEEDS</td></tr>
<tr><td>4. RATE OF RETURN</td><td>Before-tax internal rate of return (IRR)</td></tr>
<tr><td>5. REINVESTMENT RATE</td><td>*Before-tax* estimates</td></tr>
<tr><td>6. AFTER-TAX CASH FLOW</td><td>Sec. 3A-3.3, item 14</td></tr>
</table>

7. AFTER-TAX EQUITY REVERSION	Sec. 3A-3.4, item 13, AFTER-TAX NET CASH PROCEEDS
8. RATE OF RETURN	After-tax internal rate of return (IRR)
9. REINVESTMENT RATE	*After-tax* estimates
OPTIMAL INVESTOR HOLDING PERIOD IS _____ YEARS	Because internal rate of return varies with length of time property is held, program calculates number of years *after-tax* IRR is greater than previous year's IRR to determine how long property should be held by investor

3A-3.5a **Modified rate of return: reinvestment rate of ___(1)___ %**

1. Input variable REINTR

When the input variable REINTR is a nonzero percentage, the program will calculate a modified IRR. The assumption is that the annual after-tax cash flow from operations cannot be reinvested at the project's IRR but is reinvested at a rate specified by the investor, usually called the *next best investment opportunity rate.*

1. AFTER-TAX CASH FLOW	Sec. 3A-3.5, item 5
2. AFTER-TAX CASH REVERSION	Sec. 3A-3.5, item 7
3. CUMULATIVE REINVESTMENT	Sec. 3A-3.3, item 15 with 1-year lag
4. REINVESTMENT INCOME	Dollar amount of the reinvestment return
5. TOTAL CASH GENERATED	Sum of the first four items above
6. MODIFIED RATE OF RETURN	That internal rate of return which equates TOTAL CASH GENERATED to equity investment

3A-3.5b **Rate of return plot** The program prints a graph showing the after-tax IRR from Sec. 3A-3.5 and the modified IRR from Sec. 3A-3.5a on one of three scales determined by the program:

    −5 to +20 percent
    −10 to +40 percent
    −20 to +80 percent

The internal rate of return scale is on the vertical axis; the years of the holding period (1 to 30), the horizontal axis.

        I = AFTER-TAX INTERNAL RATE OF RETURN

Section 3A-3.5, item 8 is plotted with the symbol I.

    M = MODIFIED RATE OF RETURN WITH _____ % REINVESTMENT RATE

Section 3A-3.5a, item 6 is plotted with the symbol M.

3A-3.6 Depreciation Schedules

Part 1 of the following table is a summary of the input data for the depreciation calculations (subroutine DEP). Part 2 consists of the yearly data for each depreciation schedule (from 1 to the maximum of 8) as well as total figures for the depreciation allowances.

Part 1:

SCHED	Number of the depreciation schedule (1–8)
AMOUNT	Depreciable amount, $
SALVAG	Salvage value, $
LIFE	Depreciable life, years
KIND	PERSONAL = personal property
	HOUSING = low-income rental housing
	REAL = all other real property (residential and nonresidential)
METHOD	Depreciation method used
FIRST	First year in which depreciation schedule starts

Part 2:

DEPREC	Annual depreciation allowance
ADJ BASIS	Adjusted basis after year's depreciation allowance; basis for individual schedules does not include any undepreciated amount, but total for adjusted basis does include any undepreciated amount, such as land
EXCESS	Annual excess depreciation over straight-line amount
RECAPTURE	Depreciation recapture without allowance for gain
COST	Cost incurred in this year
CUM COST	Cumulative cost incurred through indicated year
UNDEP	Undepreciated amount of the cost incurred in indicated year
CUM	Cumulative undepreciated amount of all costs incurred through indicated year

---

3A-3.7   Loan(s)

This section prints the loan-amortization schedules and associated financing data for the project. The first part of the table shows most of the input variables for the loan calculations (subroutine LOAN). The second part contains the yearly data for each loan schedule (from 1 to 8) as well as totals for all loans active in each year. The total loan proceeds available in any year equal the total amounts of loan funding in that year less the total amounts of loans ballooning in that year.

Part 1:

LOAN	Number of the loan
METHOD	Amortization method used:
	1. FUL AMRT 1 and FUL AMRT 2 = fully amortized
	2. EQL PRIN 3 and EQL PRIN 4 = equal principal payments
	3. INT ONLY 5 = interest only
REF	Schedule number of the refinancing loan, which assumes unpaid balance of this loan
AMOUNT	Amount of loan, $
TERM	Term of loan, years
RATE	Interest rate, %
PERIOD	Number of periodic payments per year; effective interest rate equals RATE divided by PERIOD

PAYMEN	Dollar amount (per *period*):
	1. Constant payment for fully amortized loans
	2. Principal payment for equal-principal-payment loans
	3. Interest payment for interest-only loans
FIRST	Year in which loan funds
LAST	Year in which the loan terminates; if not specified, automatic default of 99 years is printed
END	Type of the prepayment penalty in terminating year
PPY RATE	Percentage prepayment penalty
EXCLUDE	Amount of original balance excluded from any prepayment penalty, %
Part 2:	
INTEREST	Annual interest payment
AMORTIZATN	Annual principal payment
UNPAID BAL	Unpaid loan balance at the end of indicated year
PREPAY PEN	Prepayment penalty incurred if property is sold in indicated year
PROCEEDS	Proceeds from (re)financing; if negative, this is dollar amount required for balloon payment
COST	Annual cost incurred from year 1 to LP
CUM COST	Cumulative cost incurred through indicated year
EQUITY	Annual equity investment from year 1 to LP
CUM EQUITY	Cumulative equity investment through indicated year
EQ BUILDUP	Cumulative total of all equity investments plus all principal payments through indicated year

3A-4 SECONDARY DATA SETS, ALTERNATIVE USES, AND COMPUTER SIMULATION AND SENSITIVITY ANALYSIS

Secondary Data Sets

Once the primary data set of the subroutines VALUE, REAL, LOAN, DEP data cards has been read by the REAL III program, every data item remains in the computer memory exactly as it was inputted. One or more secondary data sets allow the user to reset the value of any data item. After the secondary data set is read in, the program will compute and print the revised output. It is recommended that secondary data set(s) be Namelist input, even when the primary data set is formatted input.

In the secondary data set, the user using Namelist input data specifies only those data items whose values are to be changed. This process of changing one or more items and receiving a complete new set of printed output may be used for any number of secondary data sets in a single computer run. However, the user may have to increase the time limit and/or the page limit to process a large number of secondary data sets. (It is very important for users using formatted input for secondary data sets to remember that they must specify a value for every data item unless the instructions say that it may be left blank.)

The input data cards for the secondary data sets are identical to those for the primary data set with certain exceptions:

1. It is not necessary to include any Namelist group (VALUEL, REALL, LOANL, DEPL) whose data item values are not being changed. In this case, the Read option for that group must be punched with a zero. For example, if none of the subroutine

LOAN's input parameters are changed, the Namelist LOANL cards are omitted and a zero is punched in column 5 of the options and heading card.

2. Once a variable is reset to a new value by the secondary data set, it will retain that value unless reset again by another secondary data set. This fact is important to remember in the case of the VALUE subroutine because the variable COST(CY) will be altered during the iterations. Therefore, if the *original* value for COST(CY) is to be used with a subsequent secondary data set, this data item must be reset to that original value. Do not set AMTKEY in LOANL cards at zero when using the VALUEL subroutine to avoid having to reset the dollar amount of the loan(s) in secondary data sets; also AMOUNT(j) in DEPL cards should be entered as a percentage figure, not a dollar amount.

Alternative Uses

As noted in Sec. 3A-3.2, there are six different options codes used in the REAL III program. The "normal" operation option is 1. The alternative uses of the program are described below

Valuation

OPTIONS 2 AND 5 : In this usage, the namelist VALUEL card is the first Namelist group in the data set. *It is recommended that the user select the alternate option 5 and that the namelist VALUEL cards be handled as a secondary data set.* In this case, all data items for Namelists REALL, DEPL, and LOANL are already in the computer memory. Otherwise, for option 2 the user must input the Namelist group cards in the required sequence: VALUEL, REALL, LOANL, DEPL. The data items in Namelist VALUEL cards will retain their values after reading in unless the values are reset by a secondary data set. It is usually necessary to reset the variable COST(CY) after each present-value calculation because COST(CY) may be altered substantially during the iteration process.

OPTIONS 3 AND 4 : The REAL III program is constructed so that either the depreciation schedules or the loan schedules can be calculated and printed separately. When option 3 is used for depreciation schedules, the Read options for REALL and DEPL should be entered as 1; for option 4 the Read options for REALL and LOANL should be entered as 1. Usually, the only data items needed on the namelist REALL card are LP, holding period of the project, and COST(i), where it is the total project cost.

The calculations for either the depreciation of loan schedules are identical to those performed for the normal program sequence. In the printed output only Sec. 3A-3.6, depreciation schedules, or Sec. 3A-3.7, loans, will appear on the printout.

OPTION 6 : When using secondary data sets for rate of return analysis, it may be unnecessary to print out Sec. 3A-3.6, depreciation schedules, and/or Sec. 3A-3.7, loans, if they are unchanged from the primary data set. Selection of option 6 will cause a printout of only Secs. 3A-3.2 to 3A-3.5 and will reduce both processing time and paper costs.

Computer Simulation and Sensitivity Analysis

With the feature of secondary data sets, the REAL III computer model makes it possible for the user to determine quickly the interaction of the model's input variables under differing sets of assumptions. With the technique of computer simulation, the user can explore a wide range of alternative assumptions, such as three sets of input variables for the most likely, optimistic, and pessimistic estimates of COST, ARBSEL, INCAMT, INCRAT, ARBVAC, EXPAMT, EXPRAT, etc., to gain insights into the inter-relation of the effective gross income, operating expenses, net operating income, equity reversion upon resale, and other investment results.

Another analytic technique for which REAL III's secondary-data-set capability may be used is sensitivity analysis. With this approach, the user can compare the impact on the after-tax internal rate of return created by different assumptions about *one* input variable while holding all other variables *constant*. The sensitivity of the IRR to a directional change can be tested for key variables or ratios, e.g., the mortgage interest rate, the loan-to-value ratio, the mortgage term, the equity investment, or the improvements-to-land ratio. The effect of a change in one input variable or a key ratio can be seen readily when comparing the after-tax IRRs plotted in Sec. 3A-3.2, rates of return plot. However, the program will not plot rates of return that exceed the limits of the scale selected; exact values for the IRR can be read from Sec. 3A-3.5, item 8.

When using REAL III for sensitivity analysis, it is important to remember the relationship of the internal rate of return to the project cost [COST(i)] because of the possible effects from any change in the cost parameter on other input variables, such as dollar amounts in the depreciation and loan schedules. Testing the sensitivity of the IRR to a change in COST(i) involves much more than merely changing the dollar amount of COST(i).

In the case of the loan schedules, if the dollar amount of loan j will remain fixed while COST(i) is varied, the input variable AMTKEY(j) = 0 should be used. However, if a constant loan-to-value ratio is indicated, AMTKEY(j) = 1 should be used. The loan term or periodic payment also may be affected by a change in the loan balance resulting from the change in the cost parameter. Given varying assumptions about COST(i), the depreciable amount in subroutine DEP should be expressed as a percentage of the cost rather than as a specified dollar amount except when the land value remains unchanged for all cost assumptions.

APPENDIX 3B: Development of Compound-Interest Tables

In order to understand real estate investments and related financial instruments, facility in dealing with compound interest is desirable. This appendix is designed to further an understanding of the use of compound-interest tables. An extensive set of tables is presented in a companion volume.[1] Compound-interest tables are widely available and can be derived by using hand calculators.

SIMPLE INTEREST

Simple interest, i.e., interest for a single time period, must be distinguished from compound interest. For example, if Barnes loans Jones $10,000 at 6 percent for 3

[1] Paul F. Wendt and Alan R. Cerf, *Tables for Investment Analysis,* Special Report no. 3, University of California, Center for Real Estate and Urban Economics, Berkeley, 1966.

years and collects the interest annually, the interest is $600 each year. Note that the principal of the loan is $10,000 at the beginning of each year since the $600 is paid to Barnes at the end of each year.

COMPOUND INTEREST

Compound interest reflects the fact that if interest is not withdrawn at the end of each earning period, it is added to the previous capital amount and thereafter becomes part of the accumulation on which the next interest charge is calculated. Amounts that are not withdrawn do not lie idle but become part of the principal on which future interest is calculated.

The example below shows the growth of $10,000 invested at 6 percent compounded annually for 3 years. Interest is not withdrawn but becomes part of the principal.

Investment beginning of year 1 ....$10,000.00
Increase during year 1 (6% of $10,000)....................   600.00
Balance beginning of year 2.................................$10,600.00
Increase during year 2 (6% of $10,600)....................   636.00
Balance beginning of year 3.................................$11,236.00
Increase during year 3 (6% of $11,236)....................   674.16
Balance at end of year 3.......................................$11,910.16

If we multiply 1.06 for the first year by 1.06 for the second year, we arrive at the amount that $1 at 6 percent would accumulate to in 2 years. Multiplying this amount again by 1.06, we obtain the compound-interest factor that $1 would accumulate to in 3 years at 6 percent compounded annually. This is expressed as $(1.06)^3$, which amounts to 1.191016. When we multiply this factor by $10,000, we have a total of $11,910.16, which is the amount determined above.

Use of Tables

The compound amount of $1 at different rates of interest and for various periods is presented in column 1 of compound-interest tables. To calculate the amount of any investment earning a specified interest rate compounded annually for a specified number of years, all that is necessary is to multiply the value of the investment by the compound amount of $1 factor in the proper table.

More Frequent Compounding

If we assume that the interest was compounded quarterly as in some savings institutions, we would look in the table with interest compounded quarterly. For example, look in quarterly compound interest tables for 6 percent and for 3 years. The factor is 1.195618, and $10,000 (1.195618) = $11,956.18.

Note that compounding quarterly makes the investment grow faster than if it is compounded annually. The computation of the 1.195618 factor is determined by $S = (1 + 0.015)^{12}$.

The annual rate is 6 percent, and so the quarterly interest rate is one-fourth of this, or $1\frac{1}{2}$ percent. Interest rates are generally expressed in annual terms. To determine interest rates for periods of less than a year, the annual interest rate is divided by the number of compounding periods in the year. In each of the 3 years interest is compounded 4 times, and so the number of periods now becomes 12 instead of 3.

In detail, the computation for the first year of the quarterly compounding is as follows:

```
Investment beginning year 1 .........................$10,000.00
Interest at 0.015 for first quarter.....................   150.00
Balance beginning second quarter.................$10,150.00
Interest at 0.015 for second quarter...............   152.25
Balance beginning third quarter....................$10,302.25
Interest at 0.015 for third quarter ..................   154.53
Balance beginning fourth quarter..................$10,456.78
Interest at 0.015 for fourth quarter.................   156.86
Balance at end of fourth quarter ...................$10,613.64
```

We can express the above by saying that $10,000 compounded quarterly at an annual rate of 6 percent amounts to $10,613.64 at the end of the year.

The table below shows the rates and periods, starting from 6 percent compounded annually for 3 years.

Compounding	Interest rate	Period
Annual	0.06	3
Semiannual	0.03	6
Quarterly	0.015	12
Monthly	0.005	36

To obtain the monthly number of periods, we multiplied by 12 since there are 12 separate periods. The annual rate of 6 percent is divided by 12 to obtain the monthly rate of 0.5 percent.

Values Outside Tables

A problem may be encountered where n is larger than the number of periods listed in the table. This can be solved as follows. Assume that the limit of the table is 50 years and that we need the amount of $10,000 at 6 percent compounded annually for 70 years.

$$S = \$10,000(1.06)^{70} = \$10,000(1.06)^{50}(1.06)^{20} = \$10,000(18.420154)(3.207135)$$
$$= \$59,075.99$$

The factors for $(1.06)^{50}$ and $(1.06)^{20}$ can be read directly from the table. The factor $(1.06)^{70}$ can be obtained by multiplying $(1.06)^{50}$ times $(1.06)^{20}$.

PRESENT VALUES

The time line below shows the results of the annual compounding of $10,000 invested at 6 percent for 3 years, which amounted to $11,910.16. Note that the principal value of $10,000 at the beginning grew at 6 percent compounded annually to $11,910.16.

Values	$10,000.00	$10,600.000	$11,236.00	$11,910.16
End of year		1	2	3

We can also say that $10,000 is the present value of $11,910.16 at 6 percent 3 years hence. Recall that to arrive at $11,910.16 we multiplied $10,000 by 1.191016 or $(1.06)^3$. We can determine that $10,000 is the present value of $11,910.16 at 6 percent interest for 3 years by the reverse process. The amount $11,910.16 can be divided by 1.06 three times in succession or by $(1.06)^3$.

Note that for any given interest rate per period the increase of any given amount at some future date can be determined by multiplying by $(1 + i)^n$. Conversely, the present value of any given future amount can be determined by dividing by $(1 + i)^n$.

FORMULAS FOR ACCUMULATION AND DISCOUNTING[1]

Algebraically the above can be summarized as follows. Let
i = rate of interest per period
n = number of periods
S = compound amount

Period 1:   Interest on $1 = 1i = i$ compound amount $= 1 + i$
Period 2: $(1 + i) + i(1 + i) = (1 + i)(1 + i) = (1 + i)^2$
Period 3: $(1 + i)^2 + i(1 + i)^2 = (1 + i)^2(1 + i) = (1 + i)^3$
Period 4: $(1 + i)^3 + i(1 + i)^3 = (1 + i)^3(1 + i) = (1 + i)^4$
Period n: $(1 + i)^{n-1} + i(1 + i)^{n-1} = (1 + i)^{n-1}(1 + i) = (1 + i)^n$

General Formula for Compound Amount of $1
$$S = P(1 + i)^n$$

General Formula for Present-value Reversion of $1
The present value can be determined as follows:
$$S = P(1 + i)^n$$

where P equals the principal amount. Solving for P gives
$$P = \frac{S}{(1 + i)^n} \quad \text{or} \quad S\frac{1}{(1 + i)^n}$$

The factor $1/(1 + i)^n$ is found in the compound-interest tables. It is sometimes designated as v^n, representing the valuation of a residual amount.

For example, a supermarket enters into a sale and leaseback agreement with an insurance company. The insurance company wishes to determine the present value of its interest in the land and building 50 years hence, assuming that money is worth

[1] In this section the authors have drawn upon M. Moonitz and L. Jordan, *Accounting: An Analysis of Its Problems*, vol. 1, Holt, New York, 1963, pp. 553–576.

7 percent, compounded annually and that the land and building will be worth $100,000 in 50 years.

Present value equals $100,000[1/(1.07)^{50}]. The factor $1/(1 + i)^n$ at 7 percent for 50 years is $1/(1.07)^{50} = 0.033948$. So the present value is

$$\$100,000(0.033948) = \$3,394.80$$

PRACTICE PROBLEMS

Here are some examples of accumulating and discounting. Try them out and check your answers.

Example 1   Brown lends $20,000 at 8 percent compounded annually for 5 years. Interest and principal are due at the end of the contract. How much will he receive at the end of 5 years?

The problem may be expressed as $S = \$20,000(1.08)^5$. Looking at the annual compound-interest table for 8 percent, we find $(1.08)^5 = 1.469328$, and $\$20,000(1.469328) = \$29,386.56$.

Example 2   Investor Greene places $30,000 in a savings institution which compounds interest quarterly at 5 percent. What amount will she have at the end of 3 years?

$$S = (1.0125)^{12}$$

where $\qquad i = \dfrac{0.05}{4} = 0.0125 \qquad$ and $\qquad n = 3(4) = 12$

Looking at the quarterly compound interest table for 5 percent, we find

$$(1.0125)^{12} = 1.160755$$
$$\$30,000(1.160755) = \$34,822.65$$

Example 3   As part of the selling price for the sale of a duplex, Armstrong receives a 6 percent $10,000 note for 3 years, 4 months, with interest compounded monthly. Interest and principal are paid at maturity. What is the value of the note at maturity with interest?

This may be expressed as

$$S = (1.005)^{40}$$

where $\qquad i = \dfrac{0.06}{12} = 0.005 \qquad$ and $\qquad n = 3(12) + 4 = 40$

In the monthly 6 percent compound-interest table there is no column for 40 months, but for 3 years $(1.005)^{36} = 1.196681$ and for 4 months $(1.005)^4 = 1.020151$. Thus, $S = \$10,000(1.196681)(1.020151) = \$12,207.95$.

Example 4   A financial institution estimates that property it owns will be worth $200,000 at the end of the present lease in 30 years. Money is considered to be worth 6.5 percent compounded annually. What is the present value of this property?

$$\text{Present value} = \$200,000 \,\frac{1}{(1.065)^{30}} = \$200,000(0.151186) = \$30,237.20$$

ORDINARY ANNUITY

An ordinary annuity is a series of individual payments of equal amounts that are paid or received at the end of each of a number of successive periods of equal length. The amount of an ordinary annuity then is the total accumulation resulting from the periodic payments and interest on each of these payments.

A diagram of an ordinary annuity of $1 per period for four periods would appear as follows:

Values	$1.00	$1.00	$1.00	$1.00
Period	1	2	3	4

Note that an ordinary annuity is an annuity in which payments are made at the *end* of the period. Later we will study a series of payments which are made at the beginning of each period. Such an annuity is called an *annuity due*.

The formula for the compound annuity of $1 flows directly from the formula for the compound of $1. The amount of the annuity is the sum of the compound amounts of the several payments each accumulated to the end of the term. Assume an interest rate of 6 percent and an annuity of four payments. Then the first payment earns interest for 3 years, the second payment for 2 years, the third for 1 year, and the fourth does not earn any interest.

This can be shown as

$$S_n = (1.06)^3 + (1.06)^2 + (1.06)^1 + 1.00$$

Referring to the tables for the amount of $1, we find

$$(1.06)^3 = 1.191016$$
$$(1.06)^2 = 1.123600$$

Thus, we can substitute the values in the above formula and write

$$S_n = 1.191016 + 1.123600 + 1.060000 + 1.00 = \$4.374616$$

Algebraically this can be expressed as

$$S_{\overline{n}|} = \frac{(1+i)^n - 1}{i}$$

The process of accumulation of an ordinary annuity of $10,000 for four periods at 6 percent compounded annually is shown below:

End of period	Interest on balance	Receipt	Total increase	Accumulated total
1		$10,000.00	$10,000.00	$10,000.00
2	$ 600.00	10,000.00	10,600.00	20,600.00
3	1,236.00	10,000.00	11,236.00	31,836.00
4	1,910.16	10,000.00	11,910.16	43,746.16

The table indicates that if we deposited $10,000 at the end of each year for 4 years and money was compounded at 6 percent annually, the value of the series of payments at the end of the 4 years would be $43,746.16.

This annuity can be expressed in another manner. Recall our computation of the amount of $1 at a given rate of interest at a given number of periods in the future:

$$S = (1 + i)^n$$

The accumulation could be determined using this formula for each payment as follows:

Period

1	$10,000(1.06)^3 = $10,000(1.191016) = $11,910.16
2	$10,000(1.06)^2 = $10,000(1.123600) = $11,236.00
3	$10,000(1.06) = $10,000(1.060000) = $10,600.00
4	$10,000(1.00) = $10,000(1.000000) = $10,000.00
Total	$43,746.16

Note that the first payment which is made at the end of period one draws interest for the three remaining periods. The payment made at the end of period 4 draws no interest.

The amount of $43,746.16 can be easily determined by looking up the accumulation of $1 per period at 6 percent for four periods in column 2 of the tables. This amount of $4.374616 is then multiplied by $10,000 to obtain the answer.

ANNUITY DUE

An annuity due is an annuity in which each payment is due at the beginning instead of the end of the period. A diagram of an ordinary annuity of $10,000 for four periods looks like this:

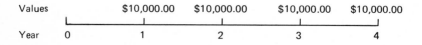

A diagram of an annuity due looks like this:

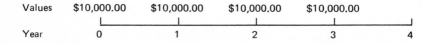

In order to calculate the amount of an annuity due, calculate the amount of an ordinary annuity for one more than the actual number of periods and subtract the last payment. This last payment will not be received, since by definition payments are made at the beginning of the period.

The formula for the amount of an annuity due of P per period is as follows:

$$S_{\overline{n}|} \text{ due} = P \frac{(1 + i)^{n+1} - 1}{i} - P$$

For an annuity due of $10,000 per period at 6 percent for four periods, the formula would be

$$S_{\overline{n}|} \text{ due} = \$10,000 \frac{(1.06)^5 - 1}{0.06} - \$10,000$$

By reference to tables showing the value of $S_{\overline{n}|}$ at 6 percent

$$\frac{(1.06)^5 - 1}{0.06} = 5.637093$$

Then $\qquad S_{\overline{n}|}$ due $= \$10,000(5.637093) - \$10,000 = \$46,370.93$

EXAMPLES OF ANNUITIES

Some examples of computations involving ordinary annuities and annuities due follow. Try each and then check the solution by reference to tables.

Example 1 Reagan deposits $20,000 at the end of each year for 10 years in an investment account which earns 7 percent interest compounded annually. What is the value of Reagan's investment account at the end of the 10 years?

$$S_{\overline{n}|} = \$20,000 \frac{(1.07)^{10} - 1}{0.07}$$

By reference to compound-interest tables

$$S_{\overline{n}|} = \$20,000\,(13.494423) = \$276,328.96$$

Example 2 Assume the same facts as in the above except that the $20,000 was deposited at the beginning instead of at the end of each period. Now we have

$$S_{\overline{n}|} \text{ due} = \$20,000 \frac{(1.07)^{11} - 1}{0.07} - \$20,000$$

Compound-interest tables give 15.783599 as the value for an ordinary annuity of 11 periods.

$$\$20,000(15.783599) - \$20,000 = \$315,671.98 - \$20,000 = \$295,671.98$$

Example 3 Martin has an account in a savings institution that pays 5 percent compounded quarterly. He deposits $5,000 in the account at the end of each quarter for 3 years. How much does he have in his account at the end of 3 years?

$$S_{\overline{n}|} = \$5,000 \frac{(1.0125)^{12} - 1}{0.0125}$$

Reference to compound-interest tables for 5 percent compounded quarterly gives us a value of 12.860361. Therefore

$$\$5,000(12.860361) = \$64,301.81$$

PRESENT VALUE OF AN ANNUITY

The present value of an annuity is the sum of the present values of the several payments, each discounted at the designated interest rate to the beginning of the term.

The present value of an ordinary annuity flows from the values of the present value of $1, which was

$$V^n = \frac{1}{(1+i)^n}$$

For example, assume the determination of the present value of an ordinary annuity of $1 per period for four periods at 6 percent. On a line diagram this can be shown as follows:

Values	$1	$1	$1	$1
Period	1	2	3	4

This can be expressed as shown below. Note that the $1 to be received in a year is discounted for one period; the $1 to be received in 2 years is discounted for 2 years; and so forth.

$$a_{\overline{n}|} = \frac{1}{(1.06)^1} + \frac{1}{(1.06)^2} + \frac{1}{(1.06)^3} + \frac{1}{(1.06)^4}$$

Referring to compound-interest tables for the present value of $1 at 6 percent, we can substitute the values in the above formula and write

$$a_{\overline{n}|} = 0.943396 + 0.889996 + 0.839619 + 0.792094 = \$3.465105$$

Algebraically the formula for the present value of an ordinary annuity of $1 can be expressed as

$$a_{\overline{n}|} = \frac{1 - 1/(1+i)^n}{i}$$

Values for this formula are presented in compound-interest tables. The $a_{\overline{n}|}$ is merely a symbol for the present value of an annuity of $1.

To illustrate the use of these tables, assume a lease agreement requiring an annual rental of $10,000 for 20 years. The tenant wants to pay the entire lease obligation in advance, and the landlord allows a discount at the rate of 7 percent compounded annually for the advance payment. Assume that rental payments are due at the end of the year. Then

$$a_{\overline{n}|} = \$10,000 \frac{1 - 1/(1.07)^{20}}{0.07}$$

Compound-interest tables give the factor for an annuity of $1 for the required periods and interest rate.

$$\$10,000(10.594014) = \$105,940.14$$

PRESENT VALUE OF AN ANNUITY DUE

If payments are made at the beginning instead of the end of the period, the series of payments becomes an annuity due. The formula for the present value of an annuity due is

$$a_{\overline{n}|} \text{ due} = R \frac{1 - 1/(1 + i)^{n-1}}{i} + R$$

The present value of an ordinary annuity is calculated for 1 less than the actual number of periods, and one payment R is added. This first payment is made immediately at the beginning of the first period and therefore requires no discounting.

Assume, for instance, a lease agreement, as in the previous example, but assume that payments are made at the beginning of the period. Thus the present value of a series of 20 annual payments of $10,000 made at the beginning of each year at 7 percent compounded annually is to be determined. This can be shown as

$$a_{\overline{n}|} \text{ due} = \$10,000 \frac{1 - 1/(1.07)^{19}}{0.07} + \$10,000$$

By reference to compound-interest tables we have

$$\$10,000(10.335595) + \$10,000 = \$113,355.95$$

EXAMPLES OF PRESENT-VALUE CALCULATIONS

Here are some examples of the determination of present values of ordinary annuities and of annuities due. Try each and then check the result against the answers provided.

Example 1 Assume that $5,000 a year is the income for 10 years for a net lease payable at the end of each year. What is its present value at 6 percent per annum? This can be expressed as

$$a_{\overline{n}|} = \$5,000 \frac{1 - 1/(1.06)^{10}}{0.06} = 5,000(7.360087) = \$36,800.43$$

Example 2 A financial institution leases land and a building to a supermarket at $20,000 payable at the end of each year for 30 years. It is estimated that the residual value of the property in 30 years will be $100,000. What are the present value of the lease and the residual value at 8 percent discounted annually?

Note that a computation is required for both the present value of an annuity and the present value of the reversion at the end of the period. This can be expressed as follows:

$$\$20,000 \frac{1 - 1/(1.08)^{30}}{0.08} + \$100,000 \frac{1}{(1.08)^{30}}$$

By reference to compound-interest tables:

$$\$20,000(11.257783) + \$100,000(0.099377) = \$225,155.66 + \$9,937.70$$
$$= \$235,093.36$$

Example 3 What is the present value of a net lease of $4,000 per year for 8 years with rentals paid at the beginning of the year, assuming an annual interest rate of 6 percent compounded annually? This can be expressed as

$$\$4,000 \, \frac{1 - 1/(1.06)^7}{0.06} + \$4,000$$

Here an annuity is due since the rent is paid at the beginning of each year. Thus

$$\$4,000(5.582381) + \$4,000 = \$26,329.52$$

SINKING-FUND PAYMENTS

Periodic payments may be made into a fund in order to accumulate to a certain amount at a given future date and at a specified interest rate. These payments are often referred to as *sinking-fund payments*.

For example, it may be necessary, assuming a 5 percent interest rate, to have $100,000 available in 10 years. What equal annual deposit will accumulate to $100,000 in 10 years at 5 percent compounded annually? A line diagram would appear as follows:

	R	R	R	R	R	R	R	R	R	R
Year	1	2	3	4	5	6	7	8	9	10

$$n = 10 \qquad i = .05 \qquad \text{Total fund} = \$100,000.00$$

The sum of the level payments plus interest on each payment will amount to $100,000 in 10 years. Reference to the tables gives the amount of an annuity of $1 at 5 percent compounded annually for 10 years to be 12.577893. We can then determine the periodic deposit by dividing $100,000 by 12.577893. The result is $7,950.50, which is the periodic annual deposit required at 5 percent that will amount to $100,000 in 10 years.

Basically we are solving for R in the following formula where R equals the periodic deposit of an ordinary annuity:

$$S_{\overline{n}|} = R \, \frac{(1 + i)^n - 1}{i}$$

To solve for R we can look up the value for the amount of an annuity of $1 at a given interest rate and number of periods and then solve for R by simple division as above.

However, sinking-fund factors are presented directly in compound interest tables. When these tables are available, the periodic deposit can be determined by multiplying the appropriate factor times the amount that the fund will accumulate to at the end of the specified time period. This is illustrated in the following example.

Example An investor desires to build a replacement fund of $40,000 in 10 years. How much would he have to invest monthly at an annual interest rate of 5 percent, assuming that interest is compounded monthly?

Reference to the monthly compound-interest table for 120 months gives a factor of 0.006440.

$$\$40,000 \times 0.006440 = \$257.60$$

Thus, an investor would have to deposit $257.60 each month for 10 years in a savings institution that pays 5 percent interest compounded monthly in order to have $40,000 at the end of 10 years.

Assume that tables were available for amounts of ordinary annuities but *not* for sinking-fund payments. The answer then could be determined by dividing the $40,000 by the amount of an annuity of $1 for the proper number of periods and the specified interest rate. The amount of an ordinary annuity of $1 for 120 periods at an annual interest rate of 5 percent compounded monthly is 155.28279. If we divide $40,000 by 155.282279, the result is $257.60.

LOAN-AMORTIZATION PAYMENTS

A common problem is to determine the level periodic installment that will amortize a loan. For example, in a mortgage on a home level monthly payment is usually made that will amortize the loan in a certain time period at the specified interest rate.

Assume that we wanted to determine what equal annual payment would amortize a loan of $100,000 received at the beginning of a period in 10 annual payments at 6 percent. A diagram of this problem would appear as follows:

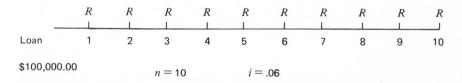

Note that the amount of the loan is the present value of an ordinary annuity. Here the $100,000 is the present value of an ordinary annuity of 10 annual payments at 6 percent, and the problem is to determine the amount of the periodic payment. The tables give the periodic installment that will amortize a loan of $1 in 10 periods at 6 percent as 0.135868. If we multiply $100,000 by 0.135868, we get the required annual payment of $13,586.80.

Many tables do not have the loan-amortization factors. However, the answer can readily be determined by using the table for the present value of an ordinary annuity. The amortization factors are reciprocals of the factors for the present value of an ordinary annuity.

To illustrate, assume the same problem as above. Reference tables give the present value of an ordinary annuity of $1 a period for 10 periods at 6 percent to be 7.360087. If we divide the $100,000 loan by 7.360087, the result is $13,586.80, which is the required annual payment to amortize the loan.

RELATIONSHIP OF COLUMNS[1]

The relationship of the amounts in the various columns will be demonstrated using the example in Table 3B-1 of an interest rate of 10 percent and data for five periods.

The first column is the amount to which an investment of $1 will grow in n periods at 10 percent. This column is, of course, determined through the use of the formula $(1 + i)^n$, described in detail at the beginning of this appendix.

Column 2 gives the amounts to which a series of individual payments of $1 per period will accrue at an interest rate of 10 percent per period. These are the figures for an ordinary annuity in which payments are made at the end of the period.

Column 2 starts with 1.000000, and each successive period adds the corresponding factor from column 1 of the table. For example,

Period 1:   1.000000 = 1.000000
Period 2:   1.000000 + 1.100000 = 2.100000
Period 3:   2.100000 + 1.210000 = 3.310000

Returning to the basic formula, we find the basis for construction of column 2 to be

Period 1: $1
Period 2: $1 + (1 + i)$
Period 3: $1 + (1 + i) + (1 + i)^2$
Period 4: $1 + (1 + i) + (1 + i)^2 + (1 + i)^3$
Period 5: $1 + (1 + i) + (1 + i)^2 + (1 + i)^3 + (1 + i)^4$

Column 1 shows the growth of $1 at 10 percent interest per period. Column 2 presents the accumulation of a series of payments of $1 made at the end of each period. Each deposit earns interest for one period less than the one that precedes it.

Column 3 presents the periodic installment that will accumulate to $1 in n periods

TABLE 3B-1

Period	Amount of $1 at compound interest (1)	Accumulation of $1 per period (2)	Sinking-fund factor (3)	Present-value reversion of $1 (4)	Present-value annuity, $1 per period (5)	Installment to amortize $1 (6)
1	1.100000	1.000000	1.000000	0.909091	0.909091	1.100000
2	1.210000	2.100000	0.476190	0.826446	1.735537	0.576190
3	1.331000	3.310000	0.302115	0.751315	2.486852	0.402115
4	1.464100	4.641000	0.215471	0.683013	3.169865	0.315471
5	1.610510	6.105100	0.163798	0.620921	3.790786	0.263798

[1] In this section the author has drawn on the pioneer work, L. W. Ellwood, *Ellwood Tables for Real Estate Appraisal and Financing,* The American Institute of Realtors, Chicago, 1967.

at 10 percent. These figures are often referred to as sinking-fund factors. Note that column 3 is a tabulation of the reciprocals of column 2. A deposit of 0.163798 per period would amount to $1.000000 in five periods at 10 percent. Division of 1 by 6.105100 (factor in column 2 for $n = 5$) yields 0.163798. Stated in another way, $1 is divided by the amount of an ordinary annuity for the specified interest rate and number of periods. This can be shown as the following for n periods:

$$\frac{1}{1 + (1 + i) + (1 + i)^2 + \cdots + (1 + i)^n}$$

Column 4 represents the present values of $1 at 10 percent deferred n periods in the future. These are the discounted values of $1 to be paid or collected n periods from the present. Note that column 4 is a tabulation of the reciprocals of corresponding factors in column 1.

Assume that unimproved land was purchased for $10,000 today and held for 3 years. It would have to be sold for $13,310 to produce a yield of 10 percent. The factor 1.331000 is found in column 1 of the table at $n = 3$. Thus the present value of $13,310 in 3 years at 10 percent is $10,000. This can be determined by dividing $13,310 by the factor 1.331000 or by multiplying $13,310 by the reciprocal of 1.331000 which is 0.751315.

$$\frac{1}{1.331} = 0.751315 \quad \text{or} \quad 0.751315 \times \$13,310 = \$10,000$$

Recall that the formula for the present value of $1 is $1/(1 + i)^n$.

Column 5 gives the present values of an annuity. These figures are the sum of the present values of the several payments, each discounted at the designated interest rate to the beginning of the term. These values are sometimes referred to as *Inwood coefficients*.

Each payment is one period further removed from the present than its predecessor. Column 5 can be produced by adding the factors in column 4 and entering the subtotal in column 5:

Period 1: $\qquad\qquad\qquad$ $0.909091 + 0 = 0.909091$

Period 2: $\qquad\qquad\qquad$ $0.909091 + 0.826446 = 1.735537$

Period 3: $\qquad\qquad\qquad$ $1.735537 + 0.751315 = 2.486852$

The present value of an ordinary annuity of $1 per period for n periods can be represented by the progression

$$\frac{1}{1 + i} + \frac{1}{(1 + i)^2} + \frac{1}{(1 + i)^3} + \cdots + \frac{1}{(1 + i)^n}$$

Column 6 is a tabulation of the reciprocals of the corresponding factors in column 5. These are the factors used for calculating the periodic installment in level-payment mortgage contracts in which the principal amount is to be amortized over the term of the contract. In such a contract the lender is purchasing the right to collect a series of future, level, periodic installments from the borrower. These installments comprise an ordinary annuity, and the amount of the loan is the present value of the annuity at the contract rate of interest. The installment required per dollar of loan can be determined by dividing 1 by the present value of an ordinary annuity of $1 per period at the specified interest rate.

For example, assume a loan of $1,000,000 which is to be amortized by five level, annual installments at 10 percent interest. Column 6 of the table at $n = 5$ gives a factor of 0.263798 per dollar of loan. Multiplying this factor of 0.236798 by $1,000,-000 gives the level, annual payment to amortize the loan as $263,798.

DEVELOPMENT OF LOAN-AMORTIZATION TABLES

In the preceding section the method of determining a level payment that would amortize a loan of a given amount over a certain number of periods at a specified interest rate was explained. A portion of each level payment applies to interest, and the remainder to reduction of the principal balance on the loan. Amortization tables indicate the principal balance of the loan at the end of each period and the amounts of the payments that are applied to principal and to interest.

TABLE 3B-2   Sample Amortization Table*

Year	Month	Balance	Principal	Interest
1	1	$9,935.601151	$ 64.398849	$ 41.666667
	2	9,870.933974	64.667177	41.398338
	3	9,805.997351	64.936624	41.128892
	4	9,740.790158	65.207193	40.858322
	5	9,675.311268	65.478890	40.586626
	6	9,609.559550	65.751718	40.313797
	7	9,543.533866	66.025684	40.039831
	8	9,477.233075	66.300791	39.764724
	9	9,410.656031	66.577044	39.488471
	10	9,343.801583	66.854448	39.211067
	11	9,276.668574	67.133009	38.932507
	12	9,209.255844	67.412730	38.652786
2		8,378.055717	831.200127	441.586056
3		7,504.329814	873.725903	399.060280
4		6,585.902435	918.427379	354.358804
5		5,620.486568	965.415867	307.370316
6		4,605.678193	1,014.808375	257.977808
7		3,538.950296	1,066.727897	206.058286
8		2,417.646575	1,121.303721	151.482462
9		1,238.974828	1,178.671747	94.114436
10		−0.000003	1,238.974831	33.811352

*Monthly amortization of $10,000 loan at 5% interest. Monthly payment $106.07. By months for first year; then annual summary of monthly amortization for years 2 through 10.

A sample table presenting monthly balances for the first year and annual balances thereafter[1] is Table 3B-2. The table is for a $10,000 loan at 5 percent annual interest for 10 years. The level *monthly* payment to amortize such a loan is $106.07.

The level monthly payment can be determined directly by multiplying the factor from column 6 of the compound-interest tables by $10,000. Alternatively, it can be computed by multiplying the reciprocal of the present value of an ordinary annuity of $1 per month at 5 percent per annum for 120 periods times $10,000. The present values of ordinary annuities are in column 5 of the compound-interest table. The loan-amortization table is derived as follows:

Beginning balance of loan	$10,000.00
Interest for 1 year: 0.05(10,000) = $500	
Monthly interest: $500.00/12 = $41.666667	
Applied to principal: $106.07 − $41.67	64.40
Balance at the end of month	$ 9,935.60

An extensive set of annual summaries of monthly amortization tables is presented in the companion volume.[2] An example of such a table is Table 3B-2. If a balance is desired within a specified year, all that is necessary is to start with the balance at the beginning of the year and calculate the yearly interest. Divide by 12 to obtain the monthly interest, and the balance of the monthly payment is allocated to principal and deducted from the principal balances. Proceed until the desired point is reached. Monthly amortization tables for specified loan amounts and interest rates can be obtained from financial publishing houses.

APPENDIX 3C: Calculating Reinvestment Rates

Many real estate investment problems require the calculation of reinvestment rates on capital released from investment projects. The formula below for calculating the rate of return earned on total cost or equity investment can be adapted to the calculation of the necessary reinvestment rate on released capital for any period of time. For this purpose, the formula can be expressed as

$$E = \sum_{i=1}^{n} \frac{NCF_i}{(1 + r)^i} + \frac{Res}{(1 + r)^n}$$

Assuming an investment problem in which a portion of capital is released during the period, the above formula can be expanded as shown below to permit calculation of the required reinvestment rate R necessary to maintain any given rate of return r over a period of years.

$$E = \sum_{i=1}^{n} \frac{NCF_i}{(1 + r)^i} + \sum_{i=x}^{t} \frac{R(NRC)}{(1 + r)^i} + \frac{NRC + Res}{(1 + r)^t}$$

---

[1] The computer program for the determination of the numerical values of the amortization tables was developed and run at the University of California, Berkeley. The authors are indebted to David Moffett and C. A. Prentice for their work in this regard.

[2] Wendt and Cerf, op. cit.

where
$$E = \text{initial equity}$$
$$NCF_i = \text{net cash flows for years } i = 1, \ldots, n$$
$$r = \text{rate of return}$$
$$n = \text{number of years of cash flows}$$
$$NRC = \text{net released capital}$$
$$R = \text{reinvestment rate}$$
$$x = \text{first year of return on reinvested capital}$$
$$t = \text{final year of calculation}$$
$$Res = \text{residual (SP} - GT - UM)$$
$$SP = \text{sales price}$$
$$GT = \text{capital gains tax}$$
$$UM = \text{unpaid mortgage}$$

Transposing and solving for R, we have

$$\sum_{i=x}^{t} \frac{R(NRC)}{(1+r)^i} = E - \sum_{i=1}^{n} \frac{NCF_t}{(1+r)^i} - \frac{NRC + Res}{(1+r)^t}$$

$$R = \frac{E - \sum_{i=1}^{n} \dfrac{NCF_i}{(1+r)^i} - \dfrac{NRC + Res}{(1+r)^t}}{\sum_{i=x}^{t} \dfrac{NRC}{(1+r)^i}}$$

The following problem illustrates the calculation of the rate of return on released capital:

Mrs. Johnson buys a motel-apartment property for $150,000. Her equity is $35,000. If she sells the property at the end of 10 years for $150,000, she will earn a rate of return of 17.94 percent. If she sells the property at the end of 5 years for the same price, at what rate does she have to reinvest this money to equal the return of the first alternative?

Accumulated depreciation, end of 5 years	$74,191
Unpaid mortgage	$96,311
Capital-gains tax rate, %	25

After-tax cash flows			
Year		Year	
1	$3,144	6	$5,832
2	6,288	7	5,653
3	6,288	8	5,527
4	6,288	9	4,531
5	6,073	10	3,731

The solution is

$$\text{Reinvestment rate} = \frac{E - \sum_{i=1}^{5} \dfrac{NCF_i}{(1+r)^i} - \dfrac{Res}{(1+r)^{10}} - \dfrac{NRC}{(1+r)^{10}}}{\sum_{i=6}^{10} \dfrac{NRC_i}{(1+r)^i}}$$

where
$$E = \$35,000$$
$$Res = 0 \text{ (at end of 10 years)}$$
$$NRC = \$35,141$$
$$r = 18\%$$
$$SP = \$150,000$$
$$UM = \$96,311$$
$$GT = \$18,548$$
$$NRC = SP - UM - GT$$
$$= \$150,000 - \$96,311 - \$18,548 = \$35,141$$
and the investment rate is 23 percent.

Calculate the capital gains tax

Purchase price	$150,000
Less depreciation	74,191
Adjusted basis	$ 75,809
Selling price	$150,000
Less adjusted basis	75,809
Capital gain	$ 74,191
Tax rate	0.25
Capital gain tax	$ 18,548

To calculate $\sum\limits_{i=1}^{5} \dfrac{NCF_i}{(1 + r)^i}$, use the tables for 18 percent:

Year
1	0.847 (3,144) =	$ 2,663
2	0.718 (6,288) =	4,515
3	0.609 (6,288) =	3,823
4	0.516 (6,288) =	3,245
5	0.437 (6,073) =	2,654
Total		$16,900

$$\sum_{i=1}^{5} \frac{NCF_i}{(1 + 0.18)^i} = \$16,900$$

APPENDIX 3D: The Use of Probability Theory in Real Estate Investment Analysis

The most common interpretation of probability is that of objective probability. When reference is made to the probability of heads given an unbiased coin, the probability of drawing a 7 from a deck of cards, or the probability that a light bulb will last 20 hours, these are all examples in which objective probability is used. In each instance the probabilities are based on a large number of repeated trials in a constant environment. Given these probabilities based on repeated trials or past experience, it is possible to calculate expected values for the uncertain future.

The question arises whether it is possible to assign objective probabilities to future outcomes in the real estate market. If each investment opportunity is unique and the market environment changes, it would not be possible to perform repeated trials in order to determine the probabilities for various outcomes. Past experience with similar investment opportunities is no guide to the future outcome of a specific opportunity in real estate because of the heterogeneous product. Given that objective probabilities are not available, can probability theory be useful? Fortunately the answer is yes. However, a different interpretation of probability is required. This new interpretation relates probability to the *degree of belief,* and is called *personal* or *subjective probability.*[1] Subjective probability is not restricted to repeatable events but applies to unique events as well. Subjective probability is intimately related to the individual making the evaluation. Thus, two individuals could have identical information and still decide on different probabilities of a certain event.

There are still a number of unresolved theoretical difficulties with the use of subjective probability; however, the concept is well enough established to be considered as a useful tool in real estate analysis. It is assumed that an investor can determine subjective probabilities and that these probabilities will satisfy the conditions set out in the next section. Given these assumptions, once the subjective probabilities are formed, the situation is similar to a problem involving objective probabilities.

Probability concepts and the statistical techniques based on them have proved to be of great value in other areas of business and economics. In fact, the usefulness of probability theory in real estate investment analysis has been demonstrated in one example by Ricks.[2] However, before attempting to apply probability theory to real estate problems, it may be useful to review some of the basic properties and theorems of the theory. No attempt will be made to derive or prove the theorems.

BASIC PROPERTIES, POSTULATES, AND THEOREMS OF PROBABILITY THEORY[3]

Postulate 1   Each probability $P(A_i)$ must satisfy the relation $0 \leq P(A_i) \leq 1$ for all *i* where A_i is a basic outcome. In other words, the probability can never be less than 0 or greater than 1.

Postulate 2   The probabilities $P(A_i)$ must satisfy the relation

$$P(A_1) + P(A_2) + P(A_3) + \cdots + P(A_n) = 1$$

given that there are *n* basic outcomes.

Postulate 3 $P(A_i \text{ or } A_j) = P(A_i) + P(A_j)$, where $P(A_i \text{ or } A_j)$ denotes the probability that either A_i or A_j will occur.

If there are only two basic outcomes A_1 and A_2, then $P(A_1 \text{ or } A_2) = 1$. Often it is useful to concentrate our attention on something broader than the basic outcomes. This broader outcome is defined as an *event*. An event consists of one *or more* basic outcomes and is denoted by *E*. The probability of any event is the sum of the probabilities of the basic outcomes constituting *E*:

$$P(E) = P(A_1) + P(A_2)$$

where A_1 and A_2 constitute the event *E*.

[1] G. Hadley, *An Introduction to Probability and Statistical Decision Theory,* Holden-Day, San Francisco, 1967.

[2] R. Bruce Ricks, *Recent Trends in Institutional Real Estate Investment,* University of California Center for Real Estate and Urban Economics, Research Report 23, Berkeley, 1964, pp. 100–105.

[3] For a more complete development of these postulates and theorems with numerous examples see J. Neter and William Wasserman, *Fundamental Statistics for Business and Economics,* Allyn and Bacon, Boston, 1966, chap. 7, pp. 187–243. A more rigorous treatment will be found in W. Feller, *An Introduction to Probability Theory and Its Applications,* vol. 1 Wiley, New York, 1966.

Theorem 1: addition theorem

$$P(E_i \text{ or } E_j) = P(E_i) + P(E_j) - P(E_i \text{ and } E_j)$$

When events are used instead of basic outcomes, it may be possible for two events to occur simultaneously, whereas two basic outcomes could not occur at the same time. Therefore, in order to avoid double counting it is necessary to subtract the probability of both events occurring at the same time. If two events cannot occur at the same time, then $P(E_i \text{ and } E_j) = 0$. Therefore

$$P(E_i \text{ or } E_j) = P(E_i) + P(E_j)$$

Events E_i and E_j are said to be *mutually exclusive* if $P(E_i \text{ and } E_j) = 0$.

Theorem 2: multiplication theorem The multiplication theorem is used to find the probability of any two events occurring together; i.e., the events are not mutually exclusive:

$$P(E_i \text{ and } E_j) = P(E_i)P(E_j | E_i) = P(E_j) P(E_i | E_j)$$

where $P(E_j | E_i)$ reads as the probability of E_j occurring given that E_i has occurred. $P(E_j | E_i)$ is the conditional probability of E_j, given E_i, where $P(E_j | E_i) = P(E_i \text{ and } E_j)/P(E_i)$. If $P(E_j | E_i) = P(E_j)$, then E_j and E_i are said to be independent. If $P(E_j | E_i) = P(E_j)$, then $P(E_i | E_j) = P(E_i)$.

Using these elementary postulates and theorems of probability theory it is possible to calculate the expected value of variables. The expected value of the variable X denoted by $E(X)$ is equal to the sum of all possible outcomes times their respective probabilities:

$$E(X) = \sum_{i=1}^{n} X_i P(X_i) \quad \text{for } n \text{ possible values of } X$$
$$= X_1 P(X_1) + X_2 P(X_2) + X_3 P(X_3) + \cdots + X_n P(X_n)$$

ILLUSTRATIVE EXAMPLES USING PROBABILITY THEORY

Case 1 Assuming that a property is offered to the investor for $100,000 subject to the lease described below, should this property be purchased if the investor requires a return of 8 percent before income taxes or depreciation? Let

R_1 = annual contract rent for original 25-year lease (= 7% of $100,000 = $7,000 per annum)

R_2 = annual contract rent for first renewal period (= $4,000 for a period of 10 years)

R_3 = annual contract rent for second renewal period (= $3,000 for a period of 5 years)

P_{n1} = residual value of property at end of original lease, given that first renewal option is not exercised

P_{n2} = residual value of property at end of first renewal period, given that second renewal option is not exercised

P_{n3} = residual value of property at end of second renewal period

P_0 = price or cost of property = $100,000

Before it is possible to determine whether the property will yield more or less than 8 percent, it is necessary for the investor to determine the probability that the tenant will exercise the renewal options. Since the investor has no objective probabilities, it will be necessary to use subjective probabilities. If the tenant is a rational individual, he will exercise the options to renew the lease if the value of the premises to the tenant is equal to or greater than the renewal rents (R_2 or R_3).[1] Therefore the investor must determine the probability (subjective) that the property will have a value greater than the renewal rent. Assume that the investor assigns a probability of 0.7 for the first renewal being exercised and a probability of 0.4 that the second option will be exercised, given that the first option is exercised. They can be written as

$$P(R_2) = 0.7 \quad \text{and} \quad P(R_3|R_2) = 0.4$$

Since there is only one other possible outcome in each period, it follows that the probability of the first residual value is $1 - 0.7 = 0.3$, and the second residual value is 0.6, given that the first option is exercised. These may be written as

$$P(P_{n1}) = 1 - P(R_2) = 0.3 \quad P(P_{n2}|R_2) = 1 - P(R_3|R_2) = 0.6$$

It should be noted the probability of receiving R_3, given that the first option is *not* exercised, is zero: $P(R_3|P_{n1}) = 0$. Similarly, the probability of receiving the second (third) residual values, given that the first (second) options are not exercised, is zero. $P(P_{n2}|P_{n1}) = 0$ and $P(P_{n3}|P_{n2}) = 0$.

In addition to determining the probability that a tenant will exercise the renewal options, it is necessary to determine the residual values if the options are not exercised. In reality the renewal values (P_{n1}, P_{n2}, P_{n3}) may take one of a large number of possible values. In order to keep the problem manageable, the investor will consider only a small finite number of possible values. To each of these values the investor attaches a subjective probability and determines the expected value of the residual at the end of 25, 35, and 40 years.[2] The investor considers all other values as unlikely; i.e., their probability is very small (but not necessarily zero). The investor's expectations are summarized as follows:

P_{n1}		P_{n2}		P_{n3}	
Value	Probability	Value	Probability	Value	Probability
100,000	0.1	90,000	0.1	80,000	0.2
90,000	0.5	80,000	0.4	70,000	0.3
80,000	0.4	70,000	0.5	50,000	0.5

From this information it is possible to calculate the expected value of P_{n1}, P_{n2}, and P_{n3}:

---

[1] Transfer costs and disturbance costs are ignored. If these are included, the tenant will exercise the option if the renewal rent is less than or equal to the value to the tenant plus transfer and disturbance costs.

[2] A larger number of future residual values is possible. However, because of the discount factor over a long period of time and the difficulty of assigning subjective probabilities, the accuracy in the final result will not be improved significantly.

$$E(P_{n1}) = 100,000(0.1) + 90,000(0.5) + 80,000(0.4) = \$87,000$$
$$E(P_{n2}) = 90,000(0.1) + 80,000(0.4) + 70,000(0.5) = \$76,000$$
$$E(P_{n3}) = 80,000(0.2) + 70,000(0.3) + 50,000(0.5) = \$62,000$$

Given this information, the investor is now in a position to determine whether the property should be purchased. There are three possible income flows. Stream 1:

$$\sum_{t=1}^{25} \frac{R_1}{(1+r)^t} + \frac{P_{n1}}{(1+r)^{25}}$$

Stream 2:

$$\sum_{t=1}^{25} \frac{R_1}{(1+r)^t} + \frac{1}{(1+r)^{25}} \left[\sum_{q=1}^{10} \frac{R_2}{(1+r)^q} + \frac{P_{n2}}{(1+r)^{10}} \right]$$

Stream 3:

$$\sum_{t=1}^{25} \frac{R_1}{(1+r)^t} + \frac{1}{(1+r)^{25}} \left[\sum_{q=1}^{10} \frac{R_2}{(1+r)^q} \right] + \frac{1}{(1+r)^{35}} \left[\sum_{s=1}^{5} \frac{R_3}{(1+r)^s} + \frac{P_{n3}}{(1+r)^5} \right]$$

If we recall the probabilities and expected values assigned earlier and use the probability theories previously discussed, it is possible to determine the probability of each of the three possible income flows, or, alternatively, these three outcomes and their respective probabilities may be reduced to one simple equation.

Probability of stream 1 = 0.3 or $1 - P(R_2)$
Probability of stream 2 = $P(R_2)P(P_{n2}|R_2) = (0.7)(0.6) = 0.42$
Probability of stream 3 = $P(R_2)P(R_3|R_2) = (0.7)(0.4) = 0.28$

Note that the total probabilities of these three income flows sum to 1. This must be so since streams 1, 2, and 3 represent the only possible outcomes.

Therefore the expected present value (EPV) to return 8 percent is

$$EPV = 0.3 \left[\sum_{t=1}^{25} \frac{7,000}{(1.08)^t} + \frac{87,000}{(1.08)^{25}} \right] + 0.42 \left\{ \sum_{t=1}^{25} \frac{7,000}{(1.08)^t} + \frac{1}{(1.08)^{25}} \left[\sum_{q=1}^{10} \frac{4,000}{(1.08)^8} \right] + \right.$$

$$\left. \frac{76,000}{(1.08)^{35}} \right\} + 0.28 \left\{ \sum_{t=1}^{25} \frac{7,000}{(1.08)^t} + \frac{1}{(1.08)^{25}} \left[\sum_{q=1}^{10} \frac{4,000}{(1.08)^q} \right] + \right.$$

$$\left. \frac{1}{(1.08)^{35}} \left[\sum_{s=1}^{5} \frac{3,000}{(1.08)^s} \right] + \frac{62,000}{(1.08)^{40}} \right\}$$

$$= \$84,461$$

The three equations could be condensed to

$$EPV = \sum_{t=1}^{25} \frac{7,000}{(1.08)^t} + 0.3 \frac{87,000}{(1.08)^{25}} + 0.7 \left[\frac{1}{(1.08)^{25}} \sum_{q=1}^{10} \frac{4,000}{(1.08)^8} \right] +$$

$$0.42 \frac{76,000}{(1.08)^{35}} + 0.28 \left[\frac{1}{(1.08)^{35}} \sum_{s=1}^{5} \frac{3,000}{(1.08)^s} + \frac{62,000}{(1.08)^{40}} \right]$$

$$= \$84,461$$

Given EPV = $84,461 and a cost of $100,000, the investor would earn less than the required 8 percent. Therefore the investor should not purchase the property. Ricks[1] has considered a variation of this problem in which he calculates the expected return using probability theory, given the purchase price and expected incomes.

Case 2 A second application of probability theory to real estate investment exists where there is a percentage lease. In order to simplify the problem, the following assumptions are made:

1. R_1, the minimum rent, is $10,000 per annum and is certain.

2. P_n, the residual value at the end of the lease, has an expected value of $50,000.

3. The term of the lease is 10 years; no renewal options are used.

In addition to the minimum rent R_1, the lease calls for an additional rent equal to 5 percent of net sales in excess of $100,000 to be paid at the end of each year. Given that the purchase price of this property P_0 is $100,000, what would be the yield before income tax and depreciation?

Before calculating the yield or return, it is necessary to determine the expected value of the additional rent for each of the 10 years of the lease. In order to calculate this, the investor must determine the possible sales levels and their respective probabilities. Assume that the investor decides on the following possible sales levels and the attached subjective probability:

Year	Sales	Probability	Expected percentage rent
1–5	<$100,000	1.0	0
6	<$100,000 125,000 150,000	0.5 0.3 0.2	0.5(0) + 0.3(1,250) + 0.2(2,500) = $875
7	<$100,000 125,000 150,000	0.2 0.5 0.3	0.2(0) + 0.5(1,250) + 0.3(2,500) = $1,375
8	$125,000 150,000 175,000	0.3 0.5 0.2	0.3(1,250) + 0.5(2,500) + 0.2(3,750) = $2,375

[1] Op. cit., pp. 100–105.

9	$150,000 175,000	0.7 0.3	$0.7(2,500) + 0.3(3,750) = \$2,875$
10	$150,000 200,000	0.7 0.3	$0.7(2,500) + 0.3(5,000) = \$3,250$

To determine the expected yield, the following equation is used:

$$P_0 = \$100,000 = \$10,000 \left[\sum_{t=1}^{5} \frac{1}{(1+r)^t} \right] + \frac{\$10,875}{(1+r)^6} + \frac{\$11,375}{(1+r)^7} +$$

$$\frac{\$12,375}{(1+r)^8} + \frac{\$12,875}{(1+r)^9} + \frac{\$13,250}{(1+r)^{10}} + \frac{\$50,000}{(1+r)^{10}}$$

where $10,000 is the rent received for the first 5 years and $10,000 + $875 is the expected rent in the sixth year, etc. Solve for r. At 7 percent the present value of the income flow is $101,690. Thus, where the cost is equal to the present value = $100,000, the return is very close to 7 percent.

It is possible to construct numerous other examples where probability theory could be applied. In cases 1 and 2 the original rent R_1 is treated as a certain income. In reality the expected value of $R_1[E(R_1)]$ should be used. This would be particularly true where the property is under only a yearly lease instead of a long-term lease. Other more elaborate cases using subjective probability for statistical decision making are possible.[1]

[1] Some application of these techniques can be found in William A. Spurr and Charles P. Bonini, *Statistical Analysis for Business Decisions,* Irwin, Homewood, Illinois, 1967; Thomas H. Wonnacott and Ronald T. Wonnacott, *Introductory Statistics,* Wiley, New York, 1969.

FOUR

Tax Considerations: Depreciation and Capital Gains

Since taxes have a significant influence on cash flows and therefore on rates of return, it is important for investors to know how taxes affect an investment's current and future cash flows. This chapter and the next should provide the reader with a basic knowledge of the tax elements involved in real estate decisions and an awareness of the potential pitfalls in the area of taxation which arise because the law changes and because certain issues of federal tax law relating to real estate are still unsettled.

An investor attempts to determine whether a potential investment is likely to provide a desired rate of return for the risk involved. Tax considerations impact upon this decision in an important way. The investor must ask: What present tax advantages do I have? What future tax liabilities will I have?

BACKGROUND FOR CHANGE IN THE TAX LAW

The United States uses a self-assessment system with an underlying progressive rate structure. Successful business and professional people find themselves in high marginal tax brackets. For many years these people and their advisors have attempted to find legal methods to reduce the high tax. Real estate, farming, oil and gas, equipment leasing, and movies are areas where there has been significant activity in tax shelters. Basically in a tax shelter an investor takes allowable deductions under the current tax law and offsets them against the investment (and if there are excess deductions against business or professional income). Often the allowable deductions are not actual economic deductions. For example, allowable depreciation on property which does not decline in value is a tax deduction but not an economic loss.

TAX REFORM AND TAX SHELTER

There is a growing legislative trend toward reduced tax shelter in real estate income investments. The 1976 Tax Reform Act resulted in severe reductions in benefits for many tax shelters such as oil and gas, movies, and equipment leasing.

For many types of tax shelters, deductions are now limited to the amount "at risk." Under prior law a taxpayer's basis in property included the portion of the purchase price which was financed, even though the taxpayer was not personally liable on the loan. Thus, deductions could be generated by the property in excess of the taxpayer's at-risk investment in such property. The at-risk rules do not apply to real estate.

There are many important changes, however, that affect real estate investment directly. A summary will be provided here, and later we will examine each area in greater detail.

Prepaid Interest

Under prior law any interest prepayment by a cash-basis taxpayer for a period of more than 1 year was considered a material distortion of income. An interest prepayment of less than 1 year generally was deductible. Thus, taxpayers might be able to deduct interest for up to 12 months past their taxable year. The Tax Reform Act provided that prepaid interest must be deducted by a cash-basis taxpayer over the period of the loan to the extent the interest represents the cost of using the borrowed money during that period.

Capitalization and Amortization of Real-Property Construction-Period Interest and Taxes

Before the 1976 Tax Reform Act, construction-period interest and taxes could be immediately expensed when paid or incurred. This benefit has been reduced since after the 1976 act generally construction-period interest and taxes must be capitalized and amortized over a 10-year period. As will be explained subsequently there is a transitional phase-in schedule of the new rules.

Recapture of Depreciation on Real Property

Residential real property formerly enjoyed favored tax treatment for the recapture of accelerated depreciation subject to ordinary income tax rates relative to commercial or industrial property. Recapture of depreciation relates to the provision which results in the taxability of a portion or all of a gain on sale as ordinary income rather than at capital-gain rates to the extent depreciation has been taken. Before the 1976 Reform Act this varied depending on type of property held, length of time held, and depreciation method used. The 1976 Reform Act treats that portion of depreciation in excess of straight-line depreciation attributable to periods after December 31, 1975, as ordinary income. This assumes there is that amount of gain.

Capital Gains

The holding period required to qualify for the more favorable long-term capital-gain treatment was increased from 6 to 9 months in 1977 and 12 months in 1978 and subsequent years. The amount of ordinary income against which capital losses may be deducted by individuals is increased from $1,000 to $2,000 in 1977 and to $3,000 in 1978 and subsequent years. It still requires $2 of long-term capital losses to offset each $1 of ordinary income. Any capital losses which are not utilized may continue to be carried forward indefinitely.

Overall Effect of Tax Reform

Tax reform may result in more emphasis on the economics of the project rather than search for tax shelter. Investors may pay greater attention to the quality of the project and to overall project yield. It is certain that benefits have been reduced by the 1976 Reform Act, but it is clear that real estate has not been hurt as much as other forms of tax shelter. Accelerated depreciation is still an effective tax-deferral method, and straight-line depreciation continues to convert ordinary income into capital gain on real property.

A review of the background of tax shelters is presented below to indicate some of the abuses which resulted in failure of many real estate projects.

INCREASED SYNDICATION OF
TAX SHELTERS

Small groups of people have joined together for many years to develop an apartment house, a medical building, or an office building. Such groups have often included doctors, lawyers, and other high-income professional and business people who have been aware of the benefits of accelerated depreciation and other aspects of the tax law. A relatively recent development has been the widespread public sales of shares in investments in real estate and other shelter areas which involve promoters passing tax-shelter benefits to passive outside investors.

Some critics of tax shelters believe that this widespread syndication of investments creates a preoccupation with current tax benefits to the neglect of future tax liabilities and the basic economics of the project. The latter half of the 1960s saw a significant increase in the amount of real estate limited partnerships. The stock market was in a period of decline. As an alternative to stock investments, the perceived low downside risk for real estate and the prospect of appreciation in an expanding and inflationary economy made real estate an attractive investment. Inflation in the early 1970s placed many taxpayers in high middle-income brackets and therefore subject to significant marginal tax rates, which in turn made them more aware of the importance of tax deductions. The Tax Reform Act of 1969 had emphasized depreciation recapture and reduced many tax benefits but did not remove the potential deferral aspects of accelerated deductions.

Promoters saw an opportunity in which investors could be sold interests in an apartment house or other real estate and could directly share in the "tax losses" generated by the project while still remaining passive investors. The basic vehicle was the limited partnership, in which the promoter or agent served as the corporate general partner and the investors became limited partners.

ABUSES IN SYNDICATIONS

Overenthusiastic promoters and syndicators often exaggerated the debt-to-equity ratios which were used. The tax law permits investors who invest with borrowed funds to claim depreciation and other deductions as though the borrowed funds were their own equity. However, along with the extensive merchandising of syndications came the attempt to create enough deductions with borrowed funds for investors to be able, in effect, to "recover" all their own equity out of tax savings on their business or professional income in the early years of the venture. This created the illusion of an economic profit with little or no capital at risk. The danger element of course is that no attention was paid to the potential tax liabilities which the tax law imposes on an unsuccessful project when the underlying mortgage is defaulted and the property is foreclosed upon.

Some promoters built in excessive markups when they resold land to the limited partnership or contracted with the partnership to construct rental building on the land. Real estate commissions and management fees were excessive in many cases. The result was that while the investors entered the project because of enthusiasm for tax deductions, much if not all of the potential profit was taken out by the promoters and an excessive amount of debt was used, so that if the project failed, investors were faced with tax liabilities for forgiveness of debt.

Areas of abuse included (1) maximum use of borrowed money; (2) maximum prepayment of interest and other financing costs; (3) maximum expense deductions for fees to brokers, promoters, lawyers, and accountants; (4) extreme allocations of the purchase price of a property between depreciable and nondepreciable assets; (5) unrealistic allocations of deductions under partnership agreements to allow deduction of the rapid write-off items by the limited partners; and (6) going to the margin of the rules which permit the partnership to be taxed as a partnership and not as a corporation.

Publicly syndicated tax-shelter offerings since the 1969 Act increased from 1970 to 1972 but decreased in 1973 and dropped off sharply in 1974 and 1975. The combination of inflation, recession, and a weak economic structure for the real estate syndicate caused the failure of many projects in the early 1970s. Recession caused owners of rental properties to face high vacancy rates together with the inability to increase rents to meet operating costs. Because of inflation and high interest rates, many real estate construction ventures experienced cost overruns which owners found difficult to finance. The wish to recover all equity through early-year tax losses encouraged investors to reduce their down payments and use excessive debt. This in turn resulted in higher mortgage payments and little cushion if revenues were not as projected. Investors preoccupied with tax shelter did not stress sound economics, and the overall result in a declining market was an increasing number of loan defaults and foreclosures on real estate partnerships.

Disenchantment with tax shelters has significantly curtailed public syndications. In addition the decline is the result of (1) shortage of investor funds because of the recession, (2) restrictive audit policies and ruling guidelines by the IRS, (3) increased disclosure requirements by the Securities Exchange Commission (SEC) and by state securities laws, and (4) a decreased supply of loan funds. High interest rates have made alternative investments such as Treasury notes and corporate bonds relatively attractive.

The significance of this background is that the investor should not be too easily enticed by tax benefits. He must appraise the economics of the project, considering the risks involved because of the use of a high proportion of debt. He must also consider the amounts taken out by the promoters and syndicators and whether these amounts will be deductible. Finally he must consider future tax liabilities. If the project fails, he must be prepared for additional liabilities. The future determination must be made in the environment of a Congress which is aware that tax shelters have become a focal point for criticism of the fairness of the federal tax system. Future tax legislation is likely to center on potential tax benefits inherent in real estate ventures. The implementation of the law by the IRS still leaves many issues unsettled.

DEFERRAL OF TAXES

Three basic elements which combine to provide tax shelter are tax deferral, leverage, and conversion of ordinary income into capital gain. Deferral is accomplished through accelerated deductions in the early years of the investment. This deferral of tax liability from early years to later years results in an interest-free loan from the federal government. This loan is repayable as the investment produces taxable income and is sold or otherwise disposed of in a taxable transaction. Deferral occurs when taxpayers choose accelerated depreciation in the beginning years of an investment transaction.

In certain cases deductions are bunched, so that in the early years not only revenues from the investment are sheltered but also the business or professional income of the investor, significantly reducing his tax liability. In later years, when the deductions are no longer available and taxable income is created, the investor may invest in another tax shelter to provide a "roll-over," or further deferral of the taxes.

Deferral can be worth significant amounts over a period of time. Thus, for example, an investor with accelerated deductions of $200,000 and in the 50 percent bracket defers $100,000 in taxes (assuming there is other offsetting income). Investors who in turn invest this $100,000 in 7 percent tax-exempt bonds will double their money in 10 years. In many cases high-bracket taxpayers can recover their investment through the acceleration of their deductions. Thus the government is helping supply the risk capital for investment to high-bracket taxpayers.

A high-bracket taxpayer is benefited proportionately more than a low-bracket taxpayer. A $100 deduction used to offset other income defers $70 of taxes for a high-bracket taxpayer but only $20 for a 20 percent bracket taxpayer.

The tax provisions also affect the risk taken by the investor. Assume that an investor invests in a project which fails and he loses all his investment. Again the tax bracket of the investor is significant. For example (assuming no borrowed money), an investor in the 70 percent bracket would lose $30 for each $100 of investment, in contrast to a taxpayer in the 20 percent bracket, who would lose $80 for each $100. This tends to make high-bracket taxpayers more willing to make riskier investments because their potential after-tax net loss is lower.

LEVERAGE

Leverage allows taxpayers to maximize their tax benefits by using borrowed funds. They may also enhance their economic situation if the cost of the borrowed funds is less than the amount earned on the borrowed funds. For certain properties the borrowing may be on a nonrecourse basis. In this situation the investor is not personally liable to repay the loan, and her personal investment risk is then limited to her equity investment. Limited partnerships are often used in real estate ventures so that the taxpayer can invest as a limited partner with no liability other than the amount of equity he has advanced from his own funds.

Borrowed funds are treated in the same manner as the taxpayer's own investment for tax purposes. This allows a taxpayer deductions based on borrowed funds as well as on her own investment. Deferral of taxes can be maximized by incurring deductible expenditures which exceed the equity investment.

EXAMPLE OF LEVERAGE FOR ALTERNATIVE TAX BRACKETS

Assume a project which requires capital of $100,000 of which $90,000 is borrowed, so that the investor's equity is $10,000. Note how the benefits are superior for a high-tax-bracket taxpayer.

	Bracket		
	70%	50%	20%
First-year deductions	$20,000	$20,000	$20,000
Tax benefit	14,000	10,000	4,000
Excess of tax benefit over investment	4,000		−6,000

Thus high-tax-bracket taxpayers recover the entire amount of their investment in the year it is made through tax deductions. Investors are financing their investment entirely by an interest-free loan from the government. It must be cautioned, however, that even if the investment fails, there is usually recovery of previous write-offs. Investors would be liable for tax on the constructive income they are required to recognize when the shelter terminates.

ORDINARY INCOME DEDUCTIONS AND CAPITAL GAIN

The third major element in the tax-shelter aspect of real estate is having a portion of the gain which reflects the accelerated deductions taxed at capital-gain rates. A benefit may also be achieved if the accelerated deductions are taken against high income and gain is taken in a low-income year. Even if the gain does not qualify as capital gain, it is taxed at a lower rate than the rate for the year in which deductions are taken. For example, assume that a taxpayer in the 50 percent tax bracket has accelerated depreciation in the amount of $20,000. This results in a deferral of $10,000. Assume that the asset is a capital asset when it is sold and that the amount realized exceeds the adjusted basis, so that there is a taxable gain of $20,000. If the gain is taxed at a capital-gains rate of 25 percent, the taxpayer would pay $5,000 tax on the $20,000 gain. Thus there is an advantage of $5,000 because of the differential between ordinary income and capital-gain tax rates.

Through the concept of *recapture* Congress has significantly limited the conversion of ordinary income into capital gains in the real estate area. Several recapture rules in present tax law will be discussed later.

TAXES

General Ways Taxes Affect Cash Flows

Because of the federal income tax law, certain kinds of gains are superior to others. Some gains, e.g., the sale of property by a dealer, yield ordinary income which is taxable at progressive tax rates from 14 to 70 percent. Other gains, e.g., the sale of investment property by an investor, yield capital gain. For sales in 1978 and subsequently the gain is a long-term capital gain and is taxed at preferential rates if the property has been held over 12 months. The tax on certain gains may be postponed, when investment property is traded for other investment property or property is subject to an involuntary conversion.

Different Types of Losses

Losses are undesirable, but certain losses are better than others. Some losses are considered ordinary, are deductible in arriving at taxable income, and give rise to operating-loss carry-forwards and carry-backs. Others are capital losses and subject to specific limitations. There are limitations on deductions of capital losses in determining taxable income. Under these circumstances, an ordinary loss is superior to a capital loss.

Important Tax Questions

Virtually all real estate investments are affected by taxes. Five important tax questions arise when real estate is purchased or sold:

1. When is gain or loss recognized, and when can gain be postponed?
2. How is the amount of gain or loss measured?

3. How is the basis arrived at for depreciation allowances and for determining future gain or loss?

4. What method of depreciation should be employed?

5. Is gain or loss ordinary or capital in nature?

These five questions are significant whether the investment is held in the form of an owner-occupied residence, a residence to rent, a fourplex, an apartment house, or a commercial investment property.

Planning Transactions to Achieve Tax Benefit

The investor must consider how to plan his transactions so that the gain, where possible, will be taxed at capital-gain rates rather than ordinary rates. He must be aware of the recent change in the tax laws which taxes as ordinary income gain formerly subject to capital-gain rates. These so-called *depreciation-recapture* rules, which relate most severely to depreciable property other than buildings, apply in modified fashion to buildings and leaseholds.

Postponement of Tax on Gain

Taxable gain can sometimes be deferred when property held for investment is exchanged for like property. This is also true for property used in a trade or business. Examples described later will show how exchanges can be repeated so that gain may be deferred indefinitely. Gain may also be postponed when property is involuntarily converted through casualty or condemnation.

Operation of Income Property

The everyday problems of operating a real estate venture have many tax consequences. When is revenue taxable? What deductions are allowed in arriving at taxable income? Deductions must have statutory authority to be allowed. Some deductions may be taken only by a taxpayer engaged in a trade or business or holding property for production of income. Other deductions, such as interest and taxes, may be taken even if the ownership of the property is strictly personal.

Taxes and Business Organization

The choice of organization of a real estate venture has many tax consequences. For example, if more than one individual is involved, the form of ownership may be a tenancy in common or a joint tenancy. A limited partnership may in some cases, be preferable to a general partnership, while in other instances the corporate form may be indicated. For certain small ventures in which rentals are *not* an important part of income, the corporate form may be used, but an alternative election may avoid the corporate income tax. This election is called a subchapter S election and is limited to firms which have a small number of shareholders and which meet certain specified requirements. Certain large ventures may choose the form of a real estate investment trust, since there is no corporate tax if certain requirements are met in respect to distributions of profits.

METHODS OF CALCULATING TAX

The law provides tax rate schedules for three categories of individual taxpayers. These are individuals other than head of household or surviving spouse, married taxpayers filing joint returns and certain widows and widowers, and heads of household. These rates rise from a low of 14 to a high of 70 percent. The rates are marginal rates, and each segment of income is taxed at a higher rate. Items that are classified as capital assets under the law receive capital-gain treatment on sale and are subject to preferential rates, as explained later.

Partnerships file informational returns and provide the partners with a report showing their share of income and specially treated items. Each partner then reports his share in the appropriate places on the individual tax return.

Corporations are special taxable entities and thus are subject to a corporation income tax. When a corporation distributes its earnings in the form of dividends, these dividends are taxed again as part of the income of the shareholders. This is sometimes referred to as *double taxation*. A considerable body of tax law is concerned with attempts by taxpayers to avoid this double taxation and the legislation that has resulted in order to block these attempts. Corporate tax rates under the 1976 Act are 20 percent of the first $25,000, 22 percent of the next $25,000, and 48 percent on the balance.

INCOME AVERAGING

Income averaging allows a portion of an unusually large amount of annual taxable income to be taxed in lower brackets than if it were treated in the normal manner. The method has the effect of taxing income of an unusually high income year as if it were earned over a 5-year period. Generally, all types of income can be averaged, including long-term capital gains and income from inherited property and from gifts. There are some exceptions, e.g., premature payouts from self-employment retirement plans. Certain tests in respect to residence and support must be met.[1]

An individual who qualifies can elect income averaging when averageable income for a current tax year is more than $3,000 and taxable income for the same tax year is more than one-fifth higher than average income for a base period of the four preceding years.[2] Persons receiving an unusually

---

[1] U.S. Internal Revenue Service, *1954 Internal Revenue Code,* sec. 1303, 1.1303-1.
[2] Ibid., sec. 1301, 1.1301-1.

large amount of income from a sale of real estate should determine whether they are eligible for income averaging.

MAXIMUM TAX ON EARNED INCOME

Congress determined that extremely high rates of tax for earned income tend to create disincentives in the tax system. A 50 percent maximum marginal rate on earned income was determined to be a method of reducing the disincentive effect of high rates for earned income.

Wages, professional fees, and compensation for personal services are examples of earned income. Capital gains and dividends do not qualify as earned income. If both services and capital are material income-producing factors, not more than 30 percent of the share of the net profit may be treated as earned income. The 1976 Tax Reform Act added pensions, annuities, and deferred compensation to the definition of personal-service income subject to the maximum tax.

COMPUTATIONS AND OFFSETS
FOR MAXIMUM TAX

The personal-service *net* income is the gross personal-service income reduced by (1) deductions allocable to, chargeable against, that income and (2) all tax-preference items for the year. Tax preferences are discussed below under minimum tax.

The following illustrates the calculation:

Salaries, bonuses, etc.	$170,000
Deductions attributable thereto	14,000
Personal-service net income	$156,000
Other income	44,000
Adjusted gross income	$200,000
Deductions from adjusted gross income and exemptions	50,000
Taxable income	$150,000

$$\text{Earned taxable income} \quad \frac{\$156,000}{\$200,000} \times \$150,000 = \$117,000$$

The maximum tax is the sum of three separate tax computations: (1) regular tax on taxable income through the 50 percent tax bracket; (2) 50 percent of the excess of earned taxable income over the amount of taxable income in item 1; and (3) the excess of the tax on taxable income (figured as if the maximum tax did not apply) over the tax on earned taxable income (figured as if this income were the taxable income). The IRS provides Form 4726 to compute the maximum tax. The purpose is to tax earned taxable income at a maximum rate of 50 percent and to tax any excess at the rates which would apply if the maximum tax rules did not apply.

MINIMUM TAX

Taxpayers receiving most of their income from capital gains or other tax-preferred activities tended to pay relatively low rates of tax compared with those who received the bulk of their income from personal services. Congress imposed a minimum tax to be sure tax preferences are taxed to a certain degree.

Some of the items of tax preference are:

1. Capital gains; this is one-half the amount by which the net long-term capital gains exceed the net short-term capital losses for the year. For corporations it is 37.5 percent of the excess.

2. Accelerated depreciation on real property; this is the amount of the depreciation deduction during the year on real property (other than the year of disposition) in excess of the depreciation deductions that would have been allowable had the straight-line method of depreciation been used.

3. Depletion; this is the excess of the depletion deduction over the adjusted basis of the property at the end of the year (determined without regard to the depletion deduction for the year).

4. Excess depreciation on personal property subject to a net lease; this applies to most taxpayers. Corporations other than Subchapter S and personal holding companies do not include this as a tax preference.

5. Fast amortization on certified pollution-control facilities, railroad rolling stock, on-the-job training expenses and child-care facilities in excess of the depreciation allowance.

6. The difference between purchase price and value when a stock option is exercised.

7. Banking institutions use the excess of the addition to their debt reserve over the reserve which would have been allowable if the excess had been based on the institution's actual experience.

The 1976 Tax Reform Act added several new tax preference items as well as increasing the minimum tax rate to 15 percent. New tax preference items for individuals and other noncorporate taxpayers include:

1. Excess of itemized deductions (other than casualty and medical deductions) over 60 percent of adjusted gross income. This may be important to the individual who has large interest and property taxes on a personal residence.

2. Certain excess intangible drilling costs.

3. Excess of accelerated over straight-line depreciation on all leased personal property.

No new items of tax preference were added for corporations.

Tax preference exemptions were lowered by the 1976 Tax Reform Act. For individuals there is an exemption of $10,000 per year or, if greater, one-half of the regular income tax for the year. There is no longer any offset available for tax carryovers from previous years. For corporations the exemption is $10,000 per year or, if greater than the regular income tax, it is computed generally in the same manner as for individuals. There is no longer any offset available for carry-overs from previous years for corporations or individuals.

Example of Minimum Tax for Individuals

The following illustrates the calculation of the minimum tax for individuals. Assume that John and Janie Jones file a joint return. They had taxable income of $50,000. Tax preferences consisting of excess accelerated depreciation allowances amount to $30,000. Their regular tax liability (not including the minimum tax) is $17,060. The minimum tax is calculated as follows:

```
Total tax preferences .................................$30,000
Less: greater of $10,000 or 50% of
    regular income tax for year...................... 10,000
Minimum tax base....................................$20,000
Tax: 15% of minimum tax base...................$  3,000
```

This is added to the regular income tax to find the tax due.

Depreciation and Cash Flow

It is particularly significant that depreciation is a deductible expense for tax purposes which does not constitute a cash outflow. Because depreciation is computed on the total cost of improvements, and because certain accelerated depreciation methods are allowed, they often result in sizable depreciation deductions. Depending on the combination of relevant factors, there may be a positive cash flow and at the same time no taxable income in the early years of a real estate venture.

Example of Positive Cash Flow and No Taxable Income

Assume that Mrs. J purchases a new apartment house with net rental income, before depreciation, interest, and income taxes, of $66,000 per annum. The relevant facts are as follows:

```
Cost..................................................$800,000
Down payment ..................................$200,000
First mortgage .....................................$600,000 (20 years at 6%)
Depreciation method...........................200%, declining-balance
Useful life .........................................40 years
Cost allocation: land ...........................$200,000
Improvements .....................................$600,000
```

Cash flow   A cash flow of $14,000 results in the first year:

Cash from operations $66,000
Loan payment...................................... 52,000
Net cash flow.....................................$14,000

Taxable income   Because of the use of the double-declining-balance depreciation method, there is no taxable income:

Income before depreciation,
  interest, and income taxes...................$66,000
Interest $36,000
Depreciation........................ 30,000

                                         66,000
                                         None

In addition to the $14,000 cash flow Mrs. J enjoys, she also has paid off $16,000 principal of her mortgage and thus has increased her equity in the apartment house by this amount, assuming no decline in the market value of the property. This is referred to in Chap. 2 as equity buildup.

The amount of the depreciation deductible and the amount of the interest charges will decline each year. If the property does not decline in value an amount equal to the depreciation deductions, the property can be sold at a gain.

Depreciation deductions offset revenue in arriving at taxable income. Thus, they reduce taxes by an amount equal to the deduction times the taxpayer's ordinary tax rate. Depreciation deductions also reduce a taxpayer's basis for determination of gain or loss on future disposition of the property. Thus it would be advantageous to deduct excess depreciation, even though it meant an equal amount of capital gain, since capital gains are taxed at a lower rate. Recapture rules limit this possibility.

Example of the Relationship of Current
Depreciation and Future Capital Gain

Assume M purchases an apartment house and deducts $50,000 depreciation in the first 10 years under the straight-line method. M is in the 50 percent tax bracket; this deduction saves him $25,000 in income taxes. After 10 years he sells the apartment house. Assuming that the apartment house did not decline in value, he has $50,000 long-term capital gain, and assuming no other capital transactions, he pays $12,500 tax on this gain.

Consider Trade of Property

Owners of appreciated real estate have another tax-planning opportunity. They may exchange, rather than sell, their property for another piece of property. Provided certain requirements are met, there is no tax recognized at the time of the exchange. Thus, taxpayers may often be able to trade for a more valuable piece of property after their equity in the original property has increased. This is discussed in detail in a later chapter.

Property That Can Be Depreciated[1]

Land is not subject to an allowance for depreciation. A deduction is not allowed for property held for personal use, but it is allowed for property used in a trade or business or property held for the production of income. For property that has a partial personal and partial business use, only the business portion may be depreciated.

Property must have a definite limited life to be depreciated. Intangible property, such as leaseholds, patents, and copyrights, may be amortized, but the accelerated depreciation methods, shortly to be discussed, may not be used.

Basis for Depreciation[2]

The basis for depreciation is the same as for determining the gain on a sale. This is usually the original cost plus additions for improvements less deductions for depreciation and deductible casualty losses.

In some cases property is first utilized for personal use and then later for business use. For example, a person may purchase shares in a cooperative and live in the cooperative. Later he may rent out his cooperative apartment. There is no depreciation deduction when the apartment is used for personal use, but when it is rented, it becomes subject to an allowance for depreciation. The basis for depreciation is the lesser of (1) the adjusted basis on date of conversion and (2) the fair market value on the date of conversion.

Different Depreciation Methods[3]

For tax purposes the following depreciation methods may be employed:
1. Straight-line method
2. Sum-of-the-years-digits method
3. Declining-balance method

A taxpayer may also use any other consistent method of depreciation for property which qualifies for the sum-of-the-years-digits method and the double-declining-balance methods. There is a limitation, however, in that the total depreciation allowances at the end of each year may not exceed the total amount that would result from the declining-balance method at twice the straight-line rate. This limitation applies for the first two-thirds of the useful life of the asset. Although these methods will be familiar to many, it will be useful to review their computation briefly and to outline the necessary qualifications.

[1] Ibid., secs. 167 (a)1, 1.167(a)-1(a), and 167(a)2, 1.167(a)-1(a).
[2] Ibid., sec. 167(g), 1.167(f)-1.
[3] Ibid., sec. 167; 1.167(b)-0.

Straight-line The annual depreciation allowance is determined by dividing the cost or other basis of the property less its estimated salvage value by its estimated useful life. For example, Miss W purchases a warehouse for $40,000 with an estimated useful life of 40 years and no scrap value. Her annual depreciation allowance is $1,000. Salvage value up to 10 percent of the cost or other basis may be ignored for personal property with at least a 3-year useful life.

Sum-of-the-years-digits method[1] The sum-of-the-years-digits method and the double-declining-balance method (discussed below) are both referred to as *accelerated methods* because they yield more depreciation deductions in the earlier years of the life of the asset and fewer in the later years. Thus, even if the same total amount of depreciation is taken during the life of the asset as under the straight-line method, the earlier, larger depreciation deductions mean that the taxpayer pays less tax and thus has more working capital in the earlier years. Even if there is a larger tax outflow in the later years under the accelerated methods, the taxpayer has benefited from the use of the money during this period.

Under the sum-of-the-years-digits method, a changing fraction is applied to the basis of the property less salvage value. The numerator of the fraction is the number of years remaining in the life of the asset, and the denominator is the sum of the numbers representing the years of life of the property.

Example of computation Assume that R, an apartment-house operator, purchases three appliances. Given the following facts, depreciation is computed as follows:

```
Cost of appliances.....................................$1,500
Useful life..............................................5 years
Salvage value .........................................None
Taxpayer's marginal tax bracket..................30%
```

Year	Fraction	Amount of depreciation
1	$5/15$	$500
2	$4/15$	400
3	$3/15$	300
4	$2/15$	200
5	$1/15$	100

The total depreciation is $1,500, which is the same as the amount R would have had under the straight-line method. However, he prefers this method because it results in the use of extra working capital. For example, in year 1 there is $500 depreciation deduction under the sum-of-the-years-digits method, whereas the straight-line method would have given a deduc-

[1] Ibid., sec. 167(b)(3),c; 1.167(b)-3.

TABLE 4-1

		Cumulative Depreciation Charged		
Year	Annual depreciation charge, declining-balance method	Declining-balance	Straight-line	Sum-of-the-years-digits
1	$600	$ 600	$ 300	$ 500
2	360	960	600	900
3	216	1,176	900	1,200
4	162*	1,338	1,200	1,400
5	162*	1,500	1,500	1,500

* Change to straight-line method in year 4.

tion of only $300. At R's 30 percent tax bracket, the $200 additional deduction means that he pays $60 less in tax. Even though he will pay more tax in years 4 and 5 under the sum-of-the-years-digits method, he has had the use of this money in the interim.

The following formula helps in computing the denominator under the sum-of-the-years-digits method, where $S =$ denominator and $N =$ estimated useful life:

$$S = N \frac{N + 1}{2}$$

In our example $\qquad S = 5 \frac{5 + 1}{2} = 15$

Not all property is eligible for the sum-of-the-years-digits method, as will be discussed below.

Declining-balance method[1] A rate of depreciation not exceeding twice the the straight-line rate may be used with the declining-balance method. From now on, the declining-balance method at twice the straight-line rate will be referred to as the *double-declining-balance method*. A uniform rate is applied to the unrecovered basis of the property each year. Salvage value is not considered in the calculation. However, salvage value must be considered when the asset is retired. Also, the asset may not be depreciated below salvage value.

Take the same example, and see how the double-declining-balance method operates. Recall that the cost of the appliances was $1,500 and the useful life was 5 years with no salvage value. The straight-line percentage rate for 5 years is 20 percent a year (100 percent divided by 5). The double-declining-balance rate is twice this, or 40 percent. Each year 40 percent is applied to the unrecovered balance. Table 4-1 shows the calculation and

[1] Ibid., sec. 167(b)(2); 1.167(b)-2.

also compares the cumulative amounts to date under the alternative methods.

For the first year 40 percent is applied to the $1,500. Subtracting the $600 from the $1,500 leaves $900, and the 40 percent is applied to yield $360 for the second year. The same process results in $216 in year 3, and a balance of $324. Continuing the process would give a deduction of $129.60 for year 4 and $77.76 for year 5.

A change from the double-declining-balance method to the straight-line method may be made without permission of the IRS. Other changes require permission. Thus in year 4, with 2 years remaining, the remaining balance of $324 is divided by 2, assuming no scrap value. If there had been a scrap value of $124, then $200 would be divided by 2 to get the depreciation for years 4 and 5 ($324 remaining balance less $124 scrap value).

REQUIREMENTS FOR USE OF ACCELERATED DEPRECIATION METHODS ON PERSONAL PROPERTY

Not all property may be depreciated under the sum-of-the-years-digits method or the double-declining-balance method. Rules are different for tangible personal property and for real property. For tangible personal property these methods apply only to property that is acquired by taxpayers after 1953 provided they are the *original user* of the property and to owners of property built or rebuilt by or for the taxpayer after 1953. The property must have a useful life of at least 3 years. The maximum rate that can be employed for used tangible personal property having a useful life of 3 years or more is 1½ times the straight-line rate. Generally changes can be made from any acceptable declining-balance method to the straight-line method without the consent of the IRS. After a change is made to the straight-line method for any property, a change cannot be made to the declining-balance method or to another method without written permission from the IRS.

150 Percent Declining-Balance Depreciation

Property not eligible for the accelerated methods discussed above may be depreciated using the declining-balance method at a rate of 1½ times the straight-line rate. For example, Mrs. R purchases equipment at a cost of $100,000 with a 25-year remaining life. She cannot use double-declining-balance or sum-of-the-years-digits methods because she is not the original user. She may, however, use 1½ times the straight-line rate. A 25-year remaining life means a 4 percent straight-line rate (100 percent divided by 25), and so the limited declining-balance rate is 6 percent (150 percent of 4 percent). Depreciation the first year is $6,000 (6 percent of $100,000), and the second year it is $5,640 (6 percent of the remaining $94,000). Note that her depreciation still exceeds that in the straight-line method, which would have resulted in an allowance of $4,000 each year.

REQUIREMENTS FOR ACCELERATED METHODS ON REAL PROPERTY

The methods that may be employed for real property depend on whether it was acquired after July 24, 1969, whether it was acquired new or used, and whether it is residential rental property or other real property. Table 4-2 defines the allowable methods. For residential rental property 80 percent of the gross income must be derived from rentals of residential units. A residential unit means a house or an apartment used to provide accommodations but does not include units in a hotel, motel, inn, or other establishment in which more than one-half of the units are used on a transient basis.

Useful Life of Depreciable Property[1]

In addition to the depreciable basis and the straight-line method, two other crucial variables determining the depreciation allowance are the useful life of the property and the salvage value. The expected useful life to the taxpayer may be very different from the physical life of the asset. The depreciation lives adopted will depend on the particular facts involved in each case. The taxpayer's experience may be used to support a particular depreciation life. Taxpayers who have not had much experience with a particular type of asset may rely on the industry experience. As noted in the next section, the Treasury Department has issued guidelines for depreciation lives.

TABLE 4-2   Allowable Methods for Real Property

Type of property	Acquired	Allowable method
Real, new	Before 7/25/69	Declining-balance at twice straight-line
Used	Before 7/25/69	Declining-balance at $1\frac{1}{2}$ times straight-line
Residential rental, new	After 7/24/69	Declining-balance at twice straight-line
Used	After 7/24/69	Declining-balance at $1\frac{1}{4}$ times straight-line
Other real, new	After 7/24/69	Declining-balance at $1\frac{1}{2}$ times straight-line
Used	After 7/24/69	Straight-line

[1] Ibid., sec. 1.167(a)-1(b).

Depreciation Guidelines

In 1962 the Treasury Department issued Revenue Procedure 62-21, more commonly known as the Depreciation Guidelines. This replaced Bulletin F, the previous basic guide for depreciation lives. The Depreciation Guidelines had the objective of providing basic reforms by shortening depreciation lives and was designed to help in the administration of depreciation for tax purposes. Whereas Bulletin F listed several hundred items with depreciation lives, the Depreciation Guidelines gives lives for approximately 75 broad classes of assets. The guideline lives are mostly by industry, and taxpayers may set any useful life they wish for the individual asset as long as the lives average out to the useful life for the particular class. A few classes of assets are not listed by industry; e.g., apartments have a 40-year life; dwellings, 45 years; factories, 45 years; garages, 45 years; hotels, 40 years; office buildings, 45 years; stores, 50 years; warehouses, 60 years; automobiles, 3 years; office furniture, fixtures, machines, and equipment, 10 years. Land improvements are given a life of 20 years. This includes such improvements as sidewalks, paved surfaces, sewers, landscaping, shrubbery, and similar improvements.

Allocation between Land and Building[1]

When land and building are purchased together for one price, the amount must be allocated between the land and the improvements. The land, of course, is not depreciable. The problem is to have an objective basis for this division, as it is, of course, to the taxpayer's benefit to place as much of the valuation as possible on the depreciable improvements. The relative assessed valuation of the tax assessor is often used in substantiating the allocation.

Example of allocation of cost K pays $100,000 for an apartment building and the surrounding land. The assessor has placed a valuation of $10,000 on the land and $30,000 on the building. Thus K can allocate $25,000 to the land and $75,000 to the building. This is a 3:1 ratio just as the assessed valuation. Sometimes a purchaser and seller specify the allocation of purchase price in a contract, but this may or may not be accepted by the IRS.

First-Year Special Depreciation Allowance[2]

Additional first-year special depreciation is allowed for tangible personal property. Note that this does *not* apply to real or intangible personal property. This is of special interest to the real estate investor in motels, hotels, or furnished residential or commercial property.

[1] Ibid., sec. 1.167(a)-5.
[2] Ibid., sec. 179; 1.179.

The allowance is equal to 20 percent of the cost of the investment. The 20 percent applies to $10,000 of investment, and salvage value is not considered in applying the 20 percent. On a joint return, the 20 percent is applied to $20,000 of cost rather than $10,000. Also, the $10,000 limit applies to each taxpayer and not to each business in which a taxpayer has an interest. To qualify, property must (1) be tangible personal property, (2) be acquired after December 31, 1957, and (3) have a useful life of at least 6 years when acquired. The property may be new or used.

For example, Ms. E, a single apartment-house operator, purchases $10,000 of furniture for an apartment house. She uses straight-line depreciation, and the furniture has a useful life of 10 years. Salvage value is $2,000. The special initial first-year allowance is $2,000. This is 20 percent of the $10,000. Her basis for depreciation is now $7,000. That is, the $10,000 cost less the $2,000 initial first-year depreciation and less $1,000 salvage. Recall that 10 percent of the cost of personal property may be ignored in computing salvage value. Under the straight-line method the allowance for the first year is $700 ($7,000 divided by 10). Her total allowance is thus $2,700. We have assumed that Ms. E purchased the furniture at the beginning of the year. This initial allowance can be taken in full, no matter how late in the year the property is acquired.

Grouping for Depreciation[1]

Taxpayers may compute the depreciation on each depreciable item. Alternatively, they may use composite accounts in which all the depreciable assets in the business are grouped in one account with one allowance for depreciation. In some cases classified accounts are used. Here the items are included in the same account, regardless of their estimated useful lives, e.g., office furniture and fixtures and machinery and equipment. Real estate investors may depreciate a building as a unit, or they may depreciate its component parts, such as the roof and foundation, separately.

Investment Credit[2]

Taxpayers receive a credit against their tax on certain qualifying property that they purchase. Note that this is a credit against their tax and not a deduction in arriving at the tax. This credit is in addition to the depreciation allowance.

Buildings excluded   The investment credit is only of limited significance to the real estate investor, since buildings and their structural components are *not* qualifying property. The credit is applicable to depreciable, tangible personal property except livestock. Real property other than buildings or

[1] Ibid., sec. 1.167(a)-7.
[2] Ibid., sec. 46.

their structural components may qualify if it (1) is used in manufacturing, production, extraction, or the furnishing of utilitylike services or (2) constitutes a research or storage facility of an activity under item 1. Examples of real property that would qualify are elevators and escalators acquired or completed after June 30, 1963, blast furnaces, storage tanks, and broadcasting towers.

CAPITAL GAINS AND LOSSES

The importance of capital gains to the real estate investor has already been indicated. The excess of net long-term gains over net short-term capital losses is taxed at a maximum of 25 percent for the first $50,000, which is ordinarily below the individual's ordinary tax rate. For corporations the excess of net long-term gains over net short-term capital losses is taxed at a maximum of 30 percent, which is below the current corporate tax rate of 48 percent for income above $50,000.

Capital assets held over the required holding period yield long-term capital gains when sold or exchanged. If the net gain from the sale or exchange of long-term capital assets is greater than the net losses from the sale or exchange of short-term capital assets, only one-half of such excess is subject to tax. If the result of sales and exchanges of both short-term and long-term capital assets is a loss, the maximum that may be deducted is limited, as explained below.

Meaning of Capital Asset

Since capital gains and losses result from the sale or exchange of capital assets, it is necessary to define a capital asset. The definition is primarily negative. *Capital assets* include any property held *except* (1) stock in trade; (2) real or personal property includable in inventory; (3) real or personal property held for sale to customers; (4) accounts or notes receivable acquired in the ordinary course of trade or business for services rendered, or from the sale of any of the properties described above, or for services rendered as an employee; (5) depreciable property used in trade or business; (6) real property used in trade or business; (7) a copyright, or a literary, musical, or artistic composition, or similar property if created by the taxpayer's personal efforts or if the taxpayer acquired it from the creator under circumstances entitling him or her to the creator's basis; (8) certain federal, state, and municipal short-term obligations.

Property for personal use Property held for personal use, such as the taxpayer's personal residence, is a capital asset, and sale yields a capital gain. However, a loss on the sale of a personal asset is not deductible.

Real property If the property is investment property, it is a capital asset and its sale or exchange yields capital gain or capital loss. If it is used in a trade or business, it is not a capital asset. Note especially that properties in categories 5 and 6 are not generally regarded as capital assets.

However, depreciable property used in a trade or business and real property used in a trade or business receive long-term capital-gain treatment if the following conditions are met: (1) the asset sold or exchanged is held over 1 year *and* (2) the recognized gains on these assets exceed recognized losses. These transactions are referred to as Section 1231 transactions after the relevant section of Internal Revenue Code. We will come back to a discussion of these transactions later. Other transactions, such as certain involuntary conversions, are also covered by Section 1231.

Rental property   There may be a question whether rental property is investment property, and therefore a capital asset, or property used in a trade or business, and therefore not a capital asset. If it is property used in a trade or business, it is covered by Section 1231, referred to above.

Stocks   Stocks, stock rights, and bonds are capital assets unless they are held for sale by a securities dealer. However, losses on stock of certain so-called "small business corporations" are treated as ordinary losses.

HOLDING PERIODS

The holding period is important in determining whether the asset sold or exchanged gives rise to a short-term or a long-term gain or loss. Before 1977 if the asset was held 6 months or less, its sale or exchange resulted in a short-term capital gain or loss. Starting in 1977, the holding period for long-term capital gain or loss treatment is extended in two steps. For tax years beginning in 1977, gain or loss on the sale or exchange of an asset that is held more than 9 months will be long-term. For tax years beginning in 1978 and later years, it will take more than 1 year before gain or loss will be long-term. In computing the holding period, the day the property is acquired is not included, but the date the property is disposed of is included.

Real property[1]   The holding period for real property starts on the day after that on which title passes or on the day after that on which delivery of possession is made and the burdens and privileges of ownership are assumed by the buyer, whichever happens first. The rule may be of significance in determining whether a gain is short-term or long-term. If a new building is erected and a part is finished before the whole, the holding period for each part would start at the time of its completion.

Gifts (after December 31, 1920)[2]   In the case of property acquired by gift, the holding period generally begins with the date when the property

[1] *Revenue Rulings,* 54-607, 1954-2 *Cumulative Bulletin* 177.
[2] *1954 Internal Revenue Code,* sec. 1223(2); 1.1223-1(b).

was acquired by the donor. There is an exception if the property had a value lower than cost at the date of the gift and the subsequent sale by the donee results in a loss. In this case, the holding period starts on the date of the gift.

Nontaxable exchanges[1]   In the case of property acquired in a nontaxable exchange after March 1, 1954, the holding period for the property acquired in the exchange is the same as that of the property given up in the exchange.

Computation of Tax on Capital Gains and Losses[2]

The first step is to merge all the short-term capital gains and losses. The result is a net short-term capital gain or a net short-term capital loss. Next, the long-term capital gains and losses are merged with each other. Finally, the total net gain or loss is determined by merging the net short-term capital gain or loss with the net long-term capital gain or loss.

Capital-gain deduction[3]   There are, of course, a variety of possible results from the merging. However, if the net long-term capital gain exceeds the net short-term capital loss, there is a deduction equal to 50 percent of the excess. The example below illustrates that the tax on a long-term capital gain may be less than 25 percent for certain taxpayers.

Example of merging of capital gains and losses   W, married, and filing a joint return, has taxable income of $12,000 after all exemptions and itemized deductions but *not* including an $8,000 long-term capital gain. To compute his tax, W adds $4,000 of the $8,000 capital gain to his $12,000 to yield $16,000 taxable income and a tax of $3,260. If he had not had the capital gain, his tax on the $12,000 would have been $2,260. Thus, he has paid $1,000 on the $8,000 capital gain ($3,260 on $16,000, compared to $2,260 on $12,000). This $1,000 amounts to only $12\frac{1}{2}$ percent of the $8,000 capital gain and is the result of the fact that only one-half of the long-term capital gain was added to his other taxable income.

Capital loss[4]   If the merging of the capital gains and losses, both short-term and long-term, resulted in a loss, the deduction for the excess loss is limited to the smaller of (1) $3,000 ($2,000 for taxable years beginning in 1977) or (2) the taxable income for the current year. For this limitation, taxable income is computed without regard to capital gains or losses and without regard to personal exemptions. Carry-forward provisions will be discussed later.

Only 50 percent of net long-term capital losses can be deducted against ordinary income, so that it will take $2 for net long-term loss to offset $1 of ordinary income. Corporations, unlike individuals, cannot deduct any capi-

[1] Ibid., sec. 1223(1); 1.1223-1(a).
[2] Ibid., sec. 1222(1)-(8); 1.1222-1.
[3] Ibid., sec. 1202; 1.1202-1.
[4] Ibid., sec. 1211(b); 1.211-1.

tal loss against other income. Capital loss for corporations must be offset against capital gain.

Alternative tax[1] It was noted earlier that the maximum tax on the excess of net long-term capital gains over short-term capital losses is 25 percent up to $50,000 of such gains. A taxpayer who approaches the 50 percent marginal income tax bracket should compute the alternative tax which gives effect to the above limitation.

Calculation of alternative tax Mrs. J, married, filing a joint return, has taxable income of $100,000, and her tax computed in the usual manner is $45,180. Included in the $100,000 is $12,000 of a $24,000 long-term capital gain. Mrs. J did not have any short-term capital gains or losses. Mrs. J computes her tax under the alternative method as follows:

Taxable income	$100,000
Capital gain included in income	12,000
Balance	$ 88,000
Tax on $88,000	37,980
Add: 25% of $24,000 long-term capital gain	6,000
Alternative tax	$ 43,980

Since her tax under the alternative method is $43,980, compared with the regular method which yielded $45,180, Mrs. J uses the alternative method.

LOSS CARRY-OVERS

Capital losses not used in the current year are allowed in succeeding years until they are exhausted. Loss carry-overs are first applied against any capital gains of the year to which carried; then $3,000 is offset against ordinary income and any excess is carried over to succeeding years. A capital loss retains its original character; i.e., if it is a long-term capital loss, it is carried over as a long-term capital loss. It takes $2,000 of long-term capital loss to offset $1,000 of ordinary income.

CORPORATIONS

Corporations may carry capital losses back 3 years and forward 5 years. Also, corporations cannot deduct a loss against other income, as an individual can. There is no capital-loss deduction for corporations, but there is the alternative tax computation.

Section 1231 Transactions

The sale, exchange, or involuntary conversion of property used in a taxpayer's trade or business is sometimes treated as the sale or exchange of a

---

[1] Ibid., sec. 1201(b); 1.1201-1.

capital asset. Included in the property used in a trade or business is real property and property subject to depreciation but not property held for sale to customers. As will be discussed later, other transactions are also included in Section 1231 transactions.

Tax treatment   If the grouping of gains and losses of all Section 1231 transactions results in a gain, all transactions are treated as long-term capital gains and losses. However, if the grouping of all the Section 1231 transactions results in a loss, all these transactions are treated as ordinary gains and losses. Before the grouping is done, any part of the gain that is ordinary gain because of the depreciation-recapture rules is segregated and enters the computation of ordinary gain.

Examples of Section 1231 transactions   Assume the sale of an apartment house with a $150,000 basis for $100,000. Since this is the only Section 1231 transaction and losses exceed gains (none), the loss would be treated as an ordinary loss.

This is why a Section 1231 loss is often preferable to the loss on a capital asset, since the latter is subject to the capital-loss limitations. Ordinary losses may be carried back 3 years and forward 5 years. Capital losses may only be carried forward and are subject to the $3,000 limitation noted earlier.

Property sold	Adjusted basis	Selling price
Apartment house	$180,000	$200,000
Furniture	35,000	25,000
Business automobile	2,000	4,000

These Section 1231 transactions are grouped as follows:

Property sold	Gains	Losses
Apartment house	$20,000	
Furniture		$10,000
Business automobile	2,000	

Since the gains exceed the losses by $12,000, each transaction is treated as a sale or exchange of a capital asset and is merged with capital gains or losses from the sale or exchange of other capital assets.

Change the situation and assume that the apartment house was sold at a $20,000 loss. When the owner aggregates his Section 1231 transactions, he will have a $28,000 net loss. This is the loss on the apartment house plus the loss on the furniture less the gain on the car. Since the losses exceed the gains, each gain or loss is treated as if it resulted from an ordinary or noncapital asset.

FORMS OF OWNERSHIP

If there is more than one owner of real property, ownership may take a variety of forms. Different kinds of co-ownership have different legal consequences. Property may be held, for example, in tenancy in common, joint tenancy, and in some states, e.g., California, as community property. Real property may also be held by a partnership or a corporation. The partnership may be either a general partnership or a limited partnership.

Joint Tenancy

The right of survivorship is an important characteristic of joint tenancy. If one of the joint tenants dies, the property passes to the remaining joint tenant. Joint tenancy and community property ownership are different forms of ownership. Property in joint tenancy may actually be community property. For example, in California a husband and wife may present evidence to indicate that property was community property rather than joint-tenancy property. Title in joint-tenancy property vests in the survivor. Thus, joint-tenancy property cannot be disposed of in a will. The characteristic of survivorship means that property does not go through probate and as such the relevant time and expense are saved. The survivor holds title to property free from debts and claims against the deceased joint tenant.

Income tax consequences of joint tenancy for a husband and wife may not be significant because they usually file joint tax returns but may have an effect on estate and inheritance taxes. If the joint tenants do not file joint tax returns, they would each report their proportionate share of gross income and deduct their share of expenses, provided that they pay their share.

Community Property

In certain states, e.g., California, property may be held as community property. Community property in California is property acquired by either husband or wife or both during their marriage, provided it was not acquired as the separate property of either of the spouses. Property owned before marriage is separate property. Similarly, property acquired during marriage by devise, bequest, or gift is separate property. Property may be community property even though the title to the property is recorded as joint tenancy or tenancy in common. If the husband dies and property is held as community property, one-half belongs to the wife. The husband has the right of testamentary disposition over his half.

Tenancy in Common

Another way for more than one individual to hold property is in tenancy in common. A joint tenant is personally liable for all expenses incurred on property. Conversely, a tenant in common is personally liable for only his proportionate share of expenses. Tenants in common who pay all the expenses on property can deduct only their share and the balance is considered to be an advance to their co-owner. When one joint tenant dies, the property passes by right of survivorship to the remaining spouse. In the case of tenancy in common, the interest of the tenant is subject to testamentary disposition.

Partnership Ownership

A partnership may acquire title to real property. If a partner dies, his right in the partnership property vests in the surviving partners. The real property of the partnership does not become part of the deceased partner's estate. The surviving partner has the right to manage the partnership business in order to terminate its operations. He must, of course, account to the estate of the deceased partner.

One partner may bind a partnership as a matter of law. However, in the case of real property, conveyances of partnership real property are either executed by all the partners or else by partners who are authorized to perform the particular conveyance.

A partnership does not pay an income tax. A partnership merely files an information tax return. Each partner reports his share of profits of the partnership and of certain specially segregated items, such as capital gains and losses and contributions, and includes them in his own tax return.

LIMITED PARTNERSHIPS

A limited partnership is a partnership composed of general partners and limited partners. Limited partners do not have control over the business and have only limited liability for debts. The limited partner's liability is limited to the amount contributed to the partnership capital. The death of a general partner terminates the limited partnership, but the death of a limited partner does not necessarily dissolve the partnership.

If a limited partnership meets specified requirements, it is subject to the partnership rules of the Internal Revenue Code. The limited partnership has been the most commonly employed form of organization in real estate tax-shelter investments.

Nonrecourse financing facilitates the use of limited partnerships because investors are able to limit their liability to the amount actually invested. Nonrecourse loans obtained by the partnership may raise the basis cost and thus increase the tax deductions. Income tax regulations provide that limited partners may include in the basis of the partnership interest their share of the nonrecourse loans to the partnership in real estate even though not personally liable on the debt.[1]

Several attributes of limited partnership make it a popular vehicle for real estate investments:

[1] Ibid., sec. 1.752-1(e).

1. A limited-partnership agreement may provide for the manner in which the partnership's items of income, gain, loss, deduction or credit will be allocated among the partners. The purpose may not be to avoid or evade tax. Recall that the partnership does not pay tax and all partners report their individual shares of gain and loss and specially segregated items such as capital gains and losses.

2. At the beginning of a partnership, the adjusted basis of the partner's partnership interest equals the sum of his capital contribution to the partnership plus his share, if any, of partnership liabilities. A limited partner's share of the partnership liabilities includes his pro rata share of all liabilities with respect to which there is no personal liability. It is this rule which allows a partner to deduct amounts in excess of his actual investment.

ADVANCE RULINGS FOR PARTNERSHIP TAX TREATMENT

The IRS has taken an active role in recent years in reviewing various aspects of tax-shelter investments. Revenue procedures have been issued setting forth certain conditions that must be met before the IRS will issue a ruling that a limited partnership will be treated as a partnership for federal tax purposes. The financial responsibility assumed and the level of participation in operations by the general partner is considered before the IRS will issue a favorable advance ruling.[1] Certain net-worth requirements are also set forth with respect to a corporation which acts as the sole general partner of a limited partnership. An additional requirement for an advance ruling is that the general partner or partners, during the existence of the partnership, should have at least a 1 percent interest in each material item of partnership income, gain, loss, deduction, or credit.[2] Another advance ruling requirement is that for the first 2 years of operation of a limited partnership the partners may not claim aggregate deductions which exceed the amount of equity capital invested in the limited partnership. This requirement has the effect of precluding the use of nonrecourse liability included in the partners' adjusted losses to absorb losses incurred during the first 2 years of operation.[3]

SECURITIES AND EXCHANGE COMMISSION

Under the full-disclosure requirements of the Securities Act of 1933 and the Securities Exchange Act of 1934, any material risks of adverse tax conse-

---

[1] *Revenue Procedures,* 72-13, 1972-1 *Cumulative Bulletin* 735.
[2] Ibid., 74-17, 1974-1 *Cumulative Bulletin* 438.
[3] Ibid.

quences must be fairly disclosed to prospective investors. SEC disclosure requirements and policies have direct application to public offerings. They have indirect application to intrastate and private offerings because the anti-fraud provisions of federal securities laws apply to private and intrastate as well as public offerings.

It is particularly important to the limited partner that the partnership be treated as a partnership for tax purposes so that the tax benefits can be passed through to the limited partners. In many cases opinion of legal counsel is obtained rather than getting an advance ruling from the IRS. The SEC requires disclosure of the fact that the opinion of counsel is not binding on the IRS, and if the limited partnership is reclassified as an association taxable as a corporation, the limited partners would lose the pass-through of tax benefits.

PARTNERSHIP ALLOCATIONS

The Internal Revenue Code (Section 704) allows flexibility in allocating among partners various partnership items of income, deductions, and credits. This permits satisfying the objectives of various partners who have different goals relative to income versus future capital gain. Thus, for example, one group of partners may have first claim on current income and the other group first claim on future capital gain. These allocations may be disregarded if their principal purpose is the avoidance or evasion of income taxes. The SEC requires an opinion of counsel that allocations do not have tax avoidance as their principal purpose and/or a disclosure to the effect that the special allocation may be disregarded upon an IRS audit of the partnership's returns.

Many investors are attracted to real estate limited partnership by special allocations. Tax- and non-tax-oriented investors can be attracted through special allocations. Greater security and first return of cash flow are allocated to the non-tax-oriented investor while the tax deductions and capital appreciation are allocated to the tax-oriented investors.

The developer is usually not interested in tax losses for himself during or after construction. Thus, he attempts to allocate all losses to the limited partners for a specified number of years. By using the special allocations, the limited partners will be able to recover a large portion of their investment through substantial tax savings during the early years of the investment.

If it can be determined that the principal purpose of the agreement is tax avoidance, the partner's share of any item will be determined by the provisions of the agreement governing the divisions of the profits and losses generally. With respect to special allocations, including retroactive allocation to new partners, the SEC requires an opinion of counsel that tax avoidance is not the principal purpose and/or a disclosure to the effect that the special allocation may be disregarded upon an IRS audit of the partnership returns. This means not that partnership allocations will not be allowed but that there must be economic substance to the allocation other than tax avoidance. Careful attention should be paid to current developments in this area.

Corporate Income Tax Considerations

The major disadvantage of a corporation from the standpoint of a small real estate investment is in the area of taxation. In an individual ownership or partnership, an operating loss may be offset against other income. As discussed earlier, many real estate ventures yield a taxable loss, particularly early in the life of a project. This may be true even though the operation yields a positive cash flow.

Corporate income is subject to a "double tax." A corporation is subject to a corporate tax, and if it distributes dividends, the individual recipient must pay tax on the receipt of the dividend. Recall that in the case of individual ownership or partnership ownership there is only one tax at the individual level.

Even though the corporate form results in what appears to be a double tax, it may still be better from the tax standpoint to choose the corporate form. If the corporate tax rates are significantly below the individual's tax brackets, it may be desirable to use the corporate form. The corporation may retain earnings, and eventually a way may be found to distribute the earnings at capital-gain rates. This may be accomplished either through sale of stock or liquidation of the corporation. Here the depreciation-recapture provisions, discussed later in this chapter, must be carefully considered.

Pitfalls in Corporate Ownership

There are pitfalls to be avoided. Among these is the accumulated-earnings tax, which may be imposed on earnings above $150,000. The personal holding-company tax is a penalty tax which is imposed on corporations whose income is primarily of certain passive sources, such as interest, dividends, personal-service contract income, and rents. However, if rents are over a certain portion of the income, the tax will not be imposed. The collapsible-corporation rules must also be considered if the corporation is dissolved before 3 years. Collapsible-corporation rules result in ordinary income rather than capital-gain treatment.

An owner-manager of an income-producing property may pay himself a salary, Provided this salary is reasonable and necessary, it is a deductible expense by the corporation. There may be certain amounts of debt in the capital structure of a corporation. Again, provided the debt is not excessive, the interest is a deductible item for the corporation. If salaries are unreasonable or interest is excessive, these expenses may be disallowed. Sometimes they will be treated as constructive dividends to the owner-managers.

Real Estate Investment Trusts[1]

The selection and management of the properties and the resources of the organization are the key to an investor's success rather than the form of organization. Some limited-partnership syndicates have fallen into disrepute, often as a result of poor management or disenchanted investors rather than because of problems inherent in the form or organization. Another important vehicle of organization for large-scale real estate investments other than the corporation is the *real estate investment trust* (REIT). This form of organization, like the public corporation, allows many small investors to aggregate their savings to purchase large-scale real estate investments. It is roughly analogous to a closed-end mutual fund with a portfolio consisting of real estate investments such as office buildings, apartment houses, hotels, motels, shopping centers, mortgages, and the like.

A REIT may be established so that many of the nontax advantages of a corporation can be achieved. These include centralized management, limited liability, continuity of interests, and transferability of ownership. The tax advantage of the REIT is of utmost importance, and provided it meets the necessary qualifications, the REIT will pay a corporate income tax only on retained income. There will be no corporate tax liability if the Reit distributes all its income as dividends. Thus small investors are able to have the advantages of increased marketability and liquidity available with transferable certificates of beneficial interest. They may have the ability to borrow against the value of their equity holdings and the advantages of investment diversification, limited liability, and continuity of life. The principal advantage of the REIT over the public corporation is the tax advantage. Corporations are taxable entities, whereas a REIT, by distributing its income in the form of dividends, can avoid this tax.

Subchapter S Corporations

A Subchapter S corporation is a corporation electing to be taxed under Subchapter S of the Code.[2] Certain requirements must be met, including the requirement that there be no more than 10 shareholders, all of whom must be individuals or estates and who may not be nonresident aliens. A corporation will not qualify for Subchapter S status if it has a corporate shareholder or if more than 20 percent of its gross receipts are derived from various types of passive income, including rental income from realty. Thus, the Sub-

---

[1] *1954 Internal Revenue Code,* sec. 856; *Treasury Regulations,* 1.856.
[2] Ibid., secs. 1371–1379.

144 / Real Estate Investment Analysis and Taxation

chapter S form is not available for a rent-producing investment. It is a possibility mainly when realty is held and used directly by an entity operating an active business. Thus, for example, hotels, parking lots, and warehouses in some cases might employ the Subchapter S form.

The shareholders of a Subchapter S corporation are taxed each year on each holder's proportionate share of the corporation's undistributed taxable income and on dividends received. The corporation itself is not subject to federal income tax. Therefore the double taxation at shareholder and then individual level is avoided.

SUMMARY

Taxes have a significant influence on cash flows and therefore on rates of return. This is the first of two chapters designed to inform the reader of major taxation elements involved in real estate decisions. The major changes of the tax reform act of 1976 indicate the legislative trend to reduce tax shelter. A review of the background for the changes in the tax law shows how excess concentration on short-term tax considerations resulted in insufficient analysis of the economics of projects and substantial financial losses for some investors. The lesson to be learned is to make a complete economic analysis of a project and realize that the tax effect is only one component of the rate of return.

The three basic elements which combine to provide tax shelter are tax deferral, leverage, and conversion of ordinary income to capital gain. Deferral is accomplished through accelerated deductions in the early years of the investment. Deferral of tax liability from early years to later years results in an interest-free loan from the federal government. Leverage allows a taxpayer to maximize his tax benefits by using borrowed funds. He is also better off if the cost of the borrowed funds is less than the amount earned on the borrowed funds. The third major element in the tax-shelter aspect of real estate is having a portion of the gain which reflects the accelerated deductions taxed at capital-gain rates. Through the concept of depreciation recapture Congress has significantly reduced the ability to convert ordinary income into capital gains by the use of accelerated depreciation. Straight-line depreciation still has the advantage of converting a portion of ordinary income into capital gain.

The 1976 Tax Reform Act did not subject real estate investments to the at-risk rules applied to many tax shelters. The law did provide for capitalization and amortization of construction-period interest and taxes which formerly could be deducted. There are separate transition rules for commercial, residential, and low-income housing. The capitalization rules do not apply to property which is not held for profit, such as a personal residence.

Provision for depreciation recapture when real property is sold at a gain in the 1969 tax law converts a portion of depreciation claimed in excess of straight-line depreciation into ordinary income. The percentage of such depreciation so recaptured depends upon the holding period of the property at time of sale. The 1976 Reform Act increased recapture on residential property other than low-income housing to 100 percent of excess depreciation over straight-line.

Alternative forms of business organization result in different tax computations. Special rules apply to partnerships, corporations, and Subchapter S corporations. In addition to the basic rules for tax computation the real estate investor needs to be aware of special rules for income averaging, the maximum tax on earned income, and the minimum tax on tax preferences. The 1976 Tax Reform Act also increased the minimum tax rate on tax preferences to 15 from 10 percent and reduced the exemption and provided that a taxpayer will have to subtract all tax-preference income from earned income before applying the 50 percent maximum tax rate.

Depreciation is a particularly important tax consideration, and the rules for use of alternative methods were reviewed. Rules on capital gains and losses and the relevant holding periods were described. Before 1977 if a capital asset was held 6 months or less, its sale or exchange resulted in a short-term capital gain or loss. Beginning in 1977, the holding period is extended to 9 months, and in 1978 and thereafter property must be held more than 1 year before gain or loss will be long-term. The last section of the chapter outlined tax considerations relative to alternative forms of business organization.

Although the Tax Reform Act reduces many tax-shelter benefits, real estate investments may still provide attractive benefits. Losses in many real estate investments are generated in part through operating deficits, and such losses are not limited. If these losses are more than offset by gain on sale, benefits will be realized through tax deferral. Appendix 4A shows the importance of various tax rules to the cash flows and rates of return in a hypothetical apartment-house investment.

APPENDIX 4A: A Case Study

IMPACT OF TAX REFORM ON APARTMENT-HOUSE INVESTMENTS

Smith and Shulman[1] illustrated the probable impact of proposed tax reforms upon cash flows and rates of return on apartment-house investments. They explored the

[1] Keith V. Smith and David Shulman, "The Impact of Tax Reform on Apartment House Investments," *Real Estate Review,* vol. 4, no. 1, pp. 37–42, Spring 1974. The following illustration and analysis is presented with the permission of the authors.

EXHIBIT 1 Investment and Financing of Apartment-Building Project

Investment:	
Land	$ 400,000
Building construction	3,900,000
Interest during construction*	195,000
Financing fees*	120,000
Property taxes during construction†	50,000
Other fees†	35,000
Total investment	$4,700,000
Financing:	
Cash down payment	$1,200,000
First mortgage‡	3,500,000
Total financing	$4,700,000

* Deductible from taxable income in year 0.
† Deductible from taxable income in year 1.
‡ 8.5% interest, 27-year amortization; annual debt service, $331,000; interest only during construction

EXHIBIT 2 Analysis of Final Sale of Apartment-Building Project*

Computing capital gain		
Sixth-year cash flow		$ 443,000
Divided by: capitalization factor		0,095
Estimated sales price†		$4,663,000
Building construction	$3,900,000	
Minus: depreciation	1,200,000	
Depreciated building	$2,700,000	
Plus: land	400,000	
Book value at sale		3,100,000
Gross profit		$1,563,000
Minus: depreciation recapture		
($1,200,000 − $867,000)		333,000
Capital gain		$1,230,000

Computing after-tax cash flow	
Sales price	$4,663,000
Mortgage principal to be repaid	3,268,000
Gross cash proceeds	$1,395,000
Minus: ordinary income taxes	
(50% × $333,000)	167,000
Minus: capital gains taxes†	
(35% × $1,230,000)	431,000
After-tax cash flow	$ 797,000

* This illustration ignores the possible effects of the minimum 15% tax on tax-preference items.
† Figure is rounded off.

probable effects of eliminating five types of preferential tax treatment for real estate investments. As noted in Chap. 4, the Tax Reform Act of 1976 did in fact eliminate some of the following:

1. The ability to deduct certain investment costs from taxable income
2. The ability to use 200 percent double-declining-balance depreciation
3. The ability to convert ordinary income into capital gains to the extent of straight-line depreciation of the property
4. The ability to avoid depreciation recapture on the accelerated portion of depreciation on property held in excess of 100 months
5. The ability to incur losses for tax purposes in excess of the total cash investment

A description of the essential financing and investment details for a newly constructed 260-unit apartment project used for case analysis is shown in Exhibit 1. For purposes of illustration, the authors assumed a 50 percent tax on ordinary income and a 35 percent tax rate on capital gains. Double-declining (200 percent) depreciation and debt service ($331,000 annually including interest at 8.5 percent) are based on a 27-year loan-amortization schedule and a 30-year useful life. They also assumed a 6-year investment horizon, at the end of which the apartment building is sold. Details of the sale are presented in Exhibit 2, where a typical 9.5 percent capitalization rate is applied to the sixth year net operating income and results in a sale price of $4,663,000. Depreciation in excess of the straight-line amount is recaptured at the 50 percent tax rate, while the remainder of the gross profit is taxed at the 35 percent rate.

COMPONENTS OF CASH FLOW

The apartment project is completed at the end of August. Net operating income (gross rent minus operating expenses) for the remainder of the first year is just enough to cover the debt service of $110,000. Thereafter, the net operating income is $443,000 annually.

Analysis of annual cash flows in Exhibit 3 is broken down into (1) cash down payment, (2) cash flow from operations, (3) cash flow from annual tax deductions, (4) cash flow from investment deductions, and (5) cash flow from the final sale of the project. The total cash flows are then used to determine that the internal rate of return for the new apartment building project is 9.7 percent. This means that the present value (using a discount rate of 9.7 percent) of the cash flows for the project is just equal to the cash down payment of $1.2 million.

Take 9.7 percent as a discount rate; then the present value of the cash-flow components based on current legislation is as shown in column 1 of Exhibit 4. Examination of these components as percentages (listed alongside the dollar present values in column 1) reveals that cash flow from operations totals 33 percent and cash flow from final sale constitutes 38 percent. The remaining 29 percent (cash flow from tax and investment deductions) is directly related to tax treatment allowed under the existing tax legislation.

EXHIBIT 3 Annual Cash-Flow Analysis of Apartment-Building Project, Thousands

	Year						
	0	1	2	3	4	5	6
(a) Cash down payment (Exhibit 1)	$−1,200	0	0	0	0	0	0
(b) Net operating income	0	$110	$443	$443	$443	$443	$443
(c) Minus: debt service	0	110	331	331	331	331	331
(d) Cash flow from operations, (b) − (c)	0	0	112	112	112	112	112
(e) Interest	0	99	294	291	287	283	279
(f) Plus: depreciation	0	87	254	237	222	207	193
(g) Tax deductions from operations, (e) + (f)	0	186	548	528	509	490	472
(h) Taxable income, (b) − (g)	0	−76	−105	−85	−66	−47	−29
(i) Cash flow from annual tax deductions [50% of (h)]	0	38	52.5	42.5	33	23.5	14.5
(j) Investment deductions (Exhibit 1)	−315	−85	0	0	0	0	0
(k) Cash flow from investment deduction [50% of (j)]	157.5	42	0	0	0	0	0
(l) Cash flow from sale (Exhibit 2)	0	0	0	0	0	0	797
(m) Total cash flow [(a) + (d) + (i) + (k) + (l)]	−1,042.5	80.5	164.5	154.5	145	135.5	923.5

IMPACT OF PROPOSED TAX LEGISLATION

Columns 2 to 5 in Exhibit 4 include comparable present values and relative proportions for each cash-flow component which would result from certain of the proposed changes in tax legislation. The proposed changes which are examined include:

1. Straight-line depreciation only (column 2)
2. Capitalization of interest and taxes during construction (column 3)
3. Full recapture of depreciation at the 50 percent tax rate (column 4)
4. All three of the above changes (column 5)

CONCLUSIONS OF ANALYSIS

A first observation is that the IRR is lower for all three of the proposed changes and drops to 5.4 percent for the illustrative project if all three tax changes are implemented. For present-value components we note that cash flow from annual tax deductions becomes negative (i.e., taxes must be paid) under straight-line depreciation (column 2) and cash flow from investment deductions becomes zero if those deductions are not allowed as immediate deductions (column 3). For full recapture of depreciation, we see that the tax reform lowers overall return but does not change the relative importance of various cash flows (column 4). And in the case of all three proposed changes, we observe that cash flow from operations and sale of the project collectively account for all the benefits (column 3). Although the relative percentages in Exhibit 4 would, of course, vary from project to project or for different assumptions about net operating incomes, the impact of the proposed changes in tax legislation upon the resulting internal rate of return is vividly seen in this illustration of an apartment-building project.

CONSIDERATION OF THE RISK DIMENSION

To examine the risk dimension of the project, it is necessary to examine possible outcomes over the 6-year investment horizon. The authors have selected three possible patterns of net operating income, each associated with a relative probability of occurrence. The likely outcome (50 percent probability) is one we have used in our example thus far; it has a level pattern of $443,000 beginning in the second year. In contrast, the pessimistic outcome (30 percent probability) has a net operating income for years 2 to 6 of 95 percent of that for the likely outcome, a result of lower occupancy rates, higher operating expenses, or both. The optimistic outcome (20 percent probability) has a net operating income that grows 3 percent annually after the second year. Exhibit 5 describes the year-by-year value of net operating income for each of the three outcomes and the total annual cash flows under existing tax rules and under the assumption that all three proposed changes in tax rules are in effect.

It is interesting to note that total cash flows decrease over time for the optimistic outcome under existing legislation but increase under the proposed changes. The absolute level of cash flows is lower under proposed legislation. An IRR is calculated for each outcome under each set of tax conditions. The estimated IRR values range

EXHIBIT 4 Impact of Possible Tax Legislation on Apartment-Building Project

Present-value component	Current legislation (1)		Straight-line depreciation (2)		Capitalize investment costs (3)		Recapture depreciation (4)		All three changes (5)	
Cash flow, from operations	$ 389,995	33%	$ 406,795	34%	$ 421,478	35%	$ 409,708	34%	$ 455,034	38%
From annual tax deductions	156,360	13	−32,172	−3	212,944	18	162,067	13	−9,401	−1
From investment deductions	196,243	16	196,672	16	0	0	196,745	17	0	0
From sale	457,239	38	628,938	53	567,884	47	432,380	36	753,470	63
Cash down payment	1,199,837*	100	1,200,233	100	1,202,306	100	1,200,900	100	1,199,103	100
Internal rate of return		9.7		8.5		7.5		8.3		5.4

* Rounding all values to the nearest $1,000 in Exhibit 3 reduces the total cash flow to slightly less than the $1.2 million cash down payment.

EXHIBIT 5 Return and Risk Tax Analysis of Apartment Building Project, Thousands

	Probability	Year						Sales price	Internal rate of return, %
		1	2	3	4	5	6		
Net operating income:									
Pessimistic outcome	0.3	$110	$421	$421	$421	$421	$421	$4,432	
Likely outcome	0.5	110	443	443	443	443	443	4,663	
Optimistic outcome	0.2	110	443	456	470	484	499	5,253	
Total cash flow under existing tax legislation:									
Pessimistic outcome	0.3	80.5	154.5	144.5	135	126.5	764		6.7%
Likely outcome	0.5	80.5	164.5	154.5	145	135	923.5		9.7
Optimistic outcome	0.2	80.5	164.5	161.5	158.5	156	1,336		15.0
Total cash flow under proposed legislation:									
Pessimistic outcome	0.3	17.5	93.5	97	90	88	1,003.5		2.8
Likely outcome	0.5	17.5	109	107	105.5	103.5	1,134.5		5.4
Optimistic outcome	0.2	17.5	109	115.5	122.5	129.5	1,465		9.7

EXHIBIT 6   Calculation of Return and Risk Measures for Apartment Building Project under Existing and Proposed Tax Legislation

Legislation	Expected return
Existing	$(6.7\%)(0.3) + (9.7\%)(0.5) + (15.0\%)(0.2) = 9.9\%$
Proposed	$(2.8\%)(0.3) + (5.4\%)(0.5) + (9.7\%)(0.2) = 5.5\%$

	Risk (standard deviation)
Existing	$[(6.7\% - 9.9\%)^2(0.3) + (9.7\% - 9.9\%)^2(0.5) + (15.0\% - 9.9\%)^2(0.2)]^{1/2} = 2.9\%$
Proposed	$[(2.8\% - 5.5\%)^2(0.3) + (5.4\% - 5.5\%)^2(0.5) + (9.7\% - 5.5\%)^2(0.2)]^{1/2} = 2.4\%$

from 6.7 to 15.0 percent under existing tax legislation but only 2.8 to 9.7 percent under the proposed changes.

For each set of tax conditions, the three possible values of IRR together with their associated probabilities can be combined into measures of return and risk. In Exhibit 6 expected return and standard deviation are calculated as measures of return and risk, respectively. For expected return, each possible IRR is multiplied by its probability, and the weighted returns are totaled. Expected return is thus a weighted average IRR. As seen in Exhibit 6, expected return drops from 9.9 to 5.5 percent while standard deviation drops from 2.9 to 2.4 percent under the proposed tax legislation including all three changes.

The standard deviation is a standard measure of the dispersion of statistical observations about the mean. It is found by (1) squaring the deviations of individual values from the arithmetic mean, (2) summing the squares, (3) dividing the sum by $n - 1$, and (4) extracting the square root.[1] The basic formula for the standard deviation is

$$s = \sqrt{\frac{\Sigma x^2}{n - 1}}$$

where s = standard deviation
x = deviation of any value of x from arithmetic mean $\overline{X}$
n = number of items or observations in sample

In a normal distribution, the proportion of items typically falling within 1, 2, and 3 standard deviations (SD) is:[2]

Number of SDs	+1	+2	+3
Items in normal distribution, %	68.27	95.45	99.73

Standard deviation decreases for the apartment-building project under the proposed taxation legislation because the range of possible outcomes becomes narrower. This in turn is due to a loss in some of the cash-flow benefits that exist under current tax statutes. A final measure for the project, the coefficient of dispersion, is

---

[1] William A. Spurr and Charles P. Bonvin, *Statistical Analysis for Business Decisions*, Irwin, Homewood, Ill. 1967, pp. 122–123.
[2] Ibid., p. 130.

obtained by dividing standard deviation (risk) by the expected return. This provides a measure of *relative risk*.[1] Under existing legislation this coefficient of dispersion is 0.29 (2.9%/9.9%), while under the proposed legislation it would be 0.44 (2.4%/5.5%). In other words, the proposed tax legislation would actually increase the risk of the apartment building project relative to the level of expected return. The reason for this is that the proposed tax legislation tends to reduce those components of cash flow that are less uncertain. Cash flows from operations are not affected, while cash flow from final sale of the project is only somewhat affected.

An illustrative case exploring the probable effects of changes in real estate tax-shelter legislation, prepared in 1974 by Smith and Shulman,[2] demonstrated the integration of discounted cash flow and probability-analysis techniques. The obvious importance of tax shelter to the real estate investor, demonstrated so clearly in this case study, emphasizes the need for the broad overview of federal taxation and its impact on real estate investment.

[1] Ibid., p. 133.
[2] Op. cit.

FIVE

Disposition of Real Estate: Tax-Free Exchanges, Installment Sales, and Involuntary Conversions

INTRODUCTION

An investor's decision concerning the timing of the sale of property must, of course, take into account the tax consequences of the sale. The importance of the holding period in obtaining long-term capital-gain treatment has already been discussed. The implications of two other important tax rules must be considered in determining when and how to dispose of property. The first of these is the set of rules for tax-free exchanges, and the second is the set of rules for condemnations and involuntary conversions. These subjects are the major concern of this chapter.

It should be noted that the result of these regulations is postponement, and not forgiveness, of tax. Provided the property qualifies, an investor should consider the alternative of a tax-free exchange relative to an outright sale. If condemnation proceedings are imminent, it is desirable to compare results with those of a voluntary sale. It is important, of course, to pay careful attention to the relevant details of the tax rules so that one does not act assuming qualification and then find out later that certain detailed rules resulting in disallowance of the transaction as planned have been overlooked.

The analyst confronted with a problem of disposal of property may well project the effects on rate of return and on cash flow under assumptions of

(1) outright sale, (2) a qualified installment sale, and (3) a tax-free exchange. If property is subject to condemnation, the probable results of this alternative should also be projected.

Generally, a sale or exchange results in the recognition of gain or loss. However, in some situations, special rules apply which result in the postponement of taxable gain. Exchanges of investment property or depreciable property used in a trade or business are examples of exchanges that may be tax-free. These nontaxable exchanges may be an important planning tool for the investor in real estate. For example, investors may start with limited funds sufficient to support a small investment. As their investment prospers, they may be able to increase their equity through payments on mortgage principal. After a time, their equity may increase to the point where it is sufficient to support a larger real estate investment. If they sell the original property, they will probably find that the proceeds are substantially diminished by income tax on the gain. However, if they exchange the property, the tax on the gain may be deferred, provided the provisions in respect to tax-free exchanges are satisfied. Thus investors may increase their holdings without paying any income tax. This procedure may be repeated.

If property is destroyed or stolen, a taxpayer usually receives insurance proceeds. In the case of condemnation, a condemnation award is received. The compensation received may be greater than the taxpayer's adjusted basis for the property if the property has appreciated in value. If certain rules are followed and the proceeds are reinvested, taxable gain may be deferred.

For both tax-free exchanges and involuntary conversions it is important to realize that tax is not forgiven but merely postponed. The basic effect is to reduce the basis of the asset acquired so that on its future disposition the gain deferred on the first asset will be realized.

NONTAXABLE EXCHANGES[1]

In the case of a nontaxable exchange the new property is considered to be substantially a continuation of the old investment. Either gain is not recognized, or it is partially recognized and loss is not recognized. Note that a nontaxable exchange may result in partial taxation of gain if either property or money is received in addition to the property that may be received tax-free. This is often the case, since it is usually necessary to add something to balance an exchange. Loss is never recognized in a nontaxable exchange, even when cash or other property is received.

The most common exchanges are exchanges of property for *like* property. The property must be business or investment property. This includes the

[1] U.S. Internal Revenue Service, *1954 Internal Revenue Code*, sec. 1031.

property given and the property received. The property cannot be property used for personal use, e.g., a car driven only for personal purposes. The property cannot be property held for sale to customers. Machinery, buildings, land, trucks, and rented houses are examples of property to which the rule applies. For example, raw materials or inventories would not come under this rule. Real estate held by dealers for sale to customers does not qualify.

DETERMINATION OF GAIN OR LOSS

To determine gain or loss, the adjusted basis of the property must be subtracted from the amount realized. Thus, it is important to know the meaning of the terms *adjusted basis* and *amount realized*. The adjusted basis of property is the original basis of the property plus additions for improvements and less deductions for such items as depreciation and casualty losses.

For example, assume that A bought property for $160,000 in 1978. This property was to be used as a warehouse in his trade or business. Other expenditures included commissions of $4,000 and title search and legal fees of $1,200. The total cost was allocated as follows: land $20,650 and building $144,550. Subsequent to acquisition a total of $19,200 depreciation was allowed, and there was an uninsured casualty loss to the building of $10,000, which was claimed as a deduction. A total of $40,000 was spent to remodel the building. The adjusted basis for the land is $20,650. The adjusted basis for the building is computed as follows:

Original cost...		$144,550
Add: improvements.................................		40,000
		$184,550
Less: depreciation..................	$19,200	
Casualty loss.................	10,000	29,200
		$155,350

Basis is increased for all items or expenditures chargeable to the capital account, which include improvements, purchase commissions, legal costs for defending or perfecting title, surveying expenses, and recording fees. Title insurance is included. Basis is decreased for items that are a return of capital, including depreciation, depletion, obsolescence, recognized losses on involuntary conversions, and deductible casualty losses.

LIKE PROPERTY[1]

It is important to consider the meaning of like property. Generally, the exchange of real estate for real estate is the exchange of like property, and the

---

[1] Ibid., sec. 1031(a), 1.1031(a)-1.

trade of personal property for personal property is an exchange of like property. However, an exchange of personal property for real property would not qualify.

Specific Examples

The exchange of business or investment real property for a lease of 30 years or more in business or investment real property is a qualifying exchange. An exchange of city business or investment property for farm business or investment property also qualifies. Similarly, the trade of improved business or investment property for unimproved business or investment property is an exchange of like property. The exchange of an apartment house for a store building or a truck for a machine are also like exchanges. Note that the like-kind requirement relates to the character rather than the grade of the property. For example, the exchange of unimproved real estate for improved real estate qualifies.

Property held for investment may be exchanged in a nontaxable exchange for property held for use in a trade or business, or vice versa. The category "property held for investment" does not include exchanges of stocks, bonds, notes, or other securities or evidences of interest. However, the exchange of securities in one corporation for stock or securities in another corporation may be tax-free in certain corporate reorganizations. Also, the exchange of common stock in a corporation for common stock in the same corporation or preferred stock in a corporation for preferred stock in the same corporation is considered a nontaxable exchange.

Other nontaxable exchanges such as the transfer of property to a corporation controlled by a transferrer, the exchange of insurance policies, and the exchange of United States bonds will not be discussed.[1] The discussion and examples that follow relate primarily to exchanges of investment property and property held for use in trade or business.

Example of tax-free exchange Assume that motel owner J has appliances which she wishes to replace. The facts are as follows:

Adjusted basis	$10,000
Cost of new appliances	56,000
Trade-in	20,000
Cash required	36,000

Even though J is allowed a trade amounting to $20,000, she does not have recognized gain on the exchange. Note, also, that if the adjusted basis of the appliances had been $25,000, she would not have been allowed a loss on the trade.

If instead of a trade, J had sold her appliances to a third party for $20,000 and then purchased the new, she would have a recognized gain or loss

[1] Ibid., sec. 351, 368(c); 1.351-1 to 1.351-3.

measured by the difference between the amount realized and the adjusted basis of the old furniture. In planning transactions, it is important to consider whether it is better to have a nontaxable exchange or to have a sale followed by a purchase. If property is voluntarily sold for cash and similar property is immediately purchased, there is a purchase and a sale, not an exchange. However, if the sale and purchase are reciprocal and mutually dependent transactions, the transaction may be treated as an exchange by the IRS. An example that might be challenged and treated as an exchange would be the sale of property to a dealer followed by the immediate purchase of similar property from the same dealer.

From a tax standpoint, an investor is interested in the time of recognition of gain. It may be desirable to postpone taxable gain so that the investor has the use of the money in the interim. As noted earlier, the exchange procedure can be repeated as a device to postpone payment of gains taxes. An investor may give property to another member of his family who is in a lower tax bracket or sell the property during a low-income year, perhaps after retirement. In a tax-free exchange, the basis of the property received is a function of the property given up. In the case of appreciated property, the new property has a lower basis in a tax-free exchange than if the old property had been sold and the new property purchased. Investors must also consider the depreciation-recapture rules and if they sell the property, how much of the recognized gain will be ordinary income rather than capital gain.

The following facts for B who has an apartment house which he wishes to exchange for C's apartment house can be used to illustrate the determination of basis in an exchange:

Basis	B's	C's
Adjusted basis	$20,000	$10,000
Fair market value	40,000	40,000

B's basis for his new apartment house is still the same as the adjusted basis of his old apartment house. It is $20,000 even though the fair market value is $40,000. He will compute his depreciation on $20,000, and if he sold it the next day for $40,000 cash, he would pay tax on a $20,000 gain.

Boot[1]

Boot in a transaction may make a transaction partially taxable that would otherwise be tax-free. The term *boot* means the cash or other property that is added to balance the exchange.

Receipt of boot   The receipt of boot will result in a recognition of gain that has a maximum limit equal to the cash plus fair market value of the

---

[1] Ibid., sec. 351(b); 1031(b); 1.351-2, 1.1031(b)-1.

boot received. Note, however, that the receipt of boot will not cause a loss to be recognized.

S owns a farm with an adjusted basis of $80,000 which she exchanges for other real estate she plans to hold for investment. S receives real estate with a value of $100,000 plus cash in the amount of $10,000, and her *realized gain* is therefore $30,000. This is the amount realized of $110,000 less the adjusted basis of the farm of $80,000. S's gain for tax purposes is *recognized* only up to the amount of boot received, which in this case is the cash of $10,000. Now, if S were a real estate dealer instead of an investor, she would have to pay tax on the entire $30,000. This is another example of the importance of property being classified as investment or trade or business property rather than as property held by a dealer.

Effect on basis[1]   Investors are, of course, interested in the basis of their newly acquired property, since this is their basis for depreciation deductions. It is also their basis (subject to future adjustments for depreciation, casualties, etc.) for gain or loss on future disposition of the property. The basis when boot is received in the form of money is the adjusted basis of the old property less the amount of money received, plus any gain recognized on the exchange.

The recapture rules of Section 1245 of the Internal Revenue Code, relating to property other than buildings, and of Section 1250, relating to buildings, extend only to the amount of boot received.[2] That is, they may convert all or a portion of the recognized gain into ordinary income rather than capital gain.

The basis of S's new investment property is equal to $80,000, which is the basis of the farm less the $10,000 cash received and plus the $10,000 gain recognized on the exchange. Loss is not recognized in a tax-free exchange, and when loss is realized and not recognized, the basis of the property acquired is the adjusted basis of the property transferred less any money received.

For example, M exchanges an apartment which has an adjusted basis of $100,000 but a fair market value of $90,000 for another parcel of real estate with a fair market value of $80,000 and in addition receives $10,000 in cash. He has realized a $10,000 loss, which is the adjusted basis of the old property of $100,000 less the $90,000 value of the assets received. The basis of the new parcel to M is $90,000.

Giving of boot   The giving of boot does not cause the transaction to become taxable. For example, W has rental property with an adjusted basis of $90,000 and a fair market value of $100,000. She adds $20,000 cash and acquires a new property with a fair market value of $120,000. W has *no*

---

[1] Ibid., sec. 1031(d); 1.1031(d)-1.
[2] Ibid., sec. 1245(b)(4), 1250; 1.1245-4(d), 1.1250-3(d).

recognized gain on the exchange. Her basis for the new property is $110,000, which is equal to the adjusted basis of the old parcel of $90,000 plus the $20,000 boot given.

Liabilities on Exchanged Property

The existence of liabilities on exchanged property affects the taxability of the transaction. If the other party to the exchange assumes liability on the property exchanged, the amount of the liability is considered as boot received. The amount of the liability is also included as boot received if the property is transferred subject to the liability.[1]

For example, D has rental property with an adjusted basis of $80,000. This property is subject to a mortgage of $30,000. D exchanges this property for property with a fair market value of $100,000 and also receives $10,000 in cash. D has *realized* a gain of $60,000. This is the amount realized ($140,000) less the adjusted basis of the property transferred ($80,000). The amount realized consists of the fair market value of the property received ($100,000) plus the cash received ($10,000) and the mortgage ($30,000) assumed by the buyer. The amount of gain that is taxed is $40,000. This is the sum of the cash received ($10,000) plus the mortgage ($30,000).

Effect on basis[2] The basis of the new property is equal to the adjusted basis of the property transferred less the amount of the mortgage that the taxpayer is relieved of plus any recognized gain. The basis of the new property in the example above is the adjusted basis of the property transferred ($80,000) less the mortgage ($30,000) and less the cash received ($10,000) plus the gain that is recognized ($40,000). Thus D's new basis for the new property is $80,000.

Mortgages on both properties Both properties to an exchange may be mortgaged. In this situation the mortgages on the properties are offset, and the net amount is considered as boot received by one party and boot given by the other party. The party relieved of the larger mortgage is considered to have received boot, and the other party is considered to have given boot.

Example of both properties mortgaged X owns a motel which he wishes to exchange for Y's apartment house. Consider the following facts:

Basis	Motel X property	Apartment Y property
Adjusted basis	$150,000	$165,000
Mortgage	30,000	18,000
Fair market value	207,000	195,000

Realized gain can be determined as follows for X and Y:

[1] Ibid., sec. 1031(d); 1.1031(d)-2.
[2] Ibid.

Basis	X		Y	
Fair market value of property received	$195,000		$207,000	
Mortgage relieved of	30,000	$225,000	18,000	$225,000
Less:				
Adjusted basis of motel	150,000		165,000	
Mortgage assumed	18,000	168,000	30,000	195,000
Realized gain		$ 57,000		$ 30,000

However, the gain that is recognized for tax purposes is limited to the boot received.

Basis	X	Y
Mortgage relieved	$30,000	$18,000
Less mortgage assumed	18,000	30,000
Boot received	$12,000	
Boot given		$12,000

The exchange is tax-free to Y. He has assumed a mortgage of $30,000 and is relieved of one for $18,000. Y is considered to have given boot in the amount of $12,000. X, however, must pay tax on the $12,000 boot received.

Basis of property   The parties to an exchange must determine the basis of the property acquired for purposes of calculating depreciation and also for the purpose of determining gain or loss on future disposition of the property.

When both properties in the exchange are mortgaged, the basis of the property acquired is equal to the adjusted basis of the property given up plus the mortgage assumed on the new property minus the mortgage on the property given up plus any gain that is recognized on the exchange.

Example of basis computation   The following illustrates the calculation of basis of the new property acquired, using the facts of the motel and apartment house exchanged by X and Y:

Basis	Motel X	Apartment Y
Adjusted basis of old property	$150,000	$165,000
Mortgage assumed	18,000	30,000
Gain recognized on exchange	12,000	
	$180,000	$195,000
Less mortgage relieved	30,000	18,000
New basis	$150,000	$177,000

Recall that Y did not have any recognized gain on the exchange since he assumed a larger mortgage than he was relieved of and therefore was considered as having given boot.

Multiple Exchanges

Our examples have considered the situation in which there have been only two parties to an exchange. More than two parties may be involved in an exchange, and the tax-free benefits may still be enjoyed. This can be illustrated by the situation of J, S, and B, each of whom owns an apartment house. J would like to trade his apartment house for S's apartment house. S does not want J's apartment house, but would like to sell her apartment house. B, however, would like to purchase J's apartment house. The solution is as follows: B purchases S's apartment house and then exchanges it for J's apartment house. If certain formalities are observed, J is able to consider this transaction as a tax-free exchange of his apartment house for S's apartment house.

Comprehensive Tax-free Exchange Example

An exchange of qualifying properties between parties F and G can be used to illustrate calculation (1) recognized gain on the exchange, (2) adjusted basis of property acquired, and (3) depreciation allowable on property acquired.

Basis	F's Property	G's Property
Cost	$50,000	$200,000
Improvements	10,000	
Depreciation	25,000	50,000
Market value	90,000	200,000
Mortgage	30,000	110,000

Adjusted basis of present property   This is calculated by taking the cost plus improvements less depreciation:

Basis	Party F	Party G
Cost	$50,000	$200,000
Improvements	+10,000	
Depreciation	−25,000	50,000
Adjusted basis	$35,000	$150,000

Equity in present property			Gain if property sold at market value		
Basis	F	G	Basis	F	G
Market value	$90,000	$200,000	Market value	$90,000	$200,000
Mortgage	30,000	110,000	Adjusted basis	35,000	150,000
Equity	$60,000	$ 90,000		$55,000	$ 50,000

Thus, if F sells her property outright, she will pay tax on a $55,000 gain, and similarly if G sells her property outright, she will pay tax on a $50,000 gain. Consideration might also be given to an installment sale, but assume that an exchange is to be completed. Since G has an equity of $90,000 in her property and F has an equity of only $60,000, it will be necessary for F to come up with additional cash or property of $30,000 to balance the exchange.

Recognized taxable gain under exchange   As stated previously, the receipt of boot makes an otherwise tax-free exchange partially taxable; the recognition of gain has a maximum limit equal to the cash plus fair market value of the boot received. If realized gain is less than boot received, then gain *recognized* for tax purposes is limited to the gain *realized.*

Assume here that F gave G $20,000 cash to balance the exchange plus a second mortgage of $10,000:

Boot received, basis	F	G
Cash	0	$ 20,000
Boot	0	10,000
Net mortgage relief	0	80,000
		$110,000

G was relieved of a mortgage in the amount of $110,000 and assumed a $30,000 mortgage, which results in a net mortgage relief of $80,000.

Since F received no boot, she does not have any recognized gain on the transaction. G, however, has a recognized gain equal to the lower of the realized gain of $50,000 and of boot received $110,000. G must pay tax on the $50,000 gain.

Basis of new property received   The basis of the new property received is important from the standpoint of calculation of depreciation deductions and, of course, for gain or loss on future sale or exchange of the property.

Basis	F	G
Adjusted basis of old property	$ 35,000	$ 150,000
Loan assumed	+110,000	+30,000
Cash paid	+30,000	
Recognized gain		50,000
Subtotal	$ 175,000	$ 230,000
Less:		
Loan relieved	$ −30,000	$−110,000
Cash received		−20,000
Boot received		−10,000
New basis	$ 145,000	$ 90,000

Allowable depreciation on new property   The allowable depreciation on the new property will be a function of the new basis and the useful life of the property. For the property acquired by F, assume a 20-year life, and for the property acquired by G, a 25-year life. Allocation of basis between land and improvements must also be made. Assume that the percentages given below can be substantiated by relative assessed valuations:

Basis	F	G
New basis	$145,000	$90,000
Allocation to improvements	80%	60%
Amount depreciable	$116,000	$54,000
Annual: straight line	$ 5,800	$ 2,160

CONDEMNATIONS AND INVOLUNTARY CONVERSIONS — zoning law changes

When property is involuntarily converted or condemned, there is a question whether gain or loss is recognized. There is also a question of determining the basis for depreciation and gain or loss on future disposition for any replacement property acquired. Generally, if certain requirements are met, a taxpayer may defer the recognition of gain resulting from the condemnation or involuntary conversion of property by replacing the property within certain time limits. This, however, is a postponement of tax and not a forgiveness. The basis of the replacement property is appropriately reduced so that future disposition will reflect the postponement.

Involuntary Conversions[1]

An involuntary conversion results when property is stolen, requisitioned, condemned, or destroyed and other property or money is received in payment. If property is destroyed, a taxpayer may receive insurance payments. If it is condemned, he may receive a condemnation payment. Destruction of property by casualty such as drought, hurricane, or flood and the receipt of insurance proceeds are examples of involuntary conversion.

Condemnation

A condemnation occurs when property is taken for public use without consent of the owner, and the owner receives a payment as compensation for the property. The property may be sold or exchanged after a condemnation occurs, or the property may be sold or exchanged under the threat or imminence of condemnation.

Threat or imminence of condemnation   It may be necessary to have written confirmation of oral statements on which a taxpayer relies in selling or exchanging property under the threat of condemnation. There is a threat or imminence of condemnation if a representative of a governmental body who is authorized to acquire property for public use informs a property owner that such body has determined to acquire the property, and it is reasonable to assume that steps to condemn will be instituted if the property is not voluntarily sold. Another example of a threat or imminence of condemnation arises if property owners learn of a decision to acquire their property for public use through a report in a newspaper or other news medium. They must, however, confirm this report with a representative of the governmental body or public official involved, and they must also have reasonable grounds for believing that steps to condemn will be instituted if they do not sell voluntarily.

---

[1] Ibid., sec. 1033; 1.1033(a)-1(a).

Severance Damages

In addition to a condemnation award, property owners may also receive severance damages to the property they retain. Severance damages are applied by the owner of the property as follows: (1) against the proportionate share of expenses of securing the severance damage award, (2) against any amount of a special assessment levied for benefits to the remaining real estate, (3) against the expenses of restoring the property retained to its former use. If there still is a balance of the severance award, it reduces the basis of the property retained by the owner and any remaining amount is taxable.

It is important that the amount of the award from the condemning authority which is for severance damages be separately stated. When it is not clear that part of the award is for severance damages, the presumption is that the proceeds were given as consideration for the property that was taken by the condemning authority.

Consequential Damages

A property owner may receive a damage award from a public body for damage done to his property even though there was no actual taking of his property. These damages may be paid, for example, as a result of flooding or erosion of property or impairment of access. The tax treatment of these damages is the same as severance damages.

Easements

When property owners grant an easement on their property, the tax treatment of the proceeds depends on whether they still have a beneficial interest in the property. If owners maintain a beneficial interest in the property, they are not considered to have disposed of the land. The amounts received for granting an easement in land are used to reduce the basis of the entire property. Any amount that is greater than the basis for the entire property is included in income and is ordinary income or capital gain, depending on the classification of the asset for tax purposes.

An owner of property may grant a perpetual easement and retain only the mere legal title while giving up all beneficial use of the property. This situation is treated differently from the situation above, as it is considered that the property on which the easement was granted has been disposed of. A portion of the basis of the entire property is allocated to the portion of the property to which the easement relates, and gain or loss is determined in the same manner as from a sale.

Gain or Loss from Involuntary Conversion[1]

There may be a gain or loss from an involuntary conversion. This is measured by the difference between the adjusted basis of the property to the

[1] Ibid., sec. 1033(a)(3)(A); 1.1033(a)-2(c).

owner and the insurance proceeds or the condemnation award received. In the case of a gain, the taxability may be postponed, as will be explained below. If these rules are not availed of, a gain is taxable and a loss is deductible.

If the property is held over 1 year, the gain or loss is treated under Section 1231. The following transactions are included as Section 1231 transactions provided the property has been held over 1 year: (1) nonbusiness property subjected to a casualty or theft, (2) business property subjected to a casualty or theft and covered by insurance in any amount, (3) property held for the production of rents or royalties subjected to a casualty or theft and covered by insurance in any amount, (4) notes, bonds, and other investment property subjected to a casualty or theft and covered by insurance in any amount, (5) property condemned for public use.

Note the phrase "covered by insurance in any amount" in several of the categories above. When property is used in trade or business or is a capital asset held for the production of income, it is not included in the Section 1231 aggregation if it is not compensated for by insurance in any amount. Instead such losses are deductible in full against ordinary income.

With property held strictly for the personal use of the owner and condemned there is no deduction for loss. If the property is destroyed by casualty, it may give rise to a casualty loss deduction, which will be explained later. This is true even if the property was held for personal use.

Recall from the discussion of basic tax considerations in Chap. 4 that Section 1231 transactions are aggregated. If the total gains exceed the total losses, *each* gain and *each* loss is treated separately in the same manner as a sale or exchange of a capital asset held for more than 1 year. Thus each is treated as a long-term capital gain or long-term capital loss. If the total of all Section 1231 transactions results in a loss, *each* gain or loss is treated as a gain or loss from an ordinary asset, which means that the gains are included in taxable income in full and losses are deducted in full. In addition to the items affected by casualty and condemnation above, the following items of interest to the real estate investor are also included in the above grouping: (1) sales or exchanges of depreciable property used in trade or business and held for more than 1 year, (2) sales or exchanges of real property used in trade or business and held for more than 1 year, (3) and sales or exchanges of leaseholds used in trade or business and held for more than 1 year.

Depreciation recapture[1] If there is a gain on involuntary conversion and part of this gain is ordinary income because of the operation of either Section 1245 or 1250 IRC, this gain is first separated and treated as ordinary income. Any balance of gain is either Section 1231 gain if it falls in the categories

[1] Ibid., sec. 1245(b)(4), 1250; 1.1245-4(d); 1.1250-3(d).

explained above or else directly capital gain. Recall that Section 1245 recapture applied to depreciable property other than buildings and their structural components in respect to depreciation taken after 1961. Section 1250 relates to depreciation recapture on buildings and their structural components and leaseholds in respect to depreciation taken after 1963. These Internal Revenue Code sections operate in a limited manner in respect to involuntary conversions and like-kind exchanges. The amount of gain that is recaptured as ordinary income is generally limited to the unreinvested involuntary conversion proceeds in the case of involuntary conversions and to the amount of boot received in the case of nontaxable exchanges.

Example of depreciation recapture The following facts relating to a motel and all the furniture therein which were completely destroyed by a hurricane illustrate depreciation recapture in the situation of an involuntary conversion:

Insurance proceeds for building	$100,000
Amount reinvested in new building	96,000
Total gain	15,000
Amount subject to recapture under sec. 1250, IRC	10,000

The result is that the $4,000 of the insurance proceeds that were not reinvested is the recognized gain. Since this is less than the $10,000 subject to recapture through the application of Sec. 1250 IRC, it is all ordinary income.

The following facts relate to the furniture:

Cost	$7,500
Depreciation taken since 1961	2,700
Insurance proceeds for furniture	7,000
Amount used to replace furniture	5,000

Realized gain is computed as follows:

Insurance proceeds	7,000	
Adjusted basis of furniture	4,800	$2,200

The amount of proceeds that were not reinvested is $2,000. This is ordinary income, as it is less than depreciation since 1961 and less than the realized gain.

In the above situations, if the recognized gain was larger than the amount recaptured and the property was held over 1 year, the amount in excess of the amount recaptured would be treated as Section 1231 gain.

The tax consequences of a recognized gain were considered above. However, even though taxpayers may have a realized gain, it may not be recognized if they reinvest the proceeds according to the relevant rules.

Direct Conversion[1]

If a property owner has his property condemned and receives similar property as compensation, there is no gain or loss recognized. A taxpayer does not have the option of electing to report the gain or loss.

For example, R owns a parking lot which is used for parking purposes in her business. This land is condemned by the state for a freeway, and R is offered and accepts a similar piece of land which can be used for the same purpose. The land that R gave up has an adjusted basis of $40,000, and the land she receives has a fair market value of $50,000. No gain or loss is recognized, and R cannot decide to recognize a gain or loss.

Postponement of Gain[2]

As a result of an involuntary conversion, property owners may receive money as insurance proceeds or as a condemnation award, and in some cases they may receive unlike property such as state bonds. Provided they follow certain rules, owners may *elect* to defer the gain. Note that this is an election and is not mandatory. A taxpayer may find it advantageous to recognize a gain rather than postpone it. It is usually preferable, however, to defer the gain.

In order to defer the gain, it is necessary to (1) make an election to do so and (2) purchase either replacement property or the controlling "interest in a corporation" owning such property within the replacement period. To obtain postponement of the entire gain, the cost of the replacement property or the controlling interest must be equal to, or in excess of, the proceeds from the involuntarily converted property. When the proceeds exceed the cost of the replacement property, gain is recognized in the amount of the unreinvested proceeds.

Example of postponement of gain on involuntary conversion The following facts relate to a resort destroyed by an avalanche:

Insurance proceeds	$110,000
Adjusted basis	90,000
Realized gain (only partially recognized)	20,000
Amount used for replacement	100,000

The $10,000 of unreinvested insurance proceeds must be reported as income. However, the balance of $10,000 of gain may be postponed at the election of the owners.

Qualifications[3]

Careful attention must be given to the terms such as "proceeds," "replacement property," "similar or related in service or use," and "controlling interest" in order for the property owner to defer his gain.

[1] Ibid., sec. 1033(a)(1), 1.1033(a)-2(b).
[2] Ibid., sec. 1033, 1.1033(a)-1(a).
[3] Ibid., sec. 1033(a)(3)(A); 1.1033(a)-2(c)(4).

Proceeds   The term *proceeds* includes money as well as the value of dissimilar property received on the involuntary conversion, less the expenses incurred in obtaining them. If there was a mortgage on the property, part of the proceeds may be paid directly to the mortgage holder. Any amount paid on the mortgage directly to the mortgage holder is still considered part of the proceeds, whether the property owner was personally liable on the mortgage or not.

H owns property which has an adjusted basis of $50,000. When the property is condemned by the state for a freeway, H receives an award of $75,000, because the property has appreciated in value. The state pays $25,000 to First Loan Company, which holds a mortgage on the property, and pays the balance to H. Similar property acquired by H costs $60,000. He is considered to have a realized gain of $25,000 ($75,000 less $50,000 adjusted basis), and the $15,000 equal to the amount of unreinvested insurance proceeds is reportable as income. The balance may be deferred if H elects. Note that the payment of the mortgage is considered part of the proceeds. A property owner does not have to use the identical proceeds for replacement.

Similar or related in use   The replacement property must be similar or related in use. There are exceptions, however, in the case of certain condemned real property discussed below. The replacement property must be acquired by purchase. A gift of property will not satisfy the requirement for replacement of property. Similar or related in use means that the property must be functionally the same as the property converted. For example, unimproved real estate is not considered similar or related in service or use to improved real estate.

Controlling interest   The replacement property requirement may be satisfied by purchasing a controlling interest in a corporation owning such property. A controlling interest for this purpose means the ownership of stock possessing at least 80 percent of the total combined voting power of all classes of stock entitled to vote and at least 80 percent of the total number of shares of all other classes of stock of the corporation.

Special rule for certain condemned real property   The rule of similar or related in service or use is relaxed in the case of certain real property that is condemned. The real property must be used in trade or business or held for investment and must be condemned, seized, requisitioned or disposed of under the threat of imminence thereof. The rule does not apply to involuntary conversions because of fire, storm, or other casualty. The rule does not apply if the replacement is by the purchase of a controlling interest in a corporation which owns the replacement property.

Gain on property in this category that is replaced within the required time limit by other real estate used in trade or business or held for investment may be postponed, even though the replacement property is not similar or related in service or use to the property converted. Property of a like kind which is held either for productive use in a trade or business or for investment is treated as property similar or related in service or use to the converted property. For example, in this case unimproved real estate would be a satisfactory replacement for improved real estate.

For example, J owns a commercial office building which she sells to the city under threat of condemnation and realizes a gain. She takes the proceeds and invests them in a hotel. Both these properties are held for production of income, but they do not meet the test of similar or related in use. However, since the office building was property used in a trade or business, and since it was sold under imminence of condemnation, it comes under the special rule and the replacement by the hotel qualifies for the deferment of gain. This replacement would not qualify if the office building had been destroyed by fire or other casualty. It would not apply if J had purchased a controlling interest in a corporation owning the hotel instead of purchasing the hotel.

Award for lease A taxpayer who leases property may receive a condemnation award if he has to give up his lease. Tax on realized gain may be postponed if replacement property is purchased. In order to qualify, a leasehold must be purchased. It is not sufficient to enter into another lease.

Replacement period There is a definite time limitation on the acquisition of replacement property in order to qualify for the postponement of gain. Property that is destroyed or stolen must be replaced on or after the date on which the old property was damaged or stolen. In the case of condemnation, the date begins on the date of threat or imminence of requisition or condemnation. The end of the replacement period ends 2 years after the close of the first tax year in which any part of the gain on the involuntary conversion is realized. An extension of the replacement period may be granted upon application. To receive an extension, reasonable cause must be shown for not being able to make the replacement within the regular period of time.

Election An election to postpone gain is made by reporting all details in connection with the involuntary conversion of property in the tax year in which the gain is realized.

Loss from Involuntary Conversion

If the adjusted basis of the property that is involuntarily converted is greater than the proceeds, the taxpayer can claim a loss. A loss is deductible if it relates to property held in a trade or business or in a transaction entered into for profit, or results from a casualty or theft.

Assume that a taxpayer has rental property and also has a personal residence, both of which are destroyed by fire. Here she has a deductible casualty loss on both. However, if both properties are condemned and the result is a loss, the loss on the rental property is deductible but the loss on the condemnation of the personal residence is not deductible.

SALE AND LEASEBACK

A sale and leaseback arrangement generally involves the owner's selling a property and leasing it back on a long-term basis. The seller, now the lessee, agrees to maintain the property and pay the property taxes and insurance and other expenses, just as if he still owned the property. A variety of financial and tax considerations may be involved in sale and leaseback arrangements.

Considerations of Seller

Leasing is an alternative to purchase as a method of acquiring the use of property. Since rental payments on the lease are a fixed obligation, the lessee must consider the risk involved in meeting these payments in a manner similar to meeting interest and amortization requirements on a mortgage.

Influence on availability of funds The sale and leaseback may increase a corporation's ability to borrow funds. It has been accounting practice not to put leases directly in the financial statements. Thus a corporation that has leased property may appear to be stronger financially, all else being equal, than a firm that has raised its capital by borrowing. However, essentials of lease obligations are put in the footnotes of the financial statements, and to an increasing extent financial liability for leases is shown directly in the balance sheets of firms.

Sale and leaseback is often a major alternative to borrowing through bonds. Bond indentures often impose restrictions on the firm, e.g., limitations on dividends and restrictions on future indebtedness and management salaries. Leases do not involve these prohibitions, and hence a firm that is hampered from raising funds because of bond indenture restrictions may find that a sale and leaseback is the only alternative way of raising funds.

Probably the most important advantage to the seller in a sale and leaseback arrangement is the working-capital effect, since the sale of property will normally yield working capital. The rate of return on these funds in the firm's operations may be greater than the lease cost and thereby yield an advantage. The firm must, of course, plan for sufficient liquidity to meet the lease payments.

Disadvantages in use of sale and leasebacks A larger amount of funds can often be raised through sale of a property than through borrowing. Sale of property will normally yield approximately the total value, whereas only 60 to 80 percent can usually be borrowed with property as collateral. The prime disadvantage to the seller is that he will no longer have the asset at the end of the lease. Property may be an excellent hedge against inflation. If the property is sold and leased back, the company has lost this inflationary hedge and may be faced with the problem of looking for more expensive property at the end of the lease. Sometimes an option to repurchase or the right to renew the lease may be included to obviate these disadvantages.

Another disadvantage is that the business may be more tied to a location under a lease than it is if it owns the property. If a location is determined to be undesirable at a later date, it may be easier to sell the property than to pay a lease-cancellation penalty or continue lease payments.

Tax Considerations[1]

Perhaps the key element determining the desirability or undesirability of leasing is the cost of leasing versus borrowing. Tax considerations affect the cost of leasing since rental payments are deductible for tax purposes. Rental payments are generally based on a return on investment to the lessor and amortization of the cost of the property including the land over the period of the lease. Depreciation, of course, is computed only on the cost of the improvements, and this gives rise to the statement that a lease allows the "depreciation of land."

Comparison of available deductions: lease versus purchase   The lease-versus-purchase decision requires a projection of the relative effects of depreciation and rental deductions. The time value of money cannot be ignored. A firm can claim deductions for depreciation and for interest on the loan on property which it owns subject to a mortgage, while on leased property, the firm has a rental deduction. In addition, a firm may be able to write off the cost of property more rapidly through rental deductions than by charging depreciation on improvements.

A number of tax pitfalls may be involved when corporations sell and lease back property. Transactions between related parties are carefully scrutinized by the IRS, and in some cases gain on sale is treated as ordinary rather than capital gain. When leases are over 30 years' duration, the transaction may be treated as a tax-free exchange rather than a sale and no loss is recognized. A loss would occur on a sale and leaseback transaction when the sales price was less than the basis of the property to the seller. If renewal clauses are included in the lease, the IRS may add these renewal terms to the original term of the lease, resulting in a lease of over 30 years' duration. The effect of this, of course, would be to disallow any loss involved.

Special situations in sale and leasebacks   Firms sometimes find themselves in a situation in which sale and leaseback has particular tax advantages. For example, they may have appreciated property with a relatively low adjusted basis for tax purposes, where depreciation deductions are not great. Depending on the selling price of the property, the rate of return it can earn on funds, and the lease terms, such a firm might find it advantageous to sell its property and lease it back. If the property has been held only a short

---

[1] There are many tax considerations of leasing other than those mentioned here. These involve, among others, deductibility of lease costs, bonuses, agreements to restore property, depreciation of improvements, cancellations, subletting, and renewal option terms.

time, the effect of the depreciation-recapture provisions must be considered so that capital gain is not converted into ordinary gain.

Subject to the pitfalls already discussed, a firm that owns property with an adjusted basis for tax purposes larger than market value may have an advantage in selling the property and leasing it back. Working capital will be increased by both the sale proceeds and the loss deduction.

Some firms find it advantageous to sell and lease back the bare site and erect their own building. Thus the depreciation deductions on the improvements are not lost.

Generalization about whether a sale and leaseback is the best alternative cannot be made in any of these situations. It is necessary to project the specifics of the alternatives involved, including the important decision with respect to the residual value of the property which it will forgo if it sells.

DEPRECIATION RECAPTURE

It has already been noted that a tax benefit accrues to an investor when he is able to depreciate an asset below its market value and sell it at a gain. The depreciation deductions offset his ordinary income, which may be taxed at rates up to 70 percent, and the gain on sale is taxable at a maximum rate of 25 percent. For property other than buildings and their structural components and livestock, this was largely stopped by the depreciation recapture rules of the 1962 Revenue Law. A less stringent version relating to buildings and their structural components and leaseholds was passed in the 1964 Revenue Law.

Depreciable Property Other than Buildings[1]

The gain on depreciable property other than buildings and their structural components is considered ordinary income to the extent of depreciation taken after 1961. For dispositions other than a sale or exchange (with some exceptions), gain is considered to be the excess of the property's fair market value over its adjusted basis at the time of its disposition. The amount of the ordinary income is generally the smaller of (1) the gain from the disposition of the property and (2) the depreciation taken since 1961 on the property.

Example of depreciation recapture on personal property   Assume that B had the following transaction in personal property used in her real estate trade or business.

```
Cost on Jan. 1, 1968 .............................................$6,000
Annual depreciation................................................   600
Adjusted basis at date of sale, July 1, 1977.................   300
Sales price .........................................................  2,000
Gain ................................................................   1,700
```

[1] *1954 Internal Revenue Code*, sec. 1245; 1.1245.

The entire gain of $1,700 is considered ordinary income since it is not more than the depreciation after 1961. Total depreciation taken after 1961 is $5,700. The amount of the gain discussed above is often referred to as a Section 1245 gain after the applicable section of the Internal Revenue Code.

DEPRECIATION RECAPTURE ON REAL ESTATE

Buildings and their structural components were excluded from the depreciation recapture rules of Section 1245 IRC, which came into effect in the 1962 Revenue Law. However, when the 1964 Revenue Law was passed, a modified version of this depreciation recapture was applied to real estate. A more stringent version was contained in the Tax Reform Act of 1969. The result of these rules is to severely limit the ability to convert ordinary income into capital gain through the use of accelerated depreciation deductions.

These recapture provisions, often referred to as Section 1250 recapture after the relevant Internal Revenue Code section, are a function of the type of property (commercial or residential), the time the property is held, and the method of depreciation use.

Depreciable real property includes all real property that is subject to an allowance for depreciation and is not or has not been depreciable personal property at any time. It also includes leased property to which the lessee has made improvements that are subject to an allowance for depreciation (such as a building) and the cost of acquiring a lease.

Under law before the 1976 Tax Reform Act residential real property enjoyed favored tax treatment with respect to the recapture of accelerated depreciation. On the sale of residential real property held less than 100 months, the taxpayer was subject to recapture as ordinary income all depreciation in excess of straight-line depreciation. Thereafter, the taxpayer was permitted a 1 percent reduction in the amount subject to recapture for each month the property was held in excess of 100 months. In the case of property held longer than 16 years, 8 months, there was no recapture.

The 1976 Tax Reform acts provided that if Section 1250 property, including residential real property, is disposed of after December 31, 1975, that portion of depreciation in excess of straight-line depreciation attributable to periods after December 31, 1975 is treated as ordinary income to the extent there is gain on the disposition of the property. Gain is considered to occur most recently, so that ordinary income will result to the extent there is accelerated depreciation after December 31, 1975 and there is gain. Certain qualified low-income housing projects allow a 1 percent deduction in recapture for each month the property is held after the first 100 months.

In summary, the depreciation-recapture rules have evolved so that now they prevent the conversion of ordinary income into capital gain through the use of accelerated depreciation on personal property and on commercial, industrial, and residential real property. The use of accelerated depreciation still provides a deferral effect on income taxes since a taxpayer who pays less tax now has the use of the money in the interim before the tax is payable.

CLASSIFICATION OF PROPERTY

Sometimes property is classified as investment property or property used in a trade or business. Property may also be classified in other categories, e.g., for sale to customers or as a personal residence. Different classifications may result in dissimilar tax consequences.

Personal Residence

A personal residence of a taxpayer used exclusively as a residence is a capital asset. A gain on the sale of a personal residence is a capital gain, while a loss is not deductible. Gains, however, may be postponed if proceeds are reinvested according to certain rules. In the case of taxpayers over 65, subject to certain limitations, gain may be entirely forgiven.

Property Held for Sale to Customers

If property is held for sale to customers, ordinary income and ordinary loss result from a sale of such property. Usually an investor in property has capital gain, and a dealer has ordinary income. This is at the backbone of the great amount of litigation concerning the question of when taxpayers are dealers and when they are investors. Obviously, sellers of property at a gain would rather be investors than dealers so that they can receive capital-gain treatment.

Property Held for Investment

Unimproved real estate or vacant improved property is classified as investment property. Investment property is a capital asset, and gain or loss from a sale or exchange of investment property is capital gain or loss. Rental property is usually classified as property used in a trade or business, although not all courts are in agreement.

Property Used in Trade or Business

Real property and depreciable property used in a trade or business and held over 1 year when sold or exchanged receive Section 1231 treatment, as discussed in Chap. 4. The result if there is a gain, and the aggregation of all gains and losses from Section 1231 transactions is a gain, is to yield a long-term capital gain. From this standpoint, there is not much concern whether property is considered as held for investment or used in a trade or business.

However, there may be a significant difference if property is sold at a loss. If it is sold at a loss and it is investment property, a capital loss results, which is subject to the capital-loss limitations discussed in Chap. 4. If it is treated as a trade or business asset and there is a loss and this is the only Section 1231 transaction, the loss will be an ordinary loss. An ordinary loss is more desirable than a capital loss because there is no limitation on the deduction and it can give rise to an operating-loss carry-back and carry-forward.

Dealer versus Investor

The most critical area of controversy in classification of real estate for tax purposes is that of dealer versus investor. If property is held for sale to customers, gain or loss on sale or exchange is ordinary in nature. In addition, a dealer may not use the tax-free exchange rules, which will be discussed later. The tax-free exchange rules allow a taxpayer to defer gain on the exchange of investment property for other investment property or property used in a trade or business for other property used in a trade or business.

The sale of investment property gives rise to a capital gain, and the sale of property used in a trade or business gives rise to a Section 1231 gain, which is usually a capital gain. Conversely, a dealer has ordinary gain. Whereas an investor has a capital loss, the employer of property used in a trade or business has a Section 1231 loss, which is usually an ordinary loss. The dealer also receives ordinary loss treatment on sales.

People in the business of buying and selling real estate are dealers, and they realize ordinary gain or loss when they sell real estate. In addition, however, others may be classified as dealers, even though they have completely different occupations. Thus a doctor or a lawyer could be classified as a dealer in certain circumstances. Because there is no conclusive test, the facts of the particular situation govern the determination. Where the dealer-investor problem may have important tax consequences for the taxpayer, the most recent court decisions and rulings should be studied. In the past, certain factors have been used to classify the taxpayer as a dealer, i.e., intention at the time of acquisition to resell the property at a profit, quick turnover of property, frequent sales, and active participation in the sales by the taxpayer.

If the records of the taxpayer indicate that the property is held for investment rather than resale or no advertising or active attempt is made to sell the property, the taxpayer will probably be considered an investor. These are only indications. For example, there have been cases where despite numerous sales the taxpayer has received investor treatment rather than dealer treatment. Also, in some instances, a dealer can segregate certain properties and hold them for investment and be treated as an investor on those specific properties.

IMPROVEMENTS AND REPAIRS

The distinction between improvements and repairs is important to the real estate investor. Provided the property is used for production of income or in a trade or business, the repairs are currently deductible. Improvements are added to the basis of the property and are recovered through depreciation allowances. Improvements generally are expenditures that increase the value of property, prolong its life, or make it adaptable to a different use. Repairs merely maintain property in an ordinary, efficient operating condition. Examples of improvements that would be added to the basis of the property are new floors, new plumbing, new electrical wiring, a new roof, and lighting improvements. Repairs include such items as repainting the inside and outside of a building, repairing roofs and gutters, mending leaks, and patching and repairing floors.

If a new roof is placed on a building, it is a capital expenditure and its cost is added to the basis of the property, but if the old roof is repaired, it is a deductible expense. If the heating equipment is changed from one system to another, it is considered a capital expenditure and recovered through depreciation allowances instead of being considered a currently deductible expense. If a road or driveway on business property is maintained, the cost is deductible as a business expense. If a private road on business property is constructed, the cost is a capital expenditure; and if a gravel driveway on business property is replaced by a concrete one, the cost is also a capital expenditure.

CONSTRUCTION PERIOD INTEREST
AND TAXES

Before the 1976 Tax Reform Act taxpayers had the option of electing to capitalize interest and certain taxes relating to real property and personal property incurred during the construction period. Alternatively they could expense them. The Tax Reform Act of 1976 requires capitalization and establishes rules for amortization of construction-period interest and taxes. Rules vary depending on whether the property is commercial or residential or qualifies as low-income housing, as shown in Table 5-1. Amortization begins in year of completion. Thus, a shopping-center developer, for example, who completed property in 1977 would amortize the costs over 5 years. Costs for 1978 would be spread over 6 years; for 1979 over 7 years; for 1980, 8 years; for 1981, 9 years; and for 1982 and thereafter, 10 years.

TABLE 5-1 Amortization of Construction-Period Interest and Taxes

	Amount paid or accrued in taxable year beginning in:		
Non-residential real property	Residential real property (other than low-income housing)	Low-income housing	% of amount allowable for each amortization year
1976			*
	1978	1982	25%
1977	1979	1983	20
1978	1980	1984	$16\frac{2}{3}$
1979	1981	1985	$14\frac{2}{7}$
1980	1982	1986	$12\frac{1}{2}$
1981	1983	1987	$11\frac{1}{9}$
After 1981	After 1983	After 1987	10

* 1976, 50%; 1977 and subsequent, $16\frac{2}{3}$%.

INTEREST DEDUCTIONS

Interest deductions have been subjected to close scrutiny by Congress and the IRS. Before the development of many restrictions, interest deductions were a substantial source of tax deferral in real estate investments. Our discussion here will be separated into deductions of prepaid interest and dollar limitations on deductions for investment interest.

Deductions for Prepaid Interest

A deduction for all interest paid or accrued in the taxable year is allowed by Section 163 of the Internal Revenue Code. Investors in the 1960s could prepay as much as 5 years' interest. The IRS in the late 1960s issued a ruling that the deduction of prepaid interest will be considered as materially distorting income if interest is prepaid for a period extending more than 12 months beyond the end of the current taxable year.[1] An interest prepayment of less than 12 months was subject to a "facts and circumstances test" of its current deductibility. Therefore, in many situations, taxpayers were able to obtain current deductions for interest payments which related to succeeding years.

Under the 1976 Tax Reform Act a cash-basis taxpayer must deduct prepaid interest over the period of the loan to the extent the interest represents the cost of using the borrowed funds during such a period. Points paid on a

[1] *Revenue Ruling*, 68-643, 1968-2 *Cumulative Bulletin*, 76.

loan must also be deducted ratable over the term of the loan, except in the case of any indebtedness incurred in connection with the purchase or improvement of, and secured by, the taxpayer's principal residence to the extent that in the area in which the indebtedness is incurred payment of points is an established business practice and the amount of such payment does not exceed the amount generally charged.

Interest paid before January 1, 1977, pursuant to a binding contract or written loan commitment which existed on September 16, 1975, and which required prepayment of such interest is not affected by the Tax Reform Act.

Limit on Dollar Deduction of Investment Interest

Investors in former times could incur a substantial interest expense on borrowed funds and use the interest deduction to shelter other income from tax. The interest deduction would offset other ordinary income with the intention that gains would result in capital gains. For all taxpayers, except corporations, interest on funds borrowed to buy or carry investment property is deductible up to an allowable limit. The law has changed several times to determine an allowable limit; pre-1970, pre-1976, and post-1975 interest-deduction rules apply.

For tax years starting after 1975 the investment interest-deduction limit is an amount equal to the sum[1] of (1) $10,000, (2) net investment income, and (3) excess deductions for business or investment expenses, interest, and property taxes on net lease property over rental income from such property.

Married persons filing separately substitute $5,000 for the $10,000 deduction. Trusts have no dollar exemption, and a special rule applies when a taxpayer owns 50 percent or more of a corporation or partnership.

Net investment income is the excess of the taxpayers' investment income over investment expenses. A taxpayer's investment income is the gross income from interest, dividends, rents, and royalties, the net short-term capital gain from disposing of investment property, and the recapture of depreciation and intangible drilling costs.

The investment expenses are expenses deductible as trade or business property taxes, bad debts, straight-line depreciation, amortizable-bond premium-cost depletion, and other deductible investment expenses.

Computation The following example illustrates the calculation of the limitation on investment income. Taxpayer X, who is married and files a joint return, had investment income from dividends, interest, and net short-term capital gains from sales of investment property amounting to $25,000. His investment expenses were $5,000. X has interest expense of $200,000 for a loan he was granted in January 1977.

[1] Ibid., sec 163(a),(d).

Investment interest expense $200,000
Exemption $10,000
Net investment income 20,000
Total deduction allowed 30,000
Disallowed investment interest $170,000

X's disallowed investment interest deduction for 1977 is $170,000, and deductible investment interest is $30,000. If X also had a net long-term capital gain from sale of investment property, this would not enter into the calculation.

Investment interest that cannot be deducted in the year paid or accrued can be carried over to succeeding tax years. Carryover of post-1975 interest is treated as investment interest paid or accrued in the succeeding taxable year.

Syndication and Organization Fees

Maximizing early deductions has been facilitated by the deduction of syndication and organization fees, which include promoter's fees, organization fees, and legal, accounting, and other similar items. The purpose was to achieve immediate deduction rather than to capitalize them and increase the basis for depreciation.

The IRS has ruled that such payments to general partners for services rendered in organizing and syndicating a partnership constituted capital expenditures which were not currently deductible.[1] The essential part of the ruling is that "payments to partners for services on behalf of the partnership may be deducted by the partnership only if such payments would otherwise be deductible if they had been paid to persons who are not members of the partnership."[2] This implies an arm's-length negotiation regarding the amount of the fees which does not exist in most tax-shelter situations. The SEC suggests risk disclosure to the effect that fees will not be deductible if they constitute a capital expenditure or if they represent unreasonable compensation.

CANCELLATION OF INDEBTEDNESS

If a real estate venture turns out to be unsuccessful, there may be a cancellation of indebtedness. Normally any cancellation of indebtedness is treated as ordinary income to the investor,[3] but in the partnership context any decrease in a partner's share of partnership liabilities is considered as a distribution of money to the partner by the partnership.[4] The partnership's

[1] *Revenue Ruling 75-214, 1975-23 Internal Revenue Bulletin* 9.
[2] Ibid.
[3] Ibid., sec. 61(a)(12).
[4] Ibid., sec. 752(b).

cash distribution to a partner reduces the partner's basis in his partnership interest and is treated as capital gain after his basis is reduced to zero.[1] Corporations may elect somewhat analogous treatment if the amount excluded for cancellation of indebtedness is applied to reduce the basis of the obligator's property.[2]

INSTALLMENT AND DEFERRED-PAYMENT SALES

Under certain conditions a taxpayer may pay tax on gain as payments for property are received rather than at the date of sale. Two types of sales are considered: those sales which meet the requirements of the installment method of reporting and those which do not, referred to here as other deferred-payment sales.

Installment Sales Method[3]

The installment method may be used for the sale of real estate regardless of the selling price, providing payments in the year of sale do not exceed 30 percent of the selling price. This method can also be used in the case of a casual sale of personal property (other than inventory) for a price of more than $1,000 if the payments received in the year of sale do not exceed 30 percent of the selling price. Note that the sale of a property at a loss cannot be reported under the installment method.

If the gain on the sale of the property is capital gain, it remains capital gain. If it is ordinary gain, it remains ordinary.

The installment method can be used if there are no payments in the year of sale, provided that there are at least two payments at some time after the year of sale.

The method is elective. A taxpayer may elect with each qualifying sale whether he will use the installment sales method or not. Taxpayers who elect the installment method are bound by this election unless there has been a material mistake in the facts involved in the sale. Note that the election must be made in a timely filed tax return for the year of the sale. This is true even though there are no payments in the year of sale.

Two factors have caused many real estate investors to be deprived of the benefits of the installment sale method even though they wanted them: (1) failure to elect the method in the first tax return and (2) having payments of more than 30 percent in the year of sale.

There are several key factors in reporting profit on the installment method. The payments in the year of sale cannot be greater than 30 percent of the

[1] Ibid., sec. 733 and 731(a).
[2] Ibid., sec. 108 and 1017.
[3] Ibid., sec. 453; 1.1453.

selling price, and the income percentage to be reported each year is the percentage that the gross profit to be realized bears to the contract price. Thus careful attention must be given to the meaning of (1) selling price, (2) payments in the year of sale, (3) gross profit to be realized, and (4) contract price. Each has a definite meaning under the law for this purpose. After each has been defined, a comprehensive example will be presented.

Selling price   For purpose of the installment sale method, the selling price includes (1) cash, (2) the fair market value of property conveyed to the seller, and (3) debts assumed or paid by the buyer. Included in debts of the seller assumed or paid by the buyer would be notes, mortgages, liens, accrued interest, and taxes. It is noted below that the 1964 Revenue Law requires the imputation of interest in certain cases where it is not stated in the contract. Whatever interest is imputed will reduce the selling price.

Payments received in the year of sale   Recall that payments in the year of sale cannot be greater than 30 percent of the selling price if the installment sales method is to be used. All other cash payments and property received in the year with the exception of evidences of indebtedness of the purchaser are included, in addition to the down payment. If the buyer pays liabilities of the seller in the year of sale, these are also included as parts of the payments. Examples would be liens, accrued interest, and taxes. Also included would be the option payments or any earnest money that the seller received in a preceding year which become part of the down payment under the contract.

Mortgages[1]   Often property is subject to a mortgage when it is sold, and the purchaser assumes the mortgage. In this case, the mortgage is not included as part of the payments received in the year of sale unless the mortgage exceeds the seller's basis of the property. A mortgage may exceed the seller's basis for the property if it has appreciated in value since he purchased the property and he has later refinanced the property.

If the mortgage exceeds the seller's basis of the property and the buyer assumes the mortgage, the excess of the mortgage over the adjusted basis of the property is considered an additional collection made on the sale. The excess is included in the amount of payments in the year of sale.

Instead of assuming the mortgage, the buyer may pay off the mortgage. In this case, the amount must be included in the payments in the year of sale. It will also be included in the contract price, as explained below.

Determining the percentage of gain   At the time of sale the gross profit percentage is determined, and each year this percentage is reported as income. The gross profit percentage is the ratio of the realized gain to the contract price. Note that the denominator is the contract price and not the selling price.

[1] Ibid., sec. 1.453-4(c).

For example, R sells property at a contract price of $200,000 and realizes a total gain of $50,000. Therefore, the gross profit percentage is 25 percent. If R receives $20,000 in the first year, she reports $5,000 as gain. The second year she receives $40,000 and reports $10,000 as income, and so on.

Contract price   The contract price is the total amount to be received by the seller of the property. Assume that X sells property to Y for a total price of $50,000. Y takes title to the property subject to an existing mortgage of $10,000. The selling price is the total amount of $50,000 whereas the contract price is $40,000.

The contract price is equal to the selling price less the amount of the mortgage, provided that the mortgage assumed by the buyer is not greater than the seller's adjusted basis for the property. If the mortgage that is assumed by the buyer is greater than the seller's adjusted basis for the property, the excess of the mortgage over the seller's basis is included both in the contract price and in the payments in the year of sale. The theory is that the seller has recovered his basis in the property plus an additional amount equal to the excess of the mortgage over the adjusted basis.

Placing a mortgage on property is not a taxable transaction. For example, a taxpayer may have property for which $100,000 was paid but which is depreciated down to $40,000. Assume that because of appreciation in the value of the property, it is still worth $100,000 and the taxpayer can place a mortgage on it of $75,000. No tax is involved in this transaction.

Example of installment sale calculation   The following illustrates the determination of the amount of gain to be reported for tax purposes in the first 2 years of an installment sale.

Facts   W sells a warehouse to X for $144,000. Terms of sale are cash $40,500; first mortgage assumed by W, $31,500; second mortgage for $72,000. The second mortgage is payable by X in 10 annual installments of $7,200 each. In addition, X will pay 7 percent interest computed annually on each installment. Selling expenses amount to $9,000. The original cost of the warehouse to W was $144,000. Depreciation taken since acquisition amounted to $54,000.

Analyze as follows:

W's basis:		
Cost	$144,000	
Less depreciation	54,000	$ 90,000
Sales price:		
Gross	$144,000	
Less expenses	9,000	$135,000
Payment in year of sale		$ 40,500
(30% of $144,000 sales price)		43,200
Gain on sale:		
Net selling price	$135,000	
Less adjusted basis	90,000	$ 45,000

Contract price:

Cash	$ 40,500	
Plus second mortgage	72,000	$112,500

Ratio calculation:

Gain	$ 45,000 = $\frac{2}{5}$
Contract price	$112,500

The recognized gain in the year of sale is determined as follows:

$$\$40,500 \times \frac{\$45,000}{112,500} = \$40,500(\tfrac{2}{5}) = \$16,200$$

The above is determined by multiplying the ratio of the total gain on sale to the contract price by the payments in year of sale.

Gain to be reported for tax purposes in the second year is calculated as below:

$$\$7,200 \times \frac{\$45,000}{112,500} = \$7,200(\tfrac{2}{5}) = \$2,880$$

The interest income is ignored in the above calculation. It would be recorded as ordinary income.

Imputed interest[1] Many installment sales transactions involve property which yields capital gain to the seller. Formerly some sellers would provide for no interest or an interest rate significantly below the market. This increased the amount to be reported as capital gain and reduced the amount to be reported as interest income which is taxed at ordinary income rates.

The law now imputes interest in certain transactions so that part of the deferred payment is treated as interest if a reasonable rate is not specified in the contract. Interest is not imputed if the stated interest is at least 6 percent simple interest.

There are additional exceptions to the imputation of interest in addition to the 6 percent rule:

1. The sales price is $3,000 or less.
2. No payment is deferred by the contract for more than a year.
3. Patents are being sold under certain conditions.
4. The property is neither a capital asset nor a Section 1231 asset (re seller only).
5. The property is exchanged for annuity payments which are based on life expectancy.
6. The buyer can take a deduction for carrying charges (re buyer only).

When there is imputation of interest, the basis of the property to the buyer does not include the portion of his payments that is treated as interest. The buyer is allowed an interest deduction for the amount of interest.

[1] Ibid., sec. 1.453.1(b).

Other Deferred-Payment Sales[1]

Certain deferred-payment sales may not qualify for reporting under the installment sales method. For example, the payments in the year of sale may be more than 30 percent of the selling price. In the case of these sales, which we will refer to as other deferred-payment sales, gain or loss has to be reported in the year of sale even though the seller will receive deferred payments. Note, however, that the buyer's obligations are considered here at their fair market value for determination of gain or loss.

Example of deferred-payment sale Assume that S sells a parcel of real estate to B.

Terms: $120,000 down, balance $6,000 a year for 5 years, plus 7% interest

Commission	$ 7,000		
Adjusted basis	75,000		
Period property held	12 yr		
Fair market value of B's note	22,500		
Gain realized on transaction:			
Sale price		$150,000	
Commission	$ 7,500		
Adjusted basis	75,000	82,500	$67,500
Gain recognized on transaction in year of sale:			
Cash	$120,000		
Fair market value of note	22,500	142,500	
Commission	$ 7,500		
Adjusted basis	75,000	82,500	$60,000

The $60,000 will be a gain from a Section 1231 transaction if the real estate was used in trade or business by S or a capital gain if it was a capital asset.

Each year S will collect $6,000 plus 7 percent interest on B's note. For each collection he makes, 25 percent will be income and the balance payments on principal. Recall that B's note was included in the calculation of gain at 75 percent of its face value. Fair market value at the time of sale was $22,500, and the face value was $30,000. All interest payments will be ordinary income.

RELEVANT TAX RATES

Under both the installment sales method and the deferred-payment method, the tax rates that are in effect when the collection is made are relevant for the collections, and not the tax rates at the time that the sale was made. Assume a qualifying installment sale made in 1978 with $10,000 taxable collections each in 1978, 1979, 1980, and 1981. The $10,000 will enter the taxable-income computation in each year at that year's rate. The $10,000 in 1981 will be taxed at the rates in effect in 1981.

[1] Ibid., sec. 1.453-6.

CASUALTY LOSSES[1]

A casualty loss is a complete or partial destruction of property resulting from an identifiable event of a sudden, unexpected, or unusual nature, e.g., fire, flood, storm, hurricane, or similar event. Note, however, that progressive deterioration through a steadily operating cause and damage from a normal process is not considered a casualty loss. For example, a steady weakening of a foundation caused by normal or usual wind and weather conditions would not be a casualty loss.

Losses resulting from hurricane, tornado, flood, storm, shipwreck, fire, or accident are casualties. These losses are deductible, even though they relate to personal property such as a personal residence. There is, however, a difference in the method of computation of a business and a personal casualty loss. Also, for losses after 1963, the first $100 of a personal casualty loss is not deductible.

Personal-Loss Calculation

The amount of loss on property used solely for personal purposes is the lower of (1) the decrease in fair market value of the entire property and (2) the adjusted basis of the property. The amount must also be reduced by any insurance recovery.

Example of personal-loss calculation The following facts relate to the partial destruction of C's personal residence by flood:

Cost of land	$ 6,000
Cost of improvement	30,000
Value of land before flood	10,000
Value of improvements before flood	50,000
Value of entire property after flood	20,000
Proceeds from insurance company	31,500

The casualty loss is computed as follows:

Adjusted basis	$36,000	
Insurance proceeds	31,500	
	$ 4,500	
Amount not deductible	100	$4,400

The adjusted basis of $36,000 is lower than the sustained loss of $40,000, and so it is used. The adjusted basis is the original cost since no depreciation is allowed on a personal residence and there have been no additions or deductions from basis.

Reporting a personal casualty loss Usually a personal casualty loss is deducted as an itemized deduction along with items such as contributions,

[1] Ibid., sec. 165(c)(3); 1.165-7.

interest, and taxes. In this case, the taxpayer may not elect the standard deduction. If, however, the taxpayer has other Section 1231 transactions, the loss from personal property subject to a casualty or theft and held for more than one year is included in this grouping. If the total of the aggregation of Section 1231 transactions yields a gain, each transaction is considered a gain or loss from a capital asset. If the result is a loss, each transaction is treated as a gain or loss from a noncapital asset.

Business Casualty Loss[1]

A casualty loss on property used in a trade or business or for production of income is calculated differently from a personal loss if the property is entirely destroyed. If it is only partially destroyed, the loss is calculated like a personal casualty loss.

In the case of complete destruction, the loss is the excess of the adjusted basis of the property over the total of any salvage value, insurance, and other compensation. For example, D owns a warehouse with an adjusted basis, exclusive of the land, of $35,000, which is completely destroyed by fire. The warehouse has a fair market value of $40,000 just before the fire. There was no insurance on the warehouse. D has a deductible loss of $35,000.

In the case of partial destruction, the loss is the lower of the sustained loss and the adjusted basis. For example, M owned a hotel with an adjusted basis, exclusive of land, of $300,000 when it was partially destroyed by a flood. Before the flood, the value was $600,000, and after the flood the value was $400,000. The deductible loss is the decline in value of $200,000, since it is lower than the adjusted basis. This amount would be reduced by any insurance proceeds received.

Effect on Basis of Property

The basis of the property that the owner still has is reduced by a deductible casualty loss and is also reduced by the amount of any insurance proceeds.

C owns an apartment building which is partially destroyed by fire. The adjusted basis of the apartment is $150,000 exclusive of land. Before the fire, it had a fair market value of $300,000, and after the fire $200,000. C collected $90,000 in insurance proceeds. Since the decline in value ($100,000) is lower than the adjusted basis of $150,000, the $100,000 is used. This is reduced by the $90,000 proceeds to give a loss of $10,000.

The basis of the apartment house is reduced by the $90,000 insurance proceeds and the $10,000 deductible loss. Thus, the adjusted basis is now $50,000.

[1] Ibid., sec. 165(b); 1.165-1(c)(4), 1.165-7(b)(1).

SUMMARY

The importance of the rules for nontaxable exchanges to the investor stems from the fact that a tax-free exchange is often an important alternative to an outright sale or an installment sale on the disposal of property. An investor usually projects the results of a tax-free exchange on rate of return and on cash flow in analyzing the preferable alternative for disposal of property.

Tax-free exchanges result in postponement, and not forgiveness, of tax. An outright sale will result in immediate taxation and loss of use of whatever taxes are paid. As an alternative, the investor may give property to a family member who is in a lower tax bracket or the investor may sell property when in a low-income bracket, as often happens after retirement.

An investor must also consider the basis for depreciation of the acquired property. In a tax-free exchange, the basis of the property acquired in the exchange is a function of the property given up. In the case of appreciated property, the new property has a lower basis in a tax-free exchange than if the old property had been sold and the new property purchased. Analysis of the effects of a sale of property must also consider the depreciation-recapture rules, which may cause a portion of the gain to be treated as ordinary income instead of as capital gain.

The meaning of like property is an important factor in determining whether property will qualify under the nontaxable-exchange rules. Generally, the exchange of business or investment real property for other business or investment real property qualifies. The trade of personal property for personal property is treated as an exchange of like property.

Attention should be paid to the character of the specific properties likely to be involved in an exchange. As stated previously, like-kind requirement relates to the character of the property rather than its grade. Thus, for example, the exchange of unimproved real estate for improved real estate is a qualifying exchange. An exchange of city business or investment property for farm business or investment property also meets the qualifications. Note that the category "property held for investment" does not include exchanges of stocks, bonds, notes, or other securities. Thus real estate cannot be exchanged for common stock in a nontaxable exchange unless an individual is contributing the real estate to a corporation he controls and meets certain conditions.

It must be remembered that boot is important in nontaxable exchange. The receipt of boot makes an otherwise tax-free exchange partially taxable. It will not cause loss to be recognized. The recognition of gain is limited to the cash plus fair market value of the boot received.

The basis of property received in a nontaxable exchange is affected by any boot involved in the transaction. The basis when boot is received in the form of money is the adjusted basis of the old property less the amount of money received plus any gain recognized on the exchange. Basis is, of course, important to the investor because it affects future depreciation deductions and also gain or loss on subsequent sale of the property.

The giving of boot does not cause the transaction to become taxable for the party to the exchange giving the boot. If the other party to the exchange assumes liabilities on the property exchanged, the amount of the liability is considered as boot received. Similarly the amount of the liability is also included as boot received if the property is transferred subject to the liability. If both properties to an exchange are mortgaged, the mortgages on the properties are offset and the net amount is considered as boot received by one party and boot given by the other party. The party to the transaction that is relieved of the larger mortgage is considered to have received boot, and the other party is considered to have given boot.

Tax-free exchanges may be set up which involve several parties to the exchange. These so-called *multiple exchanges* may help two or more parties to satisfy their objectives in respect to tax treatment and types of property received in an exchange.

The second major section of this chapter involves the subjects of condemnations and involuntary conversions. When property is involuntarily converted or condemned, gain or loss may not be recognized. Generally, if certain requirements are met, a taxpayer may defer the recognition of gain resulting from the condemnation or involuntary conversion of property. This is accomplished by replacing property within certain time limits. Note that tax on the gain is deferred; it is not forgiven.

An involuntary conversion results when property is stolen, requisitioned, condemned, or destroyed and other property or money is received in payment. The tax-deferral rules also apply when property is sold or exchanged under the threat of imminence of condemnation. Here careful attention must be paid to the meaning of "imminence of condemnation."

Gain or loss from an involuntary conversion is measured by the difference between the adjusted basis of the property to the owner and the insurance proceeds or the condemnation award received. In the case of a gain, the taxability of such gain may be postponed. However, if the rules are not followed, a gain is taxable and a loss is deductible. The depreciation-recapture rules may also apply. If so, the amount of gain that is recaptured as ordinary income is generally limited to the unreinvested involuntary-conversion proceeds.

If property owners have their property condemned and receive similar property as compensation, there is no gain or loss recognized. They do not have the option of electing to report the gain or loss.

Careful attention must be given to the meaning for tax purposes of "proceeds," "replacement property," "similar or related in service or use," and "controlling interest." An investor should be careful not to fall into the possible trap of believing that the day-to-day usage of these terms also applies for tax purposes.

There is a definite time limitation on the acquisition of replacement property in order to qualify for the postponement of gain. The beginning of these periods depends on how the property was involuntarily converted.

The last section of this chapter deals with deductibility of casualty losses. Here attention must be paid to the distinction between business and personal casualty losses.

This concludes the specific sections on tax considerations. Much of the material is technical and need not be committed to memory, but the basic implications should be kept in mind, and the references cited should be consulted when a particular problem rises.

It is important to have current information. New laws and interpretations result in changing strategies to minimize or defer taxes.

SIX

Investment in Apartments

INTRODUCTION

Because of the wide range of sizes and values, apartment houses constitute an important investment medium for many average and small investors as well as large institutional investors. Apartment houses allow the owner to take an active part in the ownership and management of a real estate venture.

The first two sections of this chapter provide some necessary background information. Later sections discuss the investment decision process with regard to apartment-house investments. Succeeding chapters will consider the larger-scale real estate investments represented by office buildings, shopping centers, and integrated community developments.

BACKGROUND OF
APARTMENT INVESTMENT

Overbuilding of apartment houses during the 1920s created an excess that continued during the 1930s. By 1940, apartment vacancies had returned to a normal 5 percent level. During World War II, shortages of rental housing, particularly in defense areas, were aggravated by rent controls. After the war, government financing aids and the removal of rent controls resulted in a rapid recovery in residential construction.

Special FHA financing played an important role in apartment-house building after World War II. The FHA 608 Program stimulated many apartment building starts during this period. A 90 percent maximum loan-to-value ratio under the FHA 608 Program helped to attract investors to these projects. In addition, it was customary to obtain a generous appraisal of land on the basis of estimating value after completion. Thus, the developer could often obtain as much loan capital as was represented by the project costs (and sometimes more). In many cases excess proceeds were taken out as capital gains. The tax law, however, was later amended so that excess proceeds of mortgages under the 608 Program were not treated as capital gains, and FHA appraisal policies were made more restrictive. A decline in apartment-building construction resulted after 1950.

Substantial increases in apartment-house building occurred again in the late 1950s and climaxed in a boom in the early 1960s. The boom reflected the increased availability of mortgage money and the tax advantages of the depreciation provisions of the 1954 Internal Revenue Code. However, by early 1966 overbuilding resulted in high vacancies in many areas. This overbuilding, together with a tightening of mortgage funds, resulted in virtual cessation of apartment construction by 1966. Privately owned multifamily housing starts dropped in 2 years from 505,000 in 1964 to 352,000 in 1966.

Statistics on two-family and multifamily housing starts from 1964 to 1976 are presented in Table 6-1.

Beginning in 1964, housing starts for privately owned structures (two units) follow a fluctuating pattern. Starts reached a peak of 67,000 in 1972 but then fell to a 12-year low of 31,000 in 1975 and recovered to 44,000 in 1976. Privately owned multifamily housing starts dropped from 505,000 to 352,000 in 1966. Multifamily housing starts increased between 1967 and 1972 (except for 1969). A steep rise from 352,000 in 1966 to 980,000 in

TABLE 6-1   Multifamily Housing Starts in Thousands

	Privately owned			Publicly owned			Total public and private*
Year	Two-family	Multifamily	Total private	Two-family	Multifamily	Total public	
1964	54	505	559	9	22	31	590
1965	51	458	509	8	28	36	545
1966	35	352	387	6	24	30	417
1967	41	406	447	6	23	29	476
1968	46	562	608	8	29	37	645
1969	43	413	456	5	27	32	488
1970	42	578	620	6	28	34	654
1971	55	845	900	9	22	31	931
1972	67	980	1,047	5	15	20	1,067
1973	54	859	913	4	8	12	925
1974	33	417	450	6	8	14	464
1975	31	235	266	5	6	11	277
1976	44	331	375	1	5	6	381

* Totals of publicly and privately owned housing do not include one-unit structures. •
Source: Department of Commerce, Bureau of the Census, Construction Reports, ser. C-20, U.S. Department of Housing and Urban Development Statistical Yearbook 1975.

1972 is followed by a rapid drop from 1972 to 1975. The 12-year high of 980,000 is in 1972. A 12-year low of 235,000 is registered in 1975. Total private housing starts for the period followed a general up-and-down pattern between 1964 and 1970, with a high of 620,000 in 1970 and a low of 387,000 in 1966. Total starts rose to 900,000 in 1971, hit a high of 1,047,000 the next year, and then dropped precipitously in 1974 and again in 1975. The 12-year low of 266,000 occurred in 1975. The high for the same period was the 1,047,000 starts made in 1972. Some recovery is shown in 1976.

Housing-start totals for publicly owned structures also appear in Table 6-1. Total publicly owned housing starts exhibited some fluctuation between 1964 and 1971, ranging from a low of 29,000 in 1967 to a high of 37,000 in 1968. The total then dropped to 12,000 in 1973, rose slightly in 1974, and hit a 12-year low of 11,000 in 1975.

Some observers feel that the rate of apartment construction will not rise at a rapid rate in the near future. Net rents, when compared with construction cost, debt-service cost, and the need for reasonable return on equity, form the basis for new-construction decisions.[1] Where communities have high vacancy rates, gross rental rates will have trouble rising enough to cover increasing costs for utilities, maintenance, taxes, and management. Where there is a high unemployment rate among young people there tends to be a slower rate of household formation, which in turn reduces the demand for new apartments. Increased tenant rights and the possibility of rent control also alarm potential investors.[2]

Rent control is certainly a risk for investors in income properties, but many observers feel that rent control has not been successful in achieving overall national housing objectives. If this belief prevails, it is unlikely that a restrictive rent control policy will prevail. The likelihood of imposition of rent control varies by specific area, depending, among other things, on the political climate in the particular area. Potential investors would consider the possibility of rent control in a specific area as one of the important factors in their decision to invest.

In addition to these factors, some suburban communities have moved to control growth in their areas. Downs noted that density and building height limitations, antiapartment zoning ordinances, and limits on the amount of land zoned each year for apartments all discourage apartment construction.

MOTIVATION OF INVESTORS

Since investment in rental property has a decidedly speculative element, it must compete with other investments involving risk capital and must offer

[1] Phillip C. Jackson, Jr., speech given before the Annual Meeting of the Real Estate Research Council, San Francisco, Jan. 9, 1976.

[2] Anthony Downs, "Real Estate Trends and Their Implications for Property Management," *Journal of Property Management,* September–October 1975, p. 225.

comparable prospects of return. For many investors, this means that the amount of risk capital will be limited to what can be recaptured in a short time. Debt financing must cover the bulk of financing needs.[1]

During two periods of this century, it was possible to build without advancing much equity money. The first was the apartment and office building boom of the 1920s and the second during the decade following World War II. During the 1920s the mortgage-bond issue was the device that made it possible for developers to commit very little equity to their projects. The period following World War II found the FHA-insured loan taking the place of the mortgage-bond issue as the instrument of allowing the developer the opportunity of "mortgaging out" his property.

Thus, real estate investment is appraised by an investor in the same manner as any other high-risk venture. The potential reward must overbalance the risk, and the opportunity for quick recapture of capital must be present for the investor to consider the investment.

Smith[2] distinguishes between the motivations of the investors and those of the developers, arguing that developers start out with little or no equity and attempt to develop one. Conversely, long-term investors who purchase the completed property usually start with substantial cash equity they wish to increase. Developers are entrepreneurs. They do not concern themselves with a reasonable rate of return on their capital in the manner of an investor but act like a manufacturer who sells a product at a markup above cost. As will be noted below, it is important to distinguish this entrepreneurial profit from normal investment returns. The entrepreneur's profit comes from the fact that the finished product is worth more than the cost of the components of land, building, and capital.[3]

In Smith's study of low-rise apartments in the Oakland, California, area, he noted that little equity was required in the development process. The developer had, however, created an equity by the time the property was completed. This profit could then be realized either through sale or by refinancing the property. The typical developer in Smith's study realized gains, but there was considerable variation in the outcome, with many losses and some rather spectacular gains.[4]

Investors were interested primarily in tax shelter through accelerated depreciation and equity buildup through amortization of the loan. Cash flow did not seem to be an important element for most of the investors in the

---

[1] Miles L. Colean, "The Realities of Today's Real Estate Investments," *Architectural Forum*, April 1955, p. 125; May 1955, p. 125; June 1955, p. 110.

[2] Wallace F. Smith, *The Low-Rise Speculative Apartment*, University of California, Center for Real Estate and Urban Economics, Institute of Urban and Regional Development, Research Report 25, Berkeley, 1964, p. 91.

[3] Ibid., p. 89.

[4] Ibid., p. 36.

study. For many of the projects, net cash flow from the property was minimal.[1]

Long-term yield was the important goal for the investors. Presumably, investors had other sources of liquidity and could ignore short-run fluctuations in the value of their property. Although current cash flow was not the primary goal, investors were concerned with the ability of the property to amortize debt. The investors came from diverse parts of the business community.[2] Most had backgrounds in the building trades.[3]

DEMAND FOR RENTAL HOUSING

Demographic factors help increase demand for rental housing. One important demographic trend that creates demand for rental housing is an increase in the number of marriages. Another important factor is a rise in the number of young adults who tend to rent rather than buy.

A gain in the number of "primary" individuals also contributes to the demand for rental housing. These are people who establish dwelling units that contain no other family members. An increase in the membership of this group develops largely from an increase in the number of older people and widows or widowers. The number of primary individual households also grows as divorce and separation rates increase and as more young unmarried people establish their own dwelling units. The main demographic factor against demand for rental housing is larger family size. Having more children seems to delay the stage in the life cycle at which housing space requirements ease.

Economic factors also affect the demand for rental housing. Factors favoring rental housing include an increase in the number of working wives, who want neither long commutes to work nor home ownership to burden them. Since job opportunities for women are more common in cities than in the suburbs, families with working wives are likely to prefer to rent an urban apartment.

The increase in professional, managerial, and white-collar workers in the labor force also favors rental housing. Professional men appear more likely to rent than others in their income class. Contributing factors include the high mobility rate and the urban location of the professional's activities.

INFLATION AND THE REAL
ESTATE INVESTOR

Increased costs are important because an investor must be able to obtain a reasonable return after considering costs and debt service in relation to

[1] Ibid., p. 36.
[2] Ibid., p. 55.
[3] Ibid., p. 47.

rents. A discussion of the impact of inflation on real estate values was given in Chap. 2. The reader may wish to review the section on the impact of inflation on multifamily housing, which reviews studies on realized rates of return on apartment-house investments.

INFLATION AND INCREASED CONSTRUCTION COSTS

Between 1950 and 1975, construction costs for apartments, hotels, and office buildings made of brick and concrete increased on an index scale from 54.3 to 183.5 with 1967 equal to 100. Costs for brick and steel construction of these same structures increased from 57.9 in 1950 to 183.8 in 1975.[1]

The cost of construction materials in general rose on an index scale from 90.4 in 1955 to 174.0 in 1975 with 1967 again equal to 100. Prices of lumber and wood products increased more dramatically than other materials, rising from 94.5 in 1955 to 192.5 in 1975. Window glass also recorded a significant increase, jumping from 78.3 in 1955 to 177.7 in 1975. Prices of prepared paint rose on the index from 82.1 in 1955 to 166.9 in 1975, and plumbing fixtures, including brass fittings, increased from 88.7 to 162.3. Miscellaneous products, including building paper and board and hard-surface floor coverings, increased relatively little in price from 1955 to 1975. Miscellaneous products rose on the index from 99.1 to 127.1 between 1955 and 1975, and floor coverings rose from 93.9 to 148.5 over the same period. Some materials, such as heating equipment, actually fell in price between 1955 and 1967, but all materials increased between 1967 and 1975 and all were significantly higher in 1972 than they had been in 1955.[2]

A significant portion of construction costs involves the wages paid to those who work in the building trades. The index of hourly wages for all building trades has risen from 75.4 in 1960 to 188.3 in 1975, with 1967 equaling 100. The wages of carpenters rose from 75.0 on the scale in 1960 to 187.0 in 1975. Electricians' wages rose from 76.4 to 193.8 over the same period. The wages of building laborers were 73.8 on the scale in 1960; by 1975 they had reached 190.7. In terms of average union hourly wages, this means that carpenters in 1960 earned $3.78 per hour. In 1975, they earned $9.24 per hour. Electricians' wages rose from $4 per hour in 1960 to $9.73 per hour in 1975. The wages of building laborers rose from $2.81 per hour in 1960 to $6.99 per hour in 1975.[3]

---

[1] The American Appraisal Company, Publication and Education Division in Housing and Urban Development, *Statistical Yearbook,* 1976.

[2] Department of Labor, Bureau of Labor Statistics, Wholesale Prices and Price Indexes, in *HUD Statistical Yearbook, 1976.*

[3] Ibid.

TABLE 6-2 Estimated Cost-Trend Indexes in Class D Apartment Houses, in San Francisco
Bay Area* (January 1967 = 100)

Date	Gross cost	Cost/ft²	Index	Date	Gross cost	Cost/ft²	Index
1/67	$281,000	$11.71	100.0	1/74	$455,200	$18.97	162.0
1/68	292,900	12.20	104.2	4/74	461,100	19.22	164.1
1/69	317,700	13.24	113.1	7/74	473,500	19.73	168.5
1/70	333,500	13.89	118.7	10/74	479,000	19.97	170.5
1/71	352,000	14.66	125.3	1/75	487,600	20.31	173.6
1/72	380,900	15.87	135.5	4/75	498,600	20.77	177.5
4/72	390,100	16.25	138.8	7/75	508,200	21.18	180.9
7/72	397,200	16.54	141.3	10/75	520,800	21.69	185.4
10/72	413,400	17.23	147.1	1/76	526,800	21.95	187.5
1/73	422,100	17.59	150.2	4/76	534,200	22.26	190.1
4/73	432,200	18.01	153.8	7/76	547,310	22.81	194.8
7/73	444,300	18.51	158.1	10/76	558,500	23.27	198.8
10/73	450,400	18.77	160.3	1/77	563,800	23.49	200.7

* These are typical costs of a hypothetical two-story, 24-unit apartment house with 10 two-bedroom and
14 one-bedroom apartments. The building is rectangular, 80 by 150 ft on each floor. The cost does not
include garages or site improvements. Building is above average quality in construction specifications.
Source: Real Estate Research Council of Northern California, Northern California Research Report, vol.
28, no. 3, 1976, p. 23; data by Marshall and Swift Publication Co.

Marshall and Swift Publication Company has computed an index of
typical building costs for two kinds of apartment buildings, a two-story
class D apartment house and a 27-story high-rise class A apartment building.
Marshall and Swift's description of the two hypothetical apartment buildings
and their gross cost, square-foot cost, and price index follows.

As the cost trend index for the class D building (Table 6-2) indicates,
construction costs increased rapidly between 1967 and 1977 and especially
between 1972 and 1977. Construction costs have doubled since 1967,
sending the gross cost of building an apartment building like the hypothetical one in this example from $281,000 to $563,800.

Construction costs for the hypothetical class A building (Table 6-3) increased somewhat more slowly for the first years following 1967. The cost-
trend index for the class D building indicates an increase from 100.0 in
January 1967 to 168.5 in July 1974. Construction costs for the class A
building, however, rose to 165.1, or 3.4 index points less, over the same
period. But between July 1974 and January 1977, building costs for the
class A building rose to 200.4 compared with the class D building costs,
which reached an index of 200.7.

Significantly, construction costs for both types of apartment buildings
increased more rapidly than rents over the same period. Rents rose on an
index from a base level of 100 in 1967 to 137.3 in 1975 and to 145 in
July 1976. In contrast, construction costs for both class A and class D apartment buildings increased from a base of 100 in 1967 to more than 185 by
October 1975.

TABLE 6–3 Estimated Cost-Trend Indexes in High-Rise Class A Apartment Houses in San Francisco Bay Area* (January 1967 = 100)

Date	Gross cost (thousands)	Cost/ft²	Index	Date	Gross cost (thousands)	Cost/ft²	Index
1/67	$ 7,819	$20.29	100.0	1/74	$12,174	$31.59	155.8
1/68	8,117	21.06	103.8	4/74	12,409	32.20	158.8
1/69	8,573	22.25	109.7	7/74	12,901	33.48	165.1
1/70	9,074.5	23.55	116.0	10/74	13,542	35.14	173.3
1/71	9,667	25.09	123.6	1/75	13,924	36.15	178.2
1/72	10,360	26.90	132.5	4/75	14,284	36.88	182.8
4/72	10,570	27.43	135.2	7/75	14,323	37.17	183.3
7/72	10,770	27.95	137.8	10/75	14,707.5	38.18	188.2
10/72	11,079.5	28.75	141.8	1/76	14,887	38.66	190.5
1/73	11,251.5	29.20	144.0	4/76	14,991	38.90	191.7
4/73	11,431	29.66	146.3	7/76	15,151.5	39.32	193.8
7/73	11,736	30.46	150.2	10/76	15,487	40.19	198.1
10/73	12,073	31.33	154.5	1/77	15,664.5	40.65	200.4

* These are typical costs of a hypothetical 26-story class A apartment building with two levels of subterranean parking. The building is a rectangular tower with exterior dimensions of 80 by 175 ft for all floors except the parking basements, which are 100 by 200 ft, and the elevator and mechanical penthouse, which is 30 by 12 ft; second through twenty-sixth stories, 9 ft, 6 in.; penthouse, 20 ft. Walls are face brick with concrete-block backup and porcelainized metal and glass panels.

Source: Real Estate Research Council of Northern California, Northern California Research Reports, vol. 27, no. 3, 1976, p. 25; data by Marshall and Swift Publication Co.

If rents lag behind construction costs as well as financing costs, there will not be a great incentive for new construction. There may be a favorable influence on investment in existing multifamily units as demand increases and there is a lag in supply of new construction.

MARKET-ANALYSIS TECHNIQUES FOR APARTMENT INVESTMENT

Apartment-house investors and developers concern themselves primarily with the future demand for, and supply of, apartment units in the local housing market area. The future demand for apartment units will depend upon population growth in the area and the income and age distribution of the population. In addition, such factors as the current housing supply, zoning regulations and their evolution, and a multitude of legal, political, and environmental considerations also affect the decisions made by investors and developers.

The U.S. Department of Housing and Urban Development has compiled the outline in Table 6-4 to aid investors in studying the many important factors involved in apartment-house investment.

The merit of this comprehensive outline is that it can be used as a checklist of important factors to be considered in market analysis. Developing an

TABLE 6-4   Real Estate Market Analysis*

I. Delineation of the market area, geography, and climate
  A. Metropolitan area
    1. Name of standard metropolitan statistical area (SMSA)
    2. Identification of entire area
      a. County or counties
      b. Principal incorporated and unincorporated urbanized areas (10,000 or more population)
    3. Geography
      a. Size (land area)
      b. Major topographical features
    4. Climate
      a. Rainfall
      b. Temperature changes (monthly, seasonal)
      c. Relative humidity
    5. General urban structure; location of facilities
      a. Significant geographic submarkets in SMSA
      b. Employment areas
      c. Shopping areas (central-business-district, regional and community shopping centers)
      d. Principal transportation facilities (air, highway, rail, water)
      e. Educational facilities
      f. Community facilities (religious, cultural, recreational)
    6. Direction of city growth
    7. Commuting patterns (journey to work)
    8. Any major community developments and/or special features or characteristics germane to the market analysis
II. Demographic analysis
  A. Population
    1. Most recent estimate for total population
    2. Past trends in population growth
    3. Estimated future population
      a. 1980, 1985, 1990, 1995 totals and average annual rate of growth
      b. Changes in population due to
        (1) Net natural increase
        (2) Migration
    4. Distribution by age groups
      a. 1970 census
      b. Most recent estimates
  B. Households
    1. Most recent estimates for household formations
    2. Past trends in household formations
    3. Estimated future total households and average annual rate of growth
    4. Current trends in household size (increasing, decreasing)
III. Economy of the market area
  A. Economic history and characteristics
    1. General description
    2. Major economic activities and developments
      a. Before 1970
      b. Recent and present
  B. Employment, total and nonagricultural
    1. Current estimates (1975 annual data, 1976 monthly)
    2. Past trends: 1960, 1970, 1971, 1972, 1973, 1974

TABLE 6-4   Real Estate Market Analysis*   (Continued)

        3. Distribution by industry groups
          a. For each period, past and present
          b. Numerical and as percent of all employment
        4. Estimated future employment
          a. Total
          b. By industry groups
        5. Trends in labor participation rate
        6. Trends in female employment
    C. Unemployment
        1. Current level
        2. Past trends
    D. Economic-base analysis
        1. Shift-share analysis: metropolitan area compared to national and state employ-
          ment data
        2. Alternative: location quotients
        3. Discussion of principal employers
          a. Primary industries (manufacturing, construction, mining)
          b. Secondary industries (TCU, trade, FIRE, services, governments)
          c. Location and accessibility
        4. Payroll data (census of manufacturers, trade, services, governments)
    E. Income data
        1. Personal income by major sources
          a. By type: wage and salary, proprietors
          b. By industry: farm, nonfarm, government
        2. Per capita personal income
        3. Family-income distribution
          a. All families
          b. Owner households
          c. Renter households
          d. Households with female heads
        4. Projections for growth in personal income
IV. Construction and real estate activity
    A. Building and construction Industry
        1. Residential building by type (single-family, multifamily, rental or sales)
          a. Historical and recent trends (past 10 years)
          b. Building permits: monthly for current and previous year
          c. Conversions and demolitions
         2. Nonresidential construction
          a. Commercial
          b. Industrial
          c. Institutional
         3. High-rise building activity (minimum height of five stories above ground)
          a. Residential
          b. Commercial (offices, stores, hotel and motels, multiple-use)
          c. Other (governmental, schools, hospitals)
         4. Heavy engineering construction
    B. Demand-and-supply analysis for properties other than residential
        1. General demand factors in metropolitan area
          a. Number of potential new employees
          b. Number of potential new tenants or owner-users
          c. Movement of firms in and out of the area
          d. Recent trends in replacement ratios

2. Existing inventory, by property type
   a. Price: sale or rental rates
   b. Quantity: net leasable square footage
   c. Year built: before 1960, 1960–1975, new
   d. Competitive status
   e. Vacancy factors
3. Projected production, by property type
   a. Price: sale or rental rates
   b. Quantity: net leasable space
   c. Probable conditions (financing, marketing, absorption rates)

C. Housing inventory, by type (single-family, multifamily)
   1. Most recent estimates
   2. Past trends including 1970 census
      a. Index of housing values and rents
   3. Principal characteristics
      a. Tenure of occupancy
      b. Value of houses and monthly contract rent
      c. Type of structure
      d. Year built
      e. Vacancy ratios: percent of total units (total, homeowner, rental)

D. Residential sales and rental markets
   1. General market conditions
   2. Major subdivision activity
      a. Current
      b. Past trends
   3. Trends in sales prices or monthly rentals
      a. Existing units
      b. New units
      c. Sales prices or monthly rentals adjusted to square-foot basis
   4. Unsold inventory of new sales housing
      a. Price ranges
      b. Number of months unsold
      c. Absorption rates
      d. Environmental ratings
      e. Competitive status with other sales properties
   5. New rental housing
      a. Date of completion
      b. Type of units and rental ranges
      c. Marketing experience to date
      d. Absorption rates
      e. Environmental ratings
      f. Competitive status with existing rental housing
   6. Residential units under construction
      a. Volume
      b. Types of units
      c. Probable environmental ratings
      d. Probable marketing schedules

E. Other housing markets
   1. Public and government subsidized housing
      a. Identification and location
      b. Existing and planned
   2. Specialized submarkets for housing demand and supply
      a. College or university housing

TABLE 6-4   **Real Estate Market Analysis***   (*Continued*)

   b. Housing for the elderly
   c. Military housing
  F. Real estate loans and mortgage markets
   1. Sources and availability of funds
   2. FHA, VA, FNMA, GNMA
   3. Interest rates and terms of mortgages
   4. Recordings of mortgages and/or deeds of trust
   5. Foreclosures
    a. Overall trend
    b. Conventional, FHA, other
 V. Political and legal aspects
  A. Land-use planning
   1. Regional
   2. County(s)
   3. Incorporated cities in SMSA
  B. Zoning
   1. Review of present zoning ordinances for county(s) and cities
   2. Zoning history and present attitudes of zoning authority
   3. Identify raw land presently zoned for land use of subject property
  C. Ordinances, codes, regulations
   1. Subdivisions
    a. Submission procedures
    b. Requirements for improvements
   2. Building codes
   3. Health and public safety
   4. Allocation of land for schools, recreational areas, open space
  D. Municipal services
   1. Public safety
    a. Fire
    b. Police
   2. Hospitals and health care
   3. Utilities
  E. Ecological
   1. Environmental-impact studies
   2. Limited growth policies
   3. Floodplains and flood control
   4. Solid-waste disposal
  F. Property taxation
   1. Tax rate per $1,000 valuation
   2. Assessment ratio as percent of market value
   3. Special assessment districts
 VI. Identify sources of information
  A. Population
  B. Employment
  C. Personal income
  D. Planning
  E. Building
  F. Zoning
  G. Other pertinent
 VII. Qualifications of the real estate market analyst(s)

VIII. Visual materials
   A. Metropolitan area road map (major traffic arteries)
   B. Topographical maps
   C. Land-use planning maps (present and future uses)
   D. Map(s) showing present urban structure and location of facilities
   E. Subdivision plots
   F. Aerial photographs of area(s)
   G. Area map showing location of subject property(s) and comparables
   H. Photographs of comparable properties

Source: U.S. Department of Housing and Urban Development, *FHA Techniques of Housing Market Analysis,* Washington, August 1970. Jordan E. Glazov, "A Market Analysis for Land Assemblage," *Real Estate Today,* March 1975, pp. 32–36; and William R. Beaton and Robert J. Bond, *Real Estate,* Goodyear Pacific Palisades, Calif., 1976.

---

apartment house requires the consideration of many factors, not all of which are of equal importance. Any development has its specific characteristics. To be profitable it must satisfy the effective demand of the market, and it must be properly financed and effectively managed. In using this checklist the developer must consider the relations of the factors considered to the specific project being developed.

ECONOMIC FORECASTING MODELS IN REAL ESTATE INVESTMENT ANALYSIS

Housing-market analysts are concerned with estimating future growth in urban and rural areas. Estimates of future growth and development are being made and used by individuals and public agencies in their decision process. Although decisions are often made on the basis of intuition and judgment, there has been an important attempt in recent years to develop operational models and techniques designed to forecast future employment, population, and land-use development for small geographic areas.[1]

The combination of an urgent need for improved techniques to aid in formulation of transportation, housing, and other urban-growth policy together with the use of the computer to manipulate data led to experimentation in the early 1960s with large-scale land-use forecasting models. The BASS model, for example, forecast future land uses for six classes of residential use as well as for manufacturing and wholesaling, service employment, commercial, public and recreational, and agriculture, mining, and construction.[2]

The objective of land-use models is to integrate existing knowledge and

[1] See for example, P. F. Wendt (ed.), *Forecasting Transportation Impacts upon Land Use,* Studies in Applied Regional Science, vol. 2, Nihoff, Leiden, 1976.

[2] *Jobs, People and Land,* Bay Area Simulation Study (BASS), University of California Center for Real Estate and Urban Economics, Special Report 6, Berkeley, 1968.

204 / Real Estate Investment Analysis and Taxation

techniques from a number of disciplines for the purpose of forecasting regional population, employment, incomes, industry structure, and housing demand. Input data include information on commuting, consumer travel, shopping behavior, residential, industrial, and commercial locational decisions as well as all important assumptions concerning government housing, public investment, transportation, and land-use policies.

Specification of the values for the numerous variables is a difficult task. In addition, the perception of the users of the models creates problems. Some users might assume they are getting an accurate one-time forecast rather than a planning tool to be used for estimating the probable impact of various public-policy assumptions. Other users are skeptical of models which do not explicitly specify the public-policy framework within which the market forces are working. Despite the problems involved, many large-scale land-use modeling projects were initiated.[1] There is considerable literature describing and evaluating urban land-use models.[2]

Considering the difficulties involved in dealing with the numerous variables and the potential misuse of the results by decision makers, it may seem that intuition and judgment might be better methods of projection. However, land-use models require the integration of the demand forces which influence future land development with the land supply as constrained by public-policy considerations. Specific assumptions concerning each of the identifiable variables which influence future land development must be provided for the computer-simulation model. This may be superior to simple trend-extrapolation assumptions, which were used in early development forecasts. Computer programming techniques allow efficient testing of the sensitivity of the output to changes in the variables used in the model. Also, the model users are required to make explicit assumptions about public and private policies and behavior.

Assuming that the quality of the projections of economic models can equal or exceed the intuitive judgments so generally relied upon in real estate investment decisions, these models seem to represent a powerful and important new tool for real estate investment analysis and for real estate valuation.

It will be assumed that the output of economic model projections or some

---

[1] For a recent review of six land-use models, see H. James Brown et al., *Empirical Models of Urban Land Use: Suggestions on Research Objectives and Organization,* National Bureau of Economic Research, Explanatory Report 6, New York, 1972.

[2] References may be found in S. R. Rosenthal, J. R. Meredith, and W. Goldner, *Plan Making with a Computer Model, Projective Land Use Model,* vol. 1, University of California Institute of Transportation and Traffic Engineering, Berkeley, February 1972, pp. 88–92 and ORNL-NSF Environmental Program, *Regional Environmental Systems Analysis, Regional Modeling Abstracts,* vol. 2, Oak Ridge National Laboratory, Oak Ridge, Tenn., June 1973. See also G. S. Goldstein and L. N. Moses, "A Survey of Urban Economies," *Economic Literature,* vol. 11, no. 2, pp. 494–515, June 1973.

alternative will provide the essential element of economic base analysis underlying the entire range of investment decisions treated in Chaps. 6 to 8.

STUDIES OF HOUSING MOBILITY AND VACANCIES

The use of macroeconomic models in real estate investment must be supplemented by detailed studies of changes in the housing inventory for small areas. Smith[1] has provided valuable insights into the process of filtering and neighborhood change. He explores the simultaneous influence of changes in income, aging of the housing stock, and market demand upon the structure of rents.

Key elements in local housing studies are trends in apartment vacancies and in the unsold inventory of single-family houses. Historically, accurate and up-to-date vacancy data have been very difficult to obtain. Fortunately, nonprofit real estate research committees organized in several leading metropolitan areas join in a common endeavor to provide current vacancy and unsold-inventory data to their membership. Examples are the reports of the Northern California Real Estate Research Committee and the Residential Research Report of the Residential Research Committee of Southern California.[2] These studies offer valuable information about the number of vacancies by neighborhoods, age of structure, size of structure, and type of facilities and provide an essential guide to the prospective investor in multifamily apartment buildings. Vacancy studies are usually complemented by analysis of the volume of the unsold inventory of single-family houses that provide an alternative supply to apartment units. The FHA usually carries on studies of the unsold inventory for most metropolitan areas annually, which are supplemented by more frequent reports for selected areas.

Together, these analytical techniques can provide the prospective apartment investor with essential information concerning the current and probable future demand for, and supply of, apartment-building units in selected areas.

APARTMENT-BUILDING INVESTMENT ANALYSIS

The task of the investor or developer is to provide the right product in the right location. This means a careful study of the present and probable future

[1] Wallace F. Smith, *Filtering and Neighborhood Change*, University of California Center for Real Estate and Urban Economics, Berkeley, 1964. Research Report no. 24. See also his *Aspects of Housing Demand, Absorption, Demolition and Differentiation*, 1966, Research Report no. 29 in the same series.

[2] Northern California Real Estate Research Committee, "Apartment Vacancy Survey," *Northern California Real Estate Report*, 1966, first quarter, pp. 14–33; second quarter, pp. 7–8.

supply in the area and a careful analysis of trends in consumer tastes. The investor must consider that successful developments will attract other developments and a favorable long-term venture must cater to the tastes of the consumer. Some developers may be able to identify an opportunity, create a development, and sell out at a handsome profit before serious competition is attracted. However, permanent investors looking for a retirement income with tax shelter in the interim must consider the long-run attractiveness of their investment. Sound construction, attractive design, soundproofing, swimming pools, and other amenities may mean the difference between full rental and excessive vacancies.

AVAILABILITY OF CREDIT

The size of the supply of new rental units depends largely upon the availability of credit. If credit is tightened, prices and the terms of loans usually become more stringent. Maisel and Roulac[1] identify the change in mortgage terms as one of the main factors influencing the level of housing starts:

> A decline in the availability of mortgage funds and an increase in interest rates are the most critical factors influencing real estate demand, construction, and jobs. . . .
>
> Credit is a major variable influencing the margin by which starts exceed or fall short of final demand. Tightening of credit affects the terms and prices of construction loans, as well as raising the points builders of single-family units must pay for financing. Movements in terms have been sufficient to wipe out all profits. For promoters of apartments, availability of credit rather than price has been a critical factor because most often their main concern is to minimize required equities.
>
> The following scenario illustrates the effect of credit terms on starts: When money is easy, builders rush starts. They have more money available, and they pay less for it. With easier terms, they can attract families from existing units. The effect is to increase inventories. Finally, the pressure of vacancies builds up. Houses cannot be sold; apartments cannot be rented. Prices fall, foreclosures rise. Lenders are more careful. Less money is available, and the number of starts falls.

Smith also identifies the availability of credit as an important stimulus to the development of low-rise apartments.[2] Recent years have seen large increases in savings, and large amounts of these savings went to institutions whose investment outlets are largely residential construction.

---

[1] Sherman J. Maisel and Stephen E. Roulac, *Real Estate Investment and Finance*, McGraw-Hill, New York, 1966, pp. 168, 179.

[2] Smith, *The Low-Rise Speculative Apartment*, pp. 19–24.

LOCATION AND VALUE

The developer or investor must give particular attention to the locational attributes of his property. Ratcliff[1] identifies three basic elements in the concept of location and its effect on values:

1. Convenience: measures in the disutilities (time, cost, aggravation) of movement of persons or goods from the site to other points to which movement is desirable or essential.

2. Favorable exposure: exposure to view, sun, breeze, and nearness to centers of prestige and fashion.

3. Unfavorable exposure: the degree of exposure to offensive influences which diminish the use value of real estate such as unsightly views, noise, smoke, smells, and disturbance.

A home for sale or income property for rent presumably will cater to the locational needs of a particular group. The investor or developer analyzes his potential investment in terms of his evaluation of the needs of his particular group. He must not only consider the present characteristics of the location but also project the characteristics of the location in the future.

Smith comments on the desires of the apartment renters in his low-rise apartment study as follows.[2]

> The acceptability of the product which has been offered indicates that renter households wish to enjoy some of the amenities of home-ownership. They want quiet, residential neighborhoods, even suburbs. This breed of apartment dweller does not walk to work; he drives on freeways. He doesn't crowd around theaters and restaurants; he has a swimming pool. He doesn't cherish the honk of traffic; he likes the sight of tree-lined streets.

ANALYSIS OF PRO FORMA OPERATING STATEMENTS

Investors contemplating the purchase of a rental property are usually presented with a pro forma operating statement by the seller or the seller's agent and will normally determine the rate of return based on their analysis of the projected figures. These pro forma operating statements can be compared with the regional averages published by the Institute of Real Estate Management. An example of such information appears in Table 6-5. These regional averages should help the uninformed investor determine whether or not the pro forma statements are reasonable and complete.

Notice that depreciation, interest, and income taxes have not been deducted because various depreciation methods may be used, the interest

[1] Richard U. Ratcliff, *Real Estate Analysis,* McGraw-Hill, 1961, New York, pp. 63–64.
[2] Smith, *The Low-Rise Speculative Apartment,* p. xiii.

TABLE 6-5 Average Income and Operating Costs for Unfurnished Garden Buildings in Two Selected Metropolitan Areas†

	Kansas City, Mo.	Los Angeles, Calif.
Number of buildings	23	69
Number of apartments	2,316	13,428
Number of rentable rooms	10,876	54,518
Gross square feet	2,315,962	9,904,706
Rentable square feet	2,131,031	12,088,217

	Buildings reporting	Annual rent/ room	% of annual gross possible total income/room	Annual gross rent/ ft²	Annual rent/ft² rentable	Buildings reporting	Annual rent/ room	% of annual gross possible total income/room	Annual gross rent/ ft²	Annual rent/ft² rentable
Income										
Rents, apartments	23	$519.76	96.4%	$2.14	$2.65	80	$651.83	95.9%	$2.67	$2.99
Garages, parking	1		3.7	0.11	0.14	14		2.5	0.04	0.05
Stores	1		8.3	0.13	0.14					
Offices						1		0.1		
Gross possible rental income	23	525.86	98.4	2.17	2.68	80	654.01	96.2	2.68	3.00
Miscellaneous other income	19	8.64	1.6	0.03	0.04	80	26.27	3.9	0.11	0.12
Gross possible total income	23	534.24	100.0	2.20	2.73	80	679.80	100.0	2.79	3.12
Less: vacancies and delinquent rents	23	32.89	6.2	0.11	0.17	80	54.59	8.0	0.25	0.25
Total actual collections	23	501.35	93.8	2.10	2.56	80	625.21	92.0	2.54	2.87

Expenses

	$	%				$	%		
Total payroll	23	$ 38.70	7.2%	$0.16	$0.20	77	$ 41.07	6.0%	$0.16	$0.19
Supplies	23	6.98	1.3	0.03	0.04	79	4.38	0.6	0.02	0.02
Painting and decorating (interior only)	23	16.56	3.1	0.08	0.08	78	13.49	2.0	0.06	0.06
Maintenance repairs (interior and exterior)	23	36.89	6.9	0.17	0.19	80	31.30	4.6	0.12	0.14
Services	22	6.98	1.3	0.03	0.04	77	12.92	1.9	0.05	0.06
Miscellaneous operating expenses	14	4.11	0.9	0.01	0.02	66	7.49	1.2	0.03	0.04
Subtotal maintenance and operating	23	110.22	20.7	0.48	0.57	80	110.65	16.3	0.44	0.51
Electricity	21	29.51	5.5	0.12	0.15	80	14.65	2.2	0.06	0.07
Water	23	10.05	1.9	0.04	0.05	80	8.63	1.3	0.03	0.04
Gas (excluding heating fuel)	21	11.68	2.1	0.05	0.06	76	8.70	1.3	0.04	0.04
Heating fuel	16	16.23	3.0	0.07	0.08	21	10.85	1.6	0.05	0.05
Subtotal utilities	23	67.47	12.5	0.28	0.34	80	42.83	6.4	0.18	0.20
Management fees	23	24.69	4.6	0.10	0.13	79	33.21	4.9	0.15	0.15
Other administrative expenses	23	5.03	0.9	0.02	0.03	74	9.54	1.4	0.04	0.04
Subtotal administrative	23	29.72	5.5	0.12	0.16	80	42.75	6.3	0.19	0.19
Insurance	23	11.14	2.1	0.05	0.06	79	5.84	0.9	0.02	0.03
Real estate taxes	23	55.83	10.5	0.22	0.28	80	101.94	15.0	0.41	0.46
Other taxes	11	0.86	0.1			65	1.70	0.3	0.01	0.01
Subtotal taxes and insurance	23	67.83	12.7	0.27	0.34	80	109.48	16.2	0.44	0.50
Total all expenses	23	264.24	49.5	1.12	1.35	80	293.69	43.2	1.18	1.34
Net operating income	23	237.11	44.4	0.98	1.21	80	332.49	48.9	1.36	1.53

† Subtotals represent the sum of all figures within a given subtotal section. Therefore, a summation of all subtotals may not necessarily add up to the figure under total expenses. The above calculations are based upon the number of rooms reporting the particular item. Averages and percents, therefore, may not total 100%.

Source: Experience and Exchange Committee, Institute of Real Estate Management, A Statistical Compilation and Analysis of Actual 1975 Income and Expenses Experienced in Apartment, Condominium, and Cooperative Building Operation Institute of Real Estate Management, Chicago, 1976, pp. 101–102.

will vary with the maturity and rate of interest, and the income tax will depend on the tax bracket of the purchaser.

Income and Expense Analysis

Additional data that are useful for the real estate investor can be obtained from the Institute of Real Estate Management.[1] The analysis of an investment would include a check with comparative data like those shown in Tables 6-6 and 6-7. This information also allows the investor to observe the trend in specific expense items and to see how expense ratios vary in different types of apartment buildings by building age and by national region. The information presented here is to show the type of data available. In a specific situation the investor would obtain the most recent information.

A high-rise elevator apartment is an elevator building four or more stories high.[2] A low-rise building, which may have more or less than 25 units, is a building three stories or less in height. A low-rise building, even though it is only three stories high, may still have an elevator. A garden apartment is an apartment complex of two- or three-story walk-up buildings situated on a sizable landscaped plot and operated under a single management. A garden apartment usually consists of 50 or more units.

Table 6-7 contains data on income and expense items per square foot of rentable area. Gross possible total income rose steadily from 1971 to 1975 for all elevator apartments. Gross possible income for elevator apartments fell in 1971, rose to its highest point in 1973, fell in 1974, and then recovered somewhat in 1975. Total actual collections followed a very similar pattern of steady rises for all but elevator apartments.

Of the major expenses, payroll as measured in dollars per square foot rose for all types of apartments from 1971 to 1975. Payroll expenses for elevator apartments rose from 1971 to 1973, dropped in 1974 to their 1972 level, and then increased in 1975. The subtotal of maintenance expenses per square foot, an important portion of the total expenses, rose for all four classifications of apartments between 1971 and 1975. Costs per square foot for electricity went up for all classifications over the 5-year period, and heating-fuel costs were generally higher as well, especially for elevator apartments.

For all four apartment types, the total of expenses per square foot for 1971 to 1975 rose between about 11 percent for 12 to 24 units low-rise and 24 percent for 25 units and over. The rise was relatively steady for all

---

[1] Institute of Real Estate Management, *A Statistical Compilation and Analysis of Actual 1975 Income and Expenses Experienced in Apartment, Condominium, and Cooperative Building Operation,* Institute of Real Estate Management, Chicago, 1976, pp. 21–22, 24.

[2] George Strauss and Harry Lewman, preparers, *Ratios and Methodology in Apartment House Valuation,* American Institute of Real Estate Appraisers, Chicago, 1975, p. 7.

TABLE 6-6 Income and Expense Items on a Rentable Area in the United States and Canada, All Building Types, Unfurnished, 1971–1975*

Year	Elevators No. reporting	Elevators Annual cost/ft²	Low-rise 12–24 units No. reporting	Low-rise 12–24 units Annual cost/ft²	Low-rise 25+ units No. reporting	Low-rise 25+ units Annual cost/ft²	Garden No. reporting	Garden Annual cost/ft²
				Gross possible total income				
1975	388	$3.74	335	$2.58	469	$2.79	1,245	$2.72
1974	355	3.49	308	2.46	444	2.64	1,045	2.58
1973	305	3.87	265	2.39	377	2.48	871	2.39
1972	317	3.44	261	2.22	381	2.41	750	2.28
1971	291	3.00	269	2.11	278	2.23	594	2.19
				Total actual collections				
1975	388	$3.59	335	$2.48	469	$2.61	1,245	$2.52
1974	355	3.33	308	2.34	444	2.49	1,045	2.37
1973	305	3.75	265	2.28	377	2.34	871	2.24
1972	317	3.33	261	2.13	381	2.26	750	2.15
1971	291	2.87	269	2.04	278	2.05	594	2.05
				Total payroll expenses				
1975	388	$0.32	251	$0.16	442	$0.18	1,175	$0.19
1974	349	0.30	249	0.14	419	0.15	971	0.18
1973	303	0.35	215	0.13	355	0.14	809	0.16
1972	317	0.30	212	0.13	364	0.15	691	0.15
1971	286	0.27	223	0.13	260	0.14	552	0.15
				Supplies				
1975	379	$0.03	291	$0.03	426	$0.03	1,157	$0.02
1974	341	0.03	270	0.02	405	0.02	979	0.02
1973	298	0.03	235	0.02	345	0.02	819	0.02
1972	313	0.03	226	0.02	344	0.02	698	0.02
1971	281	0.02	235	0.02	253	0.02	524	0.02
				Painting and decorating				
1975	383	$0.07	307	$0.06	451	$0.06	1,186	$0.06
1974	338	0.08	290	0.06	430	0.06	977	0.06
1973	288	0.08	249	0.07	354	0.06	822	0.05
1972	306	0.07	249	0.05	362	0.06	717	0.05
1971	276	0.07	239	0.06	260	0.05	551	0.05
				Maintenance and repairs				
1975	384	$0.19	333	$0.15	467	$0.14	1,237	$0.14
1974	355	0.18	308	0.14	443	0.14	1,033	0.13
1973	301	0.18	262	0.14	377	0.13	867	0.12
1972	314	0.15	259	0.13	378	0.12	742	0.11
1971	290	0.14	267	0.13	277	0.11	584	0.11

TABLE 6-6 (*Continued*)

	Elevators		Low-rise				Garden	
			12–24 units		25+ units			
Year	No. re-porting	Annual cost/ft²	No. re-porting	Annual cost/ft²	No. re-porting	Annual cost/ft²	No. re-porting	Annual cost/ft²
				Services				
1975	351	$0.05	281	$0.04	429	$0.04	1,148	$0.04
1974	324	0.05	266	0.03	388	0.04	945	0.04
1973	271	0.04	221	0.03	331	0.03	798	0.04
1972	281	0.04	207	0.03	336	0.03	678	0.03
1971	264	0.03	201	0.03	228	0.03	503	0.03
			Miscellaneous operating expenses					
1975	255	$0.04	182	$0.03	280	$0.03	807	$0.02
1974	230	0.05	137	0.02	267	0.03	624	0.03
1973	200	0.04	127	0.03	201	0.02	538	0.02
1972	230	0.03	114	0.02	181	0.02	458	0.02
1971	197	0.02	128	0.02	151	0.04	345	0.02
			Subtotal-maintenance					
1975	388	$0.70	335	$0.41	469	$0.47	1,245	$0.46
1974	355	0.66	308	0.38	444	0.41	1,045	0.43
1973	305	0.70	265	0.37	377	0.39	872	0.39
1972	317	0.60	261	0.35	381	0.37	750	0.37
1971	291	0.55	269	0.35	279	0.36	594	0.36
			Electricity					
1975	386	$0.20	322	$0.06	466	$0.10	1,219	$0.13
1974	349	0.17	299	0.05	434	0.08	1,007	0.11
1973	301	0.17	254	0.05	374	0.06	834	0.09
1972	310	0.15	248	0.05	372	0.06	728	0.08
1971	289	0.12	259	0.04	277	0.06	578	0.08
			Water					
1975	387	$0.06	327	$0.06	463	$0.05	1,222	$0.07
1974	353	0.05	295	0.05	436	0.05	1,023	0.06
1973	302	0.06	258	0.05	372	0.04	850	0.05
1972	315	0.05	254	0.04	378	0.04	733	0.05
1971	290	0.04	265	0.04	279	0.04	584	0.05
			Gas (excluding heating fuel)					
1975	244	$0.03	191	$0.04	304	$0.04	844	$0.04
1974	201	0.03	141	0.04	274	0.03	657	0.03
1973	178	0.03	114	0.04	231	0.03	574	0.03
1972	199	0.02	119	0.03	236	0.02	473	0.03
1971	187	0.02	153	0.02	168	0.03	401	0.02

Heating fuel

1975	364	$0.20	225	$0.16	347	$0.14	793	$0.12
1974	331	0.17	222	0.17	322	0.10	680	0.10
1973	274	0.13	181	0.13	248	0.10	536	0.07
1972	301	0.12	188	0.13	281	0.09	515	0.06
1971	282	0.09	191	0.13	217	0.11	425	0.07

Subtotal utilities

1975	388	$0.47	333	$0.25	468	$0.28	1,241	$0.30
1974	355	0.38	306	0.23	443	0.22	1,039	0.26
1973	305	0.37	262	0.21	377	0.19	862	0.22
1972	317	0.32	257	0.20	381	0.19	745	0.21
1971	291	0.26	267	0.19	279	0.20	590	0.20

Management and leasing fees

1975	377	$0.16	310	$0.13	458	$0.14	1,213	$0.14
1974	348	0.15	282	0.13	432	0.14	1,017	0.13
1973	300	0.17	246	0.13	365	0.13	845	0.12
1972	308	0.15	247	0.12	369	0.12	718	0.11
1971	282	0.13	253	0.11	272	0.10	565	0.11

Other administrative costs

1975	349	$0.06	216	$0.04	401	$0.05	1,161	$0.06
1974	310	0.07	195	0.04	375	0.05	939	0.06
1973	265	0.06	170	0.05	311	0.04	784	0.05
1972	286	0.05	161	0.03	322	0.03	638	0.04
1971	268	0.04	169	0.03	230	0.05	515	0.04

Subtotal administration

1975	386	$0.22	326	$0.15	469	$0.18	1,240	$0.19
1974	351	0.21	299	0.15	441	0.18	1,040	0.18
1973	305	0.22	257	0.16	373	0.16	868	0.17
1972	314	0.20	257	0.13	377	0.15	745	0.14
1971	289	0.17	262	0.13	279	0.14	590	0.14

Insurance

1975	381	$0.04	320	$0.05	458	$0.04	1,224	$0.04
1974	348	0.03	297	0.06	432	0.04	1,010	0.03
1973	294	0.04	251	0.06	361	0.04	844	0.04
1972	312	0.04	255	0.06	374	0.05	733	0.04
1971	289	0.03	262	0.06	274	0.06	589	0.04

Real estate taxes

1975	386	$0.55	334	$0.40	468	$0.41	1,242	$0.32
1974	351	0.53	303	0.39	437	0.40	1,036	0.30
1973	300	0.65	258	0.40	370	0.38	857	0.28
1972	313	0.57	261	0.37	376	0.36	743	0.29
1971	286	0.47	265	0.37	272	0.34	588	0.27

TABLE 6-6 (Continued)

| | Elevators | | Low-rise | | | | Garden | |
| | | | 12–24 units | | 25+ units | | | |
Year	No. re-porting	Annual cost/ft²	No. re-porting	Annual cost/ft²	No. re-porting	Annual cost/ft²	No. re-porting	Annual cost/ft²
				Other taxes				
1975	242	$0.04	167	$0.03	274	$0.02	707	$0.01
1974	228	0.02	153	0.01	280	0.01	577	0.02
1973	197	0.02	140	0.01	240	0.01	471	0.02
1972	209	0.02	139	0.02	222	0.02	380	0.02
1971	193	0.01	152	0.01	170	0.01	331	0.01
				Subtotal taxes				
1975	386	$0.58	335	$0.41	468	$0.42	1,244	$0.32
1974	354	0.54	304	0.39	442	0.41	1,040	0.31
1973	302	0.66	264	0.40	375	0.38	867	0.29
1972	315	0.58	261	0.38	377	0.37	745	0.30
1971	290	0.47	267	0.37	275	0.34	589	0.28
				Total all expenses				
1975	388	$2.01	335	$1.27	469	$1.39	1,245	$1.31
1974	355	1.83	308	1.19	444	1.26	1,045	1.21
1973	305	2.00	265	1.19	377	1.16	872	1.10
1972	317	1.73	261	1.12	381	1.12	750	1.06
1971	291	1.47	269	1.09	279	1.09	594	1.01
				Net operating income				
1975	388	$1.58	335	$1.22	469	$1.22	1,245	$1.21
1974	355	1.50	307	1.15	443	1.23	1,045	1.16
1973	305	1.75	265	1.09	377	1.19	871	1.14
1972	317	1.60	261	1.02	381	1.14	750	1.09
1971	291	1.40	269	0.95	278	0.96	594	1.04

* Samples reported only for buildings that have shown actual income or expense data. Categories with zero values were not counted.

Source: Institute of Real Estate Management, *A Statistical Compilation and Analysis of Actual 1975 Income and Expenses Experienced in Apartment, Condominium and Cooperative Building Operation,* Institute of Real Estate Management, Chicago, 1976, pp. 21, 22, and 24.

TABLE 6-7 Comparison of Operating Ratio by Age of Building in the United States and Canada, Investor Ownership, All Building Types, Unfurnished, %*

Building type	Year	1968 to date	1961–1967	1946–1960	1931–1945	1921–1930	1920 and before
Elevator	1975	51.2%	56.8%	59.4%	60.5%	68.6%	65.5%
	1974	51.7	54.6	58.5	60.4	65.5	60.3
	1973	49.2	52.4	57.4	58.0	58.9	62.3
	1972	49.0	50.7	55.6	58.1	62.5	65.8
	1971	45.8	49.4	53.7	54.9	60.4	66.4
Low-rise:	1975	45.9	49.0	53.6	64.1	66.6	65.4
12–24 units	1974	43.0	49.8	47.7	60.9	64.6	61.1
	1973	46.5	49.0	49.6	55.4	61.6	61.2
	1972	44.2	47.3	49.8	54.4	63.2	67.8
	1971	40.3	45.1	52.7	58.4	63.9	64.5
25 and over	1975	52.8	50.4	54.9	60.1	66.7	64.5
	1974	48.4	49.1	50.6	57.4	66.1	67.5
	1973	44.9	47.2	52.3	52.5	61.8	61.6
	1972	45.1	48.2	49.9	58.0	65.8	68.4
	1971	45.1	51.3	52.3	55.7	66.1	69.7
Garden	1975	50.8	53.2	56.5	61.5	65.4	57.3
	1974	50.0	50.5	57.4	58.1	59.3	57.0
	1973	48.4	48.5	54.3	54.3	54.9	54.8
	1972	47.7	48.7	53.8	55.1	61.4	55.2
	1971	50.0	48.3	52.1	59.0	55.0	62.7

* All expenses divided by actual collections.

but elevator apartments, which reached their expense peak in 1973 and then dropped slightly the following year.

Table 6-7 compares operating ratios of the four types of apartments in terms of the age of the buildings. For the most part, older buildings had higher ratios of expenses divided by actual collections, possibly because they required larger outlays for maintenance and repair. The ratios generally rose from 1971 to 1975, although there were notable fluctuations in this pattern, especially among the two oldest classifications of buildings. As of 1975 low-rise buildings with 12 to 24 units that were built between 1968 and 1975 had the lowest operating ratio.

Table 6-8 shows a similar comparison made on the basis of geographical regions rather than on building age. All regions experienced some fluctuations between 1971 and 1975. Operating ratios for 1975 were the highest or second highest of the 5-year period for most types of buildings in most regions. For 1975, regions 4 and 6 had the lowest operating ratio for elevator buildings. Buildings of all types in region 1 and 2 had higher operating ratios than their counterparts in any other region.

TABLE 6-8 Comparison of Operating Ratio by Region in the United States and Canada, Investor Ownership, All Building Types, Unfurnished, %*

| Building type | Year | Region† | | | | | | |
		1,2	3	5	4,6	9	7,8,10	Canada
Elevator	1975	65.2%	55.3%	54.9%	48.9%	54.2%	52.8%	57.3%
	1974	60.8	56.7	53.8	50.2	58.8	46.6	53.0
	1973	57.3	52.0	54.7	42.9	61.9	47.1	54.5
	1972	56.9	51.9	53.6	42.9	51.8	45.5	49.9
	1971	61.6	50.7	49.1	63.5	48.6	47.3	50.6
Low-rise:	1975	61.1	50.0	57.9	49.9	49.0	47.7	60.0
12–24 units	1974	64.3	47.1	58.9	43.8	45.6	43.5	54.1
	1973	58.8	49.4	57.8	47.7	47.3	45.3	53.5
	1972	50.2	54.3	58.3	46.4	48.0	46.7	49.7
	1971	64.5	58.7	63.3	43.7	45.6	46.0	49.7
25 and over	1975	57.7	57.1	56.3	53.3	50.5	48.1	50.0
	1974	57.3	50.4	53.1	49.6	47.2	48.5	45.8
	1973	56.7	48.6	53.1	43.4	44.4	48.5	44.3
	1972	54.8	48.8	55.7	48.9	45.0	45.6	41.2
	1971	59.0	47.7	58.1	60.5	44.0	43.6	51.7
Garden	1975	56.8	54.7	51.3	52.9	48.6	50.1	46.4
	1974	56.2	51.7	48.0	53.3	48.2	51.0	45.7
	1973	56.4	49.7	47.7	50.3	47.4	48.6	43.6
	1972	55.2	48.3	49.6	49.3	48.4	49.5	50.1
	1971	56.1	47.6	51.0	50.9	48.6	51.0	39.4

* All expenses divided by actual collections.
† Some region reports have more than one region represented to ensure a large enough sample size for the above data.

CASH FLOW

In addition to the income and expense analysis particular attention should be given to cash flow. The following example illustrates cash-flow analysis for a hypothetical property. Assume a $200,000 purchase price for the property. A first mortgage of $150,000 at 6 percent interest is obtained with a 25-year maturity. The owner advances $50,000 of the purchase price. The cash flow for the first year is:

Net before mortgage payments $16,600
Less mortgage payment 11,600
Cash flow before income taxes .... $ 5,000

Taxable income, of course, is different from cash flow, as was shown in Chap. 2. Only the interest portion of the mortgage payment is deductible in arriving at taxable income. Deduction for depreciation is allowed in addition to the expenses listed in the operating statement. The investor will project taxable income under alternative depreciation methods and under alternative forms of organization if the corporation is a desirable form. The income taxes resulting from this projection will, of course, determine the final cash flow.

Using the information given above and assuming no change in any of the operating incomes or costs over the next 10 years, we are able to calculate expected yields, using the various methods proposed in Chap. 2.

$$\frac{\text{Net income before depreciation and mortgage costs}}{\text{Purchase price}} = \frac{16,600}{200,000} = 0.083$$

$$= 8.3\%$$

$$\frac{\text{Cash flow after debt payment}}{\text{Original equity}} = \frac{5,000}{50,000} = 0.10 = 10\%$$

$$\frac{\text{Cash flow plus principal repayment (first year)}}{\text{Original equity}} = \frac{5,000 + 2,673}{50,000}$$

$$= 0.153 = 15.3\%$$

The yield, or IRR Here it will be necessary to make assumptions regarding the final sale price P_n at the end of 10 years. To simplify calculations, the final sales price is set equal to the original cost ($200,000), depreciation is straight-line 25-year, and income tax is ignored. $150,000 is depreciable.

$$50,000 = \sum_{t=1}^{n} \frac{R_t - I_t - A_t}{(1 + r)^t} + \frac{P_n - GT - UM}{(1 + r)^n}$$

where
R_t = annual net income = \$16,600
$I_t + A_t$ = annual mortgage payment = \$11,600
GT = capital-gains tax = 25%
UM = unpaid mortgage

Solve for r.

$$50,000 = \sum_{t=1}^{10} \frac{16,600 - I_t - A_t}{(1 + r)^t} + \frac{200,000 - GT - UM}{(1 + r)^{10}}$$

$$= \sum_{t=1}^{10} \frac{16,600 - 11,600}{(1 + r)^t} + \frac{200,000 - 15,000 - 114,500}{(1 + r)^{10}}$$

$$= \sum_{t=1}^{10} \frac{5,000}{(1 + r)^t} + \frac{70,500}{(1 + r)^{10}}$$

At 12%:
$$\sum_{t=1}^{10} \frac{5,000}{(1.12)^t} + \frac{70,500}{(1.12)^t} = \$50,948$$

Therefore the yield before income tax but after capital-gains tax is approximately 12 percent.

A typical analysis would include a projected cash flow and projected taxable income for at least a 10-year period. Each of these may be computed under a variety of assumptions. In group ownership, the tax effects of the corporate form versus the partnership form should be projected. For a corporation, the effect of notes in the capitalization may be explored. Also, the results of different financing plans may be determined. As previously noted, the use of the computer greatly facilitates this analysis.

Leverage Alternative methods of financing must be explored in relation to the risk-taking abilities of the prospective investors. In the above example, there is $50,000 of ownership equity. Additional financing might be obtained so that the amount of equity the investor has in the enterprise is reduced. *Leverage,* or trading on the equity as it is sometimes called, refers to the use of debt or other fixed-cost capital in addition to the equity capital.

Normally the investor could expect to obtain a first mortgage for 66 to 75 percent of the lending value of the property. In this example a first mortgage loan of $150,000 or 75 percent is assumed. This is equivalent to 0.75 leverage or 3.0 leverage, depending on the measure used.[1]

$$\text{Leverage} = \frac{\text{debt}}{\text{equity}} = 3.0 \quad \text{or} \quad \text{leverage} = \frac{\text{debt}}{\text{total value}} = 0.75$$

Leverage increases the rate of return on the ownership equity if the project is returning more than the cost of the debt. Conversely, if vacancies or expenses are larger than anticipated, the opportunity for losses is increased, as is the possibility of not being able to meet the amortization requirements on the debt.

For example, it might be possible to obtain a second mortgage on the illustrative property in the amount of $20,000 to $30,000 at 9 or 10 percent interest. The particular amortization requirements on the second mortgage will, of course, be an important consideration. Some mortgages might be payable at "interest only" for a period of time, whereas others may require amortization to start immediately.

Some investors may incur even more debt. For example, here we have implicitly assumed that the appliances and the furniture, if any, were included in the $200,000 purchase price. If we assume that they are not, a chattel mortgage may be added for the appliances and the furniture. Alternatively, some apartment-house operators lease their furniture instead of purchasing it. Finally, in some situations the owner may be anxious enough to sell the property to be willing to take a note for part of the purchase price.

The amount of leverage that an investor is willing to undertake is partially a function of his risk-taking ability and of his goals. The cash-flow projection

---

[1] Ezra Solomon, *The Theory of Financial Management,* Columbia University Press, New York, 1963, p. 81.

is a function of estimates of rental income and of expenses. Thus, investors are wise to project their cash flow on the assumption that they are, perhaps, 10 percent high on their estimates of cash inflow, in determining their ability to meet debt amortization.

Reliability of estimates Each element of the operating statement must be examined. Rental rates and occupancy percentages for similar properties must be carefully investigated. Rental forecasts must consider the likelihood of changing supply and demand conditions. Vacancy rates vary, depending on the type of rental property and also on management policies. Investors projecting their rental income must be careful not to project an unusually high occupancy because of the newness of a project or special concessions given to tenants. They must also give consideration to the number of leases and their expiration dates.

Operating expenses must be carefully examined individually. The first question in the examination of a pro forma income statement is whether all expenses are listed. For example, allowances for painting and decorating, replacement of appliances, and other similar items are often omitted from brokers' statements although they will be needed. Allowances may also have to be made for advertising to attract new tenants.

The probability of increases or decreases in each expense item must be carefully analyzed, particularly the likelihood of increases in taxes and management costs. With an older building, allowances for expensive replacements, such as a roof or a furnace, or the necessity of remodeling to attract tenants must be considered.

DATA SOURCES

Many different data sources dealing with various facets of apartment house investment are available to investors and developers. We will describe a few of these here briefly. Although this is not meant to be an exhaustive survey of the kinds of data sources available, it will provide examples of the types of data that can be obtained.[1]

We have referred to the income and expense analysis report on apartments, condominiums, and cooperatives published by the Institute of Real Estate Management.[2] The report is a statistical compilation and brief analysis of income and expense data, expressed in easily recognized and applied ratios, from properties throughout the United States and Canada.

For data on construction costs, two manuals[3] by the Marshall and Swift

---

[1] For example, Stauss and Lewman, *Ratios and Methodology in Apartment House Valuation*, American Institute of Real Estate Appraisers of the National Association of Realtors, 155 East Superior St., Chicago, Il 60611.

[2] Institute of Real Estate Management, op. cit.

[3] *Residential Cost Handbook* and *Marshall Valuation Service*, Marshall and Swift Publication Company, 1617 Beverly Boul., Los Angeles, Ca 90026, published annually.

Publication Company are widely used. The *Residential Cost Handbook* covers single-family dwellings and income apartment properties, and *Marshall Valuation Service* offers statistics for nonresidential properties. Other commonly used cost data sources are the Dodge Cost Services[1] and the Boeckh Manuals.[2]

Investors and developers wanting to evaluate the income potential of an apartment building must first be familiar with community and regional demographic data. The standard source for demographic data in the United States is the Census Survey of the U.S. Department of Commerce, Bureau of the Census. On the local level, chambers of commerce or planning departments can provide year-to-year data on the components of the economic base. Additional local and regional economic information may be found in *Sales Management* magazine's "Annual Survey of Buying Power." The survey presents retail sales data for cities, counties, metropolitan areas, and states, and the *City and County Data Book,* published by the Bureau of the Census, contains information on population, income, retail and wholesale trade, and manufacturing for local areas. Census data with housing statistics arranged on a block-by-block or neighborhood basis are also available. A source for data on housing-construction trends and estimates of housing-market absorption potential is the semiannual pamphlet *U.S. Housing Markets.*[3] The pamphlet contains regional statistics for the previous 6 months on private housing permits and starts, apartment completions, apartments under construction, vacancy rates, employment growth, and mortgage applications. Northern California investors will find useful information in the *Northern California Real Estate Report.*[4]

Recent changes in government policies toward land-use density, traffic, congestion, pollution, and sewage disposal make it necessary for real estate investors to keep informed about government decisions in these areas. The Department of Housing and Urban Development publishes *Housing and Urban Development Trends* quarterly to make this possible.

DEED STAMPS AS INDICATORS OF SALES PRICES

Purchasers of property are interested in comparable market values. They investigate to determine the sales price of similar properties. Many active realtors feel that deed stamps are not a reliable indicator of sales price be-

[1] *Dodge Cost Services,* McGraw-Hill Information Systems Company, 1221 Avenue of the Americas, New York, NY 10020.
[2] American Appraisal Company, Inc., 525 East Michigan St., Milwaukee, Wi 53201.
[3] Advance Mortgage Corporation, P.O. Box 146, Detroit, Mi 48232. (U.S. Housing Markets, published semiannually).
[4] Real Estate Research Council of Northern California, 57 Post Street, Room 711, San Francisco, Ca 94104.

cause there is no prohibition against extra stamps being put on the deed. Smith[1] found, however, for a sample of 38 properties of 4 to 48 units in Oakland sold between June 1958 and May 1963 that federal deed stamps were an accurate measure of the sale price.

Although these findings are not conclusive, they indicate that an examination of deed stamps on similar properties is important. Building-permit costs may also be investigated, although there is always the possibility that the permit costs are significantly different from the actual costs of construction. Lenders are another potential source of information on sales prices or construction costs of similar properties, as, of course, are appraisals. Recall, however, that the value to an individual investor may well differ from the norm determined by the appraiser because of the particular tax circumstances of the investor.

CASE PROBLEMS IN APARTMENT-HOUSE INVESTMENTS

Included in this section are several case studies to illustrate the factors that determine the viability of a real estate investment. The following market analysis and case study is based in part upon an article by Blazar and Hilton.[2] Following a review of recent apartment-house construction trends, they concluded that the rising cost of single-family housing would put upward pressure on apartment rentals and result in a decline in the apartment vacancy rate below the records of 5.3 percent in 1970.

Declining vacancies will permit increased rents in existing apartments without excessive tenant resistance and so will serve as a catalyst for new construction, according to Blazar and Hilton. However, they point out, rising construction and financing costs will continue to inhibit new construction. Thus, existing apartment buildings represent a more attractive investment opportunity than new construction.

Blazar and Hilton list the major long-term factors to be considered in analysis of such an investment:

1. The amount, timing, and full tax consequences of the initial investment.

2. All cash flows from operations over the life of the investment.

3. All tax effects, both tax shelter and tax liability, of net income produced during the life of the investment.

4. Recognition of the time value of money, i.e., that a dollar received today has more value than a dollar to be received tomorrow. Money has a time value because when its payment is deferred, the recipient must either sacrifice interest or forgo alternative investment opportunities.

[1] Smith, *The Low-Rise Speculative Apartment*, op. cit., p. 127.
[2] S. M. Blazar and H. G. Hilton, "Investment Opportunities in Existing Apartment Buildings," *Real Estate Review,* Summer 1976, pp. 47–52.

EXHIBIT 1   Summary of Purchase

Land	$ 500,000	
Building	3,500,000	
Purchase price		$4,000,000
Mortgage (30 years, 9.5% interest)		3,000,000
Equity requirement		$1,000,000

Current Assumptions

The analysis of our hypothetical investment[1] assumes an investor who is in a 55 percent income tax bracket (combined federal, state, and city income tax) and who has taxable sources of income other than from the contemplated investment. The potential investment is a 200-unit apartment building, which cost $20,000 per unit, or $4 million. (Of course, many investors have tax consequences substantially different from these assumptions. The same type of analysis can be performed for them without the tax aspects by computing the present value of all cash flows.) The land cost is $500,000. The investor can obtain a $3 million (75 percent) mortgage with a 30-year term at 9.5 percent interest, and so must provide $1 million of equity. This analysis is summarized in Exhibit 1.

The cash-flow projection (Exhibit 2) makes various assumptions. Rentals of $300 per month are used for computing gross annual rental income. Operating expenses in apartment buildings normally vary according to a number of factors, particularly the size, age, and location of the project. While in some instances they may range as high as 60 percent of revenues, the present analysis assumes that operating costs are stabilized at 40 percent, even though this ratio is at the bottom range of current experience. In the first year, after deducting operating expenses and debt service from revenues, the cash flow is $107,692.

EXHIBIT 2   Summary of Cash Flow (Year 1)

200 units at $300 per month		$720,000
Less: 5% vacancy factor		36,000
		$684,000
Operating expenses, at 25%	$171,000	
Real estate taxes, at 15%	102,600	
Total expenses 40%		273,600
Income after cash expenses		$410,400
Debt service on $3 million mortgage (10.10% constant)		302,708
Cash flow (10.8% of equity investment)		$107,692

[1] This case study comes from Blazar and Hilton, op. cit. It is hypothetical but presents a set of circumstances that could be encountered in a real situation.

Assumptions about the Future

Although the years 1973 to 1975 saw expenses increase at a rate strikingly faster than rents, during the seven preceding years (1966 to 1972) rents and expenses for garden-apartment units increased at almost identical rates, about 4 percent annually. One may assume that, as market conditions return to normal, this relationship of proportionate inflation in both costs and revenues will reemerge. Exhibit 3, which computes cash flow for 10 years, assumes annual increases of 3 percent for both rents and expenses.

However, real estate practitioners have differing opinions about the rate of future rent and expense escalations. The pessimists believe that in the immediate future expenses will continue to outstrip rent increases. The optimists believe that rents, having lagged behind inflation for 3 years, are due for a substantial increase. Exhibit 4, for the pessimists, assumes (1) that rents will remain flat during years 1 through 5 and increase by 3 percent annually starting in year 6, while (2) expenses will increase at a 3 percent rate during each of the 10 years.

Exhibit 5, by comparison, portrays the optimistic view. Rental income is projected to increase at a 6 percent rate, while expenses increase at a 3 percent rate. The widely divergent after-tax cash flows for each year under the different assumptions are compared in Exhibit 6.

Bitter experience during the last few years has taught us how treacherous our projections can be. To illustrate a worst-case scenario, the final column of Exhibit 6 computes after-tax cash flow for years 1 to 7 on the assumption that expenses and income increase by 3 percent annually for 7 years (as in the first column); however, in years 8 to 10, annual rentals are kept stable by an assumed deterioration in the market, while a projected energy crisis skyrockets costs by 10 percent annually.

At the End of 10 Years

At any moment, owners have three options: they can sell; they can refinance; or they can do nothing. If they choose to sell the property, we assume that they will be able to obtain a price equal to 10 times current cash flow (with the purchaser either assuming the remaining mortgage of $2,706,233 or providing additional cash to satisfy it). Under the assumptions of Exhibit 3, the seller will receive cash proceeds of $2,327,710 (10 times cash flow of $232,771).

The proceeds from the sale are subject to income and capital-gains taxes. Recapture of excess depreciation is taxed as ordinary income at 55 percent, while capital-gains taxes of approximately 30 percent are levied on the balance of gain from sale. The total tax due on sale is $663,556, of which $33,768 is ordinary tax and $629,788 is capital gains tax. The computations are shown in Exhibit 7. The after-tax return on investment on a present-value basis is 15.1 percent.

EXHIBIT 3 Annual Cash Flow Assuming Rent and Expenses Increase 3 Percent Per Year

	Year									
	1	2	3	4	5	6	7	8	9	10
Annual revenue:										
200 units at $300/month; 3% annual increase	$720,000	$741,600	$763,848	$786,763	$810,366	$834,677	$859,718	$885,509	$912,074	$939,437
Less: 5% vacancy factor	36,000	37,080	38,192	39,338	40,518	41,734	42,986	44,275	45,604	46,972
Net rental revenue:	$684,000	$704,520	$725,656	$747,425	$769,848	$792,943	$816,732	$841,234	$866,470	$892,465
Operating expenses* at 25%	$171,000	$176,130	$181,414	$186,856	$192,462	$198,236	$204,183	$210,308	$216,617	$223,117
Real estate taxes* at 15%	102,600	105,678	108,848	112,114	115,477	118,941	122,510	126,186	129,971	133,869
Total expense* 40%	$273,600	$281,808	$290,262	$298,970	$307,939	$317,177	$326,693	$336,494	$346,588	$356,986
Net operating income	$410,400	$422,712	$435,394	$448,455	$461,909	$475,766	$490,039	$504,740	$519,882	$535,479
Debt service on $3 million mortgage (10.10% constant)	302,708	302,708	302,708	302,708	302,708	302,708	302,708	302,708	302,708	302,708
Cash flow	$107,692	$120,004	$132,686	$145,747	$159,201	$173,058	$187,331	$202,032	$217,174	$232,771
Tax analysis:										
Cash flow	$107,692	$120,004	$132,686	$145,747	$159,201	$173,058	$187,331	$202,032	$217,174	$232,771
Plus: loan amortization	18,499	20,335	22,353	24,572	27,011	29,691	32,638	35,878	39,438	43,352
Less: depreciation (125% declining-balance)	131,250	126,328	121,591	117,031	112,642	108,418	104,353	101,711	101,711	101,711
Taxable income (loss)	$ −5,059	$ 14,011	$ 33,448	$ 53,288	$ 73,570	$ 94,331	$115,616	$136,199	$154,901	$174,412
Tax savings (55% bracket)	$ −2,782									
Tax payable		$ 7,706	$ 18,397	$ 29,308	$ 40,463	$ 51,882	$ 63,589	$ 74,909	$ 85,196	$ 95,927
After-tax cash flow	$110,474	$112,298	$114,289	$116,439	$118,738	$121,176	$123,742	$127,123	$131,978	$136,844

* Reflects 3% annual increase.

EXHIBIT 4 Annual Cash Flow Assuming Annual Increase of 3 Percent in Expenses (Beginning Year 2) and in Rent (Beginning Year 6)

	Year									
	1	2	3	4	5	6	7	8	9	10
Annual revenue: 200 units at $300/month; 3% annual increase (in rental years 6–10)	$720,000	$720,000	$720,000	$720,000	$720,000	$741,600	$763,848	$786,763	$810,366	$834,677
Less: 5% vacancy factor	36,000	36,000	36,000	36,000	36,000	37,080	38,192	39,338	40,518	41,734
Net rental revenue:	$684,000	$684,000	$684,000	$684,000	$684,000	$704,520	$725,656	$747,425	$769,848	$792,943
Operating expenses* at 25%	$171,000	$176,130	$181,414	$186,856	$192,462	$198,236	$204,183	$210,308	$216,617	$223,117
Real estate taxes* at 15%	102,600	105,678	108,848	112,114	115,477	118,941	122,510	126,186	129,971	133,869
Total expense* 40%	$273,600	$281,808	$290,262	$298,970	$307,939	$317,177	$326,693	$336,494	$346,588	$356,986
Net operating income	$410,400	$402,192	$393,738	$385,030	$376,061	$387,343	$398,963	$410,931	$423,260	$435,957
Debt service on $3 million mortgage (10.10% constant)	302,708	302,708	302,708	302,708	302,708	302,708	302,708	302,708	302,708	302,708
Cash flow	$107,692	$ 99,484	$ 91,030	$ 82,322	$ 73,353	$ 84,635	$ 96,255	$108,223	$120,552	$133,249
Tax analysis:										
Cash flow	$107,692	$ 99,484	$ 91,030	$ 82,322	$ 73,353	$ 84,635	$ 96,255	$108,223	$120,552	$133,249
Plus: loan amortization	18,499	20,335	22,353	24,572	27,011	29,691	32,638	35,878	39,438	43,352
Less: depreciation (125% declining-balance)	131,250	126,328	121,591	117,031	112,642	108,418	104,353	101,711	101,711	101,711
Taxable income (loss)	$ −5,059	$ −6,509	$ −8,208	$−10,137	$−12,278	$ 5,908	$ 24,540	$ 42,390	$ 58,279	$ 74,890
Tax savings (55% bracket)	$ −2,782	$ −3,580	$ −4,514	$ −5,575	$ −6,753					
Tax payable						$ 3,249	$ 13,497	$ 23,315	$ 32,053	$ 41,190
After-tax cash flow	$110,474	$103,064	$ 95,544	$ 87,897	$ 80,106	$ 81,386	$ 82,758	$ 84,908	$ 88,499	$ 92,059

* First year; increases 3% annually.

225

EXHIBIT 5 Annual Cash Flow Assuming Annual Increase of 6 Percent in Rent and 3 Percent in Expenses

		Year									
		1	2	3	4	5	6	7	8	9	10
Annual revenue: 200 units at $300/month; 6% annual increase in revenues		$720,000	$763,000	$808,992	$857,531	$908,983	$963,522	$1,021,334	$1,082,613	$1,147,571	$1,216,425
Less: 5% vacancy factor		36,000	38,160	40,450	42,877	45,450	48,176	51,067	54,131	57,379	60,821
Net rental revenue		$684,000	$724,840	$768,542	$814,654	$853,533	$915,346	$970,267	$1,028,482	$1,090,192	$1,155,604
Operating expenses* at	25%	$171,000	$176,130	$181,414	$186,856	$192,462	$198,236	$204,183	$210,308	$216,617	$223,117
Real estate taxes* at	15%	102,600	105,678	108,848	112,114	115,477	118,941	122,510	126,186	129,971	133,869
Total expense*	40%	$273,600	$281,808	$290,262	$298,970	$307,939	$317,177	$326,693	$336,494	$346,588	$356,986
Net operating income		$410,400	$443,032	$478,280	$515,684	$555,594	$598,169	$643,574	$691,988	$743,604	$798,618
Debt service on $3 million mortgage (10.10% constant)		302,708	302,708	302,708	302,708	302,708	302,708	302,708	302,708	302,708	302,708
Cash flow		$107,692	$140,324	$175,572	$212,976	$252,886	$295,461	$340,866	$389,280	$440,896	$495,910
Tax analysis:											
Cash flow		$107,692	$140,324	$175,572	$212,976	$252,886	$295,461	$340,866	$389,280	$440,896	$495,910
Plus: loan amortization		18,499	20,335	22,353	24,572	27,011	29,691	32,638	35,878	39,438	43,352
Less: depreciation (125% declining-balance)		131,250	126,328	121,591	117,031	112,642	108,418	104,353	101,711	101,711	101,711
Taxable income (loss)		$ -5,059	$ 34,331	$ 76,334	$120,517	$167,255	$216,734	$269,151	$323,447	$378,623	$437,551
Tax savings (55% bracket)		$ -2,782									
Tax payable			$ 18,882	$ 41,984	$ 66,284	$ 91,990	$119,204	$148,033	$177,896	$208,242	$240,653
After-tax cash flow		$110,474	$121,442	$133,588	$146,692	$160,896	$176,257	$192,833	$211,384	$232,654	$255,257

* First year; increases 3% annually.

EXHIBIT 6   After-Tax Cash Flow

Year	Exhibit 3: 3% annual increase in rent and expense	Exhibit 4: 3% annual increase in expense and after year 5 in rent	Exhibit 5: 6% annual increase in rent; 3% annual increase in expense	Worst case scenario; 3% annual increase in rent and expenses for years 1–7; stable rents and 10% expense increase thereafter
1	$110,474	$110,474	$110,474	$110,474
2	112,298	103,064	121,442	112,298
3	114,289	95,544	133,588	114,289
4	116,439	87,897	146,692	116,439
5	118,738	80,106	160,896	118,738
6	121,176	81,386	176,257	121,176
7	123,742	82,758	192,833	123,742
8	127,123	84,908	211,384	105,806
9	131,978	88,499	232,654	87,677
10	136,844	92,059	255,257	67,736

**EXHIBIT 7   Tax on Sale of Property after 10 Years,
Based on Assumptions in Exhibit 3, 1975–1984**

Cash flow from property (cumulative)	$1,677,696
Less: portion reported as taxable income	844,717
Untaxed balance of cash flow	$ 832,979
Plus: net proceeds of sale	2,327,710
Total	$3,160,689
Less: investment in property	1,000,000
Taxable gain	$2,160,689
Ordinary portion ($61,397) taxed at 55%	$ 33,768
Capital-gain portion ($2,099,292) taxed at 30%	629,788
Total tax	$ 663,556
Net proceeds of sale	$2,327,710
Less: total tax	663,556
Net cash proceeds after tax	$1,664,154
After-tax return on investment	15.1%

If the owner decides to refinance rather than to sell, tax-free dollars can be extracted from the project. Continuing the assumptions of Exhibit 3 (that rents and operating expenses increase annually at a 3 percent rate), Exhibit 8 demonstrates how, at the end of year 10, a refinancing would result in obtaining an additional $1,710,285 tax-free. The initial $1 million investment would thus be recouped, while the investor would continue to enjoy

**EXHIBIT 8 Refinancing Proceeds after 10 Years,
Based on Assumption in Exhibit 3**

Net rental revenue in year 11	$ 967,619
Operating costs	378,750
Net operating income	588,869
Capitalized at 10 times	$5,888,690
Mortgage value at 75%	4,416,518
Existing balance at end of year 11	2,706,233
Additional tax-free financing	$1,710,285

positive annual cash flow as long as the mortgage constant does not exceed 13.33.

Under the assumptions used, it is readily apparent that a well-chosen existing apartment project can indeed represent a profitable investment opportunity for an investor. Of course, in the unlikely event that rent increases cease and costs skyrocket, the opportunity for profitable resale or refinancing might not be present.

The following three cases are actual situations for which the locations and names have been changed. They are presented here so that the reader can experiment with analysis of actual situations.

After establishing goals in relation to current cash flow and equity buildup, the reader may ask: What additional information do I want in relation to the property? Assuming the results specified in the case, is the price reasonable? Some readers will want to experiment with sensitivity analysis to determine variation in rates of return given various assumptions concerning rentals and expenses.

Case Study: Bavarian Village (360 units)

Property description and area data Bavarian Village Apartments is one of the finest apartment complexes in its city. Built about 5 years ago, it is located on a major east-west artery. Bavarian Village has fabulous exposure, yet the property runs deep off the major artery, so that tenants have a quiet and serene setting. The property is about 1½ miles from a major luxury office and retail center housing several fine department and specialty stores, a hotel, a large enclosed shopping mall, and several high-rise office buildings. This section of the city is known for its sophistication. Bavarian Village attracts the young executive single population. The complex is 100 percent occupied. There is no doubt rents can be raised.

The Montebello Club is net-leased to a local operator, who is paying percentage rents over his minimum. Relevant financial information for analysis follows.

Purchase price and terms

Cash to seller.............................$1,475,000
First note to Prudential.................. 3,397,000
Total price $4,872,000

1. 9%, $28,522 monthly, plus a 10 percent participation in rents over $655,000 or 1 percent of the remaining principal balance, whichever is less. Note amortizes in 25 years.

2. Seller to pay for title issuance and escrow fees.

3. Normal rents, security deposits, vacation pay prorated as of closing.

4. Closing must occur on or before October 1, 1975. Contract must be signed without contingency except appraisal and audit by September 10, 1975.

5. Deferred maintenance estimated at $25,000 for painting and asphalt.

Unit breakdown The unit breakdown is given in Table 6-9.

Cash-flow summary The cash-flow summary is given in Table 6-10.

TABLE 6-9 Unit Breakdown

	Area, ft²	No. of units	Total ft²	Rent Monthly, per unit	Rent Annual, total
Rent income (as per current rent roll):					
Efficiency	505	144	72,720	$160	$276,480
1-bedroom flat	702	72	50,544	195	168,480
Studio, 1-bedroom	647	55	35,585	205	135,300
With fireplace	647	7	4,529	210	17,640
With patio	647	7	4,529	210	17,640
With both	647	2	1,294	215	5,160
Special	647	1	647	225	2,700
2-bedroom flat	962	72	69,264	250	216,000
Total		360	239,112		$839,400
Other income:					
Laundry rent (net-leased at $720 per month)					$ 8,640
10-year-lease restaurant rent (6% of gross income with a minimum of $1,600 per month)					22,200
Other miscellaneous income					14,400
Total					$ 45,240
Total gross income					$884,640

TABLE 6-10 Cash-Flow Summary*

		Monthly	Annual
Total gross income		$73,720	$884,640
Vacancy 3% of rents		2,099	25,188
Effective gross income		$71,621	$859,452
Expenses:			
Advertising and promotion	$ 200		
Electricity	5,000		
Gas	1,350		
Scavenger	468		
Water	1,600		
Rental fees, referrals	200		
Office expense	90		
Professional fees	100		
Other taxes and license	15		
Telephone	75		
Maintenance supplies	1,080		
Landscape supplies	100		
Recreation supplies	50		
Reserves	1,800		
Roof and parking	598		
Cleaning and painting			
Units, contract service and supplies	1,920		
Maintenance, outside service	125		
Landscape, outside service	1,440		
Pool, outside service	180		
Pest control, outside service	180		
Resident manager's staff	1,700		
Rental aids	300		
Maintenance	1,000		
Cleaning and painting (common area)	600		
Incentive pay and bonuses	300		
Payroll taxes	390		
Employee benefits	195		
Insurance	375		
Property tax	5,574		
Management fees	3,438		
Home office expenses	50		
		$30,493	$365,916
Income before debt		41,128	493,536
Debt service, note principal and interest		−28,522	
Participation I		$−1,564	$361,032
Cash flow		$11,042	$132,504
$7 rent increase, net of participation		2,200	
Projected		$13,242	$158,504

* The sellers reported actual cash flow for last year of $100,000, before two rent increases were effective.

Analysis of data

Total cost, including land and restaurants per square foot of net rentable ....$ 20.37
Cost per unit..$13,533
Gross multiplier.. 5.5
Rents per square foot...$ 0.29
Expenses per square foot ....$ 1.53
Expenses as percentage of apartment gross 44%
Debt service including participation as percentage of gross 41%
Average unit size, ft^2... 664
First-year equity buildup ($36,500) 2.5%
Downpayment as percentage of purchase price................................... 30%

Case Study: Raintree East, Raintree West, and Bayou

Located in the same southwestern city are the subjects of the next case study, the Raintree East, Raintree West, and Bayou apartment complexes. A description of the property and important financial information follows.

Property description and area data The subject complexes are located at the intersection of two major thoroughfares in the southwest section of the city. The apartments have excellent access to the freeway. The complexes are located near an athletic stadium, and a large number of the tenants appear to work at a nearby medical center. Surrounding the subject properties are several poorly maintained units that in many cases have attracted less desirable tenants. It is probable that a private partnership may be formed to acquire the nearby poorly maintained units in an effort to upgrade the immediate neighborhood.

The two-story, all-brick, Raintree and Bayou complexes were built about 14 years ago. The units themselves are in excellent condition, offering nine pools, covered parking, and modern appliances and carpeting. The units have both two- and four-pipe airconditioning systems.

Many of the tenants have lived in the complex since it was completed. Turnover has been negligible. As of June 23, there were four vacancies.

Purchase price and terms

Cash to seller..$ 500,000
Finder's fee (equity-fund advisors)............................ 50,000
Wraparound note and trust deed to seller................. 5,400,000*
Commission to Schwertferger Realty .... 320,000†
$6,270,000‡

* 7%, first 6 months ($37,011), then $500,000 principal due Jan. 5, 1977; 7¾%, next 4½ years ($37,011); 8%, next 10 years; then all due ($37,710). This amortizes as a 25-year note.
† Estimated.
‡ It is estimated that an additional $157,275 must be spent on various deferred maintenance items.

Unit mix The unit mix is given in Table 6-11.

TABLE 6-11 Unit Mix

Bedroom/bath	Number of units	Total ft²	Monthly rental
	Raintree West (177)		
1/1	4	670	$ 165
1/1	45	660	165
1/1	40	600	160
2/1	16	860	210
2/1	20	850	200
2/1	4	800	200
2/2	42	950	200
3/2	6	1,425	265
	Raintree East (155)		
Efficiency	3	384	125
1/1	43	700	165
1/1	43	700	170
2/1	48	900	210
3/2	18	1,240	265
	Bayou (240)		
1/1	80	630	165
1/1	80	650	165
2/1	64	840	200
2/1	16	880	210
	572	437,352 =	$105,875 =
		765 ft²/unit	$185/unit
			$024.2/ft²

Cash-flow projections

Rents $1,270,500
Vacancy 63,525 (5%)
                                  $1,206,975
Furniture..........................   9,210 (½)
Laundry............................ 11,000
Deposits   6,864
                                  $1,234,048
Expenses:
    Taxes............................$ 94,320 ($0.216) (7.4%)
    (+10%) Utilities.............. 205,000 ($0.469) ($29.87 per month)
    Other.......................... 336,000 ($0.77)
                                  $ 635,320 ($1.45) (50%)
Net............................. 598,728
Debt............................ 444,132 (35%)
Cash flow ....$ 154,596 (14.7%)*
Cash flow, after load 11.3%
    After deferred maintenance and load...10.1%

* Southwest Properties projects a before-load cash flow of $132,288 from operation (12.6%) and has approved of this acquisition subject to a private partnership being able to acquire a majority of the surrounding units.

Analysis of data (before commissions to realtor)

Price per unit..	$	10,402.00
Per square foot..		13.60
Multiple of gross		4.68
Rents, per unit		185.00
per square foot..		0.242
Expenses, per unit.......................................		92.56
Per square foot..		1.45
As percentage of gross...............................		50%
Debt service as percentage of gross..................		35%
Debt constant...		9.06%
Equity buildup, year 1	$	66,538
Year 2..	$	69,938 (6.62%)
Down payment as percentage of gross		$1,050,000 (17.7%)
Per unit..	$	1,836
Capitalization note......................................		10.06

Case Study: Ash Creek Apartments

The Ash Creek apartments, the last case to be studied here, comprises 1,682 units, making it by far the largest of the three complexes. The property is located in the same southwestern city as the Bavarian Village and Raintree-Bayou complexes.

Location and area data   The property is located in the southeast section, 8 miles from the center of the city at the nearly completed intersection of two freeways. An estimated 250,000 cars will pass by the property daily when the intersection is cleared of construction. The area surrounding the property is industrial and blue-collar. There are virtually no vacancies in this part of the city since most apartment building has been in the southwest.

The city itself is experiencing nearly full employment and expects rapid growth from its present population of 1.2 million.

Property description   Ash Creek Apartments consists of 1,682 units plus a full recreation complex and a bar and discotheque nightclub. All units are one- and two-bedroom. The complex also has a security entrance. Laundry equipment is owned.

The complex was designed to meet the mass-market need in the area. The units have excellent layout and full amenities. There are no carports or garages. Of five phases in the complex, the oldest phase began renting in December 1973 and the newest phase in October 1974. There are presently less than five vacancies overall.

Purchase price and terms   These are given in Table 6-12.

Cash-flow projections   These are given in Table 6-13.

TABLE 6-12 Purchase Price and Terms

Cash	$ 2,100,000 (11.4% of price)
First mortgage	15,400,000
Second mortgage	900,000
Price	$18,400,000

	Mortgages				
	Balance (thousands)	Term	Interest,%	Annual	Constant,%
A	$ 4,729	30	$8\frac{5}{8}$	$ 443,357	9.38%
B	5,387	30	$8\frac{5}{8}$	504,027	9.36
C	4,900	30	$9\frac{1}{8}$	484,120	9.88
Club	383*	3.5	$9\frac{1}{2}$	60,385†	15.77
	$15,399			$1,491,889	9.69
Second	900‡	30	$8\frac{1}{2}$	83,043	9.23
	$16,299			$1,574,932	9.66%

First-year equity buildup $135,873 = 6.5%.

* This loan must be paid off in 3.5 years. Seller will subordinate to new loan if desired.
† Payments are $6,000 per quarter plus interest.
‡ All due in 15 years. Right to pay off at 10% discount at any time within 3 years of closing.

TABLE 6-13 Cash-Flow Projections

	1975		
Rents	$3,284,220	23¢ per square foot	$163 per unit
Vacancies, 5%	164,211		
	$3,120,000		
Club and games	50,000		
Laundry	60,000	$2.97 per unit monthly	
	$3,230,000		
1975 expenses	1,390,000 = 42%		$1.17 per square foot
	1,840,000		
Loans	1,575,000 = 48%		
	$\frac{265,000}{\$2,100,000}$ = 12.6%		

	1976		
Rents + $10	$3,486,060	24.5¢ per square foot	$173 per unit
Vacancies, 5%	174,000		
	$3,312,000		
Club	50,000		
Laundry	60,000		
	$3,422,000		
1976 expenses	1,545,000 = 44%		$1.30 per square foot
	$1,877,000		
	1,575,000 = 45%		
	$ 302,000 = 14.4%		

Analysis of data and notes

1,682 units
1,187,044 ft^2
  706 ft^2 per unit
Total = $18,399,398 (1,682 × 10,939)
Price =   5.6 × gross
        5.3 × gross after increase
    $10,939 per unit
     $15.50 per ft^2
     6.2 × gross without utilities
1975 taxes $240,000; expected tax increase 10%
Utility increase of 10 to 15% expected in 1976
Club income $147,000 last 11 months; off in May $3,500
Possible problem areas: asphalt, taxes, utilities

Expenses

Off-site management, 5%	$ 156,000
Property taxes, 28 cents per square foot	330,000
Insurance, 1.5%	49,000
Utilities, 30 cents per square foot	356,000
On-site management, 5(900 + 150)	63,000
Assistant management, 5(700 + 150)	51,000
Rental aids, 6%(1,682)(12)(35)	42,000
Cleaning, 6%(1,682)(12)(50)	61,000
Advertising, 0.7%	23,000
Trash, $1.30 per unit semimonthly	26,000
Office supplies plus phone, $0.20 per unit monthly + 50	5,000
Landscape, $4.50 per unit monthly	91,000
Reserves, $5 per unit monthly	101,000
Pools, $30 per pool × 12	3,000
Security, $1 per unit monthly	20,000
Payroll tax, etc., 15% of payroll	34,000
Roof and parking and exterior, $0.03 per square foot, annually	35,000
Repairs, 3%	99,000
Total	$1,545,000

COMPARATIVE DATA ON CASE STUDIES

The subjects of these three case studies, Bavarian Village, Raintree, and Ash Creek are of different sizes. Certain significant data are presented in comparative form in Table 6-14. Current information of this sort provides useful bench marks so that an investor can compare potential alternatives; e.g., the investor can compare the gross income multiplier with that of other available properties. A comparison of cost per square foot and expenses as a percentage of apartment gross will indicate whether expenses are out of line. Obviously these bench marks are not a substitute for a complete analysis of cash flow and rate of return, as explained in earlier chapters.

TABLE 6-14 Comparative Data on Case Studies

	Bavarian Village	Raintree, etc.	Ash Creek
Total price (cost)	$4,872,000	$6,270,000	$18,399,398
No. of units	360	572	1,682
Average unit size, ft^2	664	764.5	706
Price (cost), per unit	$13,533	$10,402	$10,939
Per square foot	$20.37	$13.60	$15.50
Gross multiplier	5.5	4.68	6.2*
Rent, per unit	$192.56	$185	$173
Per square foot	$0.29	$0.242	$0.295
Expenses, per square foot	$1.53	$1.45	$1.30
As a percentage of gross	44%	50%	44%
Debt service as a percentage of gross	41%	35%	48%
First-year equity buildup	$36,500 (25%)	$66,538	$135,873 (6.5%)

* Without utilities.

SUMMARY

Over the past six decades, apartment-house starts have experienced considerable fluctuation. Changes in tax laws, mortgage rates, and availability of financing and increases in construction costs have been important factors in this fluctuation. New construction has slowed significantly since 1966, and there are indications it will continue to be slow through the end of the 1970s. As costs of material and labor increase at a more rapid rate than rents, apartment-house construction becomes a high-risk venture. However, this does not mean that investment in existing apartment buildings is unwise. Each situation must be analyzed based on the goals of the investors and the financial data.

There are motivational differences between developers and investors. Developers begin with little or no equity and try to develop one. Investors, on the other hand, try to increase the substantial equity they began with and are likely to be more interested in tax shelter and equity buildup through amortization of the loan than in current cash flow.

Market analysis for rental apartments is important to both investors and developers. An outline for market analysis prepared by the United States Housing and Urban Development indicates the many important factors to be considered.

The attempt to develop operational models and techniques designed to forecast future employment, population, and land-use development for small geographic areas is reviewed. As techniques are improved, the developer and investor may have new important planning tools. The use of macroeconomic models must be supplemented by detailed studies of changes in the housing inventory for small areas. Together, these techniques can provide the prospective apartment investor or developer with information concerning the probable demand and supply for apartment units.

Apartment investment analysis requires careful consideration of availability of credit; analysis of the specific location and future characteristics is also important.

An investor contemplating the purchase of an apartment will have a pro forma statement providing the relevant financial information. These pro forma operating statements may be compared to the regional averages published by the Institute of Real Estate Management. This and other comparative information help the investor determine whether the relationships in the pro forma statement are reasonable; e.g., whether the expense ratio or the cost per square foot is unreasonable compared with those of alternatives. Naturally it is important to compare properties of similar size, location, and amenities. The various data sources are mentioned so that up-to-date information can be obtained.

Case studies of four apartment-house complexes are included, one hypothetical and three actual situations, which allow the reader to review the data and experiment with the investment analysis techniques presented in the book.

SEVEN

Office Building Investment

Historically, the construction of office buildings in the United States has been characterized by relatively long cycles of boom, followed by collapse. High levels of office-building construction before World War I, from 1923 to 1930, and from 1960 to 1973 resulted in an oversupply of office space and were followed by declining office rents, high vacancies, foreclosure, and long periods of market absorption.

A 10-year summary of the total competitive office space and occupancy in buildings reported by members of the Building Owners and Managers Association, International (BOMA) is shown in Table 7-1. An extremely rapid expansion in office space available nationally during the past decade of expansion has been accompanied by rising vacancies. Interpretation of these reports is made difficult by the fact that reports are not received for all buildings for every year and that changes in membership and in buildings reported from year to year affect the completeness of the data.

Table 7-1 reveals an approximate fivefold increase in the number of office buildings reporting and in the total rentable area of competitive office space in United States cities over the decade. The percentage of vacant space in reporting buildings rose from 4.5 percent in 1967 to approximately 14.0 percent in 1976. It would appear that over the past decade an average of approximately 30 million square feet of competitive office space was added, while absorption of space averaged only about 25 million square feet per year, indicating surplus development of approximately 49 million square feet for the decade, or an average of 4.9 million per annum.

The most recent peak in the value of permits for national office-building construction occurred in 1973 and was followed by a 27 to 30 percent de-

TABLE 7-1 BOMA-reported Occupancy in Competitive Office Buildings in the United States, 1967 and 1976

Year	No. of cities	No. of buildings	Competitive rentable area, millions of square feet			Vacant, %
			Total	Occupied	Vacant	
1967	92	547	73.1	69.8	3.3	4.5%
1976	73	3,256	374.7	322.1	52.6	14.0
Net change, decade	−19	2,709	301.6	252.3	49.3	9.5%

Source: Building Owners and Managers Association, International, *47th Annual Office Building Exchange Report,* Washington, 1976.

cline in 1975 and 1976.[1] Several factors contribute to the traditional instability in office-building construction:

1. High financial leverage typical of office-building finance makes new construction highly sensitive to changes in mortgage-money rates and terms.

2. Tax shelter resulting from depreciation and interest deductions from taxable income provides a strong inducement to builders and investors to construct office buildings during prosperity.

3. Office-building construction often reflects nonmarket considerations, such as corporate prestige and image.

4. The elasticity of supplies of existing office space facilitates the postponement of new demand under conditions of uncertainty, high money rates, or recession.

5. The eternal optimism of developers, the naiveté of lenders, and the lack of sophisticated market-analysis techniques prolong periods of over- and underconstruction.

6. The long planning and construction period required often results in continued high construction volume long after weakness becomes apparent in the demand for office space.

Nonmanufacturing employment growth is the underlying demand generator for office space. The post-World War II surge in government and service employment spurred a phenomenal growth in office-related space demands. It has been estimated that over 80 percent of the jobs in finance, insurance, and real estate and related areas such as law are keyed to office-space use. It can also be observed that a growing proportion of the employees of manufacturing, mining, and wholesale firms actually work in offices.[2]

[1] *Construction Review,* October 1976.
[2] Charles J. Detoy and Sol L. Rabin, "Office Space: Calculating the Demand," *Urban Land,* June 1972, pp. 4–13.

Substantial increases in the number of square feet of office space required per worker have accompanied the rapid growth of metropolitan employment in recent decades. Rising office-worker productivity has been accompanied by added space requirements for office machines and related facilities, as well as for improved light, air, and space. Meanwhile, high-speed elevators and air conditioning have accelerated the rate of obsolescence of older office buildings. Transportation innovations, such as mass transit and "people movers," have permitted the integration of office and shopping areas and helped preserve the waning attraction of centrally located office structures.

However, the outward drift of employment and population associated with freeway and other transportation improvements has contributed to the decentralization of office construction in many metropolitan areas. These conflicting trends have added to the challenge and problems of office-building market analysis, long a neglected area.

Recent employment growth in major metropolitan areas of the nation

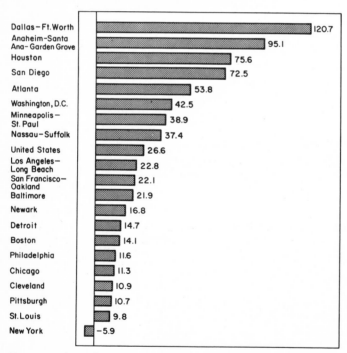

Figure 7-1 The 20 largest metropolitan areas ranked by percent growth of nonfarm employment, 1965 to 1975.

reveals wide variations in rates of growth between different metropolitan areas and regions. Figure 7-1 shows that the oldest and largest metropolitan areas of the North and Northeast have grown much more slowly than the newer and smaller metropolitan areas of the Southeast, Southwest, and the Far West. A report by the Bureau of the Census as of July 1, 1975, drew attention to a population drift away from big cities since 1970. The Bureau of the Census reported that the population of 272 metropolitan areas grew by only 4.2 percent between 1970 and 1975, while the population of non-metropolitan areas gained 6.5 percent. The wide divergence of metropolitan growth rates is shown in Table 7-2, which identifies trends in the 70 largest metropolitan areas since 1970. Growing shortages of energy and high heating costs in the northern industrial tier of states augur a continuance of the population drift to the sunbelt. For the first time in our history, more Americans live in the western and southern states than in the northern and central regions of the nation.

The rapid growth of suburban office areas has reflected the general decentralization of economic activity in large cities and metropolitan areas and has added a further dimension to the problems of office-building market analysis. The office-building market can be viewed as a number of related submarkets, representing structures of different age, building height, floor area, facilities, geographical location, occupancy, and ownership characteristics. BOMA distinguishes between office buildings in different age groups, building heights, and location, and groups reporting buildings as *competitive,* i.e., potentially available in the open market, or as *non-competitive,* i.e., permanently occupied by the owner or a single tenant lessee.

Although office-building submarkets are more or less linked, important differences in market characteristics, performance, and participants can be observed in many areas. The office-building market is also linked to the industrial building market through multipurpose buildings serving office, warehousing, and manufacturing facilities and to residential markets in some areas where older residences are converted to office use. The complexity of office-building submarkets and their interrelationships are suggested by Fig. 7-2.

OFFICE-BUILDING MARKET ANALYSIS

Trends in rents and vacancies are prime indicators in virtually all real estate market analysis. Office-building valuation and investment decisions require forecasts of the future demand and supply of office space as they will affect

TABLE 7-2 Estimated Population Changes for the 70 Largest Metropolitan Areas in the United States, 1970–1975

Metropolitan area	Population (thousands)	Change from 1970, %	Metropolitan area	Population (thousands)	Change from 1970, %
1. New York	9,635.2	-3.4	40. Sacramento	880.1	+9.5
2. Chicago	6,982.9	+0.1	41. Memphis	873.2	+4.7
3. Los Angeles–Long Beach	6,944.9	-1.4	42. Fort Lauderdale–Hollywood, Fla.	862.5	+39.1
4. Philadelphia	4,797.3	-0.6	43. Providence–Warwick–Pawtucket, R.I.	851.1	-0.5
5. Detroit	4,444.7	+0.2	44. Dayton	836.9	-1.8
6. Boston–Lowell–Brockton–Lawrence–Haverhill, Mass.	3,914.6	+1.7	45. Albany–Schenectady–Troy, N.Y.	799	+2.7
7. San Francisco–Oakland	3,128.8	+0.7	46. Bridgeport–Stamford–Norwalk–Danbury, Conn.	793.9	+0.1
8. Washington, D.C.	3,016.2	+3.6	47. Birmingham, Ala.	793	+3.4
9. Nassau–Suffolk, N.Y.	2,622.0	+2.6	48. Salt Lake City–Ogden	783.8	+11.1
10. Dallas–Fort Worth	2,552.8	+7.3	49. Toledo	781.4	+2.5
11. St. Louis	2,369.4	-1.7	50. Norfolk–Virginia Beach–Portsmouth	772.6	+5.5
12. Pittsburgh	2,315.9	-3.6	51. Greensboro–Winston-Salem–High Point, N.C.	765	+5.6
13. Houston	2,297.3	+14.9	52. New Haven–West Haven–Waterbury–Meriden, Conn.	760.9	+2.1
14. Baltimore	2,136.9	+3.2	53. Nashville–Davidson, Tenn.	753.1	+7.7
15. Minneapolis–St. Paul	2,027.5	+3.2			
16. Newark, N.J.	1,995.9	-3.0			
17. Cleveland	1,975.4	-4.3			
18. Atlanta	1,806.1	+13.2			
19. Anaheim–Santa Ana–Garden Grove, Calif.	1,710.2	+20.3			

	Population	% Change			Population	% Change
20. San Diego	1,587.5	+16.9		54. Oklahoma City	752.9	+7.7
21. Miami	1,438.6	+13.5		55. Honolulu	704.5	+11.7
22. Milwaukee	1,426.4	+1.6		56. Jacksonville	700.6	+12.7
23. Seattle–Everett	1,411.7	−0.9		57. Akron	668.2	−1.6
24. Denver–Boulder	1,404.3	+13.3		58. Worcester–Fitchburg–Leominster, Mass.	648.1	+1.7
25. Cincinnati	1,384.5	−0.2		59. Syracuse	647.8	+1.8
26. Tampa–St. Petersburg	1,365.4	+25.4		60. Gary–Hammond–East Chicago	640.4	+1.1
27. Buffalo	1,327.2	−1.6		61. Northeast Pennsylvania*	636.9	+2.4
28. Kansas City	1,287.1	+1.0		62. Allentown–Bethlehem–Easton, Pa.	621.5	+4.6
29. Riverside–San Bernardino–Ontario, Calif.	1,223.4	+7.2		63. Springfield–Chicopee–Holyoke, Mass.	597.4	+2.5
30. Phoenix	1,217.5	+25.4		64. Charlotte–Gastonia, N.C.	594.5	+6.6
31. San Jose, Calif.	1,173.4	+10.1		65. New Brunswick–Perth Amboy–Sayreville, N.J.	589.6	+1.0
32. Indianapolis	1,147.4	+3.2		66. Tulsa	585.8	+6.7
33. New Orleans	1,094.4	+4.6		67. Orlando	585.2	+29.1
34. Portland, Oreg.	1,081.8	+7.4		68. Jersey City	582.8	−4.1
35. Columbus, Ohio	1,077	+5.8		69. Richmond, Va.	581.5	+6.2
36. Hartford–New Britain–Bristol, Conn.	1,059.8	+2.4		70. Omaha	572.8	+5.6
37. San Antonio	977.2	+10.0				
38. Rochester, N.Y.	971.2	+1.0				
39. Louisville	891.7	+2.8				

* Scranton–Wilkes-Barre–Hazleton.

Source: U.S. Department of Commerce, Bureau of the Census, ser. P-25, no. 709, September 1977, table 1.

Downtown				Suburbs			
High-rise		Middle rise		Office Parks		Other	
Multiple tenant	Single tenant	Multiple tenant	Single tenant	Office use only	Mixed use	Office use	Mixed use
Further classification of each submarket by age, amenities, and location							

Figure 7-2   Office-building submarkets.

future rents and occupancy. The following generalized model for office-building market analysis was set forth by Detoy and Rabin:[1]

$$D \quad - \quad S \quad = \quad \frac{1}{1 - V_n} \quad (G \quad + \quad U \quad + \quad O_r)$$

Demand   Supply   Normal expanded demand to allow for vacancy   Net real growth from net employment   Office space for upgrading tenants   New space removed

$$- \quad (O_a \quad + \quad O_v)$$

Space added   Space overhang previous years

(7-1)

where V_n = vacancy rate (normal)

G = tenants coming from community employment growth

U = demand from present tenants for upgrading

O_r = office space removed from inventory

O_a = office space added by new construction or rehabilitation

O_v = vacent space carryover from previous years

An excess of estimated future demand over supply resulting from Eq. (7-1) reflects probable future positive absorption of space. A negative absorption estimate indicates additions to supply in excess of new demand or an increase in vacancies above normal expectations.

Describing the model, Detoy and Rabin point out that the growth in demand for office space results from:

1. Expansion of space requirements by existing tenants
2. New tenants moving from other cities
3. New business firms in the community

Increases in supply of office space may result from:

1. Existing tenants going out of business, reducing space, or moving to other cities
2. New office space being added (including remodeling)
3. Vacant office space available from previous years

Needless to say, the accuracy of the analyst's estimate of G and U in

[1] Ibid.

Eq. (7-1) is the key to a useful forecast of future space absorption. Detoy and Rabin suggest a technique for extrapolating G by multiplying expected employment increases in office-using SIC sectors by an office-space coefficient reflecting the number of square feet required per office employee. They recommend as the most satisfactory method of estimating U (the space demand for upgrading tenants) conducting a painstaking canvass of existing leases and tenants.[1]

The following case examples from Detoy and Rabin illustrate the use of the model shown in Eq. (7-1). The equation permits the analyst to estimate the probable absorption, given a target vacancy rate applicable to the growth in demand for space and new space to be added O_a and the present market overhang O_v. A negative value for $D - S$ indicates that expected increases in supply exceed growth in demand and that market overhang will rise by the amount of the negative result.

Conversely, Example 2 shows the calculation of the new space added O_a in order to satisfy growth in demand.

Example 1 It may be helpful to review the above model by working through several numerical examples. Consider a community with a 5 percent office-space vacancy target V_n, a net real growth G of 1 million square feet of space, upgraded demand U for 750,000 ft², no space removed O_r from inventory, 200,000 ft² of space added O_a to the market, and 250,000 ft² of overhang O_v:

$$D - S = \frac{1}{1 - V_n} (G + U + O_r) - (O_a + O_v)$$

$$= \frac{1}{1 - 0.05} (1,000,000 + 750,000 + 0) - (200,000 + 250,000)$$

$$= 1,392,105 \text{ ft}^2$$

This indicates that an additional 1.4 million square feet of space could be built and absorbed.

Example 2 Using the above data and not knowing the amount of space added O_a to the market, one can determine the absorption rate as follows. Set the market in equilibrium:

$$D - S = 0$$

Then

$$O_a = \frac{1}{1 - V_n} (G + U + O_r) - O_v$$

$$= \frac{1}{1 - 0.05} (1,000,000 + 750,000 + 0) - 250,000$$

$$= 1,592,105 \text{ ft}^2$$

[1] Ibid., p. 10.

Construction of 1.6 million square feet of office space will therefore keep the market in equilibrium.

Reports of BOMA provide current information on occupancy rates, new office space added, and space occupied or taken off the market. Although BOMA reports distinguish between competitive office space potentially available in the open market and noncompetitive space, representing buildings permanently occupied by an owner or single tenant lessor, this distinction is often blurred by inclusion of buildings predominantly occupied by the owner as noncompetitive, even though some space might be rented to other tenants.

Unfortunately, not all office buildings in a given city may be represented in BOMA reports, and buildings may be included in reports for one period and not for another. BOMA reports for some cities may include suburban as well as downtown office buildings. These and other problems of non-reporting and area coverage make it necessary to exercise caution in using the only continuous source of information on office-building occupancy available to the analyst.

The summary of national office occupancy data as of October 1, 1976, in Table 7-3 shows that vacancy rates in office buildings varied in a wide range from zero in some smaller cities to 43.03 percent in Austin, Texas. Approximately 29 of the 75 cities reporting had vacancy rates of under 10 percent of total available space, and only 12 cities reported vacancy rates exceeding 20 percent. The median vacancy ratio was about 15 percent. If vacancy rates in excess of 10 percent of available office space are taken as a criterion, it would appear that over 60 percent of major reporting cities in the United States had an oversupply of office space in October 1976.

The following review of recent developments in the office-building markets in Atlanta, San Francisco, and New York illustrates the varying

TABLE 7-3 BOMA National Office Building Occupancy, 1976, Comprehensive Reports by Cities

		Office space competitive rentable area				
	No. of		Vacancy		Occupancy	
Region and city	buildings	Rentable ft²	ft²	%	ft²	%
Middle Atlantic:						
Baltimore	73	3,540,480	554,903	15.67%	2,985,577	84.33%
Hartford	3	540,000	30,000	5.56	510,000	94.44
New York	99	52,050,615	8,796,646	16.90	43,253,969	83.10
Philadelphia	166	24,779,896	3,317,919	13.39	21,461,977	86.61
Pittsburgh	52	10,191,569	1,158,313	11.37	9,033,256	88.63
Rochester	5	372,951	38,744	10.39	334,207	89.61
Springfield, Mass.	*			0.00		0.00

Washington, D.C.	120	13,245,973	703,611	5.31	12,542,362	94.69
Wilmington	15	1,033,333	27,946	2.70	1,005,387	92.30
Regional total	534	105,754,817	14,628,082	13.83	91,126,735	86.17

North Central:

Akron	6	359,879	27,442	7.63%	332,437	92.37%
Battle Creek	*	7,363		0.00	7,363	100.00
Chicago	170	46,954,201	7,087,380	15.09	39,866,821	84.90
Chicago Suburban	189	11,214,028	1,615,943	14.41	9,598,085	85.58
Cincinnati	15	1,285,076	152,714	11.88	1,132,362	88.12
Cleveland, Ohio	38	5,923,055	452,562	7.64	5,470,493	92.36
Columbus	8	236,649	24,397	10.31	212,252	89.69
Detroit	33	4,690,149	608,568	12.98	4,081,581	87.02
Fort Wayne	*	70,596		0.00	70,596	100.00
Merrillville, Ind.	3	193,010	2,096	1.09	190,914	98.91
Midland, Mich.	3			0.00		0.00
Peoria, Ill.	18	680,410	112,984	16.61	567,426	83.39
Toledo	*	205,877	28,591	13.89	177,286	86.11
Youngstown	*	38,697	5,974	15.44	32,723	84.56
Regional total	488	71,858,990	10,118,651	14.08	61,740,339	85.91

Midwest, northern:

Davenport, Iowa	*	78,692	3,862	4.91%	74,830	95.09%
Des Moines, Iowa	16	907,438	118,971	13.11	788,467	86.89
Duluth	12	383,284	52,098	13.59	331,186	86.41
Kansas City, Mo.	16	1,334,824	89,778	6.73	1,245,046	93.27
Lincoln	*	182,793	30,219	16.53	152,574	83.47
Madison, Wis.	9	470,236	69,003	14.67	401,233	85.33
Milwaukee	123	7,141,327	900,312	12.61	6,241,015	87.39
Minneapolis	71	6,259,452	753,209	12.03	5,506,243	87.97
Omaha	26	1,472,196	76,618	5.20	1,395,578	94.80
Sioux City	*	77,124		0.00	77,124	100.00
St. Louis	57	8,301,611	1,610,548	19.40	6,691,063	80.60
St. Paul	25	2,149,253	376,337	17.51	1,772,916	82.49
Topeka	3	212,929	20,109	9.44	192,820	90.56
Regional total	363	28,971,159	4,101,064	14.15	24,870,095	85.85

Southern:

Atlanta	187	14,701,111	3,984,516	27.10%	10,716,595	72.90%
Atlanta Suburban	109	9,674,406	2,529,537	26.15	7,144,869	73.85
Birmingham, Ala.	3	262,666	44,464	16.93	218,202	83.07
Chattanooga	2	154,754	2,692	1.73	152,062	98.26
Jackson	10	274,123	10,757	3.92	263,366	96.08
Jacksonville	4	232,800	49,963	21.46	182,837	78.54
Knoxville	3	174,452	8,170	4.68	166,281	95.32
Lake Worth, Fla.	6			0.00		0.00
Louisville	5	530,934	72,986	13.75	457,948	86.25
Memphis	*	369,345	146,233	39.59	223,112	60.41
Nashville	5	207,184	37,312	18.01	169,872	81.99
New Orleans, La.	15	2,013,667	118,852	5.90	1,894,815	94.10
Orlando	*	107,928	13,602	12.60	94,326	87.40
Shreveport	*	58,786	2,160	3.67	56,626	96.33
Tampa, Fla.	20	1,134,025	175,800	15.50	958,225	84.50
Regional total	373	29,896,181	7,197,044	24.07	22,699,136	75.92

TABLE 7-3 BOMA National Office Building Occupancy, 1976, Comprehensive Reports by Cities (Continued)

| | | | Office space competitive rentable area | | | |
| | | | Vacancy | | Occupancy | |
Region and city	No. of buildings	Rentable ft²	ft²	%	ft²	%
Southwest:						
Austin	5	153,890	66,221	43.03%	87,699	56.97%
Dallas	202	26,564,352	3,989,831	15.02	22,574,521	84.98
Denver	114	11,932,667	2,612,604	21.89	9,320,063	78.11
El Paso	8	394,106	42,605	10.81	351,501	89.19
Fort Worth	7	785,913	170,333	21.67	615,580	78.33
Houston	582	45,599,919	3,556,919	7.80	42,043,000	92.20
Little Rock	4	282,279	26,753	9.48	255,526	90.52
Oklahoma City	34	3,348,474	406,080	12.13	2,942,394	87.87
Roswell, N. Mex.	*	87,085	21,114	24.25	65,971	75.75
San Antonio	15	731,915	151,284	20.67	580,631	79.33
Tulsa	24	1,196,650	35,000	2.92	1,161,650	97.08
Regional total	996	91,077,250	11,078,744	12.16	79,998,506	87.84
Pacific Northwest:						
Portland	51	4,559,068	403,768	8.86%	4,155,300	91.14%
Salt Lake City	12	1,029,323	141,270	13.72	888,053	86.28
Seattle	51	5,805,789	477,378	8.22	5,328,411	91.78
Spokane	19	1,025,346	166,240	16.06	859,106	83.94
Tacoma	3	203,669	44,155	21.68	159,514	78.32
Regional total	136	12,623,195	1,232,811	9.76	11,390,384	90.23
Pacific Southwest:						
Honolulu	19	2,154,480	203,686	9.45%	1,950,794	90.55%
Los Angeles	43	6,922,155	935,962	13.52	5,986,193	86.48
Phoenix	19	1,581,416	320,188	20.25	1,261,228	79.75
Sacramento	*			0.00		0.00
San Diego	10	1,350,597	402,447	29.80	948,150	70.20
San Francisco	272	22,266,846	2,344,468	10.53	19,922,378	89.47
Tucson	*	221,817	26,447	11.92	195,370	88.08
Regional total	366	34,497,311	4,233,198	12.27	30,264,113	87.72
Canada:						
Calgary	114	10,661,839	764,000	7.17%	9,897,839	92.83%
Ottawa	*	207,200	1,200	.58	206,000	99.42
Regina	3	165,563	7,668	4.63	157,895	95.37
Toronto	75	9,639,361	624,810	6.48	9,014,551	93.52
Vancouver	52	5,918,223	422,006	7.13	5,496,217	93.87
Regional total	245	26,592,186	1,819,684	6.84	24,772,502	93.16
Total United States	3,256	374,678,903	52,589,594	14.03%	322,089,308	85.96%
Grand total	3,501	401,271,089	54,409,278	13.56%	346,861,810	86.44%

* Where less than three buildings report the number is not shown, but is included in total.
Source: Building Owners and Managers Association, International, Washington, preliminary report.

degrees of overbuilding and market overhang characteristic of major cities in the mid-1970s.

ATLANTA OFFICE-BUILDING MARKET 1976

Office occupancy data published currently by BOMA of Atlanta provides a basis for estimating the absorption of space in the Atlanta metropolitan area and the magnitude of the 1976 overhang of vacant space.

Table 7-4 summarizes the changes in occupancy of competitive office space in Atlanta reported by BOMA members from 1967 to 1976. The *Office Occupancy Survey* as of October 1976 reported total office space in metropolitan Atlanta of 30,984,239 ft^2 of leasable area, of which approximately 6,608,000 ft^2 was classified as noncompetitive. Approximately 14.7 million square feet of competitive office space was located in urban Atlanta, with a 72.9 percent occupancy ratio as of October 1, 1976, while about 9.7 million square feet, or almost 40 percent of the total competitive space was located in suburban Atlanta with an occupancy ratio of 73.9 percent.

TABLE 7-4 10-Year Summary of Competitive Office-Space Occupancy in Atlanta

Date	No. of participating buildings	Total competitive space reported, ft^2	Occupancy, %	Vacancy, %
10/1/76	245	24,375,517	73.4 %	26.7 %
5/1/76	255	21,957,052	75.8	24.2
10/1/75	321	25,793,601	77.0	23.0
5/1/75	272	24,897,940	80.3	19.7
10/1/74	148	21,380,959	89.1	10.9
5/1/74	130	19,011,330	86.23	13.77
10/1/73	121	17,269,815	86.12	13.88
5/1/73	131	17,586,491	86.97	13.03
10/1/72	113	13,190,294	86.3	13.7
5/1/72	91	10,506,877	86.1	13.9
10/1/71	78	8,428,775	83.0	17.0*
5/1/71	60	6,013,615	84.83	15.17
10/1/70	61	5,901,256	85.08	14.92
5/1/70	25	3,463,710	77.04	22.96†
10/1/69	78	6,248,331	82.87	17.13
5/1/69	76	6,471,100	88.02	11.98
10/1/68	71	6,393,241	87.83	12.17
5/1/68	80	6,926,915	86.22	13.78
10/1/67	52	5,659,638	84.82	15.18
5/1/67	50	5,336,973	82.14	17.86

* Incorporates substantial suburban reports for the first time.
† Note limited number of reports.
Source: Building Owners and Managers Association, of Atlanta, Inc.

The data include suburban office space beginning in 1971, and it is significant to note in Table 7-4 that the number of participating buildings reporting occupancy increased by more than 400 percent from October 1970 to October 1976. The suburban office market accounts not only for 40 percent of the total competitive space available but also for about the same percentage of total occupancy, with a 73.9 percent current-occupancy ratio.

An admittedly crude analysis of the BOMA data shown in Table 7-4 for 1967 to 1976 reveals that the indicated absorption of office space in metropolitan Atlanta increased from 4,526,820 ft² in 1967 to 17,891,629 ft² in 1976, an increase of approximately 395 percent for the decade. During the same period the total amount of competitive office space reported available rose from 5,336,973 to 24,375,517 ft², an increase of approximately 456 percent. The net result of the relatively larger increase in supply than in demand, as shown below, was an 800 percent increase in vacant space or market overhang. The net changes in square footage calculated below reveal that the average amount of office space added per year over the decade, 1.9 million square feet, was more than double the indicated average annual absorption rate of 883,798 ft², resulting in an average annual increase in vacant space of approximately 567,373 ft². The addition of suburban office space to the reported figures in October 1971 should be considered in interpreting these 10-year averages. The effect of including suburban office buildings after 1971 was to add to the number of reporting buildings and to the visible supply of space and occupancy after that year. It can be noted in Table 7-4, however, that the major changes in available office space and occupancy occurred after 1971.

Date, Oct. 1	Total competitive space available, ft²	Total occupied competitive space, ft²	Vacant space or market overhang, ft²
1967	5,336,973	4,526,820	810,152
1976	24,375,517	13,364,809	6,483,887
Net change	19,038,554	8,837,989	5,673,735

Market analysts for Hammer, Siler, George Associates, economic consultants, estimated in January 1976 that 1.5 million square feet of Atlanta office space was leased in the 12 months ended in June 1975 and that approximately 4.9 million square feet of net space, more than a 3-year supply based upon 1975 absorption rates, remained available for lease in January 1976. A year later, January 1977, Robert W. Siler of the same firm told members of BOMA of Atlanta that his firm estimated a total supply of office space in the metropolitan Atlanta area of 39 million square feet, of which 17.6 million was in the central sections of the city and 21.4 million in the suburbs. He estimated a total of 10 million square feet of unoccupied office space in the area, with 3.8 million in the central city and 5.7 million in the suburbs. Siler predicted that smaller construction projects would add approximately 1.2 million square feet of space in 1977, about the same amount as in 1976.

It appears probable that the overhang of unoccupied office space in early 1977 represented about a 4-year supply based upon recent absorption rates. Recent projections by the Bureau of Labor Statistics indicate a rapid growth in office using activities in Atlanta by 1985.

Atlanta's total employment (employment of all civilian workers) is expected to increase by 57.4 percent from 1970 to 1985. This represents an increase of 390,107 from the 1970 census estimate of 679,300 to 1,069,407 in 1985.[1]

The two industries which are projected to grow at the fastest rate are services, up 84.1 percent from 1970 to 1985, and finance, insurance, and real estate, increasing 80.4 percent over the same period. Employment in transportation and other public utilities is expected to rise 61.4 percent from the 1970 level of 63,500 to 102,500 in 1985. Construction employment, although currently at depressed levels, is projected to reach 69,000 by 1985, a point 58.0 percent above the 1970 employment of 43,600.

Employment in wholesale and retail trade establishments will rise by 56.4 percent over the 15-year period. More of the forecast increase will occur in retail trade establishments (62.4 percent) than in the wholesale trade (46.6 percent). Forecasts of government employment show a slowdown in growth with an increase of 45.5 percent over the period—slower than the overall rate for Atlanta (57.3 percent).

From 1970 to 1985 employment in manufacturing is expected to show the slowest rate of growth (13.9 percent) of any industry except agriculture and mining. All that increase will take place in durable goods. Employment in nondurables is projected to decrease by 3.4 percent, with most of the losses occurring in textile-mill products (4,600), food products (1,300), and printing and publishing (700). Durable-goods industries with increasing employment are expected to be machinery, electrical machinery, stone, clay and glass products, and transportation equipment. The significance of these growth forecasts and the oversupply of office space in Atlanta and other cities for office building investors will be explored later in this chapter.

SAN FRANCISCO OFFICE-BUILDING MARKET, 1976

A review of the San Francisco office-space market as of May 1, 1964, revealed total space in 200 reporting competitive office buildings of 9,566,793

---

[1] U.S. Bureau of Labor Statistics, Atlanta—1965 to 1975—*Another Decade of Growth,* Regional Report No. 36, Atlanta, January 1977.

TABLE 7-5   San Francisco Office-Building Occupancy, 1964 and 1976

Date	No. of buildings	Space, thousands of square feet			Vacant to total space, %
		Total	Occupied	Vacant	
Competitive office buildings:					
5/1/64	200	9,567	9,060	507	5.3 %
10/1/76	217	22,267	19,922	2,344	10.53
Net change	17	12,700	10,862	1,837	5.23%
Noncompetitive buildings					
5/1/64	41	4,906	†	†	†
10/1/76	96	12,829	†	†	†

† Not reported.
Source: San Francisco Building Owners and Managers Association Reports. The total number of buildings surveyed as of Oct. 1, 1976, was 272, of which 217 reported data. The total number of buildings surveyed as of May 1, 1964, was 236, including 36 loft buildings not included in the data in the table. Noncompetitive office space in 1964 included 12 government-occupied and 29 company-owned-and-occupied buildings. Noncompetitive data for 1976 included 96 buildings, of which only 55 were 100% noncompetitive and 14 government-occupied. A total of 1,240,221 ft² of occupied space reported in competitive office buildings was leased for government tenancy.

ft², of which only 507,040 ft², or 5.3 percent of the total space, was reported as vacant. The San Francisco Office Occupancy Survey dated October 1, 1976 (Table 7-5) showed an inventory of approximately 20 million square feet of competitive office space in 217 reporting buildings out of a total of 272 buildings surveyed. Vacant office space reported in San Francisco as of October 1, 1976 totaled 2,344,468 ft², or 10.53 percent of the reported total space. It was estimated in October 1976 that new office buildings under construction or in advanced stages of planning would add an additional 3 million square feet of competitive office space over the next 2 years.

The survey in Table 7-5 revealed a growth of approximately 10.9 million square feet of occupied space from May 1, 1964 to October 1, 1976, an approximate average annual growth in demand of 905,000 ft² per year over 12 years. The average annual net increase in the total supply of competitive office space reported in San Francisco over this period was approximately 1.06 million square feet, after allowing for removal of buildings. Present reported vacant space in San Francisco of 2,344,468 ft² represents about a 2.5-year supply, based upon past rates of absorption. The addition of 3 million square feet of office space in the next 2 years would increase the market overhang substantially, unless annual absorption rates increase from past levels of less than 1 million square feet per year to 1.5 million or higher.

NEW YORK OFFICE-BUILDING MARKET

The New York City office-building market deserves special attention because of the concentration of office buildings of national firms in that city.

The Empire State Building, completed in 1931, was the tallest structure in the world at that time and provided 1.7 million square feet of rentable area. During the two decades following World War II, 202 office buildings were completed on Manhattan with a total of 71.4 million square feet. Approximately 3.8 million square feet per year was added from 1947 to 1957, and 6.0 million square feet per year from 1958 to 1964. Despite these high levels of new construction, the vacancy rate in New York office buildings in 1966 was only 1.6 percent, according to a survey by the New York City Real Estate Board.

Fortune reported (February 1975) that builders had added almost 80 million square feet of office space in the preceding decade at a total cost of $5 billion, including about $1 billion for land. According to *Fortune* estimates, New York City had a total of 222 million square feet of office space in 1975, of which 40 million square feet was vacant. The estimated vacancy rate of 18 percent in 1975 was the highest since 1939, although below the peak of 1934.

A reversal in the long upward trend in New York office employment following 1970 resulted in an estimated loss to the city of over 100,000 office jobs between 1969 and 1975. Figure 7-1 shows that New York was the only large metropolitan area in the nation that experienced a loss in nonfarm employment between 1970 and 1975. According to *Business Week* for November 29, 1976, employment in the New York metropolitan area continued to decline in 1976.

This stunning and persistent decline of employment in New York City has particular significance for future office-space demand. One major cause of the decline has been the exodus of large corporate headquarters from New York. *Fortune* estimated that headquarters staffs declined from a total of 84,000 in 1969 to approximately 64,000 in 1975. Jobs in business services such as advertising, computer processing, public relations, and commercial art, which had increased by 60 percent in the preceding decade to a total of 170,000, were estimated to have declined by more than 10,000 from 1969 to 1975. It was also estimated by *Fortune* magazine (February 1975) that over 30,000 jobs in the securities field were lost from 1969 to 1975 and that smaller but significant declines occurred in the insurance and publishing fields.

Confirmation of the serious extent of overbuilding in the New York City office building market is found in annual surveys by the Cross and Brown Company and by BOMA in New York. Cross and Brown reported a net absorption of 2,348,992 ft² of office space in New York in 1975 and of nearly 3 million square feet in 1976, leaving a total of 23,303,913 ft² of space available for lease or sublease as of January 1977. This compares with a reported net absorption of 1,509,592 ft² in 1974. At the 1975 indicated rate of absorption, it would require 10 years or longer to eliminate the estimated overhang in the New York market.

The combination of overbuilding and unfavorable employment prospects has resulted in near panic conditions among office-building owners and mortgage holders in New York in recent years. Carruth[1] has described the chaotic conditions in the New York City office-building market at year end 1975.

> "It's rough times," says veteran realtor Harry Helmsley. "I went through the Depression and it's the same dog-eat-dog thing now." The vacancy rate in Manhattan is now up to 18 percent, the highest since 1939 (though still below the peak of 1934). Worst of all, white-collar employment in the city has actually declined since 1969. With fewer bodies around, says Tishman, "any renting in New York now is just a shifting from one space to another."
>
> As a result, Manhattan now has a plethora not only of empty office space but dead capital as well. To the nearly 150 million square feet already standing in 1965, builders have added almost 80 million square feet, most of it coming on in just the past four years, at a total cost of some $5 billion, including about $1 billion for land. More than 30 million feet—or one square mile—is excess space, built at a cost of about $2 billion.
>
> All of that investment is not a dead loss, to be sure, since many tenants have moved from old buildings to new ones. But when viewed in a broader context, such moves simply spread the loss around. And in many cases, the same people own both kinds of buildings. The basic problem, surplus space, is not going to disappear for ten years or more, even if New York's office jobs start growing strongly again—and the prospects for that are dim.
>
> In the dogfight for tenants, developers face a painful choice. They can offer concessions to get tenants, but this locks them into long-term losses. Or they can carry the empty space at even heavier current losses, waiting for the market to turn. Developers who completed structures in the first few years of the boom have rented up and are by now well out of the woods. But the problems are acute in the 55 million square feet of space completed in the Seventies.
>
> "Most new buildings have a negative bottom line," according to Alton Marshall, president of Rockefeller Center Inc., which controls nearly a tenth of all New York's office space. That means they are not even earning enough to make their mortgage payments. A great deal of the capital invested in these buildings, obviously, can be reckoned as a loss, acknowledged or not.
>
> A building's capital value depends on its cash flow—rents minus such expenses as taxes and maintenance. To determine that value, cash flow is capitalized at the going rate for long-term money, currently around 10 percent. To this sum is added some allowance for future prospects. On this basis, valuations on a number of hardship cases among the newer buildings are from one-quarter to one-third (sometimes more) below the total investment in the structures. The average valuation on *all* of the 55 million square feet of space produced in the Seventies is less than three-quarters of cost. Since this space cost around $4 bil-

---

[1] Eleanore Carruth, "The Skyscraping Losses in Manhattan Office Buildings," *Fortune*, February 1975, pp. 78–83, 162–166; used by permission.

lion to erect, the capital loss comes to nearly $1 billion, not counting carrying losses that may be run up in the future. . . .

Fortune has tracked down the financing on 85 percent of the buildings completed by private developers in the roaring 1970's. The amount of debt held by various financial institutions on these properties, many of them actually or potentially vulnerable, is $1.5 billion. That amount is about evenly distributed among the commercial banks, the insurance companies, the savings banks, and two pension funds run for New York State employees.

The developers and their partners—in many cases the major corporate tenant for the building—made equity investments of well over $500 million. A few of the ventures were successful, but much or most of that equity has gone beyond jeopardy into the realm of lost capital, even though only about $75 million of it has been "taken" by sale, write-off, or foreclosure.

Ordinarily, the developers' equity interest in a property acts as a shield between the lender and the vagaries of the marketplace. But if the developers can't or won't pay the losses and abandons the property, then the lender gets to play. "The question is how long can the developers take it," says Donald Davis, head of Prudential's Manhattan real-estate-investment department, "because if they cannot, it is we, their lenders, who are going to be stuck. . . ."

Insurance companies have about $400 million out in mortgages for new Manhattan office buildings and much of this is at risk because, like the banks, they relaxed lending standards. They stopped requiring developers to produce signed leases before committing mortgage money. Prudential's biggest problem is another Uris-National Kinney property, the giant 3,400,000-square-foot structure downtown at 55 Water Street . . . which cost more than $175 million to erect. It has a $130-million mortgage there as well as $7.5 million in equity.

The building is racking up an annual loss of nearly $2 million for its owners, after interest payments, because it is only 75 percent occupied. If it ever should rent up fully, this behemoth would more than pay out the mortgage, but Pru's Davis admits, "When I heard they let 1633 Broadway go, the first thing I thought of was our vulnerability. The crux of the matter is, how long can they hold on?" If Kinney can't, or won't, Pru will have it, and would have to be "very patient," Davis says, ever to get back its investment. For its part, Kinney is negotiating new leases and says it has no intention of letting go.

Equitable and Metropolitan are losing money on their 60 percent equity interest in One Penn Plaza, a 2,200,000-square-foot skyscraper adjacent to Penn Station. They also hold an $80-million mortgage on the structure, which cost $90 million to erect. The mortgage is being paid partly because developer Harry Helmsley lined up Ebasco as the major tenant early on. The company merged with Boise Cascade and never moved in; instead it paid a $22 million penalty to break the lease, and most of the penalty payment was used to reduce a higher mortgage.

Even with that break, and with 75 percent of the building rented, Helmsley acknowledges that the property still shows a "substantial" loss after mortgage payments. So the insurance companies are contributing their share of the deficit at one end and collecting on their mortgage at the other. . . .

There are, on *Fortune's* estimate, 40 million square feet of space vacant out of a total of 222 million. If vacancies were at a comfortable level, they would total only seven or eight million. With employment sagging so badly and the corporate exodus continuing, the burden of that excess 30-million-plus square feet is not only growing steadily heavier but is bearing down on every segment of the city's office market. . . . Of the 28 million square feet listed for rent, nearly 40 percent is in new buildings, and *Fortune's* analysis of the data shows a vacancy rate in the 1970–74 buildings of about 20 percent. The remainder of the space is in older buildings, particularly those of pre-1935 vintage. Two-thirds of all the square footage is uptown, one-third downtown. . . .

As a major landlord for older buildings as well, Rockefeller Center has another whole set of problems on its hands. When Exxon moved to its new quarters, for example, it left behind one million square feet at eight locations within the complex. While the center made some "good" rentals of that space, e.g., to Warner Communications . . . , it still has some former Exxon space on its hands. And Marshall figures he probably won't get the rents he needs for the 184,000 feet that Uniroyal vacated last year when it moved a large contingent of employees to Connecticut. Rockefeller Center had to put $15 million into modernizing Warner's new quarters and it will have to spend a lot to make the old Uniroyal structure into "a something building," as Marshall puts it.

Losses of income and value in older buildings have by now become quite common. McGraw-Hill last year [1974] sold its old 570,000-square-foot building on West Forty-second Street (opened in 1931) for only $5.5 million after it was returned in lieu of a mortgage foreclosure. (The publisher also collected a $4 million down payment at the time of the original sale for $15.1 million in 1971.)

Older buildings, however, vary a lot in age, location, mortgage situation, vacancy rates, and other key factors. Some, like the Empire State, have no trouble at all hanging onto tenants. All, of course, have suffered a "loss" from the expectations owners put on them five or six years ago, and in many cases the financial institutions that hold the mortgages are worried. In 1969, land-lords couldn't wait for low-rate leases to run out and be replaced by higher rentals. Costs have since increased ruinously, often without adequate rent escalators. (Rockefeller Center, for instance, would have been much worse off if Uniroyal had picked up its option to renew at $5 a foot.) In some instances an older building can scrape by with rents far below those for new space, if the owner has paid off the old mortgage and doesn't need to renovate ex-tensively.

Competition is now interacting everywhere—new versus old space, land-lord versus sublessor. The key, says John L. Dowling, executive vice president of Cushman & Wakefield, the biggest renting agents in town, is this: "Rates on sublease space will continue to go down, and as they do, it will be a sig-nificant pressure on landlords of new buildings. As the squeeze comes, some-thing has got to happen.". . .

Builders fear most of all that the financial institutions may be drawn into this game by foreclosures. "Once an institution goes in, there's no bottom," says

Harry Helmsley. "They'll go down [on rents] as far as they need to." Lewis Byrne at Dollar Savings acknowledges, "We'd rent at the highest rates we could get, but we would rent as low as we needed. We could cut rents to pieces."

Institutional cut rates would wreck altogether the delicate strategy developers are following in trying to cover costs but save a stake. Tishman never rented any space at 1166 Avenue of the Americas because in 1973 he could not get a price anywhere near high enough to break even. "We did not feel it was in our best interest to lease space at rates which ensure loss. You get to a point where you can never catch up," he explains.

In other situations, developers say, the best strategy is to cut the rent a bit but also the length of the lease. Arthur Cohen, chairman of Arlen Realty & Development, which owns 50 percent of 800 Third Avenue, rented half the space in the structure to Seagram in 1971 at a low $7.50 per square foot for ten years. "Had I rented to them for longer, say thirty years, our future would be gone," he says. Three-quarters rented, the building is losing money. Cohen hopes to recoup by renting the tower floors at high rates. It's those last leases that traditionally put developers over the top. As one says when asked about supply and demand, "All *I* need is one good tenant." The trouble is, there aren't enough such good tenants to go around and probably won't be.

All strategies are based on the developers' belief that if they can keep their buildings going, rental rates will turn up again. But an examination of supply-and-demand trends does not reveal much reason for even that bleak kind of optimism. To be sure, the developers no longer have to contend with a flood of new construction. But for the last twenty years, new construction has never fallen below 2,200,000 square feet annually, and various special situations— such as the new headquarters building for American Home Products—might keep it as high in the future, adding about 1 percent per year to the total space available. Demolitions will continue to subtract about 500,000 square feet annually, although there is an outside chance they might go higher.

As for demand, developers can count on a little lift from a continuing trend of corporations to allot more space per employee. A number of studies, however, indicate that this trend is slowing and will add perhaps only half a percent per year to demand in the future. So, if white-collar employment does not pick up, new supply and demand might just about balance out, and the vacancy rate would stay at that high 18 percent. This does not preclude, of course, a general upgrading in the quality of the space rented, which would help the developers fill their new buildings.

But it will take a great increase in jobs to put the industry back on a sound footing. If the growth in white-collar employment gets back to the average increase since 1959—1.5 percent a year—all the surplus space would be absorbed in a decade. Vacancies in 1985 would then be below a normal 4 percent, and the market would be strong again. But that seems too much to expect in the light of the city's economic outlook and employment trends over the past five years. . . .

But it is not in the nature of entrepreneurs to dwell for long on gloom. The veterans among them have survived through thick times and thin. Most of the buildings they brought in during the soaring Sixties yielded handsome profits, frequently on little or no investment of their own. They are using those profits now to carry empty space and so keep rents propped up somewhere above bankruptcy levels. "The strong builders will survive this thing," says developer Harry Helmsley, "but the weaker ones — those without adequate financing — are going to go under."

Because the developers are entrepreneurs and eternal optimists, those that do survive will look beyond the mist toward a brighter future for New York. But neither they nor their financial bankers will soon repeat the speculative practices that have brought them to disaster. . . .

OFFICE-BUILDING INVESTMENT ANALYSIS

It is important to distinguish between the profitability of new office-building development and the prospects for satisfactory investment returns from the purchase of existing office structures. The relationship between existing and new supplies of office space, absorption rates, and the market overhang are determining factors in office-building development decisions.

The returns to an investor in a new or existing office building depend, as pointed out in Chaps. 3 and 4, upon the following critical factors:

1. Purchase price of the property
2. Financing terms
3. Lease terms
4. Present and future levels of operating income and expenses
5. Future selling prices
6. Applicable depreciation rules
7. Income and capital gains tax rates

Assumptions concerning the purchase price, the future sale price, and the financing terms are the most critical factors influencing an investor's returns on a prospective investment. Local market conditions influence the level of future rents and occupancy rates and the outlook for operating income. Operating expenses reflect the quality of management, characteristics of the structure, local tax policies, and wage levels.

Virtually any well-constructed and well-located office building with some prospect for future net operating income will be a "good buy" at some favorable combination of market price and financing terms. The very existence of low occupancy rates, negative cash flows, and foreclosures in the office-building market brings about lower offering prices and encourages favorable financing terms from distressed owners or former mortgagees. The prospective investor uses a pro forma schedule of rental income and operating expenses, reflecting the market conditions in any particular area and submarket, to determine the probable rate of return under the offering prices, financing terms, estimated future selling prices, and tax shelter available. The final decision will of course reflect the investor's appraisal of the probable rewards of a given investment in comparison with the probable risks, as outlined in Chap. 1 and illustrated below.

DETERMINING THE CRITICAL FACTORS IN OFFICE-BUILDING INVESTMENT ANALYSIS

The purchase price of any property represents a decision made by the investor after considering current offering prices in combination with the other investment considerations outlined above. The cash-flow models described in Chap. 3 provide a framework within which the investor can (1) estimate the probable after-tax internal rate of return on any investment, given assumptions about its economic life, operating income, financing, and tax liabilities, or (2) estimate the purchase price an investor should offer for any investment given assumptions about its future income and selling price and the investor's target rate of return on his equity investment. In other words, investors can test any set of cash-flow expectations in combination with an offering price to determine whether the probable rate of return on required equity is acceptable, or they can determine the purchase price and required equity which would provide them with a return they consider a desirable minimum for any given investment property.

For existing office buildings, present levels of operating income and expense are known and, assuming that leases are in effect, can be estimated for years in the near future. The annual *Office Building Experience Exchange Report,* published by BOMA, includes income and operating expenses expressed in cents per square foot for all reporting office buildings by city. These bench-mark figures provide valuable guidelines to the investor comparing operating statistics for a contemplated investment property with competitive buildings in the same locality. Year-to-year comparisons of BOMA operating statistics also reveal trends in major items of income and expense which are critical in projecting future operating income and expenses. Selected data from the BOMA reports from 1963 to 1974 are summarized in Table 7-6. Significant trends in these national averages can be observed, even though differing types and age groups of buildings are represented and the sample of reporting buildings is not constant over the period.

The bottom-line income figures show that total income rose from $3.95 per square foot in 1963 to $5.93 in 1974, an increase of approximately 50 percent over the 11-year period. The reported net income (before capital charges) rose during the same period from 94.5 cents per square foot to $1.686, an increase of approximately 78 percent.

TABLE 7-6 Summary of Office-Building Experience in Exchange Reports,* National
Averages, 1963–1974, Cents per Square Foot of Leasable Area

Category	1963 (572 buildings)	1964 (587 buildings)	1965 (598 buildings)	1966 (547 buildings)	1967 (564 buildings)
A1 Cleaning	55.3	55.3	55.1	54.9	57.7
A2 Electrical system	15.1	15.3	15.8	16.8	18.0
A3a Heating	13.5	13.5	13.9	13.9	15.4
A3b Air conditioning and ventilating	17.5	17.9	18.2	18.9	19.4
A4 Plumbing system†	3.8	3.8	4.0	4.1	4.2
A5 Elevators	19.2	18.0	17.1	16.3	16.3
A6a General expense, administration	18.5	19.1	18.8	19.0	19.8
A6b General expense, building	17.9	18.4	19.2	19.5	21.0
A7 Energy					
Total operating	154.3	154.7	156.2	157.1	167.1
B1 Tenant alterations	10.8	11.4	13.7	13.2	16.8
B2 Repairs and maintenance‡	10.9	11.1	10.9	11.7	11.7
B3 Tenant decorating	6.5	6.9	6.5	6.6	6.9
Total construction	22.4	23.4	24.7	25.2	27.1
C1a Fire insurance	1.9	1.8	1.8	1.9	1.9
C1b Insurance (other)	2.8	2.8	2.7	2.7	2.8
C2a Property taxes	61.4	63.9	66.0	65.6	71.5
C2b Personal-property assessment	2.2	1.8	1.9	1.8	1.5
C3 Depreciation	65.7	65.5	67.5	66.0	73.3
Total fixed charges	132.7	134.7	138.0	135.8	149.1
Total expenses (A–C)	311.3	314.7	318.6	319.0	343.1
Net (before capital charges)	94.5	104.1	99.4	103.4	109.6
Rental income	389.2	402.3	398.5	410.7	443.4
Miscellaneous income	8.8	8.8	11.9	5.9	4.3
Total income	395.1	408.2	406.4	414.4	445.9
Total rental area, ft^2	88,627,912	92,106,050	94,345,027	89,494,293	99,964,959

* Summary includes both downtown and suburban buildings.
† Included in general expense, building (A6b) beginning with 1974 report.
‡ Includes alterations and decorating in nonrentable area.
Source: Building Owners and Managers Association, International, *Office Building Experience Exchange Report,* 1976.

Operating expenses, which represented 39 percent of gross income in 1963, rose to approximately 42 percent of gross in 1974. Fixed charges, mainly property taxes and depreciation, rose from 33.5 percent of gross income in 1963 to 38.5 percent in 1974. The total expense ratio, including operating and construction expenses, and fixed charges other than debt service accounted for 81 percent of gross revenues in 1974 compared with 78.7 percent in 1963. Table 7-3 shows that the national office-building oc-

1968 (556 buildings)	1969 (607 buildings)	1970 (601 buildings)	1971 (653 buildings)	1972 (638 buildings)	1973 (676 buildings)	1974 (721 buildings)
61.4	62.6	65.0	68.3	67.2	70.0	72.8
20.2	21.1	20.6	22.4	25.2	9.2	8.5
15.1	15.5	15.3	17.3	20.4	9.0	9.9
20.5	21.0	22.3	24.0	26.8	13.1	11.9
4.5	4.7	4.9	5.5	5.5	3.1	†
17.1	16.7	17.0	18.5	18.5	16.5	16.0
20.4	20.0	21.8	23.3	23.7	25.9	22.8
21.9	23.2	24.4	26.6	26.3	28.6	39.5
177.3	181.0	189.4	204.5	208.5	227.3	249.1
14.4	15.4	14.6	14.6	13.5	15.0	15.4
10.7	10.3	11.1	12.5	12.3	13.3	†
6.3	6.0	5.9	5.9	5.9	7.5	7.5
25.0	23.8	24.3	25.7	24.9	27.8	19.0
2.0	2.1	4.4	4.9	4.8	5.3	5.0
2.8	2.9					
74.7	64.1	90.6	97.4	103.4	113.5	121.4
1.2	2.1	2.1	2.3	4.0	8.2	8.8
76.8	81.4	91.7	91.5	95.6	97.7	103.6
154.8	169.9	188.8	193.9	207.8	224.7	228.4
355.9	382.8	398.8	422.6	336.9	488.2	480.1
116.9	115.2	146.2	132.0	138.9	146.0	168.6
455.7	463.9	498.1	514.4	528.0	558.9	574.8
5.6	5.8	7.0	8.3	8.3	31.9	22.1
459.0	467.7	503.1	520.3	534.3	565.5	593.0
100,989,054	109,347,301	119,015,609	121,205,958	134,215,783	145,247,683	162,888,965

cupancy ratio for office buildings in the United States was 85.96 percent in October 1976, which compared with approximately 93.5 percent in 1975 and represented the lowest average occupancy rate since the depression years of the late 1930s.

Table 7-7 reveals significant differences in occupancy characteristics and operating ratios between "downtown" and "suburban" office buildings. The overall operating ratio for suburban office buildings was 76.9 percent for 1975, compared with 80.3 percent for downtown office buildings. Closer examination of Table 7-7 indicates that the more favorable operating ratios in suburban buildings reflect lower operating costs for cleaning, elevators, administrative, and energy expenses and significantly

TABLE 7-7 Operating Experience for Reporting Downtown and Suburban Office Buildings 1976, Cents per Square Foot Except Where Otherwise Noted

Account	Downtown, 846 buildings				Suburban, 286 buildings			
Square feet in analysis	No. reporting	Building total 237,392,311	Office total 209,710,429	Office rented 193,600,652	No. reporting	Building total 40,443,568	Office total 35,164,450	Office rented 32,714,155
A1 Cleaning	831	83.1	87.1	94.2	275	59.2	62.0	66.6
A2 Electrical systems	661	9.8	9.9	10.7	164	8.1	8.0	8.6
A3a Heating	223	10.0	10.4	11.2	45	10.2	9.8	10.4
A3b Air conditioning and ventilating	237	12.5	13.2	14.4	53	11.7	12.1	12.8
A3c Combined heating, ventilating, and air conditioning	513	28.1	28.0	30.2	209	19.1	19.2	20.8
A5 Elevators	817	19.2	21.7	23.5	250	8.7	10.0	10.7
A6a General building costs	837	44.1	43.9	47.6	282	50.6	48.4	52.1
A6b Administrative costs	804	29.5	29.1	31.6	269	27.2	27.7	29.7
A7 Energy	813	100.4	102.5	111.0	272	87.9	89.1	95.7
Total operating	813	305.8	314.2	340.4	272	250.9	255.2	274.1
B1 Tenant alterations	476	16.7	16.3	17.7	130	16.2	16.3	17.7
B3 Tenant decorating	434	5.9	5.8	6.2	110	12.7	12.5	13.3
Total construction	591	17.7	17.3	18.7	167	22.8	22.5	24.3
Total operating expenses (A + B)	568	314.1	323.2	349.6	163	276.5	280.9	302.8
C1 Insurance	731	6.3	6.3	6.9	261	6.4	6.1	6.6
C2a Real estate tax:								
Land	741	30.9	18.9	20.5	263	13.8	4.6	4.9
Building	740	111.4	113.4	122.8	267	77.1	77.5	83.6
C2b Personal property tax, etc.	285	13.3	13.2	14.8	101	10.0	9.4	9.9
Total fixed charges*	779	146.0	136.4	147.9	275	97.8	88.9	95.8
Total operating expenses* (A + B + C)	544	458.0	458.9	496.2	156	379.8	377.1	408.1

Net income,* gain	615	281.5	283.3	305.4	220	283.1	301.3	328.4
Loss	101	245.5	205.3	240.4	13	167.7	39.5	47.3
Lease expense	292	14.1	14.0	15.4	102	14.2	13.5	15.0
Amortized tenant alterations	234	28.4	28.6	31.5	59	49.6	51.4	56.1
C3 Depreciation	496	95.3	96.8	104.2	160	118.8	121.3	131.3
Total operating expenses† (A + B + C)	455	553.6	556.1	604.6	127	501.9	494.6	540.3
Net income,† gain	436	203.3	205.9	220.7	139	178.1	198.1	214.3
Loss	167	196.0	181.0	208.3	35	107.4	63.2	77.5
Rental income:								
Office area	700	786.4	695.7	756.8	232	525.3	620.1	676.3
Store area	472	250.8			67	245.6		
Storage area	296	564.6			54	446.2		
Special area	175	664.7			30	576.4		
Total rental income	709				135			
Electrical income	258	31.6			46	16.2		
Miscellaneous income	481	25.2			111	23.2		
Total operating income	736	693.7			246	589.3		
Operating ratio, %	567	82.1			170	78.8		
Management ratio, %	735	45.7			245	40.8		
Average office vacancy, %	846	7.7			286	7.0		
Average office occupancy, %	846	92.3			286	93.0		
Labor cost	563	88.6			141	60.3		
Average office tenant, ft^2	729	4,647			228	2,719		
Average store tenant, ft^2	459	2,566			54	1,514		
Average ft^2 per employee	563	11,307			141	14,089		
Average ft^2 per person	691	200.6	187.2	173.2	225	236.9	214.7	199.3

* Does not include expense for depreciation.
† Includes expense for depreciation.

Source: Reprinted by permission from *1977 Experience Exchange Report for Downtown and Suburban Office Buildings,* Building Owners and Managers Association, International, Washington. (Current editions, special studies, and related publications available from the association at 1221 Massachusetts Ave., Washington, D.C. 20005.)

lower real estate taxes. The higher expenses in downtown buildings are seen to be more than offset by the higher total operating income and net income per square foot. The cost of construction or purchase cost of downtown buildings is of course substantially higher than for suburban buildings, reflecting structural characteristics and amenities as well as higher land costs. The higher indicated net income per square foot shown for downtown buildings in Table 7-7 must therefore support the higher capital investment in such buildings.

The apparent difference in occupancy costs for office space in the suburbs probably accounts for the moderately lower vacancy rates reported for suburban office buildings in Table 7-7. It can be observed in Table 7-7 that the average number of square feet per tenant is substantially lower in suburban office buildings, reflecting smaller tenancies, while the average square feet of space per employee is higher. These measures reflect differences in employment and operating characteristics of suburban and downtown tenants.

Recent census reports that people are moving away from the nation's big cities in favor of life in smaller communities and rural areas suggest the possibility that the move of offices to the suburbs will continue. It can be argued, however, that the current large overhang of vacant office space in the larger cities will result in lower rents and values, designed to attract tenants and investors. Table 7-2 reveals the extreme diversity in metropolitan growth trends in the nation. The larger and older metropolitan areas in the northern industrial tier of states appear to be losing population, while the smaller metropolitan areas of the South and West continue to grow. It is notable, however, that suburban growth is more rapid than growth in the central cities in all metropolitan areas. These conflicting trends emphasize the importance of local office-building market analysis, as confirmed by the earlier summaries of office occupancy and vacancies in Atlanta, San Francisco, and New York.

Analysis of any specific office-building investment requires an overall analysis of the national and local office-building market as an important first step. National market analysis is of particular importance for investors considering purchase of office buildings serving tenants with national or regional offices.

The present overhang of office space in a local market is a critical factor influencing probable rents and occupancy of existing and new structures. The potential supply of new competitive space is of particular importance for investors in existing structures. It is not unusual for a new office building possessing strong locational advantages and other amenities to lease up rapidly by drawing tenants from older buildings through offering special lease terms as incentives. The customary leasing program for a new office building usually includes a detailed analysis of office space use in the vicinity, supplemented by a door-to-door canvass and a telephone survey of prospective tenants.

The rate at which vacant office space is being absorbed in the market must be weighed in comparison with the current overhang of unused space. An oversupply of office space is not necessarily worse than a lack of supply, and a substantial overhang of space may serve to attract regional and national tenants to an office center.

CASE STUDY IN OFFICE-BUILDING INVESTMENT ANALYSIS

The earlier review of recent developments in the national and Atlanta office-building markets provides the basis for a sample case study involving the purchase of an office building in suburban Atlanta. The building was completed in 1973 and was 100 percent leased in 1975, with predominantly short-term leases including escalation clauses. The office structure is on leased land with 47 years of remaining life on the ground lease, which provides for ground rent of $75,000 per year until 1980 and $85,000 per year thereafter.

The rent toll for the building, shown in Table 7-8, shows the lease terms and the fixed and escalation rents paid for 1975. Operating performance for the past three years and estimated expenses for the first projection year are shown in Table 7-9.

Following an analysis of market conditions and the economic outlook for the Atlanta suburban office market, investor B estimated that gross revenues would be $1,078,896 for 1976, operating expenses $696,800, and net operating income $382,096. B also estimated that gross income and operating expenses would probably rise at 5% per year for the next 15 years, with a 3% annual increase in selling price for the leasehold estate. Because of the uncertainties, however, B decided to project cash flows and rates of return under less optimistic and more optimistic assumptions in order to project the probable range of returns he might expect.

The property is currently offered for $3.75 million. Financing terms are uncertain, but B wishes to consider the probable returns under the following range of financing terms:

Option 2: 8 percent interest, monthly amortization, 30 years, 70 percent cost

Option 3: 9 percent interest, monthly amortization, 30 years, 75 percent cost

Option 4: 10 percent interest, monthly amortization, 25 years, 80 percent cost

Option 1: All-cash purchase

TABLE 7-8 Rent Roll for Office Purchase

Tenant name	Lease began	Lease ends	Annual fixed rent	1975 escalation billing	Total rent	Escalation clause
Ajax Industries	1/73	12/87	$ 300,000	$18,250	$ 318,250	CPI with limit of $60,000
Dean Chemical	6/73	12/88	268,000	2,500	270,500	25% pass-through of fixed and operating expenses; escalator has a limit that increases $2,500 per year; base year 1974
DRESCO	6/73	12/85	275,000	825	275,825	30% of increases in real estate taxes over $228,500
Galt & Galt	1/74	9/80	42,000	1,260	43,260	The greater of 4½% of real estate tax increases over a 1974 base year or a CPI increase
Janson	1/74	12/78	28,000	415	28,415	3% of increases in operating expenses and real estate taxes over 1974-base-year level
Kwick-Klock	10/73	12/78	20,000	277	20,277	2% of increases in operating expenses and real estate taxes over 1974-base-year level
Liberty	10/73	6/78	15,000	277	15,277	2% of increases in operating expenses and real estate taxes over 1974-base-year level
Pilgrim Airways	1/75	12/80	30,000	0	30,000	3% pass-through of real estate tax increases over 1975 base year
Regal Products	10/74	12/79	11,000	0	11,000	CPI
Rupurt Sales	1/75	3/81	21,000	0	21,000	2% of increases in fixed and operating expenses over 1975 base year
Mortons Menswear	1/73	6/92	15,000	0	15,000	5% of sales over $300,000; sales estimated at $290,000 expected to increase at 4% per year
Silers	1/73	12/92	25,000	4,800	29,800	2% of revenues; revenues estimated at $250,000 for 1976 and expected to increase at 3% each year
Total			$1,050,000	$28,604	$1,078,604	

TABLE 7-9 Operating Performance for a Suburban Office Building in Atlanta, 1973–1975

	1973	1974	1975	1976 estimated
Total fixed rent	$560,000	$1,035,000	$1,050,000	
Escalation billings	0	7,200	28,600	
Miscellaneous revenue	2,700	3,800	3,000	
Total revenue	$562,700	$1,046,000	$1,081,600	
Cleaning	50,000	90,000	90,000	$100,000
Utilities	90,500	135,000	138,200	145,000
Repair and maintenance	15,000	28,000	30,000	30,000
Other operating expenses	37,600	54,100	60,000	50,000
Real estate taxes	160,000	228,500	231,250	235,000
Insurance	5,000	5,600	5,600	5,000
Ground rent	75,000	75,000	75,000	75,000
Management and leasing				5% of revenue
Total expenses	$433,100	$ 616,200	$ 630,050	$640,000
Net income	$129,600	$ 429,800	$ 451,550	

B wanted to know:

1. What rate of return should be expected on an all-cash basis for 10 and 15 year holding based upon a continuation of current revenues and expenses and no change in selling prices.
2. What rates of return should be expected on B's equity investment for 10 and 15 year holding assuming each of the four financing options, with no changes assumed in income, expenses, or selling prices.
3. What the change in his expected internal rate of return would be under each of the financing assumptions assuming:
   a. Changes in selling prices in the tenth and fifteenth year of +10, +20, and −10 percent.
   b. Change in vacancy for each year of +10 and +20 percent.
   c. Change in purchase price of +10 and −10 percent.
4. What return should be expected under his most probable assumption that gross income and operating expenses would rise at 5 percent per year for the next 15 years and that selling prices would increase by 3 percent per year.

This problem was run on the REAL III DCF model with the results summarized in Table 7–10.

Analysis of the pro forma rates of return and other indicators in Table 7-10 reveals that purchase of the subject property on an all-cash basis under assumptions of constant income, expenses, and selling prices represents an unattractive investment opportunity with an IRR of less than 6 percent. As

TABLE 7-10 Pro Forma Internal Percentage Rates of Return and Traditional Indicators for an Atlanta Suburban Office Building under Various Assumptions

	All cash purchase $3,750,000	Financing assumptions and loan value ratio (L/V)		
		8% 30 yr 70% L/V	9% 30 yr 75% L/V	10% 25 yr 80% L/V
Internal rate of return:				
10-yr hold	5.52	8.82	8.61	6.95
15-yr hold	5.73	9.25	9.25	7.64
Traditional indicators:				
Overall rate	5.73	9.25	9.25	7.64
Cash-spendable rate:				
Before tax, 15th yr	10.19	13.42	11.79	7.33
After tax, 15th yr	6.11	7.07	6.80	6.83
Payback period, yr:				
Before tax	9.81	7.45	8.48	13.65
After tax	0.00	11.78	11.53	0.00
Equity buildup, first year	10.19	17.32	15.89	14.91
Sensitivity analysis of internal rate of return:				
Change selling price, 10th yr:				
+10%		10.31	10.43	9.18
+20%		11.62	11.98	11.04
−10%		7.03	6.38	4.08
15th yr:				
+10%		9.99	10.14	8.73
+20%		10.65	10.92	9.67
−10%		10.43	8.22	6.35
Change vacancy rate:				
+10%, 10th yr		3.60	2.20	−0.29
+10%, 15th yr		4.25	3.14	1.24
+20%, 10th yr		−1.43	−3.96	−50.00
+20%, 15th yr		−0.51	−50.00	−50.00
Change purchase price:				
+10%, 10th yr		5.38	4.02	1.72
+10%, 15th yr		6.76	5.85	4.15
−10%, 10th yr		12.44	13.39	12.13
−10%, 15th yr		12.00	13.00	11.40
Change tax rate:				
+10%, 10th yr		7.64	7.76	6.42
+10%, 15th yr		8.07	8.39	7.03
+20%, 10th yr		6.43	6.88	5.87
+20%, 15th yr		6.86	7.49	6.40

Source: Computer Runs of the REAL III DCF program.

expected, pro forma rates of return are higher with assumptions of increasing leverage although some of the advantages of high loan-to-value ratios are offset by the higher interest costs and shorter loan periods.

The sensitivity analysis of the internal rate of return in Table 7-10 indicates the degree to which the investor's pro forma returns will fluctuate with possible changes in selling prices in the tenth year, with increases in vacancies above the normal expectancy, and changes in the original purchase price of the property. It is apparent that B can influence the expected rates of return substantially for any combination of expectations concerning operating income and selling prices by the offering price B makes for the property. B can also judge from the analysis in Table 7-10 what fluctuations in yield to expect as a result of negative changes in operating income. Increasing the allowance for vacancies to 10 percent reduces returns under all financing assumptions substantially. Anticipated selling prices in the future have a significantly greater influence upon the IRR for 10-year holding than for 15-year holding, as can be observed. However, for investor B, assumed to be in a 50 percent tax bracket, the opportunity for capital gain and higher rates of return arising from future inflation in selling prices is substantial.

PROBABILITY ANALYSIS

On the basis of a review of the pro forma returns on the subject property, B's mortgage banker advised that the best loan terms B could expect were 9 percent 30 years at 75 percent of the indicated purchase cost of $3.75 million. Table 7-10 summarizes B's projected returns under these financing terms and the most probable assumptions outlined above and indicates a return of 8.61 percent for 10-year holding and 9.25 percent for 15-year holding.

From the sensitivity analysis in Table 7-10 and other runs of the REAL III model, B concluded that there was about a 50 percent chance of achieving the above rates of return, with about a 25 percent chance that the actual returns would be 20 percent above or below these returns. Using these subjective probabilities, the investor calculated the probable expected return on the office building investment for 10-year holding as follows:

$$0.25(\text{IRR}_{-20\%}) + 0.50\,(\text{IRR}_P) + 0.25\%\,(\text{IRR}_{+20\%}) = \text{expected IRR}_E$$

$$0.25(6.89\%) + 0.50(8.61\%) + 0.25(10.33\%) = 8.61\%$$

The expected standard deviation of his returns was calculated from the above range and probabilities as follows:

$$[0.25(IRR - IRR_{-20\%})^2 + 0.50(IRR_E - IRR_P)^2$$
$$+ 0.25(IRR - IRR_{+20\%})^2]^{1/2} = SD$$

where $\quad [125(1.72)^2 + 0.50(0)^2 + 0.25(1.72)^2]^{1/2} = 1.21\%$

where IRR_P = most probable estimate
$\quad IRR_E$ = weighted probable rate of return
$\quad SD$ = standard deviation of expected return

B might interpret the above calculations and the data of Table 7-10 as follows: if the expected returns from the office-building investment follow the "normal" distribution, about two-thirds of all returns would lie within ± 1 standard deviation of 1.21 percent, indicating a probable range of 7.40 to 9.82 percent. Similarly, 95 percent of all observations would be expected to lie within ± 2 standard deviations, indicating a probable range of 6.19 and 11.03 percent.

The above forecasts, based upon one set of subjective probabilities, can be reevaluated in terms of the relative effects of possible changes in future selling prices, tax liabilities, or vacancy rates over the projected holding period, and provide a basis for an investment decision.

SUMMARY

Following a fifteen-year boom, office building construction in the United States declined sharply during the early 1970s. The very high vacancy rates which prevailed in most large cities at the end of 1975 were being gradually reduced by mid-1978 through the processes of economic recovery, building removal, and market absorption.

A review of office building market developments in Atlanta, San Francisco, and New York emphasized the divergence in local market conditions, and the close relationships between urban and regional economic growth and the demand for office space.

The decline in central city employment and the continued outward movement of population and business has been reflected in a marked growth in suburban office building in many cities. Recent architectural and technological innovation and the emergence of the energy crisis as a major cost factor have added to investment risks in old and new office buildings.

High financial leverage, business, market, and local property tax risk in office building construction combine to make office building investment a highly specialized field. As pointed out in Figure 2-2, these relatively high risks are offset by high potential equity returns.

A case example of cash flow analysis for a suburban Atlanta office building revealed the critical importance of financing terms, initial purchase price, and changes in vacancy rates, as influences upon projected equity returns from office building investment. The high sensitivity of the projected rates of return to developments in the uncertain future suggested the advisability of using probability analysis in forecasting future returns from office building investments.

APPENDIX 7A: New Techniques for Use of DCF Models in Investment Analysis

Reference was made in Chap. 3 to the QUICK model which is programmed by Decisionex, Incorporated, Wilton, Conn., for use with the Burroughs B6700, located at Burroughs New York City data center. This model is designed to provide detailed analysis of the tax impact of alternative investments for a variety of investors. The program uses computer-prompted input methods and a flexible reporting facility, allowing the output detail to be tailored to the investor's needs. For established fees Decisionex provides client training, a user guide, and consulting and computer time.

The output of the QUICK model for an attorney's building is shown in the following pages. *User-entered data and commands are shown in lowercase.*

Input details and project specifications are set forth on pages 272 to 274. The program output begins on page 275. Pretax cash flows and equity yields are summarized on page 278. After-tax yield for holding periods from 1 to 7 years are shown on pages 279 and 280. The DCX yield on page 282 represents an adjusted IRR return assuming reinvestment of cumulative net spendable at an after-tax rate of 6 percent.

The remainder of the output, pages 278 to 279, is devoted to year-by-year and annual averages of pretax and after-tax returns, including overall capitalization rates, payback periods, equity buildup, and other ratios. Total returns to the equity are broken down to show the relative importance of major components, cash flow, loan amortization, appreciation, original equity, and tax benefit, on page 281. Note that the various elements of return are discounted at the pretax and after-tax IRRs to derive the dollar figures shown, which add up to the original $150,000 equity. The percentages for each category shown add up to 100 percent.

The data on page 282 illustrate the effect on the rate of return of assuming the reinvestment of cumulative cash flows beginning in year 2 at an assumed 6 percent after-tax rate. Note that the difference in the percentage DCF (IRR) for 7-year holding is approximately 1 percent (percentage DCF rate 15.839, percentage DCX rate 14.865). The calculations on page 282 provide insight into the implicit assumption in the theory of the internal rate of return (designated as percentage DCF in the Decisionex QUICK model) that cash flows are reinvested at the IRR (percentage DCF) rate. Funds assumed to be returned to the investor under the percentage DCF assumption are retained and earn a 6 percent reinvestment income under the percentage DCX assumption.

Variation in the residual sales proceeds as a function of the annual appreciation rate is shown on page 282. It can be seen that potential capital gain has a substantial effect upon the percentage DCF and percentage DCX, Ellwood, and other yields for the subject property.

Reducing the down payment or equity by increasing the loan amount by $10,000, shown on page 283 has the expected influence of increasing leverage on yields.

The versatility of the model for appraisal purposes is illustrated on page 283, showing the effect on the appraised value of setting specific target rates and projected IRRs assuming purchase at the appraised values.

The effect of changes in assumed ordinary tax rates upon IRRs is shown on page 284.

This and other examples of the increasing sophistication of DCF models and their enhanced flexibility for investment analysis and appraisal open up new levels of sophistication in real estate investment analysis.

Parallel development of simpler DCF programs for use with minicomputers promises to broaden the application of computer techniques in real estate analysis.

LOG ON, ACCESS MODEL, AND ENTER GENERAL INPUT VARIABLES

```
e*quick
#RUNNING 1301


SYSTEM QUICK
VERSION  20G ... SEP 3, 1976


     INDICATE APPROPRIATE METHOD OF DATA ENTRY

     1. INPUT WITH BASIC PROMPTING      ...TYPE  P
     2. INPUT WITH FULL PROMPTING       ...TYPE  F
     3. INPUT FROM STORED FILE          ...TYPE  READ FILENAME
     4. INPUT BY DIRECT ASSIGNMENTS     ...TYPE  YEARS=10; ETC
     5. FOR PRESENT WORTH MODEL         ...TYPE  DO PW
     6. FOR IRR% CALC (1 STREAM)        ...TYPE  IRR
     7. FOR GENERAL CASH FLOW MODEL     ...TYPE  DO CASH FLOW


#?
P

YEARS PRICE RESIDUAL COMM% REINV% ORD% LONG% INCOME INC% EXPENSE EXP%
7,700500,3.5,5,6,50,25,*

DEPREC METHOD LIFE TYPE LOAN RATE PERIOD TERM LOAN2 RATE2 PERIOD2 TERM2
579380,150,35,2,525000,7.5,12,20,25500,4,12,3,*

OTHER VARIABLES OR OPTIONS
MAY NOW BE SET .... ELSE TYPE DO

construction project

  PERIODS TO BE BYPASSED    FRONT-END LOSSES     TYPE 1 FOR TAX-     TAX
DEP(1)  LOAN(1)  LOAN(2)  YR(1)  YR(2)  YR(3)  LOSS CARRYFORWARD  CREDIT
6,6,6,22100,*

income is irregular; expense is irregular; do
```

ENTER IRREGULAR INCOME AND EXPENSE STREAMS; PROJECTION OF AFTER-TAX RATES OF RETURN

```
ENTER GR INC...., 7 VALUES
ground floor=33390/2,33390,.025,*

FLOW 2 (0,* IF DONE)
ENTER GR INC...., 7 VALUES
flrs. two&three=68140/2,68140,.025,*

FLOW 3 (0,* IF DONE)
ENTER GR INC...., 7 VALUES
basement=2025/2,2025,.025,**

ENTER OP EXP...., 7 VALUES
taxes=14600/2,14600,.06,*

FLOW 2 (0,* IF DONE)
ENTER OP EXP...., 7 VALUES
insurance=1890/2,1890,.05,*

FLOW 3 (0,* IF DONE)
ENTER OP EXP...., 7 VALUES
utilities=6426/2,6426,.08,*

FLOW 4 (0,* IF DONE)
ENTER OP EXP...., 7 VALUES
janitor=9520/2,9520,.06,*

FLOW 5 (0,* IF DONE)
ENTER OP EXP...., 7 VALUES
supply & maint=2520/2,2520,.06,*

FLOW 6 (0,* IF DONE)
ENTER OP EXP...., 7 VALUES
management=2815/2,2815,.05,*

FLOW 7 (0,* IF DONE)
ENTER OP EXP...., 7 VALUES
miscellaneous=1050/2,1050,.05,**

    7 YR BENEFITS=  234650
       IRR (DCF)=  15.839
       IRR (OPT)=  16.284  (YR 5)
       IRR (DCX)=  14.865

write attnybldg
```

WRITE BASE CASE (ATTNYBLDG) LIST OF
PROJECT SPECIFICATIONS

```
title=attorney°s building

list specifications

              ATTORNEY°S BUILDING



***  P R O J E C T     S P E C I F I C A T I O N S  ***

PREPARED BY:
             --------------------------
ATTN:
             ----------------------------------

     1.   NUMBER OF YEARS
          TO BE PROJECTED  ...   7

     2.   INVESTORS
          PURCHASE PRICE (COST BASIS)  ...   700500

     3.   LOAN    %   ANNL  INT.  # PER  # INT  # 1ST  TERM OR BALLOON
          AMT.   LV  CONST  RATE  YEAR   ONLY   PAYM.  PAYMENT PAYMENT
          525000  75  9.667 7.500   12     0      7    20.00      0
           25500   4 35.429 4.000   12     0      7     3.00      0

     4.   EQUITY
          INVESTMENT (CASH DOWN)  ...   150000

     5.   WRITE-OFFS IN YEARS    (1)      (2)      (3)
                                22100        0        0

     6. * TAX RATES
               ORDINARY INCOME  ...  50.00 %
               LONG TERM GAINS  ...  25.00 %

     7. * FIRST YEAR
          GROSS INCOME  ...    51778

     8. * FIRST YEAR
          OPERATING EXPENSES  ...   19410
```

```
9.    AFTER TAX RETURN ON
      REINVESTMENT OF (CUMUL) NET SPENDABLE  ...  6.00 %

10.   DEPRECIATION:  AMOUNT      METHOD   LIFE IN   TYPE OF    START
                     AVAILABLE   USED     YEARS     PROPERTY   MONTH
                     579380      150 %    35.00     COMML.     7

11. * RESIDUAL VALUE
      IN YEAR ( 7) IS ESTIMATED AT  ...    891232
      BEFORE SELLING EXPENSE OF  5.00 %

12.   RESIDUAL VALUE WAS OBTAINED BY
      APPLYING A   3.50 % GROWTH RATE TO PURCHASE PRICE

///   (*) ASTERISKED INPUT VARIABLES (BELOW)
      WERE SPECIFIED ON A YEAR BY YEAR BASIS:
```

YR	GROSS INCOME (*)	OPER. EXPENSE (*)	NOI	NONDED EXP	RESALE PRICE	(RATIO) NOI/DS	%TAX ORD	%TAX LONG	EQUITY PAYMNT (*)
1	51778	19410	32368	0	688767	1.08	50.00	25.00	0
2	103555	38821	64734	0	712873	1.08	50.00	25.00	0
3	106144	41218	64926	0	737824	1.09	50.00	25.00	0
4	108797	43769	65028	0	763648	1.18	50.00	25.00	0
5	111517	46481	65036	0	790376	1.28	50.00	25.00	0
6	114305	49367	64938	0	818039	1.28	50.00	25.00	0
7	117163	52434	64729	0	846670	1.28	50.00	25.00	0
TOT	713260	291500	421760						
AVE	101894	41643	60251						

LIST OF DETAIL INCOME AND EXPENSE
CASH FLOWS

```
list income-expense report for years 1-3,5,7

ENTER
0=$  1=%INC  2=%NOI  ELSE SQFT...
0
```

ATTORNEY°S BUILDING

*** INCOME-EXPENSES ***

	1	2	3	5	7
INCOME					
GROUND FLOOR....	16695	33390	34225	35957	37778
FLRS. TWO&THREE.	34070	68140	69843	73379	77094
BASEMENT........	1013	2025	2076	2181	2291
TOTAL	51778	103555	106144	111517	117163
EXPENSES					
TAXES..........	7300	14600	15475	17388	19538
INSURANCE.......	945	1890	1984	2187	2412
UTILITIES.......	3213	6426	6940	8094	9441
JANITOR.........	4760	9520	10091	11338	12739
SUPPLY & MAINT..	1260	2520	2671	3001	3372
MANAGEMENT......	1407	2815	2955	3258	3592
MISCELLANEOUS...	525	1050	1102	1215	1340
TOTAL	19410	38821	41218	46481	52434
NET OPER INC....	32368	64734	64926	65036	64729

LIST OF INCOME AND EXPENSE RATIOS
TO GROSS INCOME

```
list income-expense report for years 1-3,5,7

ENTER
0=$  1=%INC   2=%NOI   ELSE SQFT...
1
```

ATTORNEY°S BUILDING

*** INCOME-EXPENSES ***

RATIO TO GR INC

	1	2	3	5	7
INCOME					
GROUND FLOOR....	0.322	0.322	0.322	0.322	0.322
FLRS. TWO&THREE.	0.658	0.658	0.658	0.658	0.658
BASEMENT........	0.020	0.020	0.020	0.020	0.020
TOTAL	51778	103555	106144	111517	117163
EXPENSES					
TAXES...........	0.141	0.141	0.146	0.156	0.167
INSURANCE.......	0.018	0.018	0.019	0.020	0.021
UTILITIES.......	0.062	0.062	0.065	0.073	0.081
JANITOR.........	0.092	0.092	0.095	0.102	0.109
SUPPLY & MAINT..	0.024	0.024	0.025	0.027	0.029
MANAGEMENT......	0.027	0.027	0.028	0.029	0.031
MISCELLANEOUS...	0.010	0.010	0.010	0.011	0.011
TOTAL	0.375	0.375	0.388	0.417	0.448
NET OPER INC....	0.625	0.625	0.612	0.583	0.552

PRETAX CASH-FLOW REPORT

list pre-tax cash flow

ATTORNEY'S BUILDING

PRE-TAX
** CASH FLOW **

YR	EFFECTIVE GROSS INCOME	TOTAL OPERATING EXPENSE	NET OPERATING INCOME	MORTGAGE INTEREST	MORTGAGE AMORTIZATION	TOTAL DEBT SERVICE	CASH FLOW
1	51778	19410	32368	20074	9819	29893	2474
2	103555	38821	64734	39234	20553	59787	4947
3	106144	41218	64926	37945	21841	59787	5139
4	108797	43769	65028	36607	18662	55270	9759
5	111517	46481	65036	35453	15299	50752	14284
6	114305	49367	64938	34265	16487	50752	14186
7	117163	52434	64729	32985	17767	50752	13977

YR	PRE-TAX CASH FLOW	RESALE PRICE	SELLING EXPENSE	NET RESALE PRICE	LOAN BALANCE	EQUITY REVERSION	EQUITY YIELD
1	2474	725018	36251	688767	540681	148086	0.37
2	4947	750393	37520	712873	520128	192745	15.63
3	5139	776657	38833	737824	498287	239537	19.21
4	9759	803840	40192	763648	479625	284023	20.03
5	14284	831974	41599	790376	464325	326050	19.99
6	14186	861093	43055	818039	447838	370200	19.67
7	13977	891232	44562	846670	430071	416599	19.23

list p/tax cash flow

PRE-TAX
** CASH FLOW **

YR	EFFECTIVE GROSS INCOME	TOTAL OPERATING EXPENSE	NET OPERATING INCOME	MORTGAGE INTEREST	MORTGAGE AMORTIZATION	GROSS PRE-TAX CASH FLOW	EQUITY PAYM &REFINANCING	NON DED°T-IBLE EXPENSE	NET PRE-TAX CASH FLOW
0							-150000		
1	51778	19410	32368	20074	9819	2474	0	0	2474
2	103555	38821	64734	39234	20553	4947	0	0	4947
3	106144	41218	64926	37945	21841	5139	0	0	5139
4	108797	43769	65028	36607	18662	9759	0	0	9759
5	111517	46481	65036	35453	15299	14284	0	0	14284
6	114305	49367	64938	34265	16487	14186	0	0	14186
7	117163	52434	64729	32985	17767	13977	0	0	13977

YR	ADJ PRE-TAX CASH FLOW	% CASH ON CUM EQUITY	% EQUITY CAP RATE	%OVER-ALL CAP RATE	RESALE PRICE	SELLING EXPENSE	LOAN BALANCE	EQUITY REVERSION	PRE TAX EQUITY YIELD
1	2474	1.65	1.67	4.46	725018	36251	540681	148086	0.37
2	4947	3.30	2.57	8.63	750393	37520	520128	192745	15.63
3	5139	3.43	2.15	8.36	776657	38833	498287	239537	19.21
4	9759	6.51	3.44	8.09	803840	40192	479625	284023	20.03
5	14284	9.52	4.38	7.82	831974	41599	464325	326050	19.99
6	14186	9.46	3.83	7.54	861093	43055	447838	370200	19.67
7	13977	9.32	3.35	7.26	891232	44562	430071	416599	19.23

AFTER-TAX CASH-FLOW REPORT

```
list after-tax cash flow
```

ATTORNEY°S BUILDING

```
        AFTER-TAX
  **    CASH FLOW   **
```

YR	DEPREC- IATION	TAXABLE INCOME	TAXES PAID	CASH FLOW	RECAP- TURE	TAX ON SALE	EQUITY REVERSION	EQUITY YIELD
1	12415	-22222	-11111	13585	4138	6730	141356	3.29
2	24298	1202	601	4346	11883	20768	171978	13.04
3	23257	3723	1862	3278	18587	34495	205042	15.56
4	22260	6161	3080	6679	24293	47943	236080	16.23
5	21306	8277	4138	10146	29046	61140	264910	16.28
6	20393	10280	5140	9046	32885	74114	296086	16.11
7	19519	12224	6112	7864	35851	86893	329706	15.84

```
list a/tax cash flow
```

```
        AFTER-TAX
  **    CASH FLOW   **
```

YR	NET OPERATING INCOME	LOAN INT- EREST	DEPREC- IATION	WRITE OFFS	TAXABLE INCOME	TAX ON OPERAT°NS	NET PRE-TAX CASH FLOW	NET AFTER-TAX CASH FLOW
1	32368	20074	12415	22100	-22222	-11111	2474	13585
2	64734	39234	24298	0	1202	601	4947	4346
3	64926	37945	23257	0	3723	1862	5139	3278
4	65028	36607	22260	0	6161	3080	9759	6679
5	65036	35453	21306	0	8277	4138	14284	10146
6	64938	34265	20393	0	10280	5140	14186	9046
7	64729	32985	19519	0	12224	6112	13977	7864

YR	ADJ BOOK VALUE	CAPITAL GAIN	SUBJECT TO RECAPTURE	TAX ON SALE	PRE TAX REVER- SION	AFTER TAX REVER- SION	A/TAX EQUITY YIELD (DCF)	A/TAX EQUITY YIELD (DCX)	A/TAX PAY- BACK %
1	665985	18643	4138	6730	148086	141356	3.29	3.29	9.06
2	641686	59304	11883	20768	192745	171978	13.04	12.76	11.95
3	618429	100808	18587	34495	239537	205042	15.56	15.01	14.14
4	596169	143186	24293	47943	284023	236080	16.23	15.54	18.59
5	574862	186467	29046	61140	326050	264910	16.28	15.49	25.36
6	554469	230684	32885	74114	370200	296086	16.11	15.22	31.39
7	534950	275869	35851	86893	416599	329706	15.84	14.87	256.43

ANALYSIS RATIOS REPORT

list analysis ratios

ATTORNEY°S BUILDING

** ANALYSIS **

	P R E - T A X			- - - - - - - - -		A F T E R - T A X		- - - -
		%CASH	%$+AM	%EQTY	EQUITY	%	%CASH	%$+AM	EQUITY
	OVERALL	ON CUML	ON CUML	TO	YIELD	PAY-	ON CUML	ON CUML	YIELD
YR	CAP%	EQUITY	EQUITY	VALUE	(IRR%)	BACK	EQUITY	EQUITY	(IRR%)
1	4.46	1.65.	8.20	25.43	0.37	9.06	9.06	15.60	3.29
2	8.63	3.30	17.00	30.69	15.63	11.95	2.90	16.60	13.04
3	8.36	3.43	17.99	35.84	19.21	14.14	2.19	16.75	15.56
4	8.09	6.51	18.95	40.33	20.03	18.59	4.45	16.89	16.23
5	7.82	9.52	19.72	44.19	19.99	25.36	6.76	16.96	16.28
6	7.54	9.46	20.45	47.99	19.67	31.39	6.03	17.02	16.11
7	7.26	9.32	21.16	51.74	19.23	256.43	5.24	17.09	15.84
AV	8.60	6.17	17.64	39.46	.....	.....	5.23	16.70	

RELATIVE IMPORTANCE
OF YIELD COMPONENTS

list yield analysis

RELATIVE IMPORTANCE OF

** INVESTMENT YIELD COMPONENTS **

	PRE TAX ($)	AFTER TAX ($)	AFTER REINV ($)	PRE TAX (%)	AFTER TAX (%)	AFTER REINV (%)
TOTAL YIELD.......	150000	150000	150000	19.23	15.84	14.87
CASH FLOW (YR 1-3)	8588	9129	4761	5.73	6.09	3.17
CASH FLOW.........	28365	32262	24549	18.91	21.51	16.37
REFINANCING.......	0	0	0	0.00	0.00	0.00
AMORTIZATION......	35162	43027	45647	23.44	28.68	30.43
APPRECIATION......	42678	52224	55404	28.45	34.82	36.94
ORIGINAL EQUITY...	43796	53592	56856	29.20	35.73	37.90
TAX BENEFIT.......		9592	4212		6.39	2.81
TAX ON OPERATIONS.		-9651	-7935		-6.43	-5.29
TAX ON SALE.......		-31045	-32936		-20.70	-21.96
REINVESTMENT......			4203			2.80

INVESTMENT RETURNS BEFORE DISCOUNTING	($)
CASH FLOW.........	64766
REFINANCING.......	0
AMORTIZATION......	120429
APPRECIATION......	146170
ORIGINAL EQUITY...	150000
TAX BENEFIT.......	11111
TAX ON OPERATIONS.	-20933
TAX ON SALE.......	-86893
REINVESTMENT......	11089

PROOF OF DCF RATE OF RETURN

```
list roi report
```

ATTORNEY°S BUILDING

```
    %DCF = 15.839
    %RV  =  0.000
BENEFITS= 234650
```

YR	EQUITY INVEST END OF YEAR	CASH FLOW FROM R.E.	CASH FLOW AFTER EQUITY	RESID UAL ...	CUMUL REINV START OF YR	REINV INC OME ...	TOTAL CASH GENER ATED	RET ON INV EST MENT	RET OF INV EST MENT	UNREC INV END OF YR
0	150000	0	-150000	0	0	0	-150000	0	0	150000
1	0	13585	13585	0	0	0	13585	23759	-10174	160174
2	0	4346	4346	0	0	0	4346	25370	-21024	181197
3	0	3278	3278	0	0	0	3278	28700	-25423	206620
4	0	6679	6679	0	0	0	6679	32727	-26048	232668
5	0	10146	10146	0	0	0	10146	36853	-26707	259376
6	0	9046	9046	0	0	0	9046	41083	-32037	291413
7	0	7864	7864	329706	0	0	337570	46157	291413	0

PROOF OF RETURN WITH REINVESTMENT AT 6 PERCENT

```
list roi with reinvestment at 6%
```

ATTORNEY°S BUILDING

```
    %DCF = 15.839
    %RV  =  6.000
    %DCX = 14.865
BENEFITS= 245738
```

YR	EQUITY INVEST END OF YEAR	CASH FLOW FROM R.E.	CASH FLOW AFTER EQUITY	RESID UAL ...	CUMUL REINV START OF YR	REINV INC OME ...	TOTAL CASH GENER ATED	RET ON INV EST MENT	RET OF INV EST MENT	UNREC INV END OF YR
0	150000	0	-150000	0	0	0	-150000		0	150000
1	0	13585	13585	0	0	0	13585	22298	-22298	172298
2	0	4346	4346	0	13585	815	5162	25612	-25612	197910
3	0	3278	3278	0	18747	1125	4402	29420	-29420	227329
4	0	6679	6679	0	23149	1389	8068	33793	-33793	261122
5	0	10146	10146	0	31217	1873	12019	38816	-38816	299938
6	0	9046	9046	0	43235	2594	11640	44586	-44586	344524
7	0	7864	7864	329706	54875	3293	395738	51214	344524	0

SENSITIVITY ANALYSIS BASED ON RESIDUAL

```
vary residual by -.005
```

RESIDUAL FACTOR	CASH DOWN	%CAP RATE	%ELL WOOD	%CASH ON CASH	%IRR (DCF)	%IRR (DCX)
3.0000	150000	7.51	18.20	1.65	14.87	13.97
2.5000	150000	7.77	17.13	1.65	13.88	13.05
2.0000	150000	8.04	16.04	1.65	12.87	12.12
1.5000	150000	8.33	14.92	1.65	11.82	11.16
1.0000	150000	8.62	13.76	1.65	10.74	10.19

SENSITIVITY ANALYSIS BASED
ON LOAN AMOUNT

vary loan by 10000

LOAN (1) AMOUNT	CASH DOWN	%CAP RATE	%ELL WOOD	%CASH ON CASH	%IRR (DCF)	%IRR (DCX)
535000	140000	7.26	19.80	1.42	16.47	15.45
545000	130000	7.26	20.43	1.16	17.18	16.11
555000	120000	7.26	21.13	0.85	17.98	16.85
565000	110000	7.26	21.91	0.49	18.88	17.68
575000	100000	7.26	22.79	0.06	19.91	18.65

APPRAISING FOR VARIOUS TARGET RATES
OF RETURN

appraise for dcf return of 18 %

PRICE	EQUITY	CASH%	$AM%	CAP%	ELL%	DCF%	DCX%	LV%	DV%
675177	124677	1.98	9.86	7.54	21.53	17.99	16.65	81.53	85.81

```
7 YR BENEFITS=   230687
    IRR  (DCF)=  17.994
    IRR  (OPT)=  18.824  (YR 4)
    IRR  (DCX)=  16.651
```

appraise for average cash return of 10% in years 1-7

PRICE	EQUITY	CASH%	$AM%	CAP%	ELL%	DCF%	DCX%	LV%	DV%
643023	92523	2.67	13.29	7.91	25.71	22.05	19.88	85.61	90.10

```
7 YR BENEFITS=   225655
    IRR  (DCF)=  22.055
    IRR  (DCX)=  19.883
```

appraise for ellwood yield of 20%

PRICE	EQUITY	CASH%	$AM%	CAP%	ELL%	DCF%	DCX%	LV%	DV%
691187	140687	1.76	8.74	7.36	20.00	16.56	15.47	79.65	83.82

```
7 YR BENEFITS=   233192
    IRR  (DCF)=  16.557
    IRR  (OPT)=  17.093  (YR 5)
    IRR  (DCX)=  15.466
```

READ PREVIOUSLY STORED BASE CASE AND PERFORM PROJECTIONS FOR VARIOUS TAX RATES

```
read attnybldg

    7 YR BENEFITS=   234650
        IRR  (DCF)=   15.839
        IRR  (OPT)=   16.284   (YR 5)
        IRR  (DCX)=   14.865

change ordinary tax rate to 35; do

    7 YR BENEFITS=   242974
        IRR  (DCF)=   16.076
        IRR  (OPT)=   16.411   (YR 5)
        IRR  (DCX)=   15.176

ord% is 32; do

    7 YR BENEFITS=   244639
        IRR  (DCF)=   16.122
        IRR  (OPT)=   16.436   (YR 5)
        IRR  (DCX)=   15.238

do ord% is 25

    7 YR BENEFITS=   248524
        IRR  (DCF)=   16.229
        IRR  (OPT)=   16.493   (YR 5)
        IRR  (DCX)=   15.381

do ord% is 20

    7 YR BENEFITS=   251298
        IRR  (DCF)=   16.304
        IRR  (OPT)=   16.534   (YR 5)
        IRR  (DCX)=   15.482

end
#ET=27:07.4 PT=43.6 IO=1.1
```

EIGHT

Investment in
Shopping Centers

Shopping centers represent a viable investment for certain individuals, insurance companies, real estate investment trusts, and other investors. After presenting statistical information on shopping centers, we consider methods of analysis of investment opportunities in shopping centers. Case studies are included in the chapter to enable readers to perceive which factors are important in investment analysis and which are important in determining whether a particular investment is likely to meet the investor's goals.

BACKGROUND OF
SHOPPING-CENTER INVESTMENT

The rapid post-World War II growth in suburban areas, combined with declining rates of growth in central business districts, fostered an increased interest in shopping-center properties on the part of institutional and individual investors.

The outward movement of population and incomes to the suburbs led major retail chains to alter their locational policies. A trend toward larger individual store units and the provision of extensive parking areas developed to take advantage of this outward movement. In many cases, the decision by retail chains to locate in the suburbs led to the closing of outmoded downtown outlets.

The spread of purchasing power into suburban areas was accompanied by declining employment opportunities, rising public expenditures, and rising tax rates in many downtown areas. The resulting urban fiscal crisis further limited investor interest in downtown shopping areas.

General-merchandise sales outside American cities rose by 89 percent from 1958 to 1963, compared with an increase of 54 percent from 1954 to 1958. Sales of general merchandise in the central business districts (CBDs) dropped below the sales in these stores outside the CBDs for the first time in 1958. By 1963, general-merchandise sales in the CBDs were only half the volume of sales outside the CBDs.

Although shopping-center growth slowed somewhat between 1963 and 1973, shopping centers outside CBDs continued to account for an increasing percentage of total retail sales in metropolitan areas. This shift was most pronounced in metropolitan areas with populations between 1.5 and 1.9 million.

Recession, rising construction costs, and more stringent environmental standards have all served to slow shopping-center construction since 1972. Even so, the number of shopping centers—from neighborhood centers to enclosed malls of 2 million square feet—has more than doubled in the past decade to an estimated 18,540, according to the National Research Bureau. Many experts say that shopping centers have been overbuilt because retailers and developers made some bad guesses in the late 1960s about population growth.[1]

The population gain in the United States was about 2.8 million per year in the 1950s and 2.4 million in the 1960s but only 1.7 million in the 1970s.[2] The slowing growth rate, coupled with a slowing of movement into suburban areas, has hurt developers who built shopping centers on the fringes of populated areas hoping that a market would develop around them.

A study by the National Retail Merchants Association of major department and specialty stores, mostly located in shopping centers, shows that between 1965 and 1974 sales per square foot dropped 29 percent after adjustment for inflation.[3] Overexpansion has led to higher shopping-center vacancy rates and in some instances serious financial problems for developers.

Despite possible overbuilding and despite signs through 1976 that shopping-center building is slowing, at least one source reports that 1977 and 1978 should be good years for shopping-center retailing. A survey taken by the International Council of Shopping Centers indicated that retailers as a group plan to open 26 percent more stores in 1977 and 1978 than they did in 1976. By 1978, the survey said, chains will be operating 50 percent

[1] The Wall Street Journal, Sept. 7, 1976.
[2] Anthony Downs, "Real Estate Trends and Their Implications for Property Management," Journal of Property Management, September–October 1975, p. 220.
[3] The Wall Street Journal, Sept. 7, 1976.

more stores than in 1975, a growing percentage of which will be in shopping centers. Another optimistic sign reported by the ICSC survey was that 80 percent of the more than 1,000 Grant stores had been released. The vacancies were caused when the W. T. Grant retailing chain declared bankruptcy in 1976. Some of the locations were taken over by such discount chains as K-Mart and Woolworth.[1]

While the development of shopping centers will undoubtedly continue in the future, developers may well turn their attention toward building smaller centers and centers in smaller markets. Some developers are looking at small- and medium-sized markets for future expansion.

The success of a shopping center depends partially on strong anchor tenants. Consumers who shop at the major stores often patronize the smaller stores in the center as well. The strong tenants have an important advantage in negotiating lease terms because of their importance to the development.

There is extreme competition between shopping areas. Many suburban areas are overbuilt. New centers normally take business away from existing centers. Newer centers have the benefit of modern design and construction. When overbuilding takes place, vacancies occur, particularly in the older centers. These vacancies tend to diminish the attractiveness of the entire center.

Shopping centers are still being developed in the late 1970s; those which will be successful for a significant period of time are built after careful analysis involving selection and ability to attract major anchor tenants as well as consideration of the proper mix of tenants and the optimum size of the center and the commuting distance from the market it serves. Attention must be paid to continual effective management of the center once it is developed and to the advertising efforts that will make it continue to be competitive.

Certain factors have combined in recent times to make shopping-center development less attractive. Credit grantors tend to base loans on minimum rents. As they have had unfortunate experiences, the tendency is to attempt to limit loans to those with recognized names and proved credit worthiness. The bankruptcy of major national retail chains tends also to make the credit grantors more careful, resulting in less favorable credit terms and less cash flow to investors. The continual development of new centers and resultant competition also causes tenants to be reluctant to sign long-term leases because they may wish to close an outlet and move to another center at some future time.

An important consideration in the competitive environment in the late 1970s is the amount of tax shelter available from investment shopping

[1] *The Appraiser,* January 1977.

centers. Each situation must be examined separately, but in many cases the tax shelter from depreciation on improvements in shopping centers is not as significant as that from alternative real estate investments.

An investor contemplating investing in commercial property has many alternatives besides investing in shopping centers. In fact many of the major shopping centers are owned by syndicates or real estate corporations.

Many opportunities for investors in commercial property are found in individual stores. Risk and rate of return vary greatly, depending on the type of tenant and the length of lease. Some commercial properties, leased to credit-worthy tenants or to governmental agencies, bear relatively small degrees of risk. Others, leased to marginal retailers, bear high degrees of risk. The ability for a commercial property to be a satisfactory inflation hedge is not automatic even when overages are specified in a lease. If there is extreme competition, the overages may not be realized.

ANALYSIS OF SHOPPING-CENTER INVESTMENT

Investment in a shopping center essentially represents the purchase of a group of commercial properties. There are several classifications of shopping centers, however, and the guidelines for differentiation should be clarified before analysis of shopping-center investment is begun.

Shopping centers are groups of commercial establishments planned, developed, owned, and managed as a unit and related in location, size, and type of shops to the trade area served. A shopping center provides on-site parking in definite relationship to the types and sizes of stores.

This definition eliminates from the shopping-center description miscellaneous collections of stores standing on separate lot parcels along street frontages or in a contiguous area, with or without incidental off-street parking. These are shopping areas or retail shopping districts.

Three types of shopping centers have evolved, each with a distinctive function. Neighborhood, community, and regional shopping centers are distinguished by their major tenant or tenants. Neither site nor building area determines the type of center.

The neighborhood center, which takes a supermarket as its principal tenant, provides convenience goods (foods, drugs, and sundries) and personal services (laundry, dry cleaning, barbering, and so on) for the immediate neighborhood. Neighborhood centers have an average gross leasable area of nearly 50,000 ft^2. They normally serve a trade-area population of 5,000 to 40,000 within 6 minutes' driving time.

The community center, in addition to the convenience goods and personal services of the neighborhood center, provides soft lines, e.g., wearing apparel, and hard lines, e.g., hardware and appliances. Community centers are built around a junior department store or variety store, although they also provide supermarket services. They do not have full-line department stores, although they may have strong specialty stores. The community center has an average gross leasable area of about 150,000 ft² but may range between 100,000 and 300,000 ft². A trade-area population of between 40,000 and 150,000 is normal.

The largest of the three types of shopping centers, the regional center, provides general merchandise, apparel, furniture, and home furnishings in full depth and variety. Regional centers are built around a full-line department store. For even greater depth and variety, two or more department stores are sometimes included.

Regional centers range in average gross leasable area from 300,000 to 1 million square feet or more. One-third to one-half of the total gross leasable area is usually devoted to department stores. Regional centers generally draw upon a trade-area population of 150,000 to 4 million. They provide a complete range of shopping goods in terms of both depth and variety. Because it offers complete shopping facilities, the regional center can extend its trade area by 10 to 15 miles. As the largest type of shopping center, the regional center comes closest to reproducing the shopping facilities and customer attractions once available only in central business districts.

The primary source of income for a shopping center, regardless of its size, arises from the dollar volume of sales transacted. The average annual sales per square foot of gross leasable area (GLA) offers the most significant overall measure of sales volume. Table 8-1 shows the median GLA, the median sales per square foot of GLA, and the median rent per square foot of GLA for the three different types of shopping centers.

It can be seen that median rent per square foot of GLA was generally inversely related to the median GLA for each type of store in all three types of centers. The smaller stores, e.g., jewelry, card and gift, and men's wear, all paid higher median rents per square foot of GLA than the larger department and variety stores.

Another important set of data deals with the median operating results per square foot of GLA for the various types of shopping centers. As Table 8-2 indicates, sales per square foot of GLA were comparable for the four types of centers included in the table, with neighborhood centers slightly higher. However, operating receipts per unit of GLA were significantly greater for superregional centers than for the other three types. Superregional centers also incurred somewhat higher operating costs per unit of GLA than the others. They had the highest total operating balance per square foot of GLA, followed in order by regional, neighborhood, and community centers. Regional shopping centers had the highest net income per unit of GLA, and superregional centers the largest total of funds and debt service. Thus, al-

TABLE 8-1 Space, Sales, and Rent Data for Three Types of Shopping Center

	Median GLA, ft²			Median sales volume/ft² of GLA			Median rent/ft² of GLA		
	Regional	Community	Neighborhood	Regional	Community	Neighborhood	Regional	Community	Neighborhood
Department store	122,621	30,000*	†	$ 61.41	$51.97	†	$1.44	$1.64*	†
Variety store	27,750	18,000	7,500	36.74	33.67	$41.22	2.09	1.51	$1.71
Ladies' ready-to-wear	4,005	2,940	2,000	85.76	61.83	63.05	4.83	3.68	3.75
Men's wear	3,276	3,000	†	96.66	65.55	†	5.58	3.87	†
Family shoe	3,840	3,200	†	67.75	52.37	†	4.63	3.00	†
Cards and gifts	1,959	2,000	1,800	70.97	48.90	37.29	6.38	3.71	3.92
Jewelry	2,079	1,806	†	141.21	77.93	†	7.65	4.38	†
Medical and dental	720	800	850				6.00	4.27	5.00

* Junior department store.
† No data.
Source: Urban Land Institute, Dollars and Cents of Shopping Centers, 1975, Washington, 1976, pp. 70, 122, 176.

TABLE 8-2   Median Operating Results per Square Foot of GLA for 475 Shopping Centers

	33 superregional*	109 regional*	170 community	163 neighborhood
Tenant sales	$74.83	$76.82	$76.06	$78.91
Total operating receipts	5.70	3.87	2.40	2.62
Total operating expenses	1.65	1.13	0.72	0.71
Total operating balance	3.87	2.77	1.68	1.82
Net income	1.07	1.20	0.52	0.80
Funds and debt service	1.54	1.30	0.52	0.77

* These figures apply to the mall area of superregional shopping centers. The effect of department stores has been excluded from the analysis because of the varied leasing arrangements within department stores. *Source:* Urban Land Institute, *Dollars and Cents of Shopping Centers, 1975,* Washington, 1976, p. 6.

TABLE 8-3   Median GLA, Sales, and Rent of Selected Tenants in Superregional Shopping Centers

	Median GLA, ft²	Sales volume/ft² of GLA	Total rent/ft² of GLA
Department store	180,000	$ 75.03	$1.42
Ladies' ready-to-wear	3,638	87.43	5.48
Men's wear	3,435	100.88	6.00
Ladies' specialty	1,732	87.85	6.25
Cosmetics	2,100	78.16	7.25
Family shoe	4,230	73.10	5.90

Source: Urban Land Institute, *Dollars and Cents of Shopping Centers, 1975,* Washington, 1976, p. 23.

though superregional and regional centers cost more to operate, they have the highest median operating receipts, the highest median operating balance, and the highest median net income per square foot of GLA. Median gross leasable areas, sales, and rent of selected tenants in superregional centers are presented in Table 8-3.

Space, sales, income, and expense data are valuable analytical tools for prospective shopping-center investors. Data indicating percentage changes in sales, receipts, and expenses over time also provide some indication of the potential profitability of investment in shopping centers.

TRENDS IN NEIGHBORHOOD, COMMUNITY, AND REGIONAL SHOPPING CENTERS

The Urban Land Institute in its triennial editions of the *Dollars and Cents of Shopping Centers* provides a source of information for trends in shopping centers.[1] The following section summarizes some of these significant

[1] Urban Land Institute, *Dollars and Cents of Shopping Centers,* 1975, Washington, 1976, pp. 277–279. The figures used are the median of percentage change. Information is based on shopping centers which participated in both studies.

TABLE 8-4   Shopping Centers' Percentage Change (Increase) in Operating Results 1972–1975

	Regional (sample = 36)	Community (sample = 36)	Neighborhood (sample = 26)
Sales	21.9%	26.1%	23.4%
Operating receipts	22.1	13.3	18.6
Operating expenses	14.5	10.3	19.1
Operating balance	21.8	12.0	18.9

Source: Urban Land Institute, Dollars and Cents of Shopping Centers, 1975, Washington, 1976, p. 6.

changes in the 1972 and 1975 studies. Since the information is from a representative group of shopping centers which include the influence of a wide variation of circumstances and operations, one should not use it to evaluate the performance of a specific center.

During the 3-year interval between the 1972 and the 1975 studies the consumer price index (CPI) of the Department of Labor, Bureau of Labor Statistics, increased approximately 15.4 percent. This allows a determination of the percentage of increase which merely reflects keeping up with inflation and any additional increase.

Table 8-4 summarizes percentage changes in operating results for regional, community, and neighborhood centers. A total of 98 centers provided complete information for both years. It is important to remember that these figures represent changes over 3 years and that because they are medians they do not give information on the range of results.

Regional Shopping Centers

In both studies 36 superregional and regional centers participated. The median increase in sales per square foot of GLA was 21.9 percent. When we remove the inflation element insofar as it is represented by the change in the CPI, there is a change of 6.5 percent which is not due to inflation. The typical noninflationary increase was 6.7 percent for operating receipts and 6.4 percent for the operating balance.

Separation of regional shopping centers into two groups based on age provides interesting results. Expenses increased more for centers in the group 10 years old and over (15.8 percent) than for the centers 4 to 9 years old (12.5 percent). Operating receipts increased more for units 4 to 9 years old (25.6 percent) than for those 10 years old and over (21.1 percent). Operating balances increased 19.7 percent for the newer centers and 23.9 percent for the older centers. Again it must be remembered these are median figures and do not take into account the wide variability in results of some centers. In fact the average percentage change in the operating balance of newer centers was significantly greater than the average change in centers 10 years and older. These figures indicate that some centers showed extremely large increases in operating balance but only half the centers less than 10 years old increased by more than 19.7 percent.

Community Shopping Centers

In both studies 36 of the community shopping centers provided complete information. Comparing the actual increase in Table 8.4 shows that the increase in median operating balance was 12.0 percent, which was 3.4 percent less than the change in the CPI. Operating receipts increased by 13.3 percent, which was 2.1 percent less than the CPI. This was in spite of the fact that the median or typical increase in sales per square foot was 26.1 percent, or 10.7 percent higher than the change in the CPI.

Community shopping centers were also broken down into one group 4 to 9 years old (newer group) and another group 10 years old and over (older group). Operating receipts increased for the newer group (14.1 percent) and the older group (13.2 percent), but neither kept up with inflation (15.4 percent). Median operating expenses showed a greater increase for centers 10 years old and over (12.1 percent) than the newer (5.3 percent) centers. Neither the newer centers (14.8 percent) nor the older centers (9.7 percent) kept up with inflation in respect to increase in operating balances.

Neighborhood Shopping Centers

For both studies 26 neighborhood shopping centers presented complete information. The typical increase in sales was 23.4 percent, or 8 percent better than the CPI. Receipts typically increased 18.6 percent, or 3.2 percent better than the CPI. Expenses increased 19.1 percent, or 3.7 percent more than inflation. The 18.9 percent increase in operating balance is 3.5 percent better than the CPI.

Of the centers 10 fell into the 4- to 9-year old group (newer group) and 16 fell into the group 10 years old and over. It is interesting that the newer centers showed a significantly greater increase in expenses (27.3 percent) than the older centers (6.8 percent). Operating receipts for the newer centers increased 19.5 percent compared with 13.7 percent for the older centers. The operating balance showed an increase of 15.5 percent for the newer centers compared with nearly double, or 32.1 percent, for the older centers.

VARIABLES FOR THE INDIVIDUAL CENTERS

This information covers general trends insofar as they are represented by median percentage changes. As the Urban Land Institute properly emphasizes, individual centers are impacted by different variables, and operating results will vary accordingly.

Dissimilar economic changes may take place in the area serviced by the shopping center. For example, a shopping center may be in an area of population growth or population decline. There may be significant changes in the industrial activity and employment opportunities in the area. Other possible significant economic changes may include development of commercial office buildings or research facilities or a change in the composition of the consumer group shopping at the center.

Competition is an important element, as new centers may be developed

TABLE 8-5   Report of Net Operating Income and Median Funds after Debt Service, Percent of Total Receipts

	29 superregional	95 regional	137 community	130 neighborhood
Operating receipts:				
Rental income, minimum	67.4%	72.3%	83.8%	85.1%
Average	10.6	12.9	10.5	11.2
Rent-escalation charges	2.8	1.6	2.6	3.2
Income, from common-area charges	9.9	8.1	3.4	3.7
From sale of utilities	12.5	5.3	2.0	2.0
Miscellaneous	7.0	0.7	0.5	0.7
Total operating receipts	100.0%	100.0%	100.0%	100.0%
Operating expenses:				
Building maintenance	0.7%	1.1%	2.6%	1.6%
Parking lot, mall, and other public areas	9.2	8.7	3.8	3.9
Central utility systems	7.2	4.2	2.3	1.4
Office-area services	0.4	0.8	1.0	1.8
Financing expense	34.2	29.0	30.8	31.9
Advertising and promotion	1.5	1.2	0.9	0.7
Depreciation and amortization of deferred costs	18.7	19.2	21.3	19.6
Real estate taxes	11.7	11.1	12.3	12.2
Insurance	0.6	1.2	1.8	2.0
General and administrative	4.2	5.0	5.2	4.9
Total expenses	86.2%	83.9%	85.5%	74.6%
Net operating income (loss)	13.7%	16.0%	14.4%	25.3%
Add: depreciation and amortization of deferred costs	18.7	19.2	21.3	19.6
Deduct: mortgage and other loan principal payments	8.0	11.9	15.7	13.2
Funds after debt service (net cash flow)	21.0	21.0	21.1	31.0

Source: Urban Land Institute, Dollars and Cents of Shopping Centers, 1975, Washington, 1976, pp. 20, 67, 119, 173.

in the trade area serviced by the centers. Transportation changes are important factors, as access may be improved or adversely affected, e.g. by a new limited-access freeway bypassing the shopping center.

Table 8-5 gives still greater detail of the operating receipts, operating expenses, and net operating income of the four major shopping-center classifications. Minimum rental income constituted a higher percentage of total operating receipts for neighborhood centers than for the other three types. Income from the sale of utilities, however, represented a higher percentage of total operating receipts for superregional centers than for the other types. Income from common-area charges was also more important to superregional centers than to the others.

With regard to expenses, neighborhood shopping centers paid a smaller percentage of their total receipts for parking lots, malls, and other public areas than the other three types of centers. Neighborhood centers also paid a smaller percentage of their operating receipts for central utility systems. In fact, neighborhood shopping centers paid a significantly smaller expense total, in percentage terms, than any of the other types of centers. Thus, neighborhood centers enjoyed a higher net operating income percentage and a higher percentage total of funds after debt service.

DETERMINATION OF INVESTMENT VALUE

It has often been said that the appraised value of any parcel of real estate will vary with the purpose of the appraisal, the method of valuation employed, and the personality of the appraiser. The appraiser usually tries to ascertain the *fair market value* of real estate. This represents a complex exercise in the application of skill and judgment to a wide variety of cost, market, and income data.[1]

The determination of investment value represents a special case in valuation. Investors often know the cost or market price of a property but seek to determine what the property is worth to *them* as an investment. The same property may have a different investment value for different individuals, depending upon their expectations, target yields, holding periods, and tax status.

Table 8-6, calculated with the aid of the REAL III computer program, shows the estimated values of a proposed shopping center for different investors based upon alternative target yields, holding periods, and expectations concerning future income, expenses, and resale prices. It can be seen that different individuals and institutions might have widely differing views concerning the investment value of this proposed shopping center.

[1] This section is based on Paul F. Wendt, "Real Estate Investment," chap. 30 in Leo Barnes and Stephen Feldman (eds.), *Handbook of Wealth Management*, McGraw-Hill, New York, 1977.

TABLE 8-6 Estimated Investment Values of a Proposed Shopping Center for Different Investors Based upon Alternative Target Yields and Holding Periods

Type of investor	Holding period, years	Assumed target yields, %	Estimated inventory value	
			Assumption A*	Assumption B†
Individual, 50% tax bracket	10	0.15	$2,198,220	$1,688,358
		0.12	2,367,446	1,788,546
		0.10	2,483,708	1,855,933
	20	0.15	2,321,392	1,664,011
		0.12	2,650,755	1,806,535
		0.10	2,910,538	1,913,095
Life insurance company, 30% tax bracket	10	0.15	2,305,750	1,796,775
		0.12	2,454,339	1,880,481
		0.10	2,556,101	1,936,206
	20	0.15	2,482,954	1,795,829
		0.12	2,779,290	1,914,806
		0.10	3,010,658	2,002,118

* Assumption A: cost $2 million; operating income first year, $325,000 increasing 3% annually starting year 1, 5% vacancies, operating expenses $75,000, increasing 3% annually. Building-to-land ratio 80 to 20%. Residual sale price = 6 times gross income after fourth year. Financing 75%, 9% first mortgage 25 years.

† Assumption B: change assumptions to zero growth in gross operating income, 5% increase in operating expenses. Residual sale price = 5 times gross after fourth year.

The person assumed to be in a 50 percent tax bracket and the life insurance company in a 30 percent bracket might be prepared to pay approximately $3 million for the proposed center if they both accept the assumption A forecasts. However, it can be seen that a modification of these to assumption B would imply that they would each be prepared to offer approximately $1 million, or one-third less for the property.

The market for investment real estate includes a wide variety of people and institutions with varying assumptions about the future and with differing yield objectives. It can be seen from Table 8-6 that a person accepting assumption A would be justified in offering $2,198,220 for the proposed shopping center while under the less optimistic assumption B the offer might be only $1,688,358.

Fig. 8-1 illustrates the sensitivity of cash-flow returns to changes in estimated future gross income, operating expenses, and sale prices. The rise in federal tax liabilities as the tax shelter from interest and depreciation declines gradually is also apparent under assumption A. The negative cash flows under assumption B after the fourteenth year of holding reflect the decline in net income and assumed residual sale prices. This emphasizes once again that the failure of future growth in income to meet expectations has the same adverse effect upon real estate values and yields as in growth-

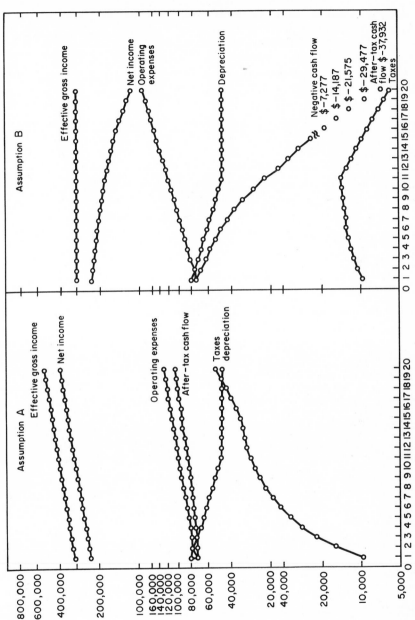

Figure 8-1 Cash-flow analysis for proposed shopping center (see Table 8-6 for assumptions A and B).

297

stock investment. Unfortunately, the problems of income forecasting are no easier for the average new real estate development project than for the "hot issue" in Wall Street. This accounts for the large yield spread between "safe" real estate investments secured by long-term leases to established tenants, with conservative loan-to-value ratios, and the high pro forma yields on new real estate development projects, with thin equities and uncertain future income and expense trends.

CASE STUDIES IN SHOPPING-CENTER DEVELOPMENT

Delineation of a trading area and forecasting of potential sales volume are important elements in planning a shopping center. An example of the problems to be met is presented using a shopping center in Monterey, California. Following this, the Canyon Shopping Center case provides actual data on a shopping center.

PLANNING AND DEVELOPMENT OF SHOPPING CENTERS

The essential element in planning a shopping center is the forecast of potential sales volume in the area under consideration. A variety of techniques can be used in developing this vital forecast. The simplest and most naïve method involves the delineation of a *trading area* for the proposed center, a forecast of population growth in that area, and the assumption that some fraction of total consumer expenditures for the area will accrue to the proposed center.

More sophisticated market-research techniques require detailed analysis of consumer shopping behavior in the area, patterns of present and planned competitive shopping facilities, and probable future changes in transportation. Freeways or throughways may increase access to a particular center. Conversely, new thoroughfares which pass the center by may have an adverse influence. Including the area in a rapid-transit district may provide a significant change in number and nature of consumers served.

Applebaum[1] outlines the market-research efforts employed before building the Del Monte Center, a shopping center in Monterey, California. He provides examples of how market research is used in planning shopping-center development and also a critical analysis of what was done in the case of the Del Monte Center.

In 1963, the city council of Monterey voted to rezone 15.2 acres of land,

---

[1] William Applebaum, *Shopping Center Strategy*, International Council of Shopping Centers, New York, 1970 (see Appendix 8A).

adding these to 32 acres already commercially zoned, to make way for the Del Monte Center. The Draper Companies were proposing to build and manage a 400,000-ft² regional shopping center on land owned by the Del Monte Properties Company. Once zoning approval was obtained, the Draper Companies began, in the spring of 1963, to examine the feasibility of the project.

Part of the examination included market analysis. A number of market studies were commissioned to delineate a trade area, to estimate sales for the center as a whole, and to estimate sales for the department store alone. Studies were also undertaken to attempt to predict population growth in the area and to identify the income levels of the consumers. Four of the research studies commissioned by the several groups interested in the development of the Del Monte Center are presented in Appendix 8A.

These four market surveys, all relating to the Del Monte Center project, contain obvious differences in the conclusions they reach about that center. Applebaum noted that reputable researchers are expected to find facts and interpret them objectively. When researchers have (presumably) the same facts at their disposal and yet arrive at very different conclusions, they must either be using widely varying methodologies or else compiling reports for greatly different purposes.

The four reports presented here all delineated the potential trade area from which the Del Monte Center could expect to draw. Reports B and C, however, delineated a much more limited area of trade than reports D and E. While reports B and C considered the Monterey Peninsula and the Carmel Valley as the potential trade area, reports D and E extended their estimates far beyond those limits. Reports D and E included Watsonville, Hollister, Bitterwater, King City, and Santa Lucia in their projected trade area. A survey of customers was made in the Del Monte Center over a 5-day period in February 1968. Of the more than 1,400 customers interviewed, only 4 percent had come to the Del Monte Center from outside the Monterey Peninsula and Carmel Valley. Thus the trade area of the center was not likely to expand beyond these limits in the future because the major retailing "magnets" were already operating in the center and because new important shopping centers were being projected for the nearby Salinas and Santa Cruz areas within 2 years.

There are discrepancies between the research reports in their estimates of sales volume for the major department store. Estimates of the projected sales volume for the entire center also varied from one report to another. For example, while reports D and C estimate approximately the same potential sales volume per square foot of shopping-center space, report C delineated a much smaller trade area for the center than report D.

There are other points of criticism regarding the Del Monte Center reports. How valid is it to apply annual national per capita expenditures to determine the spending pattern of population within a specific small geographic area?

Other problems with the research reports have to do with the researchers' methods of projecting sales and with the use of driving time to delineate the trade area. There is danger in using unadjusted sales estimates that assume a shopping center will enjoy a constant percentage of the total retail sales for a given trade area.

Interviews carried on in the home of the subject do not always yield accurate information. When people are asked at home what stores they shop in, they may well name the "prestige store" rather than the less prestigious ones they patronize. A better technique than home interviews is to interview people in the store to find out where they came from.

Buyers of research services may not receive adequate research results if they are not specific enough about what they want or not critical enough of the product they receive. The buyers should expect reports that can be studied with an open mind, not reports intended to support a previously held opinion.

Further analysis of the Del Monte Center experience was made in mid-1969 by seven experienced shopping-center developers. They met for two days in Carmel under the auspices of the International Council of Shopping Centers. The group of developers interviewed Jerome C. Draper, Jr., developer of the Del Monte Center, toured the center, visited competitive centers and retail business districts in the trade area, and visited alternative shopping-center sites. In addition, they interviewed E. P. Anderson, president of six Draper companies in which title to the center was vested at the time, and John Egan, regional vice president of R. H. Macy & Co., the key retailer in the Del Monte Center.

The group's approach to the analysis was to define a series of *decision points* at which significant alternative action had been possible. They then compared what was actually done at these points to what might have been done.

One decision point was expressed this way: Was the research adequate to permit correct decisions to be made concerning the use of the Del Monte site for a shopping center? In answering that question, the panel members noted the same discrepancies Applebaum had pointed out. They emphasized discrepancies between reports regarding sales estimates for the department store and for the whole center and regarding trade-area delineation. They pointed out that the methodology and sources of information were poorly documented, that there had been no consideration of the type and character of stores planned for the site, and that there had been no evaluation of the type of merchandising needed to achieve the projected sales results.

After analyzing the research reports and completing their tours and interviews, the panel drew some conclusions about the Del Monte Center experience. To sell as much merchandise as the surveys predicted, the members said, the developers of the Del Monte Center would have to build a downgraded center. Such a center would sell low-priced goods to lower-income customers. Actually, however, the Del Monte Center was a medium-to-high-line shopping center.

Although the research reports made sales estimates for the center, they did not specify what type of merchandise would be involved. This suggests an assumption, the panel said, that any type of store selling any kind of merchandise would have achieved the same sales volume. The panel was also critical of the reports' omission of residual purchasing power, i.e., money that could be spent in the area but is not being spent there.

Perhaps most important of all, the panel criticized the research reports for failing to be specific in their analysis of the competition the Del Monte Center had to face and how the center's location would affect that competition. The surveys were incomplete, for example, in their descriptions of what stores already existed in Carmel. One of the surveys said, without specifying the kind of department store, that there was $12 million available in purchasing power annually for a department store in the Del Monte Center. The report did not state what portion of the $12 million would be taken from sales of competitive stores and what portion would be residual. In any case, the panel noted, the survey assumed a trade area far beyond what seemed feasible.

The panel concluded that the research reports had not been adequate to permit correct decisions regarding the use of the Del Monte site for a shopping center. The research did not clearly indicate how large a center the site could support, what type of merchandise should be carried, what price-level lines should be emphasized, or how large the trade area actually was.

Determinants of Shopping Behavior

Bucklin,[1] in a study of shopping in metropolitan Oakland, concludes that spatial models based only upon center size and distance do not fully explain the vagaries and diversities of consumer purchasing behavior. He found, for example, that not all consumers perceive the values of the central business district and the suburban shopping centers in precisely the same way. Much depends upon the importance of the product to the consumer and the availability of time to search for precisely what is wanted. For higher social classes, since clothing, personal accessories, and home furnishings provided important outlets for expressing status, purchases were carefully made and the respondent was more likely to visit the central business district for this

---

[1] Louis P. Bucklin, *Shopping Patterns in an Urban Area,* University of California Institute of Business and Economic Research, Berkeley, 1967, pp. 23–27.

reason. Conversely, for other social classes and where products were relatively low-priced or of little social significance, more conveniently located centers served equally well. Such centers were also likely to be chosen when the presence of small children in the family made long trips to major downtown areas a considerable chore. In still other cases, where the value of the product was high and savings from careful purchase were substantial, the husband was likely to play a more important role in the shopping decision. If he and his wife went together, they were more likely to visit specialty shops and discount houses in outlying locations than either the downtown or the suburban centers. In sum, Bucklin found consumer spatial decisions to be far more complex than those depicted by traditional models and suggested that future models ought to include variables which represent the social and demographic determinants of shopping behavior.

EVALUATION OF SPECIFIC CENTERS

Data on a specific center are provided in the following case.[1] A potential investor would review studies of population trends in the area, purchasing power, present and probable future competition, kind, size, and type of stores, customer characteristics, and present and future transportation facilities.

The case to be considered is the Canyon Shopping Center, a neighborhood center located near a major metropolitan area in a southwestern state. The Canyon Shopping Center accommodates eight tenants, including a pharmacy, an automobile-parts store, a real estate office, and a veterinary clinic. A major chain supermarket, a major department store, and a regional shopping center are all located within 1 mile of the center but are not tenants of the center.

How would a prospective investor analyze this investment? Although the order might differ, the following considerations are typical. The financial analysis is detailed in the case itself and will not be repeated here. An inspection indicates that the center is well-designed and attractive. There appears to be a correlation between attractive centers, good merchants, and attraction of customers.

The buildings are examined to determine that the quality of construction is good. Sounder buildings are likely to require less maintenance. There appears to be no prohibitive competition in the trading area for the tenants of the center and it does not appear likely that strong competition will be forthcoming for the particular tenants of this center. The eight tenants of the shopping center appear to be helped by the chain supermarket that adjoins

---

[1] The name of the shopping center, its tenants, the buyers, sellers, and realtors, have been changed; the names appearing here are meant to be entirely fictional.

the subject property since it serves as a major attraction for convenience shoppers.

The businesses of the eight tenants are compatible. There is no duplication; two variety stores in the same center, for example, would be an unnecessary duplication. The center is located in a metropolitan suburb which appears to be a dynamic growth area. Parking in the center is ample.

Analysis of the leases is of course critical. The eight tenants pay an annual total of $51,602 in rent. Of this total, $21,661, or 41.977 percent, comes from tenants who had lease terms of 3 years at the time of the property analysis. Tenants with lease terms of 5 years paid 30.392 percent of the yearly rent. The tenants with 10-year lease terms paid 22.204 percent of the total, and tenants with 2-year lease terms paid 5.4 percent of the yearly rent. Thus, tenants with short-term leases of 2 or 3 years accounted for 47.377 percent of the Canyon center's yearly rent. Should these tenants decide not to renew their leases, $24,461 in yearly rent would be in jeopardy.

Other factors which are detailed in the body of the case are concerned with the specifics of each lease. There are provisions for overages in certain leases. The level of current rents is competitive with rents in the area. There is a good possibility of continuance of overages in those leases which specify overages. If leases do not contain restrictive clauses, that makes it difficult to effect changes in tenancy when necessary. The prospective investor has examined the sales trend of the various merchants in the center, which indicate that the merchants have stable businesses and are able to afford the prescribed rentals.

The merchants contribute to the maintenance of the common areas. Common-area electricity is prorated among all the tenants once per year. Water is included in common-area expenses. All the leases have a provision for the tenants to pay taxes over and above the base year, or first full calendar year following the start of their lease.

The case begins by presenting a property analysis for 1977, the first year, followed by projections for 1979 and 1981. Scheduled gross income and operating expenses are shown. A value is estimated by the three standard approaches. The income approach yields a value of $440,196, the cost approach $541,552, and the market-data approach $440,167. The operating income of $44,900 is adjusted to cash flow by adjusting for principal and interest payments on the loans.

As shown in the case, each item must be supported by specific data. Scheduled gross income is supported by the details of each lease. An allowance for vacancy and credit loss is made. Major items of expense such as common-area proration, taxes, insurance, utilities, advertising, and management are examined in detail.

The analysis shows the application of the three methods of valuation. Note that the depreciation of the building uses separate rates for the components of the building. Percentage allocations for different components are based on a comparison with another shopping center. The use of component depreciation often allows more depreciation in early years than the use of the total building as a base. A 10-year projection of income, expenses, cash flow, and taxable income is presented to enable investors to see the results of their investment if in fact the assumptions of the projections are realized. A prospective investor may consider alternative assumptions and determine the results.

Canyon Shopping Center

This center is located in a metropolitan suburb in a southwestern state. The neighborhood is upper middle class. A department store is located ¾ mile to the west of subject property, together with regional shopping facilities. A chain supermarket adjoins the subject immediately on the west and serves as a major attraction for convenience shoppers. The center has the stability of good local tenants—pharmacy, dentist, veterinarian, auto supply, etc., *plus* a dynamic growth area. The growth in rent and cash flow is built into the leases, but the market itself is demanding higher rates than almost all tenants are now paying, giving the center protection against vacancies.

List price

Equity cash..................................$100,000
Vendor's lien note........................ 66,000
First mortgage 274,247
Total price.............................$440,247

Projections of income for 1977, 1979, and 1981 appear in Figs. 8-2, 8-3, and 8-4. The determination of the numbers is explained in Notes to Property Analysis, which follows.

Notes to Property Analysis
SCHEDULED GROSS INCOME

Tenant	Area, ft²	Lease term, yr	Expiration date	Options	Annual total	Rent/ft²
1. Arthur Real Estate	700	5	10/78	None	$ 2,175	$3.11
2. Canyon Pharmacy	3,508	5	11/77	2 5-yr	9,823	2.80
3. O'Reilly Veterinary Clinic	1,808	10	12/83	None	6,418	3.55
4. Cost Mart Carpet	4,496	3	10/77	1 3-yr	15,061	3.35
5. Davis and Associates	700	2	9/76	2 2-yr	2,800	4.00
6. John Fosdick, D.D.S.	1,100	5	8/78	1 5-yr	3,685	3.35
7. Harton-Boswell Cleaners	1,200	10	12/82	None	5,040	4.20
8. Jeff's Auto Stores	1,750	3	9/78	None	6,600	3.77
	15,334				$51,602	

Annual Property Operating Data

1977 projection

Purpose __Evaluation__

Name __Canyon Shopping Center ·__

Location ____

Type of Property __Retail Center__

Assessed/Appraised Values xx Ratios of county:

Land	$ 70,439	16.0 %
Improvement	$ 369,808	84.0 %
Personal Property	$	%
Total	$ 440,247	100 %

Adjusted Basis as of ____ $ ____

Date __4/26/76__

Price	$	440,247
Loans	$	340,247
Equity	$	100,000

FINANCING

	Balance	Payment	Period	Interest	Term
Existing	$274,247	29,298		9.25 %	
1st	$			%	
2nd	$			%	
3rd	$			%	
Potential					
1st	$ Vendor's lien due and payable in 2 yr			%	
2nd	$ 66,000	5,610		8.50 %	

		%	2	3	Comments
1	GROSS SCHEDULED RENTAL INCOME	100		51 811	includes increases
2	Plus: Other Income			1 878	common area pro rate
3	TOTAL GROSS INCOME			53 689	
4	Less: Vacancy and Credit Losses	2		1 036	
5	GROSS OPERATING INCOME			52 652	
6	Less: Operating Expenses				
7	Accounting and Legal				
8	Advertising, Licenses and Permits				
9	Property Insurance		620		1975 actual
10	Property Management		1 616		
11	Payroll - Resident Management				
12	Other				
13	Taxes-Workmen's Compensation				
14	Personal Property Taxes				
15	Real Estate Taxes		3 984		base year only
16	Repairs and Maintenance				
17	Services - Elevator				
18	Janitorial				
19	Lawn				
20	Pool				
21	Rubbish				
22	Other		766		5¢/ft^2/yr roof
23	Supplies				
24	Utilities - Electricity				
25	Gas and Oil				
26	Sewer and Water				
27	Telephone				
28	Other				
29	Miscellaneous				
30	Common area expenses		766		estimate
31	TOTAL OPERATING EXPENSES			7 752	
32	NET OPERATING INCOME			44 900	
33	Less: Total Annual Debt Service			34 908	
34	CASH FLOW BEFORE TAXES			9 992	

Figure 8-2 Property analysis: 1977 projection (first year).

Annual Property Operating Data

1979 projection

Purpose __Evaluation__

Name __Canyon Shopping Center__

Location _____

Type of Property __Retail Shopping Center__

Date ____4/26/76____

Price $____440,247____

Loans $____274,247____

Equity $____166,000____

Assessed/Appraised Values Ratios of county:

Land	$ __70,439__	__16.0__ %
Improvement	$ __369,808__	__84.0__ %
Personal Property	$_____	____%
Total	$ __440,247__	__100__ %

Adjusted Basis as of _____ $_____

FINANCING

	Balance	Payment	Period	Interest	Term
Existing	$274,247	29,298		9.25 %	
1st	$(Balance at	closing	June 1976)	%	
2nd	$			%	
3rd	$			%	

Potential

1st $ Vendor's lien note to be paid %

2nd $ off June 30, 1978 %

		%	2	3		Comments
1	GROSS SCHEDULED RENTAL INCOME	100		56	602	
2	Plus: Other Income			1	878	
3	TOTAL GROSS INCOME			58	480	
4	Less: Vacancy and Credit Losses	2		1	132	
5	GROSS OPERATING INCOME			57	348	
6	Less: Operating Expenses					
7	Accounting and Legal					
8	Advertising, Licenses and Permits					
9	Property Insurance		717			1975 + 5%/yr per
10	Property Management		2 320			contract
11	Payroll - Resident Management					
12	Other					
13	Taxes-Workmen's Compensation					
14	Personal Property Taxes					
15	Real Estate Taxes		3 984			base year only
16	Repairs and Maintenance					
17	Services - Elevator					
18	Janitorial					
19	Lawn					
20	Pool					
21	Rubbish					
22	Other		886			1977 est. + 5%/yr
23	Supplies					
24	Utilities - Electricity					
25	Gas and Oil					
26	Sewer and Water					
27	Telephone					
28	Other					
29	Miscellaneous					
30	Common area expenses		866			1977 est. + 5%/yr
31	TOTAL OPERATING EXPENSES 57¢/ft^2			8	793	
32	NET OPERATING INCOME			48	555	
33	Less: Total Annual Debt Service			29	298	
34	CASH FLOW BEFORE TAXES			19	257	

Prepared by_____

Figure 8-3 Property analysis: 1979 projection.

Annual Property Operating Data

1981 projection

Purpose __Evaluation__

Name __Canyon Shopping Center__

Location ____

Type of Property __Retail Shopping Center__

Date __2/26/76__

Price $__440,247__

Loans $__274,247__

Equity $__100,000__

Assessed/Appraised Values

Land	$ 70,439	16.0 %
Improvement	$369,808	84.0 %
Personal Property	$	%
Total	$440,247	100 %

Adjusted Basis as of _____ $ ____

FINANCING

	Balance	Payment	Period	Interest	Term
Existing	$ 274,247	29,298		9.25%	
1st	$			%	
2nd	$			%	
3rd	$			%	
Potential					
1st	$ Vendor's lien note to be paid			%	
2nd	$ off June 30, 1978			%	

		%	2	3	Comments
1	GROSS SCHEDULED RENTAL INCOME	100		63 252	
2	Plus: Other Income			1 878	
3	TOTAL GROSS INCOME			65 130	
4	Less: Vacancy and Credit Losses	2		1 265	
5	GROSS OPERATING INCOME			63 865	
6	Less: Operating Expenses				
7	Accounting and Legal				
8	Advertising, Licenses and Permits				
9	Property Insurance		791		
10	Property Management	3	099		per contract
11	Payroll - Resident Management				
12	Other				
13	Taxes-Workmen's Compensation				
14	Personal Property Taxes				
15	Real Estate Taxes	3	984		
16	Repairs and Maintenance				
17	Services - Elevator				
18	Janitorial				
19	Lawn				
20	Pool				
21	Rubbish				
22	Other				
23	Supplies		977		
24	Utilities - Electricity				
25	Gas and Oil				
26	Sewer and Water				
27	Telephone				
28	Other				
29	Miscellaneous				
30	Common area expenses		977		1976 est. + 5%/yr
31	TOTAL OPERATING EXPENSES 64¢/ft^2			9 828	
32	NET OPERATING INCOME			54 037	
33	Less: Total Annual Debt Service			29 298	
34	CASH FLOW BEFORE TAXES			24 739	

The statements and figures presented herein, while not guaranteed, are secured from sources we believe authoritative.

Prepared by____

Figure 8-4 Property analysis: 1981 projection.

Projected Increases and Terms

1. *Arthur Real Estate.* Upon expiration of this lease, the market for this space is expected to increase to $5 per square foot on November 1, 1978.

Increase	Dollars per year
1978 income for 2 months	$ 583
1979–1981	1,325

2. *Canyon Pharmacy.* This is a 5-year lease with a 3 percent percentage rent until November 1, 1977. The guaranteed rate can only be increased 110 percent for each 5-year renewal period. No allowance is given for percentage rent.

Increase	Dollars per year
1977 income for 2 months, 110%	$163
1978–1981	982

3. *O'Reilly Veterinary Clinic.* This lease graduates each year over the first 5 years and then remains constant for 5 years. Current year (November 1, 1975 to November 1, 1976) rate is $3.55 per year, increases to $3.71 per square foot on November 1, 1976, then to $3.87 per square foot on November 1, 1977, then to $4.05 for the remaining 5 years of the lease.

Increase	Dollars per year
1976, 2 months	$ 48
1977	632
1978	904
1979–1981	904

4. *Cost Mart Carpet.* On October 1, 1977, this lease increases to $15,816, or $3.52 per square foot, at option of tenant, for an additional 3-year term. After October 1, 1980, the market for this space should be no less than $4.50 per square foot for such a large space.

Increase	Dollars per year
1977, 3 months	$ 188
1978–1980	755
1981	5,171

5. *Davis & Associates.* The current lease at $4 per square foot expires September 1, 1976, and the tenant has an option to renew at a rate which increases proportionately to the cost-of-living index. The new rate applies to the renewal period of 3 years. The second renewal will be increased by the same method. Assume a 10 percent increase in the index for September 1976 over September 1973.

Increase	Dollars per year
1976, 4 months	$ 93
1977 and 1978	280
1979	406
1980–1981	588

6. *John Fosdick, D.D.S.* This lease graduates each year in its rate over the primary 5-year term. The current rate for the year (August 1, 1975 to July 31, 1976) is $3.35 per square foot, or $3,685 per year. This rate increases to $3.50 on August 1, 1976, and $3.66 on August 1, 1977; then the tenant has an option to renew for 5 years (August 1, 1978 to July 31, 1983) at $3.83.

Increase	Dollars per year
1976, 5 months	$ 68
1977	238
1978	418
1979–1981	528

7. *Harton-Boswell Cleaners.* This is a 10-year lease at a low rate of $4.20 per square foot. Since the lease does not expire until December 31, 1982, no increase is projected herein, even though the lease provides for percentage rent at 5 percent of sales less the guaranteed rent.

8. *Jeff's Auto Parts.* This is a 3-year lease which terminates on September 30, 1978. At that time, a market rate for the space should be $5 per square foot at the expiration of the present lease.

Increase	Dollars per year
1978, 3 months	$ 538
1978–1981	2,152

Summary of Schedule Gross Income

Year	Schedule	Plus increases	Total
1976	$51,602	$ 209	$51,811
1977	51,602	1,501	53,103
1978	51,602	4,460	56,602
1979	51,602	7,052	58,645
1980	51,602	7,234	58,836
1981	51,602	11,650	63,252

VACANCY AND CREDIT LOSS: Although the center has no vacancy or credit loss, it is good business practice to include a 2 percent reserve for such losses for the future.

COMMON AREA PRORATION: The expenses for the maintenance and upkeep of the common area (common area expenses) are paid by the tenants on a pro rata basis up to a limit of 15 cents per square foot. The total prorations currently total approximately 12 cents per square foot. The current prorations by tenants are as follows:

Monthly charge

Arthur Real Estate ....$	6.25
Canyon Pharmacy...	29.23
O'Reilly Veterinary Clinic..	15.67
Cost Mart Carpet	56.20
Davis & Associates...	6.00
John Fosdick, D.D. S..	9.17
Harton-Boswell Cleaners..	12.00
Jeff's Auto Stores	22.00
Total monthly common-area maintenance.........................$	156.52
Annual common-area maintenance $1,878.24	

No increase in common-area maintenance prorations are expected during first 5 years.

TAXES: All the leases have a provision for the tenants to pay taxes over and above the base year, or first full calendar year following the start of their lease. Therefore, the landlord's effective property tax expense is $3,984.

INSURANCE: Actual insurance costs for 1976 are used, but increases of 5 percent per year are used for the projections.

UTILITIES: The tenants pay their own utilities expenses. Common-area electricity is prorated among all the tenants once per year. Water is included in common-area expenses.

ADVERTISING: No advertising expense is anticipated for the center.

MANAGEMENT: This is set up according to a contract to be executed at closing between the landlord (or purchaser) and R. J. Harris Management, Inc., whereby all off-site management will be provided for the center (collecting and depositing rents, renegotiating existing leases, disbursing checks for all expenses, negotiating new leases, disbursing mortgage payments, rendering quarterly statements of income and expenses, disbursing quarterly checks to landlord of cash flow from operations, and arranging maintenance contracts as needed). The fee will be based upon 3 percent of all collected rental income (excluding common-area prorations or tax prorations) up to $50,000 per year, then 15 percent of all amounts collected above $50,000 per year up to a limit of 5 percent of collected income.

SUPPLIES, SERVICES, AND MAINTENANCE: These expenses apply to the roof and structure only since the tenants maintain their own premises and the common-area expense is prorated among the tenants. The reserve for the roof and structure is estimated to be 5 cents per square foot, or $766, a current guideline for such expenses in the industry. An increase of 5 percent per year from the current expense is projected for future years.

Common-Area Expenses: These expenses are prorated among the tenants. Current charges to tenants of $1,878 per year exceeds estimated expenses. A limit to tenants' proration is 15 cents per square foot, or $2,300. On a current basis, these expenses are expected to be 5 cents per square foot, or $766 per year. These expenses cover water for two restrooms (semiprivate), mopping a hall twice per month, weekly sweeping of parking lot. Projections of 5 percent per year increases are utilized for future years.

Estimates of income have been projected for the years 1977, 1979, and 1981 in Figs. 8-2, 8-3, and 8-4. This income becomes the basic information which is used to project estimated market values using alternative valuation approaches. The results are shown in Tables 8-7, 8-8, and 8-9. The procedure is explained under Computation of Capitalization Rate, which follows.

TABLE 8-7   Canyon Shopping Center, 1977 Projection

Estimated market value		
Income approach:		
Capitalized at rate of 10.21%		$440,196
Cost approach:		
15,334 ft² at $25	$383,350	
Less: accumulated depreciation,		
3 yr at 1%-3%	12,719	
Depreciated value of improvements	$370,631	
Plus: site improvements	0	
Plus: land, 56,973.75 ft² at $3	170,921	
Estimate of market value by cost approach		$541,552
Market-data approach:		
10% yield/equity of $99,920 (cash flow of $9,920 capitalized at 10%); equity of $99,920 + mortgage of $340,247 = $440,167		$440,167

Income adusted to financing		
Income before interest		$ 44,900
Loan payments		
First loan:		
Interest	$ 25,197	
Principal	4,101	$ 29,298
Second loan (principal)		5,610	34,908
Cash flow		$ 9,992
Plus: principal payment (10-yr average)		4,101
		$ 14,093
Depreciation		20,302
		$ (6,209)

TABLE 8-8 Canyon Shopping Center, 1979 Projection

Estimated market value		
Income approach $48,555 income:		
Capitalized at rate of 10.21%		$476,019
Cost approach:		
15,334 ft² at $25	$383,350	
Less: accumulated depreciation	12,719	
Depreciated value of improvements	$370,631	
Plus: site improvements	0	
Plus: land	170,921	
Estimate of market value by cost approach		$541,552
Market-data approach 10% yield based on cash flow of $19,256 gives equity of $192,560 + mortgage		$466,807

Income adjusted to financing 1979 projection		
Income before interest		$ 48,555
Loan payments:		
First loan:		
Interest	$ 24,368	
Principal	4,930	29,298
Cash flow		$19,257
Plus: principal payment (10-yr average)		4,930
		$ 24,187
Depreciation		−20,302
		$ 3,887

COMPUTATION OF CAPITALIZATION RATE: The income stream represented by the net operating income is capitalized by a rate to determine the value of the property based on the income approach. Capitalization rates must require a return *on* and a return *of* the total investment in the property. The building investment is represented by the mortgage portion of the total investment, or 75 percent. The equity portion (25 percent) of the investment represents the land which requires only a return *on* that portion of the investment, since there is no need to recapture the land investment. The building requires both a recapture rate and an interest rate which is adequately represented by the mortgage constant (ratio of debt service to debt). Since the building was financed with a 9¼ percent loan, $285,000 original loan over 25 years, the annual mortgage constant of 0.1028 is used.

The required return on equity in the current market is 9.5 to 10.0 percent for comparable properties; therefore, we use 10 percent as the required rate for the equity.

TABLE 8-9 Canyon Shopping Center, 1981 Projection

Estimated market value		
Income approach $54,037 income:		
Capitalized at rate of 10.21%		$529,255
Cost approach:		
15,334 ft² at $25	$383,350	
Less: accumulated depreciation	12,719	
Depreciated value of improvements	$370,631	
Plus: site improvements	0	
Plus: land	170,921	
Estimate of market value by cost approach		$541,552
Market-data approach		$521,637

Income adjusted to financing		
Income before interest		$ 54,037
Loan payments:		
First loan:		
Interest	$ 23,370	
Principal	5,928	29,298
Cash flow		$ 24,739
Plus: principal payment (10-yr average)		5,928
		$ 30,667
Depreciation		20,302
		$ 10,365

Source of investment	Portion, %	Required return	Weighted average
Mortgage (building)	75	0.1028	0.0771
Equity (land)	25	0.10	0.0250
Capitalization rate			0.1021

THE COST APPROACH: The value of a property is generally limited to its replacement cost. Based on costs of $25 per square foot for the building, $3 per square foot for the land, less a nominal amount of accumulated depreciation, the replacement cost of the center is estimated to be $541,560.

THE MARKET APPROACH: The broker's approach is utilized. Accepting the market condition that a maximum of 10 percent is required on equity, the cash flow is capitalized at 10 percent to give an equity value to the center of $99,920. To this must be added the mortgage being serviced; the first year the mortgages are $340,247, to give a total value of $440,167.

CORRELATION OF MARKET VALUE: According to the income approach and the market approach, the estimated market value the first year supports the list price of $440,247. This market value is expected to increase in future years as the net operating income increases with rent increases. Estimated market value for future years is:

TABLE 8-10 10-Year Projection of Income, Expenses, Cash Flow, and Taxable Income

Year (ending June 30)	Rental income at 98%[a] (1)	Common-area maintenance prorations[b] (2)	Total gross income (3)	Less expenses[c] (4)	Net operating income (5)	Less debt service[d] (6)	Cash flow (7)	Cash return on equity invested, % (8)	Principal reduction[e] (9)
1977	$50,744	$1,878	$52,652	$ 7,752	$44,900	$34,904	$ 9,992	9.92%	$4,101
1978	52,040	1,878	53,918	8,272	45,646	34,908	10,738	10.73	4,496
1979	55,476	1,878	57,348	8,793	48,555	29,298[f]	19,257	11.60[f]	4,930
1980	57,480	1,878	59,358	9,310	50,048	29,298	20,750	12.50	5,406
1981	61,987	1,878	63,865	9,828	54,037	29,298	24,739	14.90	5,928
1982	64,733	2,300	67,033	10,354	56,679	29,298	27,881	16.49	6,500
1983	67,602	2,300	69,902	10,908	58,994	29,298	29,696	17.89	7,128
1984	70,597	2,300	72,897	11,493	61,404	29,298	32,106	19.34	7,815
1985	73,726	2,300	76,026	12,108	63,918	29,298	34,620	20.86	8,572
1986	76,993	2,300	79,293	12,757	66,536	29,298	37,238	22.43	9,398

Year (ending June 30)	Gross equity income[g] (10)	Total return on equity invested, % (11)	Less depreciation (12)	Taxable income (loss) (13)	Estimated resale value[h] (14)	Less mortgage balance[e] (15)	Estimated equity value (16)	Equity profit on resale[i] (17)	Profit on resale to equity investment, % (18)
1977	$14,903	14.09%	$20,302	$−6,209	$439,764	$270,145	$169,619	$ 3,619	3.62%
1978	15,234	15.23	20,302	−5,608	447,071	265,428	181,643	15,643	9.40
1979	24,187	14.57	20,302	3,885	475,563	260,717	214,846	48,846	29.40
1980	26,156	15.76	20,302	5,854	490,186	255,310	234,876	68,876	41.49
1981	30,667	18.47	20,302	10,365	529,255	249,215	280,040	114,040	68.70
1982	33,881	20.41	20,302	13,579	555,132	242,880	312,252	146,252	88.10
1983	36,824	22.18	20,302	16,522	577,806	235,751	342,055	176,055	106.06
1984	39,921	24.05	20,302	19,619	601,410	227,935	373,475	207,475	124.99
1985	43,192	26.06	20,302	22,890	626,033	219,363	406,670	240,670	144.98
1986	46,636	28.09	20,302	26,334	651,674	209,963	441,711	275,711	166.09

[a] Rental income is estimated to be 98 percent of scheduled gross income to make allowance for vacancy and credit losses, if any. For increases in tenant rates for the first 5 years, refer to Notes to Property Analysis. After 5 years, an annual increase of 4.43 percent per year in rental income is assumed, which is the average estimate for the first 5 years.

[b] Common-area (CAM) prorations are estimated to be constant at 12 cents per leasable square foot for the first 5 years, then increased to 15 cents per square foot, or $2,300 per year.

[c] See the property analysis (Figs. 8-2 to 8-4) for the expenses for 1977, 1979, and 1981. Those expenses were used for the first, third, and fifth years. The second and third were interpolated. Years 6 to 10 were increased at the rate of 5.36 percent, the average 5-year increase for years 1 to 5.

[d] Debt service for the first two years is $5,610 more than the last 8 years because of the interest on a $66,000 vendor's lien note paid at the end of the first and second year. The vendor's lien is to be paid off by additional equity contribution at the end of 2 years.

[e] Principal reduction is the amount of reduction in the first mortgage only which is paid from the total gross income; therefore, it is taxable to the extent that such debt reduction and cash flow exceeds depreciation.

Balance
Beginning balance (rounded) = $274,247

Date (June 30)	Amount	Debt reduction	Date (June 30)	Amount	Debt reduction
1977	$270,145	$4,101	1982	$242,880	$6,500
1978	265,648	4,496	1983	235,751	7,128
1979	260,717	4,930	1984	227,935	7,815
1980	255,310	5,406	1985	219,363	8,572
1981	249,381	5,928	1986	209,965	9,398

[f] Additional equity contribution of $66,000 is made; see note d.

[g] Depreciation: For detail, see Notes to Property Analysis.

[h] Resale value; the income approach is used where the net operating income (column 5) is capitalized by 10.21 percent. Rate is explained under Notes to Property Analysis.

[i] Equity profit on resale: the total equity cost of $166,000 is used in calculating the profit on a resale at any given time throughout the 10-year period.

Year	1976	1979	1981
Value (rounded)	$440,000	$476,000	$529,000

PRINCIPAL REDUCTION: This is the amount of reduction in the first mortgage during the expected 10-year holding period. Since the mortgage is reduced from approximately $274,247 at closing to $209,965 in 10 years, or $64,281, the average debt reduction per year is $6,428. The amounts shown are calculated by computer (see assumptions to 10-year projection in Table 8-7, column 9).

GROSS EQUITY INCOME: This is the total of the cash flow and principal reduction.

DEPRECIATION: The cost of the building is divided into components of the building and the land. Amounts used for the land is the pro rata amount used by the taxing authorities of the county where the center is located in evaluating values for property taxes:

	Tax evaluation	Percent of total
Building	$103,580	84.0%
Land	9,400	16.0

The land value for tax purposes will be 16 percent of the total cost of the property ($440,247) to the purchaser. The building as a whole represents the balance, or $369,808. Building components are compared percentagewise to the known cost of a comparable property.

Western Shopping Center (in a Nearby Southwestern City)

Component	Cost	%	Economic allocation of dollars Life, yr	Canyon	Depreciation
Building shell	$364,170	74.6%	25	$275,876	$11,035
Electrical system	26,650	5.5	15	20,339	1,355
Roof	37,681	7.7	10	28,475	2,847
Plumbing system	25,772	5.3	10	19,600	1,960
Paving	24,356	5.0	10	18,490	1,849
Heating and air conditioning	2,587	0.5	10	1,849	185
Floor covering	4,197	0.9	5	3,328	665
Carpets	1,464	0.3	3	1,109	369
Interiors	1,220	0.2	2	742	37
	$488,097	100		$369,808	$20,302

A ten-year projection of important financial statistics relating to the Canyon Shopping Center is given in Table 8-10.

SUMMARY

The post-World War II boom in shopping-center construction has slowed. Nevertheless, shopping centers remain an important investment alternative for individuals, insurance companies, real estate investment trusts, and other investors. Shopping centers outside CBDs continue to account for an increasing percentage of total retail sales in metropolitan areas.

Of obvious importance to investors is the size of the shopping center in which they consider investment. Comparative data have been included in the chapter to enable investors to perceive what different sizes of shopping centers have to offer by way of investment possibilities. Regional shopping centers have recently experienced the largest increase in operating balance of all three types of centers. On the other hand, neighborhood centers have recently enjoyed the highest net operating income percentage and the highest percentage of total funds after debt service.

Of critical importance to shopping-center investors is the trade area for the center. The case of the Del Monte Center illustrates the difficulty of delineating a trade area and of using market research to arrive at conclusions about population growth, potential competition, and sales projections. Nevertheless, these factors must be considered.

The Canyon Shopping Center case illustrates the factors which are important in investment analysis.

Rates of return on shopping-center properties vary widely according to the financing terms under which properties are held. Here, as in real estate investment generally, the degree of leverage and the associated tax shelter are important determinants of the investor's rate of return.

Appendix 8A: Del Monte Shopping Center[1]
Research Report B

Research Report B, prepared in 1957 for the Del Monte Properties Company, was made available to The Draper Companies when the latter was invited by the former to take over the development of the Del Monte Shopping Center.

The report estimated, for the proposed shopping center, potential sales of $14.8 and $16.8 million for 1959 and 1961 respectively. The following methodology was used and data developed.

The trade area was determined on the basis of driving time. The report stated,

> Experience has shown that the average customer will not hesitate to drive to any given shopping location, provided that driving time does not exceed a fifteen-minute period. . . . Executives of the research company drove from the site on all major roads in

[1] Appendix 8A is reproduced from William Applebaum, *Shopping Center Strategy*, International Council of Shopping Centers, New York, 1970. The copyright is held by the President and Fellows of Harvard College; publication herein is by express permission.

order to determine the distances that could be traveled in 5, 10 and 15 minutes, at normal speeds. The distances were rechecked during light and heavy traffic.

The trade area was divided "into five logical" segments, according to the characteristics of each area and its geographical position with respect to the proposed Del Monte Shopping Center. The potential shopper traffic to the proposed shopping center, from the five districts, was expected to vary, depending on the district's distance from the center, the availability of other retail facilities, and the over-all appeal of the new shopping center. . . .

The report analyzed the size, growth and quality of the trade area. "Because a shopping center appeals to all members of the family through extensive merchandise assortments, the family unit was used rather than number of people." Trade area growth was shown "by means of the long-term and short-term population growth" (see Exhibit 10).

The quality of the trade area was "analyzed in terms of total after-tax income, the family after-tax income, and the estimated purchases of retail goods and services." The report "estimated that 54 percent of total after-tax income is spent on the general category of retail goods and services, including food, purchased meals, alcoholic beverages, tobacco, clothing, shoes, accessories, household appliances, and miscellaneous personal services" (see Exhibit 11).

The report stated (without any further explanation) that "a detailed analysis was made of the spending habits of the residents" in the trade area, and the following factors "were carefully weighed":

1. Where the people now shop and their evaluation of the existing facilities
2. The ease of travel to existing shopping areas
3. The specific need for a large, one-stop shopping center within the trade area
4. The road network within the area

EXHIBIT 10   Del Monte Shopping Center, Trade-Area Size and Growth of Proposed Shopping Center*

| Trade area district | Size, families | | Growth, % | | | |
| | | | Long-term | | Short-term | |
	1959	1961	1940–1959	1940–1961	1950–1959	1950–1961
I	6,850	7,200	140	154	59	69
II	6,450	6,600	159	174	55	64
III	950	1,000	146	154	54	58
IV	4,000	4,200	238	256	79	88
V	8,100	8,850	806	898	98	118
Total	26,350	27,850	243	267	72	84
Comparative growth in:						
Monterey County			168	190	50	62
State of California			126	146	47	61
United States			35	40	18	22

* The report gave no information on the sources of data and methods used in projecting size and growth to 1959 and 1961.

EXHIBIT 11 Del Monte Shopping Center, After-Tax Income and Family Expenditures for Shopping-Center Goods

Trade area district	1959			1961		
	Total (millions)	Per family	Expenditures for shopping-center goods (millions)	Total (millions)	Per family	Expenditures for shopping-center goods (millions)
I	$ 49.7	$ 7,250	$ 26.8	$ 55.8	$ 7,750	$ 30.1
II	44.2	6,850	23.9	48.8	7,400	26.4
III	13.2	13,900	7.1	15.9	15,900	8.6
IV	37.4	9,350	20.2	41.8	9,950	22.6
V	44.6	5,500	24.1	53.5	6,050	28.9
Total	$189.1	$ 7,200	$102.1	$215.8	$ 7,750	$116.6

EXHIBIT 12 Del Monte Shopping Center, Percent of Department Store Type Expenditures

Where did you spend your money for department store type goods during the past year?

	District, %					Total all districts, %
	I	II	III	IV	V	
Monterey	48	31	17	17	38	33
Pacific Grove	22	43	33	18	10	24
Carmel	4	3	18	40	2	11
Seaside	3	1	2	—	17	6
Salinas	11	11	4	4	24	12
San Francisco	7	5	19	12	1	7
Other locations outside trade area	3	4	7	8	2	4
Post exchange	2	2	—	1	6	3
	100	100	100	100	100	100

5. The location of each spending unit in relation to existing retail facilities and the proposed shopping center.

A questionnaire survey was conducted in the trade area, but the report gave no information regarding how many families were questioned, when and how. Five questions were asked and all the answers were tabulated in percentage figures only (see Exhibits 12 through 15).[1] The text explanations merely restated the obvious.

The report presented (Exhibit 16) the figures used in making the estimates of potential sales for the proposed shopping center, without any precise

[1] Additional questions were asked but findings were not included in report B. The researcher who prepared report B informed the author in January 1970 that the report recommended a shopping center of 246,980 square feet at the proposed site.

EXHIBIT 13 Del Monte Shopping Center, Shoppers' Attitudes toward Shopping Center

Do you feel there is a need for a modern one-stop shopping center in this area?

	District, %					Total all districts, %	Civilian, %	Military, %
	I	II	III	IV	V			
Definitely needed	50	42	59	31	67	50	48	56
Nice to have	30	28	27	27	21	24	25	29
Not needed	20	30	14	42	12	26	27	15
	100	100	100	100	100	100	100	100

EXHIBIT 14 Del Monte Shopping Center, Customer Charge Accounts

a. *Do you have a charge account?*
b. *If yes, in what stores do you have a charge account?*

	Percent of respondents by weekly income				
a. Have a charge account	Under $60	$60–$100	$100–$120	$120 and over	Total
Yes	43	52	61	72	60
No	57	48	39	28	40
	100	100	100	100	100

	Percent of respondents having a charge account by weekly income				
b. Have a charge account with:	Under $60	$60–$100	$100–$120	$120 and over	Total
Holman's	30	33	44	66	49
Sears, Roebuck	23	39	30	15	26
I. Magnin	2	3	4	23	10
Montgomery Ward	18	20	7	5	10
City of Paris		1	6	12	7
White House		1	4	15	7
Emporium		4	7	8	6
Macy's	3	1	3	10	5

EXHIBIT 15 Del Monte Shopping Center, Advertising Information

What newspapers do you read regularly?

Read daily papers, %		Read Sunday papers, %	
Monterey Peninsula Herald	91	San Francisco Examiner	29
San Francisco Examiner	11	San Francisco Chronicle	17
San Francisco Chronicle	9	All other newspapers	8
All other newspapers	9	No paper	50
No paper	6		

EXHIBIT 16   Del Monte Shopping Center, Estimated Potential Sales
of the Proposed Shopping Center

Trade-area district	1959			1961		
	Expenditures for shopping-center goods (millions)	Share to proposed shopping center, %	Sales at proposed shopping center (millions)	Expenditures for shopping-center goods (millions)	Share to proposed shopping center, %	Sales at proposed shopping center (millions)
I	$ 26.8	24.6	$ 6.6	$ 30.1	24.8	$ 7.5
II	23.9	7.4	1.8	26.4	7.3	1.9
III	7.1	21.1	1.5	8.6	21.0	1.8
IV	20.2	13.3	2.7	22.6	13.3	3.0
V	24.1	9.1	2.2	28.9	9.0	2.6
Total	$102.1	14.5	$14.8	$116.6	14.5	$16.8

explanation as to how the figures in the column "Share to proposed shopping center" were developed.

RESEARCH REPORT C

During 1961, consultants to the Monterey Peninsula Area Planning Commission submitted a detailed analysis of the Monterey Peninsula for use by the Planning Commission in preparing their future urban redevelopment program. The major portion of the report was an economic analysis prepared by a nationally known market research company. Included in the economic analysis was a forecast of the need for additional retail facilities in the Monterey area. Although the research study had been prepared for use in planning the redevelopment of downtown Monterey, the study stated that the same considerations and market potential would be applicable to a shopping center located on the proposed site near Monterey. This report was made available to The Draper Companies by the Monterey Planning Commission.

The study defined two trade areas, primary and secondary. The primary trade area was defined as that area from which shoppers for all types of retail merchandise could be attracted. The secondary area was considered to be that area from which comparison shopper traffic (apparel, accessories, furniture, appliances, and other department store type merchandise) could be drawn, although not to the same extent as from the primary trade area. . . .

The principal criterion for selecting the boundaries of the trade area was distance from the retail center. Since the focal point of the study was the central business district (CBD) of Monterey, the primary trade area was outlined by drawing a circle with a radius of 2½ miles. The selection of the secondary trade area boundary was on the basis of the researcher's judgment of the likelihood of attracting shoppers beyond such distances. The report stated that some shopper traffic might come from areas beyond these boundaries, but not in sufficient quantity to warrant the inclusion of those areas in the total trade area.

In the analysis of the trade area, three categories of population were considered — military personnel, retired residents, and the civilian labor force. The population of the trade area was projected by these categories, as given in Exhibit 18. . . .

To forecast the military population, the study analyzed the future use of each of the four major military installations in the trade area. Fort Ord became a permanent Army training center in 1940 and had an average strength of 35,000 with a high of 50,000 during World War II.

The 1960 census showed the population of Fort Ord to be 28,237. Future estimates of the Fort Ord population were based on a statement by the Commanding General of Fort Ord in which he indicated that the military personnel at Fort Ord was expected to increase in the future.

The other major military installations on the Monterey Peninsula included the Army Language School, the U.S. Naval Post Graduate and General Line School, and the Naval Air Facilities. In 1960, the Army Language School had 1,650 military personnel and the two naval facilities 3,000. Future forecasts were based on statements from the U.S. Department of Defense which indicated that these facilities would continue to be used.

The Public Information Officer at Fort Ord estimated that there were between 5,000 and 6,000 retired persons living on the Monterey Peninsula who were eligible to use military commissary privileges. Also, the 1950 U.S. census showed that there were approximately 6,000 residents of the area who were over 60 years of age. Selecting 6,000 as the estimate for 1960, the study assumed that the percentage of retired residents to total population would gradually increase in the future. The assumed attractiveness of the Monterey Peninsula to retiring people was given as support for the increased percentage estimates.

The projection of the future civilian labor force was based on the analysis of economic activity on the Monterey Peninsula, other than the military activity, as summarized in Exhibit 19. The California Department of Employment was given as the source for this information.

The study concluded that, in the future, the civilian labor force would continue to grow in those industries that had shown growth in the recent past. The revival of the fishing and canning industry was not expected to take place in the near future. Generally, the economy was expected to be supported by tourism and government activities in the area. Because of the sizable unemployment ratio in the area, the report predicted that some light industry and research-oriented facilities would move into the area to take advantage of the unused labor force.

EXHIBIT 18   Del Monte Shopping Center, Population Projection for Study Area

	1950	1955	1960	1965	1970	1975
Military personnel	11,000	21,000	30,000	33,000	37,000	41,000
and dependents	4,000	11,000	14,000	16,000	18,000	21,000
Retired residents	6,000	10,000	12,000	15,000	18,000	23,000
Civilian labor force						
and dependents	29,000	43,000	49,000	58,000	70,000	80,000
Total	50,000	85,000	105,000	122,000	143,000	165,000

EXHIBIT 19   Del Monte Shopping Center, Projected Study Area Labor Market

Industry	July 1950*	July 1955*	July 1960*	1965	1970	1975
Agriculture, forestry, fishing	†	200	200	200	200	200
Mining	95	50	100	100	100	100
Construction	1,135	1,300	1,900	2,400	3,000	3,500
Manufacturing:						
Durable goods	50	100	200	400	800	1,300
Food products	1,120	400	300	200	200	200
Other nondurables	225	500	500	1,000	2,000	3,000
Transportation, communication, and utilities	440	850	1,000	1,200	1,400	1,600
Wholesale and retail trade	3,035	4,400	5,000	6,000	7,000	8,000
Finance, insurance, and real estate	465	1,000	1,000	1,200	1,400	1,700
Service	2,810	5,800	5,400	6,300	7,400	8,400
Government	765	3,600	5,100	6,000	6,500	7,000
Total	10,000	18,200	20,700	25,000	30,000	35,000

† Not available.
* *Source:* California Department of Employment.

In addition to presenting the population forecasts by occupational industries, the study also gave population forecasts by geographic location, and for Monterey County and the State of California (see Exhibit 20). . . .

The study stated that the apportionment of the population was

> largely based upon the Master Plans and other publications of the Monterey County Planning Commission and the City Planning Commissions in Carmel, Del Rey Oaks, Monterey, Pacific Grove, and Seaside. An analysis of the holding capacity of each area under existing zoning regulations and construction levels has been used as a cross-check to the reasonableness of the population dispersion. . . . The Monterey County Planning Department has made estimates of the future population of the County. . . . The population projections for the State of California have been made by the U.S. census, several departments of the state government, and various Chambers of Commerce throughout the state. These projections vary somewhat, especially for the later years of this century.

(No specific source references were given.)

An appendix to the study (Exhibit 21) gave estimates of the current income levels of various geographical locations, based on data "published annually on a state basis by the U.S. Department of Commerce . . . adjusted to small areas by applying the data on effective buying income published in *Sales Managements' Survey of Buying Power.*"

To estimate per capita retail expenditures, the study adjusted upward state-wide data taken from the 1958 U.S. Census of Retail Trade for the State of California, "to

EXHIBIT 20 Del Monte Shopping Center, Study Area Population Projections (in Thousands) by Geographic Location

Location	1960	1965	1970	1975
Carmel and vicinity	12	14	16	17
Carmel Valley	3	6	10	15
Del Rey Oaks	2	2	2	2
Fort Ord	28	32	34	37
Monterey	23	27	32	38
Pacific Grove	12	13	15	16
Seaside	19	22	25	29
Sand City	1	1	1	1
Unincorporated peninsula areas	5	6	8	10
Total	105	123	143	165
Monterey County population	198	240	300	370
Monterey County population on Peninsula, %	53	51	48	45
California population	15,717	18,500	22,000	25,000
State population, in county, %	1.25	1.30	1.36	1.48
On peninsula, %	0.67	0.67	0.65	0.66

EXHIBIT 21 Del Monte Shopping Center, per Capita Income for State, County and Local Population Groups

	Per capita annual income		Per capita annual income
State of California	$2,661	Carmel	$4,330
Monterey County	2,650	Monterey	2,870
Monterey Peninsula	2,350	Pacific Grove	2,940
Monterey Peninsula (civilian population)	2,950	Seaside	2,030
Fort Ord	1,100		

account for increases in the cost of living and for the study area's relatively high per capita income" (Exhibit 22).

The study assumed that 90 percent of the purchases made by military personnel living on post would be at the on-post commissary and post exchange, and only 10 percent of the purchases would go to off-post retail facilities. The study also gave consideration to the retail sales to tourists. The Monterey County Planning Commission estimated that the tourist business on the Monterey Peninsula had amounted to 3.5 million tourist days in 1959. During the heavy tourist season—June to October—hotel and motel occupancy was 90 percent, occupancy in the off-season was only 50 percent to 60 percent. Most tourist facilities operated all year. Future emphasis on attracting conventions during the off-season was expected to increase the tourist business.

The study assumed that tourist trade would be tied directly to the population growth of the State of California. According to interviews with local officials, at least 85 percent of the Peninsula tourist trade came from residents of California. To reflect the expected future flourishing tourist business, the percentage of tourist days to state population was increased each five-year period by ½ percent. Exhibit 23 summarizes the report's estimates of future tourist trade.

The per capita tourist expenditures was "based on *The Tourist Trade in California*, published by the Bureau of Public Administration, University of California, and upon estimates by the Monterey Planning Commission," as shown in Exhibit 24.

EXHIBIT 22   Del Monte Shopping Center, Estimated 1960 per Capita Retail Expenditures (Excludes Persons Living on Military Reservations)

Type of store	Per capita annual expenditures	Type of store	Per capita annual expenditures
Food	$ 370	Lumber, building material, and	
General merchandise	160	farm equipment dealers	$ 65
Apparel and accessories	95	Automotive dealers	285
Furniture and appliances	95	Gasoline service stations	115
Hardware, paint and glass	25	Other retail	110
Drug	55	Personal services	50
Eating and drinking places	115	Auto repair, service, and garages	30
Total	$ 915	Miscellaneous repair services	20
			$ 675

EXHIBIT 23   Del Monte Shopping Center, Estimated Tourism on Monterey Peninsula 1959–1975

Year	California population (millions)	% of Monterey Peninsula tourists to state population	Estimated no. of tourist days on peninsula (millions)
1959	15.3	23.0	3.5
1960	15.7	23.5	3.7
1965	13.5	24.0	4.4
1970	22.0	24.5	5.5
1975	25.0	25.0	6.5

EXHIBIT 24   Del Monte Shopping Center, Estimated per Capita per Day Tourist Expenditures

Kind of business	Per capita expenditures	Kind of business	Per capita expenditures
Food	$0.20	Other retail	$0.20
Eating and drinking places	1.35	Hotels and motels	2.50
General merchandise	0.40	Personal services	0.30
Apparel and accessories	0.30	Auto repair, services, and garages	0.10
Drug	0.10	All other services	1.00
Gasoline service stations	1.00	All other expenditures	1.15
Total	$3.35		$5.25

EXHIBIT 25   Del Monte Shopping Center, Total Potential Expenditures for Downtown Type Retail Goods (Thousands)

Location	Food	General merchandise	Apparel and accessories	Furniture and appliances	Hardware, paint, and glass	Drug	Other retail	Total
1960:								
Residents	$27,750	$12,000	$7,125	$7,125	$1,875	$4,125	$7,500	$67,500
Military	2,775	1,200	710	710	185	410	750	6,740
Tourists	740	1,480	1,110			370	740	4,440
Total	31,265	14,680	8,945	7,385	2,060	4,905	8,990	78,680
1965:								
Residents	32,930	14,240	8,455	8,455	2,225	4,899	8,900	80,100
Military	3,295	1,420	850	850	220	490	890	8,015
Tourists	900	1,800	1,350			450	900	5,400
Total	37,125	17,460	10,655	9,305	2,445	5,835	10,690	93,515
1970:								
Residents	39,590	17,120	10,165	10,165	2,675	5,885	10,700	96,300
Military	3,960	1,710	1,015	1,015	270	590	1,070	9,630
Tourists	1,100	2,200	1,650			550	1,100	6,600
Total	44,650	21,030	12,830	11,180	2,945	7,025	12,870	112,530
1975:								
Residents	46,620	20,160	11,970	11,970	3,150	6,930	12,600	113,400
Military	4,660	2,020	1,200	1,200	315	695	1,260	11,350
Tourists	1,300	2,600	1,950			650	1,300	7,800
Total	52,580	24,780	15,120	13,170	3,465	8,275	15,160	132,550

The total potential expenditures for downtown type retail goods within the trade area was developed from the preceding analysis of the buying power and expenditures of the area's civilian residents, military personnel living on post, and tourists, as shown in Exhibit 25.

To determine the need for additional retail facilities, a field survey was conducted in November and December 1960 of all existing retail stores. The sales capacity of these existing retail facilities was estimated by assigning per square foot sales levels

> which would be expected of such facilities under normally good management and average competitive conditions. The dollar amounts, therefore, do not necessarily reflect the maximum dollar volume levels possible by such facilities, nor do they represent estimates of the actual volume levels of these facilities in any one year. For forecasting purposes, the retail sales capacity by store category provides the most meaningful basis for estimating the potential currently being satisfied by existing facilities and, consequently, the amount of additional retail facilities which appear to be required in future years, after allowing for the full competitive volume capacity of existing stores.

By applying this technique, the study developed the "effective sales capacities of downtown and shopping center type retail facilities," as shown in Exhibit 26.

The potential for additional downtown and shopping center type retail facilities was

> calculated by subtracting the volume capacity of existing stores from the total market potential which existed in 1960. This is the *residual* method of approach which estimates future market opportunities under the implication that existing facilities could continue to enjoy normal volume levels after the completion of new shopping facilities on the Peninsula. Therefore, the market potential available can be attributed to either or both of the following factors: (1) present under-merchandising of the study area, and (2) the anticipation of future growth.

Thus, the report calculated the additional downtown or shopping center type retail facilities needed, as shown in Exhibit 27.

The estimated additional space requirements were "derived by applying a per square foot sales volume range, calculated for each type of facilities, against the total unsatisfied sales potential. The per square foot sales volume assumes average efficiency."

From a special automobile license plate survey taken in Salinas at the Sears store in the shopping center parking lot, and in the area near the Montgomery Ward store, the study found "that 12 percent of the apparent shoppers with cars at these two general locations were residents of the Monterey Peninsula study area." After commenting briefly about the various types of stores in the study area, and in particular about those selling department store type goods, the report concluded that

> a major full-line department store at a strong location would have the capability of creating and then serving a new department store market on the Peninsula which is presently being served, in part, by the smaller general merchandise stores, as well as by non-Peninsula department stores, such as those in Salinas and the San Francisco Bay area.

The report gave no specific estimate of potential sales for such a department store; instead, it referred to "the unsatisfied market potential for the overall general merchandise category" indicated in Exhibit 27.

EXHIBIT 26 Del Monte Shopping Center, Effective Sales Capacities of "Downtown" or "Shopping Center Type" Retail Facilities (Thousands)

Location	Food	General merchandise	Apparel and accessories	Furniture and appliances	Hardware, paint, and glass	Drug	Other retail	Total
Carmel	$ 3,010	$ 280	$3,844	$ 650	$ 264	$ 713	$ 3,598	$12,359
Pacific Grove	1,405	4,449	558	915	218	429	341	8,315
Forest Hills	4,573	32		32	125	168	176	5,106
Monte Vista Village	459	56					104	619
New Monterey	4,254	96	142	1,309	239	108	905	7,053
Seaside	5,994	3,533	756	2,684	625	740	1,480	15,812
Fremont Ave., Monterey	545			288			682	1,515
Carmel Valley	916		539	132	105	54	427	2,173
Downtown Monterey	3,855	2,372	2,840	1,280	712	600	2,311	14,100
Total	$25,011	$10,913	$8,679	$7,290	$2,288	$2,812	$10,024	$67,052

EXHIBIT 27 Del Monte Shopping Center, Additional Market Potential and Space Requirements for "Downtown" or "Shopping Center Type" Retail Facilities

	Existing retail capacity	Unsatisfied market potential (thousands)				Sales vol./ft²	Additional space demand, 1,000 ft²			
		1960	1965	1970	1975		1960	1965	1970	1975
Food	$25,011	$ 6,254	$12,114	$19,639	$27,569	$85–120	52–74	101–143	164–231	230–324
General merchandise	10,948	3,732	6,512	10,082	13,832	40–55	68–93	118–163	183–252	251–346
Apparel and accessories	8,679	266	1,976	4,151	6,441	45–65	4–6	30–44	64–92	99–143
Furniture and appliances	7,290	545	2,015	3,890	5,880	35–50	11–16	40–58	78–111	118–168
Hardware, paint, and glass	2,288		157	657	1,177	40–55		3–4	12–16	21–29
Drugs	2,812	2,093	3,023	4,213	5,463	35–50	42–60	60–86	84–120	109–156
Other retail	10,024		666	2,846	5,136	40–60		11–17	47–71	85–128
Total	$67,052	$12,890	$26,463	$45,478	$65,498		177–249	363–515	632–893	913–1,294

	1960	1965	1970	1975
Parking area required, at ratio of 3 ft²/ft² of retail facilities, 1,000 ft²	531–747	1,089–1,545	1,089–2,679	2,739–3,882
Total area requirements, 1,000 ft²*	708–996	1,452–2,060	2,528–3,572	3,652–5,176
Acreage requirements*	16–23	33–47	58–82	84–119

* Ratios and standards commonly applied in suburban shopping centers.

RESEARCH REPORT D

In addition to the two market research reports made available to The Draper Companies, the latter engaged another, regionally known market research firm to study the potential market support for the proposed Del Monte Shopping Center. The market research firm was to assume that the shopping center would have a total building floor area of 400,000 square feet, of which 150,000 square feet would be taken by a nationally known department store. Also, it was to be assumed that the planned Monterey freeway would be completed by the time the Del Monte Shopping Center opened in late 1965. This market research study was completed in the fall of 1962.

The trade areas that this research firm defined varied considerably from the trade areas shown in Reports B and C. Report D defined a primary trade area that embraced all of the Monterey Peninsula, including Carmel Valley, and the secondary trade area included most of Monterey County and parts of San Benito and Santa Cruz Counties. The definition of primary and secondary trade areas was similar to that stated in Market Research Report C. The primary trade area included both convenience (food, drug, etc.) and comparison (department store type goods) shoppers; the secondary trade area included only comparison type shoppers. . . .

In reply to some questions, the senior analyst who wrote Report D stated:

> Our primary trade area was delineated on the basis of logic and judgment. The limits of the primary trade area (which are co-extensive with the original trade area for the community shopping center) correspond to the accepted limits of the Monterey Peninsula. We made no attempt to quantify this through consumer or other research. The secondary trade area was delineated on the basis of geographical factors (mountains, oceans, rivers, etc.), competitive facilities, distance, and results of consumer research. We established the outer limits of the trade area by taking sample cities or communities at various points and ascertaining people's shopping habits at these points. Considerable weight was given to the percentage of people's budgets being spent at principal department stores in various communities. For example, in critical areas like Hollister (San Benito County), the percentage of people's department store expenditures going to San Jose stores compared with the percentage going to Sears and other department stores in Salinas were carefully analyzed.

Access to the proposed shopping center site was assumed to be excellent from all of the primary trade areas with the exception of Pacific Grove; residents of this community would have to travel around or through downtown Monterey in order to reach the shopping center. Access from the secondary trade area was considered to be good with the exception of Route 1 from the North, past Fort Ord; this road was considered to be in relatively poor condition and heavily traveled. Access from Salinas and the Salinas Valley was considered to be excellent.

Report D estimated future population levels for the trade area, "based on growth trends established from the U.S. Census of 1930, 1940, 1950, and 1960, local city planning departments and Chambers of Commerce, U.S. Post Offices, and the California Department of Finance's report, *California's Population in 1962*." Future economic activities of the study area were also considered in making the population estimates. Thus, the report considered:

1. The possibility of industrial growth in the vicinity of Salinas
2. The predicted trend toward more leisure time and greater expenditures for

recreational activities and the continued growth of the Peninsula for retired senior citizens and families who could afford a second home

3. The favorable residential, cultural, and scenic environment offered on the Peninsula as an attraction for light manufacturing and research facilities

The population projections developed were:

Trade area	1960	1965	1970
Primary	107,900*	133,500*	159,000*
Secondary	126,800	156,800	196,900
	234,700	290,300	355,900

* Includes 32,000 military personnel constant over the years.

From data received through consumer surveys, the median annual family income in the primary trade area was estimated to be $7,000; in the secondary trade area, $6,520; and for the total study area, $6,706. The report stated that these figures were higher than the Census figure of $5,770 because the consumer surveys did not include military personnel living on post.

Consumer interview surveys were conducted to ascertain demographic, economic, and shopping habits information. A random sampling technique was used and 475 interviews were completed in the primary trade area and 725 in the secondary trade area. Exhibits 29 and 30 illustrate some of the findings.

The estimated 1965 potential sales and the supportable square footage of store space for the proposed shopping center were computed as shown in Exhibit 31. The sales per square foot figures used in the computation of supportable square footage were "based on national averages for regional shopping centers."

EXHIBIT 29   Del Monte Shopping Center, Shoppers' Attitudes

Would you please look at this card and tell me which statements best describe your shopping experiences at stores and shopping districts on the Monterey Peninsula? Please read them all before making your selection.

	No.	%*
The merchants are friendly	323	68.0
It is hard to find a parking place and traffic congestion is a real problem	285	60.0
There is no one shopping area you can visit to get everything	256	53.9
Shopping is a real chore in this area; what we need is one good shopping center	202	42.5
There is no one shopping area you can visit to get everything you'd want to buy	141	29.7
Traffic congestion and parking don't seem to be real problems in our shopping areas	108	22.7
Stores are old and inadequate	91	19.2
It is easy to get from one shopping area to another	75	15.8
Shopping is a real pleasure; I wouldn't change anything	52	10.9
The merchants are unfriendly	28	5.9

* Percent of total respondents (475) who selected each statement.

EXHIBIT 30   Del Monte Shopping Center, Where Department Store Purchases Were Made

The last time you bought anything in a department store anywhere, at which store did you make your purchase?

Store	Location	Trade area, %	
		Primary*	Secondary†
Sears, Roebuck	Salinas	15.3	50.9
Holman's	Pacific Grove	53.5	7.3
Ford's	Watsonville		25.9
Penney's	Monterey	5.1	
Macy's	San Jose		4.7
Emporium	San Jose		2.1
Hart's	San Jose		1.4
MBS Discount	Seaside	4.0	
Montgomery Ward	Monterey	3.2	
MIDCO Discount	Seaside	2.3	

* 475 Interviews.
† After purchase.

EXHIBIT 31   Del Monte Shopping Center, 1965 Estimated Sales Potential for Proposed Shopping Center

Type	Annual sales, 1965	Supportable gross store space, ft²
Supermarket	$ 3,920,000	35,636
Drugs	1,282,000	29,814
Hardware	322,000	10,733
Variety	874,000	33,615
Other convenience goods	774,000	19,350
Department store	12,267,000	219,054
Apparel	6,859,000	149,109
Shoes	1,430,000	33,256
Restaurant	1,759,000	30,860
Other shoppers' goods	2,483,000	49,680
Total	$31,970,000	611,107

Report D provided summaries of the computations used to develop the estimated figures. It also projected department store sales and supportable gross store space for each year 1965 to 1970, except 1969 (Exhibit 32). Exhibit 33 shows the computations for the department store and supermarket. Similar computations were developed and given in the report for each of the types of stores listed in Exhibit 31.

The report stated that these estimates were based on such considerations as accessibility to the proposed site, present shopping habits of families in the trade

EXHIBIT 32 Del Monte Shopping Center, Estimated Department Store Sales and Square Footage Needs in Del Monte Shopping Center* 1965–1970

	1965	1966	1967	1968	1970
Population	258,300	271,420	284,540	297,660	323,900
Per capita department store expenditures	$126	$126	$126	$126	$126
Department store potential figures	$32,616,000	$34,198,920	$35,852,040	$37,505,160	$40,811,400
To Del Monte, %	33.8%	33.8%	33.8%	33.8%	33.8%
Dollars	$11,040,000	$11,559,234	$12,117,990	$12,676,744	$13,794,253
From beyond trade area	10%	10%	10%	10%	10%
Total sales of department store	$12,267,000	$12,843,590	$13,464,430	$14,085,270	$15,326,888
Sales/ft²	$56	$56	$56	$56	$56
Supportable square feet	219,054	229,350	240,436	251,522	273,694

* Assumes a constant rate of population growth of 13,120 per year. This is based on population growth projected for 1965 and 1970.

EXHIBIT 33 Del Monte Shopping Center, 1965 Estimated Sales Potential for a Department Store and a Supermarket in Proposed Shopping Center (SC)

Section no.*	Population, 1965	Distance from SC miles	Department store			Supermarket		
			Total potential business (thousands)	% to SC	Sales to SC (thousands)	Total potential business (thousands)	% to SC	Sales to SC (thousands)
1	23,500	1.5	$ 3,807	60	$ 2,284	$ 8,648	18	$1,557
2	16,000	3.0	1,360	40	544	4,160	8	333
3	5,500	3.0	900	65	644	2,090	18	376
4	21,100	3.0	3,798	60	2,279	8,018	10	802
5	35,400	4.0	3,009	45	1,354	9,204	5	460
6	5,150	15.0	834	33	275	$32,120		$3,528
7	37,300	16.0	5,595	26	1,455			
8	20,400	17.0	1,836	15	275			
9	6,500	17.0	975	30	293			
10	7,800	19.0	827	20	165			
11	6,750	23.0	608	23	140			
12	35,200	25.0	4,928	11	542			
13	8,550	25.0	855	23	197			
14	14,900	32.0	1,490	20	298			
15	4,350	32.0	461	18	83			
16	3,900	40.0	449	14	63			
17	5,300	50.0	689	14	96			
18	700	30.0	105	50	53			
Total	258,000		$32,616		$11,040			

Additional sales from outside (+10%) Department store 1,227 Supermarket 392

Total $12,267 $3,920

* For divisions of trade area see Exhibit 28.
† Reduced 20% to allow for expenditures at Fort Ord commissary.

area as reflected by the consumer surveys, and the pattern of retail trade in Monterey County.

In answer to questions regarding the sales estimated for the department store, the analyst who wrote Report D stated:

> In arriving at the percentage of business that a department store could achieve in various parts of the trade area, we relied heavily on the results of consumer interviewing. There are two primary department stores serving this area. Holman's serves the Monterey Peninsula while Sears in Salinas serves the rest of the trade area. We therefore had to consider the shopping habits of people in various parts of the trade area with regard to the percentage of their department store expenditures. They said went to each of these two principal stores. We started with a conceptual image of a major department store of the Macy's or Emporium type, assuming that such a store would have at least twice as many square feet as either of the present stores serving the area. With this in mind we then evaluated each of the population segments into which the trade area had been divided, making a value judgment as to the percentage of expenditures a department store at the Del Monte Shopping Center could expect to achieve.

Research Report E

While Report D was being prepared, The Draper Companies engaged another nationally known market research organization to make an independent

> estimate of the amount of additional department store space that could be supported in the Monterey-Salinas area in the 1965–1970 period; and specifically to estimate the year in which sufficient economic support will be available for an additional 250,000 gross square feet of department store area, assuming the department store would be a nationally or regionally known firm offering a wide range of merchandise. Report E was completed in late 1962.

The study undertook

> to (1) delineate the market area; (2) establish the present size and character of the residential population in the market area and to project population growth and character to 1970; (3) analyze present family and per capita income and to project same to 1970; (4) establish total potential department store expenditures in the market area, present to 1970; (5) analyze the characteristics and sales of present and proposed department stores within the market area; and (6) to calculate net potential retail expenditures available to new department store space, and the supportable square footage.

Report E stated

> The market area from which present and proposed major department stores in the Monterey-Salinas area will draw their primary support was established on the basis of the relative drawing power of these and major competitive retail and department store complexes in other areas, and by estimating distance and topographical limitations to the boundaries of the market area. The only major retail complex at present competing with the Monterey-Salinas retail locations is that located at San Jose, California. The amount of department store area in each of these two retail locations and the related annual dollar volume per square foot of selling space determine the relative pull of one retail complex in comparison with a competing complex. It has been established that the size or total selling area of a department store is a primary factor influencing the attraction of a particular store to the potential retail customer. This has been formulated as "Reilly's Law of Retail Gravitation." Therefore, it is possible to mathematically delineate the boundary points of market area along major arterial ways between any two major competing retail locations.

EXHIBIT 35 Del Monte Shopping Center, Family Population, Median Family Income, and Department Store Expenditures in Total Trade Area, 1960, 1965, and 1970

Location		Family population			Median family income			Family department store expenditures (millions)		
		1960	1965	1970	1960	1965	1970	1960	1965	1970
Alisal	Urban	15,575	18,670	23,810	$5,126	$5,577	$6,065	$1.74	$2.27	$3.42
Blanco Spreckels	Rural	536	640	820	8,000	8,704	9,469	0.07	0.09	0.13
Carmel	Rural	1,317	1,580	2,010	5,448	5,927	6,448	0.16	0.21	0.32
	Urban	3,424	4,100	5,240	6,654	7,240	7,876	0.65	0.88	1.20
Carmel Valley	Rural	8,110	9,720	12,400	8,932	9,718	10,573	1.85	2.43	3.36
	Urban	2,772	3,320	4,220	7,293	7,935	8,633	0.45	0.59	0.79
Castroville	Rural	2,684	3,220	4,100	4,347	4,730	5,146	0.21	0.27	0.39
	Urban	2,705	3,240	4,140	5,733	6,259	6,809	0.27	0.38	0.53
Coastal	Rural	308	370	460	6,003	6,531	7,106	0.04	0.05	0.07
	Urban	3,198	3,830	4,880	4,352	4,735	5,151	0.27	0.35	0.49
Fort Ord	Rural	9,617	9,617	9,617	4,229	4,601	5,006	0.74	0.80	0.90
Gonzales	Urban	7,043	8,440	10,760	5,070	5,516	6,001	0.35	0.46	0.70
Greenfield	Rural	2,839	3,400	4,350	4,968	5,405	5,880	0.28	0.37	0.51
King City	Urban	2,688	3,220	4,100	5,624	6,119	6,657	0.31	0.46	0.62
	Rural	1,361	1,630	2,070	4,218	4,589	4,992	0.11	0.14	0.20
Monterey	Urban	19,642	23,540	30,040	5,884	6,402	6,965	2.69	3.82	5.25
Monterey Peninsula	Rural	4,456	5,340	6,800	8,547	9,299	10,117	0.88	1.26	1.73
Pacific Grove	Urban	10,848	13,000	16,590	5,848	6,363	6,923	1.55	2.21	3.05
Pojaro	Rural	5,684	6,810	8,670	5,266	5,729	6,232	0.56	0.72	1.09
Salinas	Urban	25,457	30,510	38,850	7,035	7,654	8,327	4.38	5.62	7.34
San Juan	Urban	6,068	7,270	9,270	5,233	5,694	6,195	0.59	0.73	1.11
Seaside	Urban	18,428	22,100	28,100	4,592	4,996	5,435	1.96	2.64	3.62
Soledad	Rural	2,592	3,100	3,950	5,138	5,590	6,082	0.22	0.29	0.44
Toro	Rural	1,021	1,230	1,580	4,670	5,081	5,527	0.09	0.12	0.17
San Juan Bautista	Urban	1,647	1,970	2,510	8,523	9,273	10,089	0.32	0.42	0.58
	Rural	2,188	2,188	2,188	5,613	6,107	6,644	0.25	0.29	0.32
Hollister	Urban	5,491	5,780	6,040	5,663	6,165	6,707	0.70	0.84	0.90
	Rural	3,996	4,220	4,340	5,588	6,080	6,615	0.46	0.58	0.64
San Juan, Bitterwater*	Urban	425	425	425	5,442	5,921	6,442	0.04	0.05	0.06
Bitterwater	Rural	3,394	4,347	5,050	5,838	6,352	6,912	0.54	0.64	0.80
Watsonville	Rural	8,437	9,323	10,800	5,507	5,992	6,519	0.99	1.19	1.61
	Urban	11,815	13,050	15,125	5,710	6,212	6,758	1.56	1.96	2.46
Total		196,306	229,200	283,305				$25.28	$33.13	$44.80

* Part of area.
Source: U.S. Census 1960 (urban and rural breakdown given where available); research company data.

EXHIBIT 36   Del Monte Shopping Center, Population,
Median Income, and Department Store Expenditures of
Unrelated Individuals in Market Area, 1960, 1965 and 1970

	1960	1965	1970
Population [in market area]:			
Monterey County	35,867	39,100	44,500
San Benito County	1,056	1,090	1,125
Santa Cruz County	2,319	2,560	2,965
Total	39,242	42,750	48,590
Median income:			
Monterey County	$1,814	$1,974	$2,147
San Benito County	1,946	2,117	2,304
Santa Cruz County	1,594	1,734	1,886
Department-store expenditures (millions):			
Monterey County	$1.76	$1.94	$2.69
San Benito County	0.23	0.27	0.34
Santa Cruz County	0.08	0.09	0.11
Total	$2.07	$2.30	$3.14

Source: U.S. Census 1960; research company data.

Analysis was also made of the variety of merchandise offered, promotional effort, character and reputation, and "other factors such as effectiveness of management and general pricing policies" of each competing department store. The results of this analysis provided the basis for estimating sales per square foot of existing stores. "Store size and annual sales per square foot of selling area were weighed to establish the market boundary between competing department store complexes. . . . The eastern boundaries of the market area are relatively well determined by the mountain ranges." The report further stated that in the remote, sparsely populated outer areas, exact delineation of the market area boundary "is not crucial . . ."

Report E gave estimated family population and unrelated population (single military personnel and institutionalized persons) of the area for 1960 and the 1965–1970 period, based on data obtained from the U.S. Bureau of the Census and the California Department of Finance (see Exhibits 35 and 36).

Income levels for the trade area were developed from the 1960 U.S. Census. The average 1960 income was given as $5,863 for families and $1,807 for unrelated individuals. The estimated incomes projected to 1965 and 1970 were $6,395 and $7,117 for families and $1,963 and $2,134 for unrelated individuals, respectively. An average family size of 3.7 persons was assumed throughout. Projections for beyond 1960 were based on the assumption of a 3% annual increase in income, compared with the national growth rate of 4.9%. This was deflated to a constant rate of 1.7% to reflect constant dollars.

Report E stated that annual potential department store expenditures by the population in the trade area were computed on the basis of different percentages for different income groups by small areas (see Exhibits 35 and 36). The report indicated that these percentages (not given in the report) were derived from the research company's past experience and from literature in the retail field (no sources given). The projections assumed an average per capita department store annual expenditure of $100 in 1960, $125 in 1965, and $144 in 1970. The estimated potential annual department store expenditures in the market area by families and unrelated individuals combined for the years 1965 through 1970 (in constant 1960 dollars) were as follows:

Year	1965	1966	1967	1968	1969	1970
Millions	$35.43	$37.70	$39.95	$42.21	$44.51	$47.94

The annual sales of existing department stores within the market area were deducted from the total potential department store expenditures in the selected market area. . . . Existing department stores in the immediate Monterey area were discounted approximately 80% of 1962 sales and the Salinas area 92%. . . . This was based on observations of the effects of nearby competition on existing stores in many Southern California and Southwestern regions. . . . Total 1962 department store sales in the selected market area were estimated to be $31.3 million (see Exhibit 37). This was discounted by the method described to approximately $27.3 million and held constant for the 1965–1970 period.

The report gave the estimated discounted annual department store sales by urban areas within the market area.

Net annual expenditures potentially available to new department stores were estimated by subtracting the existing discounted department store sales ($27.3 million) from the total potential department store expenditures available in the market area in a particular year, as follows:

Year	1965	1966	1967	1968	1969	1970
Millions	$8.13	$10.40	$12.65	$14.91	$17.21	$20.64

Report E translated the potentially available department store expenditures into supportable department store selling space. Selling space was calculated as being two-thirds of gross space. Annual sales of $60, $85, and $100 per square foot of selling space were selected. The report stated that $60 is generally considered a minimum for entry and that this "will increase to a normal return of $80 to $90 within a three- to five-year period after construction of the department store." The $85 was considered normal for the Monterey-Salinas area where present sales were

EXHIBIT 37 Del Monte Shopping Center, 1962 and Discounted
Sales of Competing Department Stores by Urban Areas

	1962 actual sales (millions)	Discount, %	Discounted sales (millions)
Monterey	$12.0	20	$ 9.5
Salinas	15.4	8	14.0
Watsonville	3.3	5	3.1
Hollister	0.4		0.4
King City	0.2		0.2
Total	$31.3		$27.3

EXHIBIT 38 Del Monte Shopping Center, Potential Additional Amount of Department Store Space in Market Area, Thousands of Square Feet*

Year	$60/ft² Selling space	$60/ft² Gross area	$85/ft² Selling space	$85/ft² Gross area	$100/ft² Selling space	$100/ft² Gross area
1965	135.5	202.2	95.6	142.7	81.3	121.3
1966	173.3	258.7	122.4	182.7	104.0	155.2
1967	210.8	314.6	148.8	222.1	126.5	188.8
1968	248.5	370.9	175.4	261.8	149.1	222.5
1969	286.8	428.1	202.5	302.3	172.0	256.7
1970	344.0	513.5	242.8	362.4	206.4	308.1

* Gross area estimated at 1.49 times sales area.

estimated at $88, while San Jose showed an average of $83.5. (No details were given to support the estimates for Monterey-Salinas and San Jose.) The $100 sales per square foot of selling space was considered to be "strong." "However, some department stores, such as Sears, may often exceed this figure and reach $140 to $170." Thus the potential additional amount of department store area in the Monterey-Salinas area for the 1965–1970 period at different annual sales per square foot of selling space was estimated as given in Exhibit 38.

NINE

Land Development
and Investment

Land ownership was traditionally reserved to the upper classes in most European nations, with the monarchs and feudal lords sharing control. The opportunity for ownership of land was probably the most important single factor attracting European immigrants to the United States during the eighteenth and nineteenth centuries. Reflecting the strong concerns of American settlers for property rights, the Constitution of the United States provided specific protection to owners of private property under the Fifth and Fourteenth Amendments.

The many opportunities for homesteading in the nineteenth century and the rapid growth in home ownership in the United States in the twentieth century have resulted in a nation of land and real estate owners. Approximately 75 percent of the households with family heads 35 years old or older owned their own homes in 1970, and approximately 63 percent of the total number of dwellings in the United States were owner-occupied.

URBAN-LAND-VALUE THEORY

The traditional view in economic writings, summarized by the author in 1958, has been that urban land values were certain to increase with general economic growth.[1] In 1880 in support of the single tax on land values Henry George is reported to have said:

[1] Paul F. Wendt, "Urban Land Value Trends," *The Appraisal Journal,* vol. 26, no. 2, pp. 254–269, April 1958.

Go, get yourself a piece of ground and hold possession. You may sit down and smoke your pipe; you may lie around like the lazzaroni of Naples or the leperos of Mexico; you may go up in the balloon or down a hole in the ground, and without doing one stroke of work, without adding one iota to the wealth of the community, in ten years you will be rich.

John Stuart Mill expressed similar views in his *Principles of Political Economy:*

Now, the labors of the nation at large do add daily and yearly to the value of the land, whether the landlord plays the part of an improver or not. . . . The income from rural lands has a constant tendency to increase; that from building lands still more.

Several writers concluded in the early post-World War II years that urban land values were declining because of the forces of decentralization set in motion by the automobile.

The author presented the following theoretical model of urban land values in 1957.[1]

$$V = \frac{f_x(P,\ Y,\ S,\ P_u,\ PI) - (T + O_c + I_{im} + D_{im})}{f_x(i,\ R,\ C_g)} \qquad (9\text{-}1)$$

where V = value of urban land
f_x = expectations
P = population
Y = average incomes
S = supply of competitive land
P_u = competitive pull of area
PI = public investment
T = local taxes
O_c = operating costs
I_{im} = interest on improvements
D_{im} = depreciation on improvements
i = interest rates
R = investment risk
C_g = capital-gain possibility

The model was based on the theory that the total market value of urban land will equal the discounted value of future expected net annual returns attributable to urban land. These returns are expressed in the formula as the difference between expected gross income and the costs incurred in securing that income.

[1] Paul F. Wendt, "Theory of Urban Land Values," *Land Economics,* vol. 33, no. 3, pp. 228–240, August 1957.

TABLE 9-1 Required Rent at Varying Land Values

Land value/ft² of land area	Capital costs/ft² of building area			Net return on capital cost at 9%	Add real estate taxes, operating expenses, and vacancies	Required gross rent/ft²
	Building	Land*	Total			
$200	$45	$11	$56	$5.04	$4.50	$ 9.54
300	45	17	62	5.58	4.50	10.08
400	45	22	67	6.03	4.50	10.53
500	45	28	73	6.57	4.50	11.07
600	45	33	78	7.02	4.50	11.52
700	45	39	84	7.56	4.50	12.06

* Land value expressed in square feet of permissible building area, assuming a floor-area ratio of 18 times the lot size.

Source: John R. White, "Have Central City Land Values Fallen?," The Appraisal Journal, vol. 40, no. 3, p. 353, July 1972.

CENTRAL-CITY LAND-VALUE TRENDS

Based upon a review of land-value trends in Chicago and selected San Francisco Bay Area cities, the author concluded in 1958 that urban land values in major cities had continued their long-run upward trend in the post-World War II years. It was observed, however, that the rapid rise during the postwar period had not served to carry values of downtown and commercial property up to or much beyond the peaks reached during the speculative boom of the late 1920s.[1]

An authority on New York City land values reported in 1972 that it took Manhattan 40 years, from 1930 to 1970, to regain the peak levels of land values reached before the 1929 depression.[2] Observing that central-city land values had doubled from 1966 to 1969, White drew attention to a significant deflation during the early 1970s from unsupportable speculative peaks. He predicted a long-term downward adjustment in New York City central-city land values that "may extend well beyond the expected restoration of a reasonable supply-demand balance in 1976."

White attributed the rapid rise in land values during the late 1960s to a 50 percent increase in rents for prime office space during the "frantic" 4-year period from 1966 to 1969. He presented a model (Table 9-1), showing the relationships between land values and required office rents. Using this model, which is an ingenious adaptation of the residual method of valuation, he demonstrated that an increase in rents per square foot of build-

[1] Paul F. Wendt, "Economic Growth and Urban Land Values," The Appraisal Journal, vol. 26, no. 3, July 1958, pp. 427–443.

[2] John R. White, "Have Central City Land Values Fallen?," The Appraisal Journal, vol. 40, no. 3, pp. 351–355, July 1972.

ing area (assuming no changes in capital costs and floor-to-area ratio) from $9.54 to $12.06 might justify an increase in land values from $200 to $700 per square foot.[1]

White's illustration underscores the extreme volatility in central-city land values which has been observed over time by Hoyt and others.[2] His demonstration of the direct relationship between rents and land values is consistent with the generalized model of urban land values presented above. The sensitivity of central-city land values to changes in office rents has increased as the ratios of office space to land area have risen with new building technology and high speed elevators. The subscript x in f_x in the urban land-value model [Eq. (9-1)] reflects the fact that it is the *expectations* of investors and speculators in the urban land markets which influence values in the market place. White's portrayal of the "frantic" demand for office space and land during the late 1960s in New York shows the importance of inflationary expectations and explains the extreme volatility of urban land values.

Review of a random sample of properties in the Chicago Standard Metropolitan Statistical Area, for which front foot-value estimates were reported in *Olcott's Land Values Blue Book of Chicago* for 1950, 1960, and 1970, revealed that, on the average, Chicago land values increased more than 3 times from 1950 to 1960 and approximately doubled from 1960 to 1970.[3] Considerable variation was observed in the rates of increase for individual properties included in the sample.

NATIONAL LAND-VALUE TRENDS

Manvel[4] estimated that the market value of privately owned land in the United States rose from $269 billion in 1956 to $523 billion in 1966, an increase of 95 percent for the decade and a compound annual increase of 6.9 percent per annum. Table 9-2 summarizes the estimated growth in values of all taxable real estate and of nine classes of land.

Manvel's estimates were made by multiplying census data on locally assessed taxable realty by average assessment ratios. For these and other reasons outlined in the study, the estimates must be regarded as imprecise judgmental estimates. Manvel's estimated land values for 1956 are higher

---

[1] Ibid., p. 353.

[2] Homer Hoyt, *100 Years of Land Values in Chicago*, University of Chicago Press, Chicago 1933. See also *Olcott's Land Values Blue Book of Chicago, 1910, 1921, 1928, 1935, 1947, 1957*, University of Chicago Press, Chicago, 1933.

[3] The above are rough approximations only, based upon examination of raw data assembled by C. F. Sirmans of the University of Illinois, and James M. Kau of the University of Georgia.

[4] Allen D. Manvel, "Trends in the Value of Real Estate and Land, 1956 to 1966," *Three Land Research Studies*, National Commission of Urban Problems, Washington, 1968, pp. 1–18.

TABLE 9-2 Trends in the Value of Real Estate and Land, 1956-1966

	Amounts (billions)			% increase	
	1956	1966	Increase	Total	Per year
Assessed valuations	$207	$ 393	$186	90%	6.6%
Estimated market value:					
Total	697	1,261	564	81	6.1
Land	269	523	254	95	6.9
Structures	428	739	311	73	5.6

	Amounts (billions)		%		% increase	
Type of property	1956	1966	1956	1966	Total	Per year
Total	$269	$523	100.0%	100.0%	95%	6.9%
Acreage and farms	112	203	41.6	38.8	81	6.1
Urban property	157	320	58.4	61.2	104	7.4
Residential	86	181	32.2	34.7	110	7.7
One-family	77	159	28.8	30.5	106	7.5
Multifamily	9	22	3.4	4.2	141	9.2
Commercial and						
industrial	49	95	18.3	18.1	92	6.7
Commercial	36	69	18.3	13.2	93	6.8
Industrial	14	26	5.0	4.9	90	6.6
Vacant lots	21	44	7.9	8.5	109	7.6

	Average land value per parcel		% increase	
Type of property	1956	1966	Total	Per year
Nonfarm one-family houses	$ 2,569	$ 3,942	53%	4.4%
Commercial and industrial	21,419	37,998	77	5.9
Vacant lots	1,665	3,102	86	6.4
Acreage and farm properties	7,880	14,377	82	6.2

Source: Allen D. Manvel, "Trends in the Value of Real Estate and Land, 1956 to 1966." *Three Land Research Studies*, The National Commission on Urban Problems, Washington, 1968, pp. 1–2.

than earlier estimates of Goldsmith.[1] Explanation for the discrepancies is found in higher assumed ratios of land to improvements in Manvel's study. Confirmation of his higher land-value ratios and the 1956 estimates shown in Table 9-2 is found in a 1961 study of land values.[2]

A notable finding of the study was that the indicated upward trend in real estate values from 1956 to 1966 was far more rapid than the rate of increase

[1] Raymond W. Goldsmith, *The National Wealth of the United States in the Post-war Period*, Princeton University Press, Princeton, N.J., 1962. Goldsmith estimated that total private land in the United States increased in value from $2.7 billion in 1956 to $354 billion in 1966, an average annual increase of 5.5 percent per year.

[2] Joseph F. Keper, Ernest Kurnow, Clifford D. Clark, and Harvey Segals, *Theory and Measurement of Rent*, Chilton, Philadelphia, 1961.

TABLE 9-3 Annual Rates of Increase in Selected Economic Variables, 1956–1966

	%
Total United States population	1.5%
Wholesale prices, all commodities	1.0
Consumer prices, all items	1.8
Composition construction cost index	2.3
Implicit price deflator, private fixed investment	1.7
Index of common stock prices	6.2
Gross national product	6.0
National income	5.9
Personal income	5.8
Total value of ordinary taxable realty	6.1
Excluding measurable effect of shifts between major property classes	3.8
Total value of urban property	6.3
Total value of urban residential property	6.5
Land value, all ordinary taxable realty	6.9
Excluding effect of assumed rise in land value proportion for various property classes	6.0
Land value of urban property	7.4
Land value of urban residential property	7.7
Structural value of all ordinary taxable realty	5.6
Average total value per property of nonfarm one-family houses	3.2
Average land value per property of nonfarm one-family houses	4.4
Average per property value of vacant lots	6.4

Source: Allen D. Manvel, "Trends in the Value of Real Estate and Land, 1956 to 1966," *Three Land Research Studies,* The National Commission on Urban Problems, Washington, 1968, p. 5.

in population or in consumer and wholesale prices. Table 9-3 shows that the comparative annual growth rates in real estate and land values were closely similar to those in the gross national product, national income, and personal income.

This finding is consistent with the theoretical model cited earlier, which identified future expectations of population and income growth, interest rates, inflation, and changes in the supply of land as key determinants of future land value trends.[1]

The results of a study using multiple regression analysis to determine changes in the total market value of land in California between 1957 and 1966 by counties revealed average annual growth rates between 6 and 10 percent. The variables used in the study of California land values for the National Commission on Urban Problems were:

1. Enrollment in grades 1 to 8 in public and parochial schools
2. Wages of persons covered by unemployment insurance, exclusive of wages paid to agricultural workers

[1] Wendt, "Theory of Urban Land Values," loc. cit.

TABLE 9-4 Estimated Values of Land in California, 1957–1966

	Estimated value (millions)			% change from preceding year		
As of March	Urban	Urban and rural	All*	Urban	Urban and rural	All*
1957	$29,477	$35,699	$39,727			
1958	31,636	37,664	41,441	7.3%	5.5%	4.3%
1959	34,310	40,952	44,183	8.5	8.7	6.6
1960	36,999	44,660	47,842	7.8	9.1	8.3
1961	41,183	49,288	52,163	11.3	10.4	9.0
1962	45,327	55,162	57,758	10.0	11.9	10.7
1963	49,786	60,587	63,713	9.8	9.8	10.3
1964	53,913	66,118	69,315	8.3	9.1	8.8
1965	58,601	71,762	75,205	8.7	8.5	8.5
1966	63,427	77,895	81,352	8.2	8.5	8.2

* Includes timber, mineral rights, and water rights in addition to urban and rural land.
Source: Robert H. Gustafson and Ronald B. Welch, "Estimating California Land Values from Independent Statistical Indicators," Three Land Research Studies, The National Commission on Urban Problems, Washington, 1968, p. 65.

3. Taxable sales of personal property by retail and service establishments plus estimated tax-exempt sales of food for off-premise human consumption
4. Population
5. Income

The regression equation that performed the best in predicting 1966 land values in California used the 3-year changes in the variables expressed as natural numbers.[1] The estimated values, by years, based upon the equation which gave the best fit, are shown in Table 9-4.

SUPPLY OF LAND

According to the most recent estimates, approximately 2.2 percent of the total land area in the United States is devoted to "urban and related" uses, which include highways, roads, railroad rights-of-way, and nonmilitary airports.[2] Although the total land area in the United States is virtually unchanging, the supply of land suitable for urban utilization is constantly increasing.

Table 9-5 summarizes the estimated growth in the supply of urban land in the United States from 1949 to 1969 and projected land supplies for 1980 to 2000. It can be observed that the supply of urban land increased about

[1] Robert H. Gustafson and Ronald B. Welch, "Estimating California Land Values from Independent Statistical Indicators," in Three Land Research Studies, The National Commission on Urban Problems, Washington, 1968.
[2] U.S. Department of Agriculture, Economic Research Service, Our Land and Water Resources, Current and Prospective Supplies and Uses, Miscellaneous Publication 1290, Washington, 1977, p. vii.

TABLE 9-5 Major Uses of Land in the 48 States; Historic and Projected, 1949–2000, Millions of Acres

	Historic		Projected[a]	
Land use	1949	1969	1980	2000
Cropland used for crops[b]	387	333	320	298
Cropland harvested	(352)	(286)	(292)	(272)
Forest and woodland[c]	601	603	591	578
Pasture, range, and other agricultural land[d]	768	767	771	782
Urban and related[e]	42	60	66	81
Other special uses and miscellaneous uses[f]	106	134	149	158
Total land area[g]	1,904	1,897	1,897	1,897

[a] Land-use projections are derived from projections prepared for the Water Resources Council by the Economic Research Service, and the Bureau of Economic Analysis, Department of Commerce. Exclusion of data for Alaska and Hawaii significantly affects acreage of noncommercial forest, wasteland, and total land area, but has little effect on agricultural and commercial forest acreages.

[b] Cropland harvested, crop failure, and cultivated summer fallow.

[c] Excludes reserved forest land in parks and other special uses of land. The total acreage of forest land in the 48 contiguous states was approximately 627 million acres in 1949 and 632 million acres in 1969.

[d] Permanent grassland pasture and range in farms and not in farms, land in crop rotation but used only for pasture or idle, and miscellaneous other land in farms.

[e] Area in urban places, highway and road rights-of-way, railroad rights-of-way, and nonmilitary airports.

[f] Includes national and state parks and wildlife areas, national forest wilderness and primitive areas, national defense lands, state institutional sites, miscellaneous other special uses, and unclassified areas such as marshes, open swamps, bare rocks, sand dunes, and deserts.

[g] Change in total land area is attributable to changes in methods used in occasional remeasurements by the Bureau of the Census, and increases in the area of man-made reservoirs.

Source: U.S. Department of Agriculture, Economic Research Service, Our Land and Water Resources Current and Prospective Supplies and Uses, Miscellaneous Publication 1290, Washington 1977, p. vii.

50 percent from 1949 to 1969 and is expected to increase further in future years in response to demand influences.

It is of some interest to speculate about the effect of federal environmental legislation and state and local economic growth policies upon the future increments to the supply of urban land in the United States. Land-development procedures and policies have undergone significant changes over the past decade. Public concern over the deterioration of the environment in the United States resulted in the enactment of the Environmental Policy Act of 1969, followed by the Clean Air Act Amendments of 1970, the Water Pollution Control Act Amendments of 1972, the Noise Control Act and the Coastal Zone Management Act of 1972. A 1976 report from the Urban Institute identified 13 states with natural-areas-protection legislation and 22 states with special siting and location-controls legislation. According to the report, most of the states with coastal areas are expected to enact protective legislation in the near future. A list of the states with growth-management and specific land-use legislation is shown in Table 9-6. In view of the huge supplies of land available for potential urban use, it appears likely that the major effect of this legislation may be to guide and direct future increments to supplies of urban land rather than to limit urban growth.

TABLE 9-6   State Adoptions of Specific Land-Use Statutes

Legislation	Number	States
Growth management:		
Mandatory local comprehensive planning	13	Ariz., Calif., Colo., Fla., Idaho, Mont., Neb., Nev., Oreg., R.I., S.D., Va., Wyo.
Mandatory local subdivision controls	9	Calif., Colo., Idaho, Neb., Nev., N.M., Oreg., Va., Wyo.
Mandatory local zoning regulation	7	Ariz., Calif., Hawaii, Idaho, Neb., Nev., Oreg.
Siting (location controls):		
Power plants and transmission lines	22	Ariz., Ark., Calif., Conn., Fla., Ky., Md., Mass., Minn., Mont., Nev., N.H., N.M., N.Y., N.D., Ohio, Oreg., S.C., Vt., Wash., Wis., Wyo.
Large-scale industrial and commercial development	6	Del., Fla., Maine, N.J., Vt., Wyo.
Surface mines	5	Calif., Mont., N.D., S.D., Tex.
Protection of natural areas:		
Wetlands	14	Conn., Del., Ga., Maine, Md., Mass., Mich., Miss., N.H., N.J., N.Y., N.C., R.I., Va.
Shorelands	14	Ala., Calif., Del., Hawaii, Maine, Mich., Minn., Mont., N.C., Oreg., R.I., Vt., Wash., Wis.
Critical environmental areas	9	Colo., Fla., Maine, Mass., Minn., Nev., Oreg., Utah, Wyo.

Source: *Search/A Report from the Urban Institute*, vol. 6, no. 3-4, summer 1976.

Restrictions upon new supplies of urban land of special classes may result in higher prices for available land approved for development. On the other hand, overall restrictions upon economic growth in various states may reduce the demand for new urban land development, and have an adverse effect on land prices.

FARMLAND VALUES

The average value per acre of farmland in the United States fluctuated in a general range between $30 and $70 per acre between 1910 and 1950, reaching a low of $30 in 1934.[1] Farmland values rose in every year since 1942 and during the period from 1950 to 1970 increased at a compound annual rate of approximately 5.50 percent.[2] Growth in the average dollar

[1] U.S. Department of Agriculture, Economic Research Service, *Farm Real Estate Historical Series Data: 1850–1970,* ERS 520, Washington, June 1973.
[2] Ibid., p. 2.

value per acre of farmland has accelerated since 1970 in the United States and rose from $195 per acre in 1970 to $456 in February 1977, representing a compound rate of increase of 0.5 percent per year.

Table 9-7 summarizes average values of farmland per acre by states and regions and for 48 states from 1971 to 1977. Very large absolute and percentage increases in land values can be noted during the past 5 years, particularly for 1974. The large increases for some of the heavily populated states in the Northeast, the corn belt, and in the Northern plains states probably reflect the combined influences of increasing prices for farm products and inflationary expectations of purchasers during these years.

TABLE 9-7   Farm Real Estate Values: Average Value per Acre[a]

State	Mar. 1971	Mar. 1972	Mar. 1973	Mar. 1974	Mar. 1975	Feb. 1976	Nov. 1976	Feb. 1977[b]
Northeast:								
Maine[c]	$ 187	$ 218	$ 255	$ 306	$ 345	$ 373	$ 393	$ 405
N.H.[c]	286	341	407	498	570	617	650	669
Vt.[c]	256	295	341	402	452	489	515	530
Mass.[c]	623	693	775	886	976	1,054	1,111	1,143
R.I.[c]	854	997	1,166	1,392	1,578	1,707	1,799	1,852
Conn.[c]	1,034	1,171	1,332	1,549	1,725	1,866	1,967	2,024
N.Y.	288	325	359	452	520	560	575	591
N.J.	1,135	1,232	1,352	1,611	1,850	2,051	2,051	2,051
Pa.	393	422	497	631	747	830	927	1,000
Del.	553	564	640	800	956	1,138	1,272	1,322
Md.	688	736	851	994	1,078	1,300	1,361	1,371
Lake states:								
Mich.	333	373	450	530	563	615	710	782
Wis.	255	275	331	394	441	498	559	591
Minn.	231	241	270	341	436	530	591	664
Corn belt:								
Ohio	416	439	506	630	711	861	1,032	1,131
Ind.	423	436	496	596	726	886	1,071	1,167
Ill.	494	523	570	728	857	1,066	1,345	1,450
Iowa	392	414	467	600	725	911	1,103	1,228
Mo.	236	261	294	385	399	449	488	529
Northern plains:								
N.D.	95	99	110	146	196	229	245	258
S.D.	85	87	94	120	146	164	182	188
Neb.	157	170	194	244	285	359	399	407
Kans.	162	174	200	256	301	335	366	381
Appalachian:								
Va.	309	345	392	502	560	623	627	677
W.Va.	151	174	206	266	305	383	401	401
N.C.	372	398	466	560	603	648	654	684
Ky.	268	297	330	391	435	512	542	603
Tenn.	277	303	349	421	477	507	539	556

TABLE 9-7   Farm Real Estate Values: Average Value per Acre[a] (Continued)

State	Mar. 1971	Mar. 1972	Mar. 1973	Mar. 1974	Mar. 1975	Feb. 1976	Nov. 1976	Feb. 1977[b]
Southeast:								
S.C.	277	316	340	425	475	494	510	541
Ga.	256	292	333	432	486	488	499	524
Fla.[d]	378	404	466	613	692	732	747	783
Ala.	227	238	270	337	370	410	424	437
Delta:								
Miss.	238	242	271	344	386	388	388	411
Ark.	255	297	339	409	421	470	505	527
La.	350	382	406	474	518	545	572	590
Southern plains:								
Okla.	183	195	221	267	307	339	356	374
Tex.	156	174	199	248	252	278	296	298
Mountain:								
Mont.	63	68	76	97	114	134	143	154
Idaho	188	206	230	289	343	373	404	419
Wyo.	42	48	56	72	84	98	104	105
Colo.	103	116	139	170	193	225	249	262
N.M.	46	51	59	77	82	86	91	95
Ariz.	77	89	96	119	120	123	126	129
Utah	111	132	146	179	197	222	231	246
Nev.	60	69	79	92	92	94	94	94
Pacific:								
Wash.	224	239	276	313	358	428	454	500
Oreg.	168	189	209	240	258	274	279	288
Calif.	471	495	511	581	669	684	692	686
48 states	202	218	245	303	343	390	430	456

[a] March 1971 to November 1976 revised on the basis of the 1974 Census of Agriculture. Percentage changes indicated by the dollar value estimates may not coincide with the index due to rounding.
[b] Preliminary.
[c] The average rate of change for the six New England states was used to project dollar values for each of these six states.
[d] Values based upon the average percentage change in the Georgia and Alabama index.
Source: Farm Real Estate Market Developments, suppl. 2 to CD 81, March 1977, p. 3.

CHANGES IN RESIDENTIAL LOT VALUES

Maisel estimated that average single-family residential-lot values in California rose from $1,420 in 1950 to $3,796 in 1961.[1] During this period the ratio of site value to combined house and site value rose from 16.1 to 21.1 percent. Maisel estimated that approximately 50 percent of the increase in sale prices of lots in California was attributable to higher raw land costs, the balance reflecting higher improvement costs.

[1] Sherman J. Maisel, "Land Costs for Single-Family Housing," California Housing Studies, Center for Planning and Development Research, Berkeley, 1963, pp. 1–47.

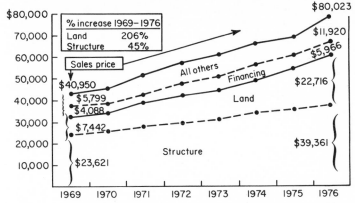

Figure 9-1 Environmental costs (not just brick and mortar) are responsible for increases in the cost of new housing. Bad laws cost a lot: the consumer is stuck with picking a bill for environmental "protection." As a result, the cost of land has tripled since 1969. (*Edward R. Carr and Associates, Inc., Annandale, Va.; National Association of Homebuilders, Economics Department.*)

Sumichrast and Frankel[1] reported that the average finished lot price in the United States rose from $2,851 in 1960 to $6,217 in 1969, an increase of 118.1 percent or a compound rate of increase of slightly above 8 percent per year. Their study revealed substantial variations in lot-price changes between different states and for individual cities, with the most rapid price increases occurring in cities and states experiencing rapid economic and population growth.

Data made available by the National Association of Homebuilders (Fig. 9.1) reveal that lot prices doubled from 1969 to 1976. According to an NAHB report,[2] land costs rose from 18 percent of total new house costs in 1969 to 31 percent in 1976. It is significant to note the emphasis in Fig. 9-1 upon environmental "protection," which reflects larger lot sizes as well as improvement costs in the NAHB data.

The trade-off between the environment and economic growth promises to be the subject of debate for many years to come. Many urban communities have adopted limited-growth policies to protect agricultural and recreational land resources. The effect of these policies often is to place restrictions upon the supplies of developable land, with the expected result of spiraling land costs.

Limited supplies of developable land inevitably lead to increased public controls over development, which have a dual effect upon the land investor and developer: (1) the range of permitted uses for individual parcels is

---

[1] Michael Sumichrast and Sara A. Frankel, *Profile of the Builder and His Industry,* National Association of Homebuilders, Washington, 1970, pp. 43–50.

[2] *Washington Post,* Jan. 1, 1977.

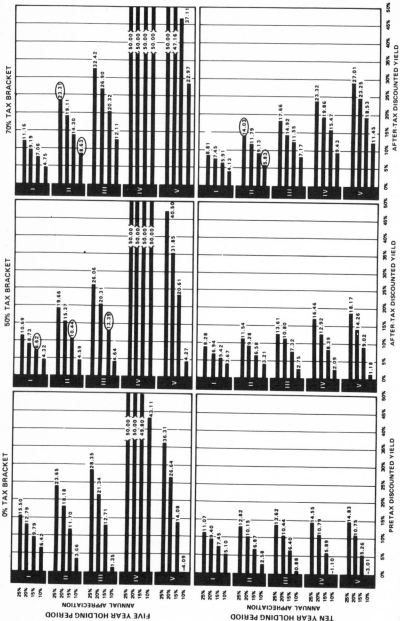

Figure 9-2 Projected annual after-tax discounted yields on land investment. Exhibit I: all cash; Exhibit II: 25 percent down, 75 percent loan, 8.5 percent interest, fully amortized in 15 years; Exhibit III: 15 percent down, 85 percent loan, 8.5 percent interest, interest only first 3 years, fully amortized over next 15 years; Exhibit IV: 5 percent down, 95 percent loan, 8.5 percent interest, interest only first 5 years, fully amortized over next 15 years; Exhibit V: 1 year's prepaid interest down, 100 percent loan, 8.5 percent interest, no payment first year, interest only at 8.5 percent for next 9 years, interest and equal principal next 5 years. Note the following general assumptions: (1) expenses = 2 percent of appreciated value; (2) annual appreciation (25, 20, 15, 10) based on noncompounding rate; (3) 39.857 percent federal capital-gains tax paid by investors in the 50 and 70 percent brackets. (*Robert M. Ellis, Real Estate Investment Analysis, Coldwell Banker Company, Los Angeles, 1976, p. 38.*)

narrowed, and the standards of required improvements and infrastructure are raised; and (2) the time required for securing development approval is greatly extended.

Time is the essence of land development, as shown in Fig. 9-2. The lower indicated returns for 10-year holding in Fig. 9-2 primarily reflect the costs of holding land over a longer period before sale. Longer holding periods increase risk and uncertainty, while higher improvement standards add to the investor's capital at risk.

The environmental costs shown in Fig. 9-1 are portrayed as falling upon the consumer. Their initial impact is upon the developer and investor, who must risk the possibility that they may not be able to pass all these environmental costs to the consumer in the short run. The alternative of holding developed property adds further to the developer's costs.

OPPORTUNITIES IN LAND INVESTMENT

The preceding discussion of land-value trends in the United States emphasizes the diversity of opportunities in land investment. It is useful to distinguish between the following types of land and potential uses in discussing land-investment strategies.

1. Land as a productive resource
   a. Farming
   b. Timber and paper
   c. Cattle raising
   d. Oil, gas, coal lands
2. Land as a speculation
   a. Changing accessibility
   b. Changing zoning and permitted uses
   c. Effect of public or private investments
3. Land development and packaging
   a. Residential subdivision
   b. Industrial development
   c. Recreational land
4. Land as a long-run investment

The purchase of land for agricultural uses or timber growing often provides an income during the investor's holding period to offset interest and other costs of holding land and property taxes. In many instances, investors with other sources of taxable income can offset losses on farm operations against other income, thus providing tax shelter to the investor during the holding period.

Recent evidence of the attractiveness of farmland as an investment is found in a proposal by the Continental Illinois Bank and Merrill Lynch,

Pierce, Fenner and Smith, Inc., for the formation of an agricultural land trust fund open to employee pension funds. According to news announcements, the bank would buy farmland outright, lease the land to farmers, and oversee its management while holding it for long-term gain. The primary investment objective would be to make money on the expected continuation of long-term upward trends in the price of farmland, with modest expectation of current cash returns.[1]

Long-term holdings of timberland provide opportunity for capital gains on sale of timber plus a possible gain in the land due to inflation or to possible changes to utilization for residential, recreational, or other use.

Land speculation in anticipation of changes in permitted use or accessibility has strong attraction for purchasers willing to assume the risks of error in forecasting political decisions with respect to zoning, transportation, or other public investment. The risks of loss in land speculation are heightened by the uncertainties regarding the degree to which future developments affecting specific properties is already discounted in current market prices. Delays in realization of future anticipated development and related carrying costs can often cause anticipated speculative profits in land to vanish.

LAND DEVELOPMENT

Land development and packaging encompass a wide range of activities using raw land as a base. Splitting farmland up into smaller units for recreational, residential, industrial, and commercial use is a common form of land packaging.

The planned-unit development represents a more complex type of land development, often involving construction, rental, and sale of various classes of improved property in a large development. New communities represent the ultimate in land development requiring large front-end capital investments and long planning, development, and holding periods. The relative importance of the land component as a percentage of the total financial element in the total project diminishes as land development and packaging projects become more capital-intensive.

The total risk in vacant land tends to increase with the degree of leverage and with the political and market risk, as discussed earlier and as shown in Figs. 2-1 and 9-2. Needless to say, the business and cyclical risk increases with the size of the capital investment and with the length of the planning, development, and selling period. It can be noted in Fig. 9-2 that land prices

---

[1] "Opposition Might Keep Farmland Fund from Leaving Ground as Hearings Start," *The Wall Street Journal*, Tues., Feb. 22, 1977, p. 40. More recent reports indicate that the bank and its underwriters, Merrill Lynch, Pierce, Fenner and Smith, withdrew the proposal because of political opposition in Congress.

must increase by over 10 percent (not compounded) per annum to provide acceptable IRRs.

ANALYZING LAND-DEVELOPMENT PROJECTS

The general analytical framework for determining the valuation and future rates of return on land-development projects outlined below is based upon the DCF formulation in Eq. (3-5). The returns from land development are represented by land-sales revenues, which are offset by outlays for development expenses and carrying charges. A large land-development project may result in a retention of a portion of the land as an investment by the developer, which is represented as a reversionary interest at the current value or selling price:

$$V - D = E = \sum_{t=1}^{n} \frac{NCF}{(1 + r)^t} + \frac{reversion}{(1 + r)^n} \qquad (9\text{-}2)$$

where
V = present value of land-development project
D = mortgage or other debt
E = investor's equity

$\sum_{t=1}^{n} NCF$ = anticipated annual or monthly net operating revenues (selling prices of lots less costs of development)
n = holding or development period, years
r = investor's target rate of return on project IRR
reversion = estimated cash value to investor at end of period n

CASE STUDIES IN LAND DEVELOPMENT

A simple illustration of the use of the land-development model shown in Eq. (9-2) follows. A prospective land investor is considering the purchase of a 200-acre tract of recreational land for subdivision into ten 20-acre parcels for high-income second-home development. The land is currently offered at $1,190 per acre, a total price of $238,000. A loan in the amount of $180,000 is available at 8 percent interest on the declining balance, with 120 equal monthly payments of principal and interest in the amount of $2,183.94 ($26,207 per year).

Land-improvement and operating costs, including property taxes, are estimated at $4,400 per year for the first 3 years, $3,000 per year for the next 4 years, and $2,000 per year for the last 3 years.

The individual investor plans to sell off nine of the ten parcels over a 10-year holding period at prices of $45,000 to $50,000 each. He plans to retain one parcel of 20 acres for his own personal residence and estimates it will have a value at the end of the holding period of $60,000. He is in a

TABLE 9-8 DCF Analysis for a Second-Home Development*

| | Year | | | | | | | | | | |
	1	2	3	4	5	6	7	8	9	10	Sum
Gross sales revenue	$45,000	$45,000	$45,000	$46,000	$50,000	$50,000	$50,000	$50,000	$50,000	$60,000	$500,000
Less 10% selling costs	4,500	4,500	4,500	5,000	5,000	5,000	5,000	5,000	5,000	5,000	43,000
Net sales revenue	40,500	40,500	40,500	41,500	45,000	45,000	45,000	45,000	45,000	60,000	457,000
Less operating and improvement costs	4,440	4,440	4,440	3,000	3,000	3,000	3,000	2,000	2,000	2,000	31,200
Net operating income	36,100	36,100	36,100	38,500	42,000	42,000	42,000	43,000	43,000	58,000	416,800
Less interest	13,957	12,940	11,838	10,647	9,355	7,956	6,442	4,801	3,025	1,101	82,062
Net taxable income	22,143	23,160	24,262	27,853	32,645	34,044	35,558	38,199	39,975	56,899	334,738
Tax (40% first 4 yr, 30%, 6 yr)	8,857	9,264	9,704	11,141	9,793	10,213	10,667	11,459	11,992	17,069	110,159
Tax shelter	5,582	5,176	4,735	4,258	2,806	2,386	1,932	1,440	907	330	29,552
Net operating income	36,100	36,100	36,100	37,500	42,000	42,000	42,000	43,000	43,000	58,000	415,800
Less loan payment (interest and amortization)	26,207	26,207	26,207	26,207	26,207	26,207	26,207	26,207	26,207	26,207	262,070
Before-tax cash flow	9,893	9,893	9,893	11,293	15,793	15,793	15,793	16,793	16,793	31,793	153,730
Less taxes	8,857	9,264	9,704	11,141	9,793	10,213	10,667	11,459	11,992	17,069	110,159
After-tax cash flow (ATCF)	1,036	629	189	152	6,000	5,580	5,126	5,334	4,801	14,724	43,571
× discount ATCF at 12%	0.8928	0.7971	0.7117	0.6355	0.5764	0.5066	0.4523	0.4038	0.3606	0.3219	
	$ 925	$ 501	$ 134	$ 96	$ 3,404	$ 2,826	$ 2,318	$ 2,153	$ 1,731	$ 4,739	18,827
ATCF + tax shelter	6,618	5,805	4,924	4,410	8,806	7,966	7,058	6,774	5,708	15,054	73,123
Present value ATCF + shelter discount at 12%	5,908	4,627	3,504	2,802	4,996	4,035	3,192	2,735	2,058	4,845	38,702
at 4%	6,353	5,363	4,376	3,769	7,237	6,293	5,357	4,945	3,995	10,168	$ 57,856

* See text for assumptions.

50 percent tax bracket now but expects to be in a 30 percent tax bracket after the fourth year.

Table 9-8 summarizes the sales revenues, development, and other expenses and the carrying costs for the 10-year land development project. The present-value calculations at the bottom of Table 9-8 show that the after-tax rate of return to the potential investor in this project, based upon an assumed initial equity of $58,000 ($238,000 − $180,000) would be approximately 4 percent under the above assumptions. Since alternative investments are probably available to the investor, producing higher after-tax rates of return, it can be assumed that the investor would offer a lower price for the land or reject the development project entirely. The calculations in Table 9-8 show that, assuming that the investor has a minimum after-tax target rate of return of 12 percent for 10-year holding, he would be justified in offering only $218,702 for the property ($180,000 + $38,702). It can be seen that the DCF model can be used to determine purchase price given a target rate of return or to measure the IRR on a land-development project given assumptions about the purchase price, debt terms, and probable sales of land in the future.

LARGE-SCALE LAND DEVELOPMENT

The many new constraints upon land development by state and federal agencies have added to the costs of developing land and extended substantially the normal period of time required to secure public approvals for land subdivision. The sequence of steps required for a large-scale land-development project in a typical state exercising subdivision controls is summarized below:

1. Land acquisition
   a. Economic-feasibility studies
   b. Options
2. Engineering and planning
   a. Preparation of overall plan and tentative maps
   b. Survey and financing of utilities
   c. General engineering and improvements studies
   d. Filing tentative map with county recorder
   e. Dedication of streets
   f. County, city, and state requirements
   g. State water-pollution board
   h. Federal environmental impact statement
   i. Questionnaire and inspection by division of real estate
   j. Filing of final map with county recorder

    k. Installation of utilities
    l. Grading and preparation of land
3. Land development and/or sale
    a. Construction loan financing and permanent loan commitments
    b. FHA, VA, or California Department of Veterans Affairs financing approvals
    c. Sales and/or development schedule

CASH STUDY IN LARGE-SCALE LAND DEVELOPMENT

The determination of cash flow for a large-scale land-development project identifies the rate at which money will have to be made available for investment in the project and (later, when sales provide revenue in excess of expense) the rate at which money will be available for other uses.

The basis of the cash-flow statement, as illustrated above, is gross income minus all expenses involved, calculated on a yearly basis. The list of expenses will vary with each project, but the following items are usually included:

1. Cost of land
2. Loan or mortgage interest and amortization
3. Utility costs
4. Property taxes on land
5. Operating expenses of the development company
6. Land-development expenses
7. Sales expenses
8. Income taxes

The generalized model shown as Eq. (9-2) can be used for estimating (1) the internal rate of return on the development, assuming an original cost and equity investment, or (2) the net present value of the project assuming a target rate of return desired by the investor.

CASE PROBLEM IN PLANNED-UNIT DEVELOPMENT: MARKVILLE LAND PROJECT

Development Strategy

The village consists of approximately 2,726 acres of land to be developed in six phases over a 10-year period, 1975 to 1986. The group will act as master developer, selling development tracts to selected subdevelopers. These subdevelopers are being chosen from among the top residential, office, institutional, and commercial developers in the country and will develop their respective tracts under a comprehensive set of development guidelines established and enforced by the group. The lot-sales programs are the only exceptions to the above. Under these programs, the group will sell single-family detached lots to builders and individuals. The lots will be fully developed including streets and all utilities.

The group will assume responsibility for all village development outside the subdeveloper tracts. Road access and total utility service will be provided to the boundary of each tract to the extent that each parcel will be ready for development when sold.

Village and community recreational facilities will be constructed by the group. Operational and security management of all recreational facilities will be provided by the group for a period of 1 to 5 years after activation, at which time they will be turned over to the Village Association or to private ownership.

The Village Association will be established the first year of development to provide a framework for continuing involvement by the village residents in the affairs of their community. The association will be organized by an independent professional community-management firm under contract with the group. The association, ultimately supported totally by assessments from the residents, will be controlled by a board of directors, on which the group will have decreasing representation as development progresses. The association will own and maintain all community-owned recreational facilities, in addition to providing coordination for community recreational, cultural, educational, and social activities.

The group will also provide overall marketing support for the village. A Village Preview Center will be constructed, outfitted, and staffed by the group in the first phase to provide a focal point for all prospective village residents. A comprehensive advertising campaign will be designed and carried out. The advertising program will be designed to focus attention on the specific development activities within the village as well as attracting general interest.

Revenue

Except for the lot-sales programs (country homes lot sales at retail and to builders), all revenues are based on the sale of unfinished tracts to subdevelopers. In order to generate momentum, it is assumed that subdevelopers and builders will require the following financing terms in 1975 and 1976: the group will receive cash at closing of 10 percent down payment and 81 percent from hypothecation of the note under a line of credit established with a financing institution. The 10 percent balance will be received two years after sale.

Residential The existing master plan provides for the ultimate development of 8,138 housing units. While the housing mix is considered optimum for today's market, it is quite likely that adjustments in the plan will be necessary to respond to changes in market demands over the coming years. Fortunately, the plan provides for this flexibility, particularly among the cottage-home, town-home, and garden-apartment categories. The following types of housing will be offered in the village:

Type	Dwelling units per acre	Finished price
Country homes, owner, detached	2	$ 75,000–$150,000
Owner, detached, patio	4	55,000–$85,000
Cottage homes, owner, patio, zero lot line	6	45,000–$75,000
Town homes, condominium, townhouse, attached	8	35,000–$65,000
Garden apartments, rental, flats, and townhouse	12	$200–$400 per month
Town apartments, rental, midrise	20	$300–$500 per month

This land-development model assumes no revenues from the group's building and selling residential units. The model assumes revenues only from land sales, according to the following guidelines:

OWNER HOUSING: Includes tract sales for garden, cottage, and town homes; does not include the lot-sales programs (country-home lot sales at retail and to builders). All revenue is generated by the sale of development tracts to subdevelopers. It has been estimated that for all forms of owner housing, undeveloped land as a percentage of the finished price of the living unit averages over 10 percent. Assuming an overall average in the village of 10 percent, the sale price of each tract is calculated by taking 10 percent of the anticipated average finished price of all living units in the tract A and multiplying by the anticipated number of units per acre in the tract B:

$$\text{Tract sales price} = 0.10AB$$

OWNER HOUSING (RETAIL LOT SALES ONLY): Approximately 688 lots on 344 acres will be sold directly to the ultimate user. The lots will be sold for $25,000 to $30,000 per lot, over half being located on a major amenity. The lots will be offered with 10 percent down payment and financing made available through the group. For the purposes of this model, it is assumed that the average sales price of these lots is $27,500 and that cash flow realized at the time of sale is $25,000 per lot. The above is based on the following additional assumptions:

1. The group will receive cash at the time of sale of 10 percent down payment and 81 percent from hypothecation of the note under a line of credit established with a financing institution. Initial service charges will be paid by the purchaser. Initial cash flow = $27,500 × 91% = $25,000 per lot.

2. Monthly payments made by the purchaser will be handled by the financing institution and will be applied in total as a reduction to the out-

standing loan. Interest paid by the purchaser will offset interest charged the group by the financing institution.

3. To provide for charges, expenses, and early-year price reductions not anticipated by the above, it is assumed that the remaining 9 percent of the selling price is *not* received by the group.

All lots sold under the retail lot-sales program will be developed within 3 years from date of sale.

OWNER HOUSING (BUILDER LOT SALES ONLY): Approximately 416 lots on 208 acres are identified in the development model as country homes, builder. Assuming that the average finished price of living units in these tracts will be $100,000 and assuming that a builder will pay 20 percent for a developed lot, the lot prices are estimated at $20,000 each, or $40,000 per acre. These lots will be fully developed by the group before sale to the builder.

RENTAL HOUSING: Includes garden and town apartments. It is assumed that these tracts will be sold to subdevelopers at $2,500 per unit for garden apartments and $3,000 per unit for town apartments. Garden apartments (12 units per acre) selling price = $30,000 per acre. Town apartments (20 units per acre on a single 15-acre tract in the village center) selling price = $60,000 per acre.

Business center   Includes seven development tracts in phases I to III, totalling 250 acres producing 2 million square feet of office space. It is assumed that six of these tracts (200 acres) will be sold to subdevelopers at $50,000 per acre. For the purposes of this model, it is assumed that tract 1, phase I, will be sold at $35,000 per acre during 1976 in order to create initial momentum in the business center. Although it is likely that the group may develop a portion of the business center for its own account, no revenue beyond the land sales revenue is included in the land-development model.

Health center   In phase I (tract 2) 30 acres have been set aside for a health center, to include a hospital, medical office space, and convalescent facilities. It is assumed that this tract will be sold to a subdeveloper in 1975 at $40,000 per acre.

Convenience centers   Includes five convenience centers located in phase I (tracts 3 and 23), phase V (tract 4), and phase VI (tracts 25 and 26). Each convenience center contains 4 acres and will be sold to subdevelopers starting in 1978 at $80,000 per acre, with the exception of tract 3 of phase I, which will include a building constructed in 1975 at group expense for use as an interim preview center. This building and site will be sold in 1978 for $500,000 for use as the first convenience center.

School sites   The first elementary school site will be dedicated to Fulton County at no cost. In addition, we have included $250,000 toward the construction of the first elementary school. The remaining four elementary school sites and one high school site will be sold to the county at our cost, $8,500 per acre.

EXHIBIT 1 Cash-Flow Summary, Compounded at 10% (Thousands)

	1975	1976	1977	1978	1979	1980	1981	1982	1983	1984	Total
Land-sales revenues*	$ 2,748	$ 9,248	$ 6,765	$20,639	$15,643	$ 9,359	$11,512	$12,574	$ 9,167	$23,336	$120,991
Land-acquisition costs†	-17,783	-5,331	-875	-259	-119						-24,367
Land-development costs	-4,110	-3,949	-2,829	-5,966	-5,109	-5,870	-3,278	-3,633	-3,471	-2,870	-40,194
Cash flow before equity and financing, annual	-19,145	-32	3,061	14,414	10,415	3,489	8,234	8,941	5,696	20,457	55,530
Cumulative	-19,145	-19,177	-16,116	-1,702	8,713	12,202	20,436	29,377	35,073	55,530	
Equity	5,000				-5,000						
Cash flow before financing, annual	-14,145	-32	3,061	14,414	5,415	3,489	8,234	8,941	5,696	20,457	55,530
Cumulative	-14,145	-14,177	-11,116	3,298	8,713	12,202	20,436	29,377	35,073	55,530	
Financing costs‡	-808	-1,796	-1,830	-1,001							-5,435
Net cash flow, annual	-14,953	-1,828	1,231	13,413	5,415	3,489	8,234	8,941	5,696	20,457	50,095
Cumulative	-14,953	-16,781	-15,550	-2,137	3,278	6,767	15,001	23,942	29,638	50,095	

* Compounded analysis assumes compounded growth rate of 10% per year for both sales revenues and development costs. Only exception is revenue from sale of sewer taps, which is shown at present value: 1976, $100,000; 1977, $200,000; 1978, $200,000.
† Assumes that all purchase money mortgages are paid off with development lenders placed in first security position upon activation of a land parcel.
‡ Used effective rate of 12% compounded annually. Weighting as follows: sales, 50% all years; land acquisition, 100% for 1975, 50% all other years; development, 50% all years.

Nonprofit producing land uses   To provide a conservative economic model, it was assumed that certain land would generate revenue at or less than cost. These nonprofit uses are summarized below:

Use	Acres
Village center, shops and offices	15
Conference center	8
Club and recreation, Private	120
Community	7
Community centers, recreation	25
Elementary schools	75
Family center	60
Open, stables, trails	488
Roads	159
	957 = 35%

Financial analysts for the group prepared two pro forma cash-flow schedules for the Markville land project. Exhibit 1 was based upon the assumption that sales revenues and costs would increase at a compound rate of 10 percent for the decade from 1975 to 1984 with financing costs estimated at 12 percent per annum.

It can be seen in Exhibit 1 that under these assumptions the development project would be expected to generate positive net cash flows beginning in 1977. Based upon these assumptions and a $5 million beginning equity, the pro forma IRR was 20.5% for 1975 to 1984.

Exhibit 2 was based upon the assumption of no change in sales prices or costs over the period. Based upon these no "inflation assumptions," the pro forma IRR was approximately 7.75 percent. The group and its equity investors decided not to proceed with the project when it became apparent that a major real estate recession was under way in 1975.

Exhibit 3 shows the pro-forma percentages of revenue expected from the project annually for the period from 1975 through 1984, with a peak in revenues expected in the year 1978.

Exhibit 4 shows the predominance of residential and retail development in the planned project, with these categories of land use accounting for 78 percent of the total expected revenues. Revenues from the business center, which was to have been developed from 1976 to 1982, were projected to account for revenues over the decade of $11,750, or 16 percent of the total.

Land acquisition costs, summarized in Exhibit 5, averaged approximately $8,800 per acre for the total planned development of 2,726 acres. The high cash equity requirements for land acquisition costs in the first two years were critical factors influencing the negative pro-forma cash flows for the project for the years 1975 through 1978.

Comparison of Exhibits 3 and 6 reveals that 42% of the land area and total

EXHIBIT 2 Cash-Flow Summary, 1975 Constant Prices and Costs (Thousands)

	1975	1976	1977	1978	1979	1980	1981	1982	1983	1984	Total
Land-sales revenues	$ 2,748	$ 8,416	$ 5,626	$ 15,568	$ 10,715	$ 5,813	$ 6,504	$ 6,448	$ 4,284	$ 9,888	$ 76,010
Land-acquisition costs*	−17,783	−5,331	−875	−259	−119						−24,367
Land-development costs	−4,110	−3,590	−2,338	−4,486	−3,499	−3,646	−1,852	−1,863	−1,622	−1,220	−28,226
Cash flow before equity and financing, annual	−19,145	−505	2,413	10,823	7,097	2,167	4,652	4,585	2,662	8,668	23,417
Cumulative	−19,145	−19,650	−17,237	−6,414	683	2,850	7,502	12,087	14,749	23,417	
Equity	5,000					−1,000	−4,000				
Cash flow before financing, annual	−14,145	−505	2,413	10,823	7,097	1,167	652	4,585	2,662	8,668	23,417
Cumulative	−14,145	−14,650	−12,237	−1,414	5,683	6,850	7,502	12,087	14,749	23,417	
Financing costs†	−808	−1,846	−1,961	−1,461	−507						−6,646
Net cash flow, annual	−14,953	−2,351	452	9,362	6,527	1,167	652	4,585	2,662	8,668	16,771
Cumulative	−14,953	−17,304	−16,852	−7,490	−963	204	856	5,441	8,103	16,771	

* Assumes that all purchase money mortgages are paid off with development lenders placed in first security position upon activation of land parcel.
† Used effective rate of 12% compounded annually. Weighting as follows: sales, 50% all years; land acquisitions, 100% for 1975, 50% all other years; development, 50% all years.
‡ Present-value analysis assumes 1975 selling prices and development costs.

EXHIBIT 3 Revenue Summary by Phase (Thousands)

| | Year | | | | | | | | | | | | Cumu- |
	1975	1976	1977	1978	1979	1980	1981	1982	1983	1984	Total	%	lative %
Phase I	$2,748	$ 8,416	$ 2,126	$ 1,472	$ 300		$ 1,000				$16,062	21%	21%
II			1,500	2,250	2,000						5,750	8	29
III				3,688	675	$ 2,625	960	$ 2,300			10,248	13	42
IV			2,000	1,808	2,300	3,188	1,440				10,736	14	56
V				6,350	340		3,104	2,968			12,762	17	73
VI					5,100			1,180	$ 4,284	$ 9,888	20,452	27	100
Total	$2,748	$ 8,416	$ 5,626	$15,568	$10,715	$ 5,813	$ 6,504	$ 6,448	$ 4,284	$ 9,888	$76,010	100%	
Cumulative total	2,748	11,164	16,790	32,358	43,073	48,886	55,390	61,838	66,122	76,010			
Percentage	4%	11%	7%	20%	14%	8%	9%	8%	6%	13%			
Cumulative percentage	4	15	22	42	56	64	73	81	87	100			

EXHIBIT 4 Revenue Summary by Use (Thousands)

	Acres	1975	1976	1977	1978	1979	1980	1981	1982	1983	1984	Total	%
Residential:													
Country homes, builder	208		$ 1,440		$ 160					$ 800	$ 5,520	$ 7,920	10%
Retail	344	$ 500	2,500	$ 2,750	6,350	$ 5,100						17,200	23
Garden homes	121		252		348	1,400		512	700	280		3,492	5
Cottage homes	197	265	853	29	95	900	$ 900	672	450	864	1,920	6,948	9
Town homes	485	675	1,008	655	4,560		2,160	4,000	2,720	1,720	2,000	19,498	26
Rental	114	108	513	492	657	975			825	300		3,870	5
Subtotal	1,469	$1,548	$ 6,566	$ 3,926	$12,170	$ 8,375	$ 3,060	$ 5,184	$ 4,695	$ 3,964	$ 9,440	$58,928	78%
Office and institutional:													
Club and recreational, private	120							$ 1,000				$ 1,000	1%
Business center	250		$ 1,750	$ 1,500	$ 2,250	$ 2,000	$ 2,625		$ 1,625			11,750	16
Health center	30	$1,200										1,200	2
School site*	115				128	340	128		128		128	852	1
Subtotal	515	$1,200	$ 1,750	$ 1,500	$ 2,378	$ 2,340	$ 2,753	$ 1,000	$ 1,753		$ 128	$14,802	20%
Commercial:													
Convenience center	16				$ 320			$ 320		$ 320	$ 320	$ 1,280	2%
Preview center	4				500							500	
Subtotal	20				$ 820			$ 320		$ 320	$ 320	$ 1,780	2%
Other:													
Sewer-tap sales			$ 100	$ 200	$ 200							$ 500	
			$ 100	$ 200	$ 200							$ 500	
No revenue	722												
Total	2,726	$2,748	$ 8,416	$ 5,626	$15,568	$10,715	$ 5,813	$ 6,504	$ 6,448	$ 4,284	$ 9,888	$76,010	100%
Cumulative		2,748	11,164	16,790	32,358	43,073	48,886	55,390	61,838	66,122	76,010		

* First elementary school site given to Fulton County; other sites sold at $8,500 per acre.

EXHIBIT 5   Land-Acquisition Costs (Thousands)

| | | Projected cumulative cost as of July 1, 1975 | | | | Year activated | Cash funding | | | | | |
Parcel	Acres	Cash equity	Debt	Total	Per acre		1975	1976	1977	1978	1979	Total
GA	244	$ 1,375	$ 972	$ 2,347	$ 9.6	1975	$ 2,347					$ 2,347
EE	651	4,232	2,327	6,559	10.1	1975	5,560	$1,070				6,630
RC	158	386	2,269	2,655	16.8	1976	1,033	1,762				2,795
GI	667	3,382	1,186	4,568	6.8	1977	3,439	413	$584	$127	$119	4,682
CH	1006	5,024	2,746	7,770	7.7	1978	5,404	2,086	291	132		7,913
Total	2726	$14,399	$9,500	$23,899	$ 8.8		$17,783	$5,331	$875	$259	$119	$24,367

EXHIBIT 6   Land Inventory, Acres

| Parcel | Phase | | | | | | Total | % |
	I	II	III	IV	V	VI		
GA	244						244	9%
EE	245	163	243				651	24
RC	158						158	5
GI			77	386	90	114	667	25
CH					350	656	1,006	37
Total	647	163	320	386	440	770	2,726	
Percentage	24	6	12	14	16	28		100

revenues were to be accounted for in the first three phases of the project.

Individual members of the group purchased land for the first phases of the development in the amount of $2.3 million. Title to this land passed to the mortgage lender in 1977, when it became evident that the project could not be financed and sold under the prevailing depressed real estate market conditions.

SUMMARY

A theoretical model was presented based upon the general principle that land values represent the discounted present value of future revenues attributable to land. Historical data revealed a close association between population and income growth and land-value trends. Total estimated land values in the United States have risen at compound rates of 6 to 8 percent since World War II. Farmland values, which increased at 5½ percent per annum before 1970, rose much more rapidly during the 1970s.

Several institutional and economic factors appear to account for rising farmland prices: (1) the continued rise in economies of scale in farming provides stimulus for farmers to acquire additional land; (2) the relative profitability of farming in recent years has attracted and held the farm entrepreneur on the land; (3) the growing worldwide demand for farm products provides a seemingly assured market for United States farm output, and government price supports and other farm subsidies undergird farmers' expectations; (5) the continued prospects for worldwide inflation encourage the purchase of land as an inflation hedge.

Empirical investigations in San Francisco, Chicago, and New York revealed that central-city land values more than doubled in the two decades following World War II and climaxed in a speculative surge between 1969 and 1973. Empirical studies have revealed the importance of changing expectations as a major factor accounting for the rapid speculative moments characteristic of central-city land values. The recognition by investors of the cessation of economic growth in many central cities in recent years resulted in major downward adjustments in the peak values of the late 1960s and early 1970s. Market observers have forecast declining land-value trends in some central cities. The coming years may test the hypothesis that suburban and rural land values may resume their upward trend while central-city land values remain stationary.

Studies of residential-lot values underscore the higher lot improvement and environmental standards adopted by many jurisdictions in recent years. Higher raw-land costs have also been a significant factor in rising improved-lot values.

The supply of urban land represents only about 2.2 percent of all land in the United States and is expected to continue to increase as the demand for urban land encroaches on rural and farmland. The future impact of environmental and other controls over land development was explored. In the short run, it appears likely that public controls will restrict increments to the supply of urban land. In view of the large supplies of unused land in the nation, it appears unlikely that any shortages of urban land will be experienced over the long run.

Two land-development case studies underscored the risks in land development during periods of rapidly changing economic conditions and investor psychology. Profits in land development are particularly sensitive to changes in financing and improvement costs, and consumer and/or investor demand.

Land, which in many ways appears as an ideal long-term investment and inflation hedge, can and often does involve exceedingly high short-term risks under conditions of high leverage, business recession, and/or general economic uncertainty.

TEN

Real Estate Investment and Portfolio Policy

Real estate investment analysis focuses upon the expected returns, selling prices, and risks associated with specific properties. Portfolio analysis is concerned with the selection of different classes of property and other investment instruments for inclusion in a real estate investment portfolio. Previous chapters have identified the diverse factors influencing real estate investment decisions for various property types. This chapter will endeavor to articulate how legal constraints, tax laws, alternative forms of ownership, management skills, special risk characteristics, leverage, the economic outlook, and other important investment considerations influence real estate portfolio decisions.

The summary of the real estate portfolio holdings of major classes of institutions presented in Table 1-2 revealed a total of approximately $269 billion in mortgage investments and $45 billion in real estate equities held by the major classes of institutional investors in 1977. Federal and state laws specify limitations upon the investments of banks, insurance companies, real estate investment trusts, pension funds, and other institutions.

The wide-scale formation of bank and insurance holding companies in the United States over the past decade has greatly broadened the range of permitted investments in real estate by affiliates and subsidiaries of bank holding companies. The Federal Reserve Board is empowered under the Bank Holding Company Act of 1970 to review the possible benefits and adverse effects of business activities of banks unrelated to banking. An application of the Bank of America to engage directly in real estate syndication was rejected by the Federal Reserve Board in 1970 under this statute. How-

TABLE 10-1 Assets of Private Noninsured Pension Funds, Market Value, End of Year (Millions)*

	1967	1968	1969	1970	1971	1972	1973	1974	Sept. 30, 1977
Cash and deposits	$ 1,320	$ 1,592	$ 1,619	$ 1,804	$ 1,641	$ 1,857	$ 2,336	$ 4,286	$ 3,242
U.S. government securities	2,207	2,615	2,568	2,998	2,772	3,700	4,474	5,582	19,939
Corporate and other bonds	22,612	22,437	21,262	24,919	26,111	26,232	27,664	30,825	44,531
Preferred stock	1,027	1,351	1,598	1,631	2,014	1,869	985	703	1,229
Common stock	50,077	60,105	59,827	65,456	86,636	113,369	89,538	62,582	97,144
Own company	5,000	5,764	5,775	6,038	7,691	8,750	6,947	5,230	N.A.
Other companies	45,077	54,341	54,052	59,418	78,945	104,619	82,591	57,352	N.A.
Mortgages	4,001	3,578	3,461	3,504	3,184	2,427	2,108	2,063	2,485
Other assets	4,206	4,332	4,295	4,422	4,560	4,908	5,140	5,681	9,887
Total assets	$85,452	$96,013	$94,632	$104,737	$126,921	$154,363	$132,247	$111,724	$178,457

* Includes deferred profit-sharing funds and pension funds of corporations, unions, multiemployer groups, and nonprofit organizations.
Source: U.S. Securities and Exchange Commission, *Statistical Bulletin,* January 1968–January 1978.

ever, Regulation 9 of the Comptroller of the Currency permits the commingling of bank fiduciary accounts, and bank-sponsored collective investment funds including real estate investments have been an important investment vehicle for pension and trust funds.

Insurance companies are primarily regulated at the state level, and ownership of real estate by insurance companies is permitted in some form in every state. Equity participations, joint ventures, development loans, and investments are usually carried on through subsidiaries of affiliates not subject to limitation under state laws. Virtually all the major life insurance companies pursue aggressive real estate investment programs, either under the name of the parent company, as a joint venture with another corporation, or through real estate investment or services corporations.

Passage of the Employee Retirement Security Act of 1974 (ERISA) had far-reaching effects upon the investment policies of pension funds, which are the most rapidly growing investment institutions. According to the Securities and Exchange Commission, the combined assets of all private and public pension funds, including state and local government retirement funds and pension plans administered by the United States Government, totaled $372.5 billion at the end of 1974. The assets of private noninsured pension funds increased from $85.4 billion in 1967 to $178.5 billion in September 1977, as shown in Table 10-1. It can be noted that common stock and corporate bonds represented approximately 80 percent of total investment holdings. Real estate equities, included in "Other Assets," and mortgages accounted for less than 7 percent of total assets.

Regulations by the Department of Labor under ERISA require diversification in pension-fund portfolios and have stimulated increasing interest in real estate investment by pension-fund managers. A review of pension-fund investment in real estate[1] drew attention to the increasing participation of corporate and other pension funds in real estate and to the diversity of investment media used.

Real estate investment trusts   REITs, the darlings of Wall Street in the early 1970s, were fighting for survival in the late 1970s. Establishment of REITs was initiated in the 1960 congressional amendment to the Internal Revenue Code of 1954. Basically, under Section 856 of the Code, a REIT is an unincorporated trust or unincorporated association which is (1) managed by one or more trustees; (2) owned beneficially by evidence of transferable shares or by transferable certificates of beneficial interest; (3) except for special tax provisions taxed as a regular corporation if these provisions are not met; (4) not involved in the holding of property primarily for sale to customers in the ordinary course of business; and (5) held beneficially by 100 or more individuals at least 335 days of a taxable year.

---

[1] "Pension Forum," *Institutional Investor*, June 1974, pp. 21–22.

REITs have been likened to closed-end mutual funds and have primarily been limited to investments in real estate and related areas. Similarity to mutual funds was the main purpose of the enabling legislation. Many investors have for years been attracted to real estate because of possible higher returns. It has been noted that in good markets, investments in real estate will yield returns far in excess of going interest rates in the money markets.

Before the trust years, one obvious answer to the individual's real estate investment was to acquire an income property and then retain the services of a qualified property manager. With the advent of the REIT, however, small investors could obtain not only a share of one real estate investment but also a portion of a portfolio of investments in real estate which were professionally managed.

The legislation provided an additional source of funds to the real estate market as a whole. Traditionally, real estate mortgage funding has flowed from commercial banks, savings and loan associations, insurance companies, mortgage bankers, and other financial institutions. During periods of tight money, the REITs were to provide an important addition to real estate finance. Compared with two other financial institutions (commercial banks and savings and loan associations), REITs have no restrictions imposed upon the interest rates they can pay on borrowings; they can therefore compete more effectively for funds in the money markets.

REITs tend to fall into either of two categories, mortgage trusts or equity trusts. Mortgage trusts are involved in the financing of both short-term and long-term real estate investment projects. Short-term mortgage trusts focus on construction and development loans which rarely endure for periods longer than 18 months. On the other hand, long-term mortgage trusts concentrate on financing permanent mortgages. In effect, the long-term mortgage trust functions like the savings and loan associations, lending long and borrowing short. The difference traditionally has been that the trust's money is obtained primarily by issuing securities rather than by inviting deposits.

Equity trusts go a little farther than long-term mortgage trusts, investing directly in depreciable property. Their income then is derived from rents, while mortgage trusts make their money from interest, fees, and discounts. A third hybrid class of trust has a combination of both mortgage and equity characteristics. Hybrid REITs have had a more successful investment experience compared with the short-term mortgage trusts, according to Hines.[1]

REITs by law must be passive repositories for investments, and the day-to-day operations of the business are conducted by an independent contractor termed the *investment advisor*. The advisor, working for a fee which

[1] Mary Alice Hines, "Bank Loans and Sponsors of Real Estate Investment Trusts," *The Real Estate Appraiser*, May–June 1975, pp. 5–11.

averages about 1 ¼ percent of the value of managed assets, has the responsibility for originating and recommending loans to the trust management. The trustees of the trust, on the other hand, have the responsibility of raising the capital which is invested by the advisor and exercise liability management.

The first wave of REITs began in 1961, with the founding of First Mortgage Investors and Continental Mortgage Investors. Both these trusts were involved in short-term construction and development loans of the type which had previously been provided by the commercial banks. Growth within the trust industry remained slow throughout the early and mid-1960s. Between 1961 and 1967, there were only six issues by REITs in excess of $10 million, and between 1964 and 1967 there were none.[1]

Monetary policy is known for its uneven effects on the real estate industry as a whole. The construction industry in general and the housing component in particular are typically hit harder than other sectors of our economy during periods of tight money. It was in 1969, a time of tight money, that REITs enjoyed a period of unprecedented change and growth. Mortgage-lending opportunities were quite plentiful beginning in 1968 because banks were concerned about their total loans and were curtailing their construction and development activities. Within this environment, the trusts were able to command good rates on their advances to eager builders and an attractive spread over their cost of funds.

The summer of 1969 saw the start of a "second wave of trusts," namely, the long-term mortgage trusts. According to Rose,[2] the traditional sources of long-term mortgage money, the life insurance companies and the savings and loan associations, were affected by "chronic and endemic structural problems," which raised questions about their ability to provide the volume of mortgages which was likely to be necessary in the 1970s. Savings and loan associations, for instance, tend to suffer from disintermediation, especially during periods of tight money such as the "credit crunch" of 1966 and the period 1969 to 1970.

Eyeing possible future gains, many of the large commercial banks in the United States saw the advantages of diversifying through their holding companies into the REIT industry. In 1969, of the nation's 50 largest banks, Continental Illinois, Crocker-Citizens, and Union Bank sponsored public offerings of over $95 million for three new trusts. The earliest REITs had remained independent of most financial institutions with the exception of mortgage companies. The major motive of the banks for entering this industry was to increase their earnings. Another consideration was the fact

---

[1] Ibid.

[2] Cornelius C. Rose, Jr., "Real Estate Investment Trusts: How They Grow and Go," *The Journal of Commercial Bank Lending,* September 1972, pp. 10–20.

that many of the larger banks which had built gigantic mortgage departments during the 1960s needed a device to utilize their personnel in the real estate area. The REIT seemed to fit the bill.

During 1969 to 1971 growth within the trust industry was so great that more than 100 new REITs came into existence.[1] In the latter part of 1969 and the early part of 1970, the REITs with good management tended to be increasingly profitable as abnormally high construction and development loan yields were received. Construction and development investments as a percentage of total investments of the REITs rose from 28 percent in 1969 to 58 percent in 1971. Even though REITs did generally well during the money crunch of 1969, the demand for construction loans in the entire economy far outweighed the supply. As credit improved in the latter part of 1970, the pent-up demand for construction and development funds began to be satisfied. Because the REITs could process loan applications quickly and offer better services to developers, they were able to improve their market share while generally charging higher rates than other lenders.

Early competition between the REITs for loans and investments was severe. Eventually the supply of new construction started to exceed the demand in many regions of the country. The first real blow within the industry came in November 1971, when Continental Mortgage Investors (then the nation's second largest trust, with assets of $512 million) announced that earnings would drop in the following two quarters, due to the proliferation of new competition.[2] On the same day as the announcement, 16 REITs listed on the New York Stock Exchange lost $262 million on paper. Further problems plagued the trusts throughout 1973 to 1976, and several REITs were in default with creditors by early 1977.

A major problem within the industry lies in the area of its unusual taxation. As provided for in the amended Internal Revenue Code of 1954, a real estate investment trust can be taxed differently from a corporation. In fact, REITs pay taxes only on income and capital gains retained. The inherent problem is in the tax-exemption provisions of the tax law. If violation of any one of seven rules occurs, sudden death occurs; i.e., the REIT status will be revoked, and all income will be taxed just as if the trust were a corporation. The seven rules are as follows: (1) under the 75 percent gross-income test REITs must realize 75 percent of their gross income from passive real estate sources; (2) the 90 percent gross income test requires that at least 90 percent of gross income be derived from income of the 75 percent type plus dividends from any source; (3) the negative 30 percent gross-income test requires that less than 30 percent of gross income be derived from either short-term capital security gains or from the sale of real property

[1] Mary Alice Hines, "Risks, Yields, Capitalization and Management Fees of Mortgage Trusts," *The Appraisal Journal,* October 1973, pp. 484–503.
[2] "Real Estate Investment Trusts Return to Favor," *Business Week,* Oct. 28, 1972, pp. 82–84.

held for less than 4 years; (4) the 90 percent income-distribution test requires that shareholders receive at least 90 percent of the REIT's taxable income; (5) REITs must not hold any property primarily for sale to customers in the ordinary course of business; (6) REITs must meet all organizational requirements previously mentioned as under Section 856 of the Code; and (7) REITs must correct any violations of the asset-diversification test within 30 days after the close of the quarter. The test says that 75 percent of the total asset value is to be held in real estate, government securities, cash, and receivables.

The problem of overbuilding became apparent in 1973, when vacancy rates soared to very high levels on multifamily residential and office structures in several cities. The nationwide glut of office space in the mid-1970s was discussed in Chap. 8. The worst area of overbuilding was in Florida, with its many empty and unfinished condominiums.[1] Developers overbuilt in response to abnormal demand, and the propensity of many REITs was to unload money wholesale without pausing to analyze local realty conditions. According to Reinhold Wolff Economic Research Company, followers of Florida sales, there were 44,000 unsold condominiums in the three counties of Dade, Broward, and Palm Beach in the fall of 1974.

A long period of high interest rates and increasing building costs created special problems. The bank prime interest rate increased from 4.75 percent in January 1972 to 12 percent in July 1974. The construction-cost index in May 1974 was increasing at a per annum rate greater than 10 percent, compared with 9 percent in 1973 and about 7 percent in other recent years. One of the big reasons for high building costs was a widespread shortage of building materials such as nails, bricks, steel reinforcing rods, and bath fixtures in isolated areas of the country for certain periods of time.[2] Although materials shortages were alleviated in 1975, building costs continued to rise, as shown in Fig. 2-6.

Areas of the greatest concern have been mortgage defaults and builder bankruptcies.[3] The prime event that brought REIT problems in this category to light in the financial community was the fall of the Kassuba Development Corporation in December 1973. Kassuba, little known in real estate until the mid-1960s, was one of the largest apartment developers in the nation when it defaulted on its obligations and went into Chapter XI proceedings under the Bankruptcy Act. As it turned out, a dozen or so different REITs had made loans to Kassuba worth around $130 million. Table 10-2 shows the

[1] Wyndham Robertson, "How the Banks Got Trapped in the REIT Disaster," *Fortune*, March 1975, pp. 113–115, 168–176.
[2] David Gumpert and Mark Starr, "How Two Realty Trusts Gave Backers Big Gains—And Then Big Losses," *Wall Street Journal*, Mar. 14, 1975, pp. 1, 21.
[3] Mary Alice Hines, "What Has Happened to the REITs?," *The Appraisal Journal*, April 1975, pp. 252–260.

TABLE 10-2 Aggregate Balance-Sheet Data for REITs (Billions)

	1969 IV	1970 IV	1971 IV	1972 IV	1973 IV	1974 IV	1975 IV	1976 IV	1977 II
Assets:									
Land, development, and construction loans	$0.85	$2.58	$4.25	$ 7.56	$10.92	$10.98	$ 8.24	$ 4.61	$ 3.57
Other loans	0.26	0.64	1.51	3.07	4.19	4.90	4.72	4.14	3.64
Loan loss reserves						−0.78	−2.08	−2.26	−2.10
Property owned	0.70	0.95	1.35	2.48	3.31	4.28	7.03	9.14	9.13
Other assets	0.22	0.56	0.61	1.07	1.77	1.64	1.28	0.92	0.97
Total assets	$2.03	$4.73	$7.72	$14.18	$20.19	$21.02	$19.19	$16.55	$15.21
Liabilities:									
Bank borrowings and commercial paper	$0.23	$0.80	$2.24	$ 6.22	$10.47	$11.76	$11.17	$ 9.03	$ 7.83
Mortgages on property owned	0.43	0.55	0.68	1.16	1.48	1.65	2.03	2.44	2.43
Other liabilities	0.13	0.49	0.83	1.70	2.40	2.59	2.51	2.33	2.20
Total liabilities	$0.79	$1.84	$3.75	$ 9.07	$14.35	$16.00	$15.71	$13.80	$12.46
Shareholders' equity	1.24	2.89	3.97	5.11	5.84	5.02	3.48	2.75	2.75
Total liabilities and equity	$2.03	$4.73	$7.72	$14.18	$20.19	$21.02	$19.19	$16.55	$15.21

Source: Research Department, National Association of Real Estate Investment Trusts, *REIT Statistics, 1977, II,* Washington, 1978.

combined balance sheets of real estate investment trusts from 1972 to 1976. The National Association of Real Estate Investment Trusts reported that nonearning assets rose from $5.2 billion as of December 1974 to $9.9 billion as of December 1975. Foreclosed properties as of July 1977 totaled $5.5 billion, representing approximately 30 percent of total assets of REITs as of that date.[1] According to the most recent financial data of the hundred largest REITs, five of the ten largest REITs reported that over 50 percent of their total real estate investments, measured in terms of total assets, were represented by foreclosed property in the third quarter of 1977.[2]

Another major problem of the REITs is rooted within the management of the trusts. As the REITs quickly grew to their $20 billion volume, some loan managers and trust advisors of REITs were accused of exercising poor management. This allegation can best be supported by the heavy losses incurred in many areas of development and investment mentioned above.

The last major problem is that of raising capital. The earliest trusts obtained their money mainly through the issuance of securities. Because of general stock market conditions in the early 1970s and because of the increased competition for construction loans from banks, REITs sought financial leverage in the form of commercial paper and lines of credit from major banks. It can be noted in Table 10-2 that over half the assets of REITs were financed by bank loans or commercial paper as of September 1976. Many of these loans were in default and earning no interest for the banks.

Some relief for the REITs was provided by the Tax Reform Act of 1976. The following is a brief summary from the House Report describing the major features of Chapter 44 of that Act dealing with Real Estate Investment Trusts.

1. As discussed, under present law, a REIT generally is required to distribute 90 percent of its taxable income each year to its shareholders. If it does not meet this requirement, the trust will be disqualified and a REIT thus must pay tax on its income as if it were a regular corporation. Under the bill, a REIT will not be disqualified if it is determined, on audit, that the failure to meet the 90 percent distribution requirement was due to reasonable cause. In this case, the REIT is to be allowed to distribute deficiency dividends to its shareholders to avoid disqualification. However, interest and penalties are to be imposed on the amount of the adjustment under this procedure.

2. Under present law certain percentages of a REIT's income must be from designated sources. The bill provides that if a REIT were found to have failed to meet the income-source tests, it would not be disqualified but

---

[1] Research Department, National Association of Real Estate Investment Trusts, *REIT Statistics, 1977 II*, Washington, 1977.

[2] Research Department of the National Association of Real Estate Investment Trusts, *REIT's Quarterly, 1977 III*, Washington, 1978, p. 4.

would be allowed to pay tax on the amount by which it failed to meet the source test. This provision would be available only if the REIT initially had reasonable ground to believe that it had met the income-source tests.

3. Present law prohibits a REIT from holding property other than foreclosure property for sale to customers. This rule has been difficult to apply because of the virtually absolute prohibition on holding such property and because of problems involved in determining when a REIT holds property for sale. The bill eliminates the "holding" prohibition and substitutes a limit on the amount of income a REIT can derive from property so held. Under the bill, a REIT could have a de minimis amount (up to 1 percent) of its gross income from such sources, and this income would be subject to corporate tax. Any income from such sources in excess of 1 percent would be subject to an additional tax under the provisions discussed in paragraph 2 above, and would not disqualify the REIT, provided the REIT had reasonable grounds to believe that the excess income was not holding-for-sale income.

4. The bill also provides that certain types of income that customarily are earned in a real estate business but which do not now qualify under the income-source tests are to be treated as qualifying income. These include (1) certain rents from personal property leased together with the real property, (2) charges for services customarily furnished in connection with the rental of real property whether or not such charges are separately stated, and (3) commitment fees received for entering into agreements to make loans secured by real property. Because these and the other amendments discussed previously remove a significant portion of income from the category of unqualified income (which now may be 10 percent of a REIT's gross income), the income-source requirements are increased by the bill so that unqualified income could be only 5 percent of gross income. Also, all unqualified income would be subject to corporate tax.

5. Under the bill, a REIT would be permitted to operate in corporate form; under present law, a REIT must operate as a trust or association.

6. Certain other changes are made concerning technical rules applicable to REITs, including changes in the rules regarding income from sale of mortgages held for less than 4 years and regarding options to purchase real property.

Review of Selected Real Estate Portfolios

Chase Manhattan Mortgage and Realty Trust   The uncertain future of REITs can best be illustrated by examining the balance sheet and portfolio of the Chase Manhattan Mortgage and Realty Trust as of May 31, 1976, shown in Tables 10-3 to 10-6. The concentration of nonearning assets in Florida, New York, and Puerto Rico is immediately apparent. It can also be noted that construction and land-development loans accounted for over one-half

TABLE 10-3 Chase Manhattan Mortgage and Realty Trust Loans and Investments by Location as of May 31, 1976 (Thousands)

	Earning		Nonearning			Earning		Nonearning	
	No.	Amount	No.	Amount		No.	Amount	No.	Amount
Ark.	0	0	2	$ 1,943	Mo.	0	0	2	1,750
Calif.	2	$ 52,308	3	11,073	N.H.	0	0	1	1,887
Conn.	0	0	1	2,897	N.J.	1	4,132	6	26,036
Del.	1	1,411	0	0	N.Y.	4	24,058	18	112,703
Fla.	6	23,292	34	135,904	N.C.	1	20,674	3	3,752
Ga.	2	5,886	5	33,814	Ohio	1	4,546	1	750
Ill.	0	0	5	22,506	Pa.	0	0	2	4,275
Kans.	0	0	1	8,633	P.R.	0	0	6	83,037
Ky.	0	0	2	2,790	S.C.	1	850	3	16,068
La.	0	0	6	19,030	Tenn.	2	8,164	1	1,069
Md.	2	4,440	9	12,870	Tex.	0	0	6	16,843
Mass.	1	31,713	3	6,916	Utah	1	1,059	0	0
Mich.	0	0	2	25,964	Total	25	$182,533	122	$552,510

TABLE 10-4 Chase Manhattan Mortgage and Realty Trust Loans and Investments by Type as of May 31, 1976 (Thousands)

	Earning		Nonearning	
	No.	Amount	No.	Amount
Construction loans:				
Residential:				
Condominiums	0	$ 0	16	$ 64,695
Other	0	0	7	26,477
Office buildings	1	1,228	0	0
Shopping centers	0	0	8	27,510
Hotels and motels	0	0	2	11,994
Nursing homes and hospitals	0	0	1	1,456
Total	1	$ 1,228	34	$132,132
Land and land-development loans	2	$ 5,633	26	$137,362
Permanent mortgages	15	140,325	15	115,559
Second mortgages	6	17,347	14	42,103
Property acquired by foreclosure	0	0	23	113,362
Leasebacks	1	18,000	1	5,594
Real estate-related investments	0	0	6	4,286
Other	0	0	3	2,112
Total	25	$182,533	122	$552,510

TABLE 10-5 Chase Manhattan Mortgage and Realty Trust, Balance Sheets (Thousands), May 31, 1976 and 1975

	1976	1975
Assets		
Loans and investments:		
Real estate loans:		
Earnings	$164,533	$236,382
Nonearning, including $148,221,000 in process of foreclosure ($114,929,000 in 1975)	429,268	547,897
Total real estate loans	593,801	784,279
Property acquired by foreclosure	113,362	26,602
Other real estate-related investments, at cost	4,286	9,445
	711,449	820,326
Less allowance for possible losses	174,000	159,150
	537,449	661,176
Investments in real estate, at (less accumulated depreciation and amortization of $204,000 in 1975)	23,594	25,690
Total loans and investments	561,043	686,866
Real estate assets exchanged for debt subsequent to May 31, 1976	13,194	
Receivable from Chase Bank	131,000	141,706
Short-term investments (secure performance of contracts)	2,390	
Cash	7,764	18,250
Accrued interest receivable	2,505	3,530
Other assets	790	642
	$718,686	$850,994
Liabilities and shareholders' equity (deficiency)		
Liabilities:		
Accounts payable and accrued expenses	$ 4,147	$ 4,760
Unearned income		1,187
Long-term debt:		
Restated credit agreement, including $17,325,000 exchanged for real estate assets subsequent to May 31, 1976	644,939	761,000
7⅞% notes due 1978	49,903	49,852
Subordinated notes and debentures	83,903	83,810
Total long-term debt	778,745	894,662
Total liabilities	782,892	900,609
Shareholders' equity (deficiency):		
Preferred shares, 2 million authorized shares; none issued	—	—
Common shares, $1 per value, 6 million authorized shares; 4,885,601 issued and outstanding shares (4,885,571 in 1975)	4,886	4,886
Additional paid-in capital, less cumulative distributions in excess of income of $15,331,000	111,954	111,953
Accumulated deficit	−181,046	−166,454
Total shareholders' equity (deficiency)	−64,206	−49,615
Commitments and litigation		
	$718,686	$850,994

TABLE 10-6 Chase Manhattan Mortgage and Realty Trust, Statements of Operations (Thousands) Years Ended May 31, 1976 and 1975

	1976	1975
Income:		
Interest on real estate loans	$ 24,553	$ 68,594
Interest on receivable from Chase Bank	5,501	
Rental income from investments in real estate	2,408	2,425
Fees and other income, net	264	624
	$ 32,726	$ 71,648
Expenses:		
Interest on short-term debt		$ 32,213
Interest on long-term debt	$ 25,170	56,430
Amortization of debt discount and expense	229	545
Advisory fees		1,134
Trustees' fees and expenses	140	189
Other expenses	6,371	3,910
Provisions for possible losses	30,774	143,676
	$ 62,654	$238,097
Loss before extraordinary gain	$−29.928	$166,454
Extraordinary gain on exchange of assets for debt	$ 15,336	
Net loss	$−14,592	$166,454
Net loss per common share (dollars):		
Loss before extraordinary gain	$ −6.13	$−34.07
Extraordinary gain	3.14	
Net loss	$ −2.99	$−34.07

of the total nonearning assets of $429.3 million. The balance sheet shows that $113 million in value of property had been acquired through foreclosure, with an additional $148 million in the process of foreclosure. Table 10-6 also shows an additional allowance of $174 million for "possible losses." Total assets of $718 million are offset by $782.9 million in long-term debt and other liabilities, leaving a net deficiency in shareholders equity of $64.2 million in Table 10-5.

The statement of operations shown as Table 10-6 indicates losses before extraordinary gain of $238 million in 1975 and $62.6 million in 1976. The most startling figure in the income statement is the rental income from investments in real estate, a mere 2.4 million on properties valued at approximately $150 million.

The accompanying notes to the 1976 financial statements for Chase Manhattan Mortgage and Realty Trust are omitted in Tables 10-3 to 10-6. Effective as of Oct. 6, 1975, the trust entered into a restated credit agreement with 40 bank lenders and the Federal Deposit Insurance Corporation which consolidated, amended, and restated the terms of the trust's two earlier bank-credit agreements. Under these agreements the maturity date for $761 million in notes due these banks was automatically extended to June 30, 1977 and to Dec. 31, 1977 under certain provisions for reductions in principal by June 30, 1977. The effective limitation on nonearning assets of the trust by these credit agreements was $557 million. The total of nonearning assets had reached $552 million by May, 1976, and represented 75 percent of total assets.

Chase Manhattan Mortgage and Realty Trust announced a plan on Feb. 28, 1977 to restructure and reduce its public and senior bank debt through a complex asset-exchange program. Under the plan the trust and its creditors agreed to the following:

1. The trust offered to acquire $50 million face value of 7⅞ percent publicly held notes due 1978 at $800 for each $1,000 face value.

2. The generation of $108 million in cash was to be effected through sale of trust assets and loan repayments.

3. Bank indebtedness was to be reduced by $275 to $330 million by a new asset exchange program involving 90 properties.

4. The trust would make a cash repayment of the remaining bank indebtedness to be financed by a new $100 million 5-year bank term loan and a $75 million revolving-bank-credit agreement.

5. The creditor banks would receive warrants to purchase common shares of the trust, exercisable until June 30, 1987.

6. Holders of the trust's 7½ percent notes due 1983, 6¾ percent convertible debentures, and its 6½ percent convertible subordinated debentures would be offered the right to exchange their existing securities for a new issue of convertible subordinated debentures to be due in 1977. The principal amount of new debentures issued would not be more than the market price of the current issues.

According to news reports, the trust expected by this plan to reduce its bank debt to no more than $175 million from $556 million presently owed and to extend the term of the remaining debt substantially. The success of the plan from the point of view of the trust's stockholders and debenture holders will depend, in the last analysis, upon the quality of the assets given up and upon the present and future value of those retained. According to news reports, the assets given up to the banks in the asset-exchange program will be priced at not less than 113 percent of their *estimated net realizable value.*

Prisa The Prudential Insurance Company's Property Investment Separate Account PRISA is the largest single holder of real estate investments in the United States, with total assets of $831.7 million and mortgage and other indebtedness equal to approximately $151 million as of Sept. 30, 1976. The distribution of investments by geographical areas and types of properties is shown in Table 10-7. Approximately 44.6 percent of properties held were under 5 years of age, with only 9.1 percent over 20 years. Office buildings

TABLE 10-7   Real Estate Investment Portfolio of PRISA as of Sept. 30, 1976

Class	West No.	West %	South No.	South %	Midwest No.	Midwest %	East No.	East %	Total No.	Total %	Value Millions	Value %
Offices	10	4.5	10	6.1	7	3.7	7	15.8	34	30.1	$217.6	30.1
Industrial	29	8.1	24	7.2	88	10.8*	5	1.5	146*	27.6	199.0	27.6
Commercial	4	2.2	5	4.4	6	4.1	3	6.8	18	17.5	126.5	17.5
Hotels and motels			7	3.7			6	11.1	13	14.8	107.1	14.8
Apartments	2	2.9	1	3.1	2	1.2	2	2.5	7	9.7	70.3	9.7
Farms					1	0.2			1	0.2	1.3	0.2
Land under lease	1	0.1							1	0.1	0.9	0.1
Total	46	17.8	47	24.5	104	20.0	23	37.7	220	100.0		

* Includes 62 industrial properties, representing 4.2% of total property value, acquired as a group.
Source: PRISA, The Prudential Property Investment Separate Account, Annual report for the Year Ended Sept. 30, 1976, p. 27.

and industrial buildings accounted for 57.7 percent of the total dollar volume of investments.

The average net return to PRISA shareholders averaged approximately 8.5 percent per year for 1974 to 1976. These returns reflect investment income after deduction of operating expenses, federal income taxes, and management fees, plus the unrealized gain or loss on investments.

Prudential, like other institutional real estate investors, can purchase or make loans on a wide range of property types. They are not interested in long-term leased fees unless they have "meaningful rental escalation" provisions and an "upside" potential. The portfolio shown in Table 10-7 reflects a limited investment in apartment properties.

Table 10-8 illustrates the wide range of potential real estate investments and the reported interest of major investment institutions in early 1977 in particular types of investments. It can be noted that all institutions appear willing to invest in shopping centers, office buildings, and industrial buildings. Only a few appear interested in short-term or speculative loans, "purchase net lease credit deals" (standby commitments), or construction loans, reflecting the unfavorable recent experience with these types of investments.

GENERAL PORTFOLIO CONSIDERATIONS

It has been noted that institutional and individual investors have a wide range of ownership forms available for real estate investment. The limited-partnership syndicate, the Subchapter S corporation, equity participation and joint-venture agreements, purchase leasebacks, commingled and

TABLE 10-8 Income Property Finance Report

Company (see key below)

	1	2	3	4	5	6	7	8	9	10	11	12	13	14	15	16
Reviewed in issue no.	2	1	2	1	3	2	5	3	4	5	1	5	1	3	4	4
Long-term first mortgages	N	N	N	N	Y	N	Y	N	Y	Y	N	Y	Y	N	N	Y
Interim 2- to 5-yr first mortgages	Y	N	N	N	N	Y	N	N	N	Y	N	N	N	Y	N	N
Sale leasebacks	N	Y	Y	Y	P	N	Y	N		P	P	N	Y	Y	N	N
Subordinated land-sale leasebacks	N	N	Y	Y	P	N	N	N	P	N	P	N	N	Y	N	Y
Second mortgages	Y	N	Y	Y	N	Y	N	N	N	N	N	N	N	Y	N	Y
Special loans	Y	N	N	N	Y	Y	F	N	F	Y	N	Y	Y	Y	N	N
Joint-venture developments	N	Y	Y	Y	N	Y	F	N	F	F	N	Y	Y	Y	Y	N
Acquisitions of real estate	N	Y	Y	Y	Y	N	Y	Y	Y	Y	Y	Y	Y	Y	Y	N
Joint-venture acquisitions	N	Y	Y	Y	Y	N	P	N	P	N		Y	Y	Y	Y	N
Shopping centers	Y	Y	Y	Y	Y	Y	Y	Y	Y	Y	Y	Y	Y	Y	Y	Y
Office buildings	Y	Y	Y	Y	Y	Y	Y	Y	Y	Y	Y	Y	Y	Y	Y	Y
Apartment buildings	Y			N	N	Y	F	Y	Y	Y	Y	Y	Y	Y	N	N
Industrial buildings	Y	Y	Y	Y	Y	Y	Y	Y	Y	Y	Y	N	Y	Y	Y	Y
Hotels, motels	Y	Y	N	N	N	N	Y	N	N	N	N	Y	Y	OWC	N	N

	1	2	3	4	5	6	7	8	9	10	11	12	13	14	15	16
Special-purpose real estate	Y	Y	N	N	N	N	OWC	N	N	N	N	Y	N	N	N	OWC
Purchase net-lease credit deals	N	N	Y	N	N	Y	N	N	Y	N	Y	N	Y	N	N	Y
Standbys	Y	Y	N	N	N	Y	N	N	Y	Y	N	N	N	N	N	Y
Gap loans	Y	N	N	N	N	Y	N	N	N	N	N	N	Y	N	N	Y
Construction loans	N	N	N	N	N	Y	N	Y	Y	N	N	N	Y	N	N	N
Wraparounds	Y	N	N	Y	Y	Y	N	N	N	Y	Y	N	Y	N	N	Y
Minimum purchase		3 MM (L)	1.5 MM (L)	4 MM (L)	1 MM (L)		500 M F/C	3 MM (L)	1 MM F/C		1 MM (L)	1 MM F/C	500 M F/C	3 MM (L)	NL	1 MM
Maximum purchase		24 MM (L)	20 MM (L)	75 MM (L)	20 MM (L)		NL	20 MM (L)	40 MM (L)	NL	5 MM (L)	NL	10 MM F/C	NL		
Minimum mortgage loan	1 MM				500 M	500 M			1 MM	1 MM	1 MM		500 MM			1 MM
Maximum mortgage loan	5 MM		20 MM	7.5 MM	15 MM		NL		NL	5 MM	5 MM	NL	10 MM		NL	8 MM

Key: 1 = Aetna Business Credit, Inc.
2 = American Property Investors
3 = BankAmerica International Realty Corp.
4 = Citibank Direct Placement Dept.
5 = Connecticut Mutual Life Insurance Co.
6 = General Electric Credit Corp.
7 = John Hancock Mutual Life Insurance Co.
8 = Robert A. McNeil Corporation
9 = Mutual Benefit Life Insurance Co.
10 = Mutual Life Insurance Co. of New York
11 = New Plan Realty Trust
12 = Phoenix Mutual Life Insurance Co.
13 = Prudential Insurance Co.
14 = Realty Income Trust
15 = Schroder Real Estate, Division of Schroder Trust Co.
16 = US Life Real Estate Services Corp.

F = few
P = perhaps
Y = yes
N = no
M = 1,000
MM = 1,000,000
OWC = only with credit
NL = no limit
(L) = leveraged
F/C = free and clear

Source: Income Property Finance Report, March 1, 1977.

pooled funds, pension funds, retirement funds, and trust funds are among the ownership vehicles available to investors seeking management expertise and diversification in real estate investment. These several vehicles for investment represent a tribute to the ingenuity of the real estate and investment banking community in creating investment-ownership media to meet a wide range of needs and criteria.

The types of property selected for a portfolio and the forms of ownership used will vary with the legal constraints, liabilities of the institutions, overall investment objectives, management and analytical capabilities, and risk-return profiles. Answers to the following basic questions underlie portfolio decisions by institutions and individuals:

1. What are the legal or other constraints upon investment?

2. What are the goals of the investment program?

3. How should the investor allow for uncertain future economic and political developments?

4. What analytical techniques and investment criteria should be used in the selection of investments?

Legal constraints upon institutional investments are based upon the general principle that the assets held must be related to the nature of the liabilities of the institution. For this reason, commercial banks with large short-term liabilities in the form of demand deposits generally confine investments to short-term securities or loans, matching investments in bonds and mortgages to levels of stable time deposits. Conversely, life insurance companies and pension funds, whose liabilities are long-term in nature and predictable, can and do seek out higher-yielding, long-term investments. Fire and casualty insurance firms generally confine investments to readily marketable securities because of the nature of their business risks.

The critical importance of matching asset and liability management has already been evident in the financial crisis facing many REITs which made long-term and high-risk real estate investments in the early 1970s, financed in large measure by short-term bank credit. Some observers have pointed out that successful liability management is of equal importance to proper asset management in REITs.[1] This principle can be applied to individual investment policy as well. Savings needed for family or business emergencies, educational expenses, or family protection are generally not committed to long-term high-risk assets with limited marketability.

Legal constraints and the nature of liabilities act as important factors in the determination of the goals of any investment program. Figure 2-2, showing the relative risks and rewards associated with various types of real estate

---

[1] Fred Gale and Robert Lattin, "Successful Liability Management for Mortgage Trusts," *Real Estate Review*, vol. 3, no. 3, pp. 82–85, Fall 1973.

investment, demonstrates that individuals and institutions are presented with a wide range of potential returns in various classes of real estate investment. Varying the degree of leverage in any specific real estate investment can alter the potential returns as well as the risks. Matching investment goals to opportunities in real estate investment presents the familiar trade-off between risks and rewards in any investment-decision framework. The choice of investments involving high business, market, and political risk is obviously inconsistent with a set of investment goals emphasizing safety of principal. The assumption of a highly leveraged investment position in high-risk investments accentuates their risk characteristics and should eliminate them from consideration for many classes of investors.

All investment decisions involve some prediction concerning the uncertain future. Will the borrower be able to meet mortgage payments? Will properties owned generate the expected rentals? Will shopping-center investments generate increasing income under rent-escalation leases? These and many other questions underlie real estate investment decisions.

Investors unwilling to limit investments to fixed-income investments guaranteed by the United States government or by some other insurer or guarantor must form some judgments about future economic and political developments affecting their portfolios. The outmoded dictum that in the absence of better information the investor should assume that past economic trends will continue, is no longer acceptable in today's dynamic era of economic and political change.

Econometric modeling is a widely used analytical tool of government and business. The president's annual budget for fiscal 1977 included 6-year projections of gross national product, personal income, pretax corporate profits, average consumer price rise, and average unemployment rate, in addition to summaries of government revenues and outlays. The budget summary included in President Ford's budget message for fiscal 1977 was based upon the near-term assumptions and long-term projections shown in Table 10-9. This forecast of rising personal income and gross national product, accompanied by declining inflation and unemployment, was generally regarded as a highly optimistic scenario of future events. President Carter's recommended budget assumed somewhat higher outlays and a budget deficit approaching $60 billion for the fiscal year 1977 to 1978.

The Wharton Economic Forecast Associates, one of the leading university-sponsored economic-consulting firms, forecast in December 1976 that the current economic recovery would continue through 1977 and 1978, followed by a brief "growth recession" in 1979, with slower growth continuing thereafter through 1985. The selected indicators from the Wharton model forecast growth rates in the real GNP measured in 1972 dollars of about 4.2 percent from 1976 to 1980 and of only approximately 3.2 percent per

TABLE 10-9   United States Budget Summary 1976–1978 and Underlying Economic
Projections 1975–1982, Billions of Current Dollars

Budget Summary, 1976–1978			
	Fiscal year ending		
	June 30, 1976	Sept. 30, 1977*	Sept. 30, 1978
Revenues	$300.0	$354.0	$393.0
Outlays	366.5	411.2	440.0
Deficit	66.5	57.2	47.0
"Full employment" surplus	−24†	−26	−18
Total new authority	415.3	435.9	480.4

Underlying economic projections, 1975–1982			
	Calendar year		
	1975	1976	1977	1978
Gross national product	$1,516	$1,693	$1,880	$2,092
Personal income	1,250	1,375	1,521	1,684
Pretax corporate profits	114	150	172	194
Average consumer price rise	9.1%	5.7%	5.1%	5.4%
Average unemployment rate	8.5%	7.7%	7.3%	6.6%
	1979	1980	1981	1982
Gross national product	$2,334	$2,579	$2,784	$2,963
Personal income	1,879	2,075	2,242	2,389
Pretax corporate profits	218	243	263	280
Average consumer price rise	5.0%	4.6%	3.8%	2.9%
Average unemployment rate	5.7%	4.9%	4.8%	4.7%

* Total omitted for July 1 to Sept. 30, 1976, transition period to new fiscal year.

† This analytical balance assumes that revenues are as large as they would be if the economy were operating at the "full employment" level, defined as a jobless rate of 4% of the labor force. It also assumes correspondingly lower outlays for jobless benefits.

Source: The Budget of The United States Government Fiscal Year 1978, Executive Office of The President, Office of Management and Budget, Washington, pp. 41–42.

annum for 1980 to 1985. These forecasts were based upon an assumption of gradually declining rates of inflation from 6.7 percent in 1977 to less than 5 percent in 1980 and to 3.7 percent in 1985.

The Wharton Economic Forecast Associates provide a range of forecasts based upon varying assumptions concerning government monetary and fiscal policies. The following summary of the estimated annual rate of increase in selected indicators for the 5-year period ending in 1982 reflects an interpretation of alternative econometric forecasts for this period by a consulting economist advising the Real Estate Advisory Department of the First National Bank.

Economic index	Estimated annual rate of increase 1977–1982
GNP, current dollars	8%
1972 dollars	3%
Price-level deflator	5%
Wages	8%
Personal-consumption expenditures	8%
Interest rates	Irregular, no major change
Residential building:	Slightly higher to 1980, declining thereafter
Single-family starts	1.2 million per annum
Multifamily	0.5 million per annum
Total government expenditures	3%
Corporate profits	10%

A forecast like that above, if it is accepted as credible, provides highly significant information for the real estate investor or portfolio manager. First, it portrays a future scenario of continued economic growth accompanied by relatively modest inflation. It implies no major boom in residential construction, with a probability of rising house prices and rents. Rising corporate profits and consumer incomes are usually accompanied by high rates of industrial and business investment, while the outlook for rapidly rising consumer income seems to augur well for retail sales and shopping-center investments. The forecast of rising wages, inflation, and continued high interest rates suggests the probability of future rises in building costs, which might lead the real estate analyst to infer that new construction would not be stimulated to any large degree. This conclusion might lead to emphasis upon investment in existing buildings to avoid risks of new investment during a period of rising prices and construction costs.

National econometric forecasts are supplemented by regional forecasts for many areas, which endeavor to relate probable national economic growth to developments in smaller geographic areas. Chase Econometrics, a subsidiary of the Chase Manhattan Bank, provides periodic forecasts for the major regions of the United States. The director of regional economics for Chase Econometrics predicted in March 1977 that interregional differences in the rates of economic growth in the nation will probably decline over the next decade. He forecast, however, that the South would continue to have advantages in terms of lower labor costs, climate, lower energy costs, and other amenities, which would favor more rapid growth in that region. These regional forecasts often provide useful guidelines to the analyst seeking to determine the regional selection of real estate investments. Advance Mortgage Company, a subsidiary of Citibank, makes forecasts of

TABLE 10-10 Selected Economic Indicators, Georgia Annual Forecasting Model, Revised Control Solution, Jan. 25, 1977

Year	Gross state product (GSP) Current dollars (billions)	Change, %	1958 dollars (billions)	Change, %	Private nonagricultural GSP 1958 dollars (billions)	Change, %	Manufacturing output 1958 dollars (billions)	Change, %	Employment Millions	Change, %	Unemployment rate, %
1976	$35.36	13.93%	$18.33	8.29%	$15.67	8.75%	$5.04	12.51%	2.02	1.73%	7.58%
1977	39.97	13.03	19.66	7.29	16.89	7.81	5.40	7.00	2.10	3.92	5.77
1978	44.80	12.10	20.98	6.68	18.12	7.25	5.77	6.87	2.17	3.36	5.11
1979	49.02	9.41	21.81	3.97	18.86	4.12	5.95	3.19	2.23	2.70	4.94
1980	53.10	8.32	22.53	3.30	19.46	3.13	6.08	2.14	2.28	2.32	4.91
1981	58.14	9.50	23.69	5.14	20.46	5.17	6.37	4.72	2.33	2.39	4.74
1982	63.64	9.47	24.89	5.08	21.43	5.21	6.66	4.60	2.39	2.41	4.60
1983	69.22	8.76	25.91	4.11	22.42	4.14	6.90	3.58	2.44	2.24	4.67

Year	Personal income Total Current dollars (billions)	Change, %	Per capita Current dollars (thousands)	Change, %	Retail sales Current dollars (billions)	Change, %	1958 dollars (billions)	Change, %	Population (millions)	Atlanta consumer price index 1958 = 100	Change, %
1976	$27.59	11.21%	$5.52	10.22%	$15.92	12.74%	$ 8.25	7.15%	5.00	192.94	5.21%
1977	31.33	13.55	6.18	11.88	18.01	13.15	8.86	7.41	5.07	203.26	5.35
1978	35.25	12.50	6.85	10.85	20.19	12.09	9.45	6.66	5.15	213.59	5.09
1979	38.59	9.46	7.38	7.85	22.14	9.67	9.85	4.21	5.23	224.78	5.24
1980	41.77	8.26	7.88	6.67	23.96	8.23	10.17	3.21	5.30	235.71	4.86
1981	45.55	9.05	8.46	7.45	26.00	8.49	10.59	4.18	5.38	245.47	4.14
1982	49.48	8.63	9.06	7.03	28.21	8.48	11.03	4.14	5.46	255.71	4.17
1983	53.26	7.62	9.60	6.04	30.32	7.51	11.35	2.92	5.54	267.12	0.46

Source: Reproduced by permission of The College of Business Administration, University of Georgia.

regional housing-market conditions which provide further useful information for the real estate portfolio analyst. Supplementary analyses of the economic outlook in various Federal Reserve Bank districts are published in the *Monthly Review* for individual banks.[1]

State econometric models linked to the Wharton national model have been developed for Georgia, Mississippi, Kentucky, and Tennessee. California, Florida, Alabama and other states have similar models useful for state forecasting. These so called *piggy-back models* are designed to show the probable effects upon employment, incomes, and business activity in individual states which are likely to arise from national economic growth, energy, fiscal and monetary policies. Table 10-10 summarizes selected economic indicators for the Georgia economy from 1976 to 1982, based upon the Wharton model control solution assuming modest stimulation policies in 1977, referred to above. It can be noted that the anticipated growth rate for the Georgia economy is significantly higher than the summary interpretation of national indicators based upon the Wharton model December 1976 national projections. According to the Georgia model projections, personal income, population, and retail sales are expected to rise more rapidly for Georgia over the next 5 years than for the national as a whole. This type of economic analysis is of course highly relevant for the real estate portfolio analyst.

Past history has amply demonstrated, however, that even the best economic forecasts often prove unreliable. It should therefore be emphasized that the use of models and other forecasting aids requires skillful interpretation, a knowledge of their shortcomings, and evaluation of the assumptions implicit in the models used. These and other limitations impress upon the real estate portfolio analyst the need for diversification among various classes of investment as well as within each class.

IMPORTANCE OF DIVERSIFICATION

The basic uncertainties associated with the prediction of future economic, social, and political events place great emphasis upon the diversification of investment risks. The principle of diversification is embodied in the common adage that an investor should not put all his eggs in one basket. Many large corporations are able to achieve industrywide, regional, and international diversification through their very size and vertical and horizontal integration. The prospect of offering diversification and expert management in real estate investment was a prime selling point in the formation of REITs in the late 1960s. Unfortunately the investor was often disappointed to find

---

[1] An interesting review of population migration to the South is contained in the *Monthly Review*, Federal Reserve Bank of Atlanta, February 1977.

that many of these trusts became specialized funds, with emphasis upon construction loans, mortgages, or new development projects rather than upon a diversified portfolio of long-term real estate investments.

Diversification of investments has long been a principle of prudent investing. The Employee Retirement Income Security Act of 1974 (ERISA) provides in Section 404 that fiduciaries shall diversify investments under retirement or pension plans "so as to minimize the risk of large losses." This injunction should probably be interpreted as requiring diversification among different classes of securities (bonds, stocks, real estate) as well as diversification within each investment class by type of industry or property and diversification regionally.

Markowitz[1] has pointed out that effective diversification is achieved only if the various components of the portfolio tend to fluctuate in opposing fashion, so that the volatility of the portfolio's rate of return is significantly less than that of the individual components. The relationship between real estate returns and returns from other classes of investments will be discussed below.

CRITERIA FOR SELECTION OF REAL ESTATE INVESTMENTS

The criteria to be used for the selection of specific investments in each general class will vary with the availability of analytical techniques and data. It was argued in Chap. 3 that the internal rate of return, calculated by use of the discounted after-tax cash-flow technique, represented the most acceptable criterion for measuring returns from real estate investments. It was concluded, however, that the use of the IRR should be supplemented by other measures, e.g., overall rate of return, before-tax IRR, present values, gross income multiplier, net income multiplier, payback period, and cash on cash. Each of these measures, as explained more fully in Chap. 3, provides significant information to the real estate analyst and the investor.

Intelligent use of these measures of real estate investment returns requires careful interpretation and judgment. Appendix 3D illustrated the use of probability analysis in determining the most probable income stream from a real estate investment and the most probable reversionary value at the end of a holding period. The case study included in Appendix 5A illustrated how the analyst can use subjective probability analysis to deal with uncertain political events which lie in the future to determine the mean average return and the range and standard deviation of returns an investor might estimate in the future.

[1] Harry Markowitz, *Portfolio Selection*, Wiley, New York, 1959.

A CASE STUDY IN PORTFOLIO CONSTRUCTION

The Real Estate Advisory Department of the First National Bank has been asked to recommend a portfolio of real estate investments for clients of the bank wishing to invest $100 million in a diversified portfolio of real estate loans and equities. The clients have specified the following broad investment objectives:

1. The investors have $25 million in cash and plan to borrow $75 million at approximately 10 percent for 15 years, secured by mortgages.

2. A minimum after-tax return of 10 percent is expected on the portfolio for 5-year holding.

3. Equity interests should represent 75 percent of the assets, with 25 percent in mortgage loans and construction loans.

4. All mortgage loans are to be secured by first mortgages.

5. No investments shall be made in unimproved land or non-income-producing property.

6. The clients expect to be in a 40 percent tax bracket and will probably hold the portfolio as a limited partnership.

7. Investments are to be concentrated in the "sunbelt" states.

The Real Estate Advisory Department of the bank submitted the following proposed portfolio program for the fund, based upon the 5-year economic forecast provided by their consulting economist using the Wharton Forecasting model projections, summarized above:

Classes of investment and/or loans	Percentage of total assets
Joint ventures	15
Apartments (used)	20
Shopping centers	20
Office buildings	20
Long-term mortgages	15
Short-term construction and development loans	10
Total	100

Joint Ventures (15 Percent of Total Assets)

Many projected single-family subdivisions, apartment projects, and planned-unit developments were shelved during the early 1970s because of high financing costs, shortages of materials, and the lack of sufficient equity capital. In many cases architectural and land planning for these projects was completed and zoning permission granted. Housing markets in most sections of the nation have improved in the mid-1970s with rising sales prices and rents, declining vacancies, and improved mortgage-financing terms. It is recommended that the fund invest 15 percent of total assets in joint-venture residential property development in suburban areas of the South close to city, shopping, and transportation facilities. The economic forecast developed by our consultants indicated an average of 1.2 million single-family and 500,000 multifamily starts for the next 5 years, with an estimated 8 percent per annum increase in wages and personal consumption expenditures. An after-tax return of 15 percent can be expected on these proposed joint-venture investments, assuming good planning, construction, and marketing by the joint-venture partnership. The basis for the expected 15 percent after-tax returns is set forth in the accompanying tables.

Apartment Buildings (Used) (20 Percent of Total Assets)

Apartments are regarded as traditional prime investments because of their long economic life, stability of income, and interest and depreciation tax shelter. The changing age and family distribution of the population foretells high demand for apartments in future years. High and rising prices for single-family homes, increasing mobility of young professional people, high rates of divorce and separation, and the energy crisis all support the conclusion of an increased demand for apartments, particularly in suburban areas near transportation, recreation, and shopping facilities.

It is recommended that the fund invest approximately 20 percent of total assets in apartments for middle- and upper-income groups, with emphasis upon some of the more rapidly growing areas of the South, which are not presently overbuilt. Lease and rental contracts should be for short terms or include escalation clauses linking rent increases to inflation rates. The accompanying cash-flow analysis (Schedule 1) indicates a most likely return of 13 percent on used-apartment building investment.

Shopping Centers (20 Percent of Total Assets)

Despite overbuilding and vacancy problems in some localities, investors continue to be strong buyers of shopping-center investments because of their tax-shelter and inflation-protection features. Recent studies by the Urban Land Institute indicate that neighborhood centers have outperformed regional centers in some areas. It is recommended that the fund invest approximately 20 percent of total assets in well-located, established neighborhood centers with a record of or potential for increasing sales. The lease terms should include provision for a percentage rent above the specified rent, based upon gross sales of the center. As the economy improves and as personal-consumption-expenditures forecasts are realized, well-located

SCHEDULE 1 Pro Forma Cash-Flow Statement (Thousands) 0% inflation, 3-5-7 inflation,* 5% inflation

Assumed rates of inflation, %	Probability	Year					After-tax IRR, %	Total invested	Assumptions		
		1	2	3	4	5			Mortgage interest, %	Ratio mortgage loan to value, %	Depreciation, %
Joint ventures:											
0	0.1	$1,740	$1,680	$1,560	$1,500	$12,120	5.4	$15,000	10%	75%	200%
3-5-7	0.6	1,740	1,786	1,798	1,838	19,827	15				
5	0.3	1,740	1,860	1,920	1,980	25,380	20.1				
Apartments (used):											
0	0.1	1,920	1,840	1,760	1,680	18,000	5.6	20,000	10	75	125
3-5-7	0.6	1,920	1,997	2,078	2,162	25,497	13				
5	0.3	1,920	2,080	2,240	2,320	35,680	19.8				
Shopping centers:											
0	0.1	2,200	2,000	2,000	1,800	14,400	2.8	20,000	10	90	150
3-5-7	0.6	2,200	2,592	2,794	3,085	35,650	21.5				
5	0.3	2,200	2,600	3,200	3,600	58,400	32.7				
Office buildings:											
0	0.1	1,680	1,680	1,600	1,600	18,640	5.5	20,000	10	75	100
3-5-7	0.6	1,680	1,805	1,950	2,098	25,748	12.5				
5	0.3	1,680	1,920	2,080	2,320	36,320	19.5				
Long-term mortgages	9%	750	750	750	750	750	4.5	15,000	10		†
Short-term construction and development loans	12%	600	600	600	600	600	6.0	10,000			‡

* 3% sales price inflation, 5% gross income inflation, 7% expense inflation.
† 25-year loan.
‡ 12-month loan.

centers in growth areas should benefit. A high after-tax return of 21.5 percent can be expected if future economic developments follow the optimistic national forecasts cited above. It will be noted in the accompanying schedules and in Chap. 8 that this element of the portfolio can be expected to have a wide range of returns, owing to the importance of expected sales growth and expected selling-price increases. Competition between investors for purchase of the most successful centers can be expected to drive yields downward as the economy improves, and there are reasons to regard this forecast of returns over 20 percent as somewhat optimistic, even though a 90 percent loan-value ratio is assumed.

Office Buildings (20 Percent of Total Assets)

Expected cash flows from office-building investment have been lower than anticipated in many large cities over the past 5 years. Vacancy problems have been particularly acute in many large cities such as New York, Atlanta, Boston, Chicago, and Los Angeles. However, the economic climate looks brighter for office-building occupancy with projected future economic growth of the economy. Many new office structures are presently held by banks and other mortgage-lending institutions which were acquired under foreclosures. Relatively new office buildings in good suburban locations away from the path of city decay are prime candidates for purchase. It is recommended that approximately 20 percent of total assets be invested in office buildings acquired under joint venture or other arrangements to assure strong and continuing management. Rental-escalation clauses should be included in lease contracts as a hedge against rising operating costs and inflation. The accompanying schedules project that an average return of 12.5 percent on office building investment should be achieved.

Long-Term Mortgage Loans (15 Percent of Total Assets)

The economic forecast for the next 5 years indicates a continuing demand for mortgage loans at or close to present interest rate levels. In some cases mortgage loans may be made, providing for equity participations. However, all mortgage loans should represent first mortgages, and the prime consideration should be safety of principal and continuity of interest payments. Analysis of individual borrower characteristics and financial strength should supplement careful analysis of the property, its location, earnings, and future outlook. Loans should be limited to a maximum ratio of 75 percent of market value, with a minimum debt coverage of 1.5:1. An average before-tax yield of 9 percent is forecast in schedules for this portion of the portfolio.

**Short-Term Construction and Development
(C & D) (10 Percent of Total Assets)**

Short-term interim loans to developers with permanent "take-out" loans should provide the fund with some measure of liquidity. The forecast of an average total level of 1.7 million housing starts over the next 5 years indicates a continued demand for this type of credit. Although the commercial banks have traditionally dominated this market, unfavorable recent experience with some borrowers has caused some banks to withdraw from their leading role in construction loans and provided opportunities for others to enter the field. The analysis in the accompanying schedules is based on the assumption that returns on short-term construction loans including interest charges, fees, and discounts would range from 12 to 14 percent before taxes.

ANALYSIS OF PORTFOLIO RETURN

The pro forma 5-year cash-flow statement and rate of return analysis in Schedule 1 is based upon the percentage division of the portfolio described above and the assumed mortgage terms on investments and depreciation rates shown in Schedule 1. After-tax cash flows and rates of return are presented under three probability assumptions concerning future inflation: (1) zero inflation, (2) inflation of 3 percent in sales prices, 5 percent in gross income, and 7 percent in operating expenses, and (3) 5 percent inflation in sales prices, gross income, and operating expenses. Each of these assumptions has been assigned a probability in the analysis. It can be seen that a 60 percent probability is assigned to the second assumption identified as 3-5-7 percent in Schedule 1, with lower probabilities assigned to the other two assumptions. The analysis presents a range of returns for each class of investment shown in the column headed IRR.

Schedule 2 presents the returns for each class of investment as weighted average probable IRRs. A calculation of the probable standard deviation for each class of investment is also shown in Schedule 2, using standard statistical formulations discussed in Chap. 3.

Schedule 3 summarizes the weighted probable average after-tax returns for each class of investment for 5-year holding, the standard deviation for each class of investment, and the probable expected range of returns falling within the range of ±1 and ±2 standard deviations. It can be seen that the range of returns and the expected IRRs are both considerably higher for shopping centers than for other classes of investment, due in some measure to the assumption of a higher leverage (90 percent) for that category of investment.

SCHEDULE 2   Calculations of Return and Risk

Return (expected return)	Weighted average probable IRR, %
Joint ventures $(5.4\%)(0.1) + (15\%)(0.6) + (20.1\%)(0.3) =$	15.5
Apartments (used) $(5.6\%)(0.1) + (13\%)(0.6) + (19.8\%)(0.3) =$	14.3
Shopping centers $(2.8\%)(0.1) + (21.5\%)(0.6) + (32.7\%)(0.3) =$	23
Office buildings $(5.5\%)(0.1) + (12.5\%)(0.6) + (19.5\%)(0.3) =$	13.9
Long-term mortgages	4.5
Short-term C & D loans	6.0

Risk (standard deviation), %	
Joint venture: $[(5.4\% - 15.5\%)^2(0.1) + (15\% - 15.5\%)^2(0.6) + (20.1\% - 15.5\%)^2(0.3)]^{1/2} =$	4.09
Apartment (used): $[(5.6\% - 14.3\%)^2(0.1) + (13\% - 14.3\%)^2(0.6) + (19.8\% - 14.3\%)^2(0.3)]^{1/2} =$	4.20
Shopping centers: $[(2.8\% - 23\%)^2(0.1) + (21.5\% - 23\%)^2(0.6) + (32.7\% - 23\%)^2(0.3)]^{1/2} =$	8.39
Office buildings: $[(5.5\% - 13.9\%)^2(0.1) + (12.5\% - 13.9\%)^2(0.6) + (19.5\% - 13.9\%)^2(0.3)]^{1/2} =$	4.32
Long-term mortgages: $[(4\% - 4.5\%)^2(0.1) + (0)^2(0.6)^2(0.6) + (5\% - 4.5)^2(0.3)]^2 =$	0.1
Short-term C & D loans: $[(5\% - 6\%)^2(0.1) + (0)^2(0.6) + (7\% - 6\%)^2(0.3)]^{1/2} =$	0.4

Schedule 4 shows the weighted average portfolio return under the three inflation assumptions described above, with the most probable return indicated as 13.73 percent, with a standard deviation of 3.87 percent. This weighted-average standard deviation assumes that the rates of return on the various classes of real estate investments vary directly with each other and will not be inversely correlated over the holding period.

The portfolio in Schedule 4 appears to meet the general criteria set forth by the clients of the bank and should be satisfactory if they are willing to accept the basic assumptions in the consultant's economic analysis that inflation in the economy will proceed at a rate of at least 5 percent over the next 5 years and that it will be accompanied by relatively stable levels of employment and income growth. It also assumes that the Real Estate Advisory Department of the bank or some other expert management-consulting services are available to the client in selecting and managing the investment portfolio.

SCHEDULE 3 Recap of Expected Return and Risk Analysis

Outcome	Inflation, %	Prob- ability	Joint venture	Apartments (used)	Shopping centers	Office buildings	Long-term mortgages*	Short-term C & D loans*
Pessimistic	0	0.1	5.4%	5.6%	2.8%	5.5%	4%	5%
Most likely	3-5-7	0.6	15.0	13.0	21.5	12.5	4.5	6
Optimistic	5	0.3	20.1	19.8	32.7	19.5	5.0	7
Expected return			15.5	14.3	23	13.9	4.5	6

Risk analysis	Standard deviation, %	Range ±1 SD, 66% confidence interval, %		Range ±2 SD 95% confidence interval, %	
Joint ventures	4.09%	19.59%	→ 11.41%	23.68%	→ 6.97%
Apartments (used)	4.20	18.5	→ 10.10	22.70	→ 5.90
Shopping centers	8.39	31.39	→ 14.61	39.78	→ 6.22
Office buildings	4.32	18.22	→ 9.58	22.54	→ 5.26
Long-term mortgages	0.1	4.6	→ 4.4	4.7	→ 4.3
Short-term C & D loans	0.4	6.4	→ 5.6	6.8	→ 5.2

* Probabilities for long-term mortgages and short-term C & D loans are (0.25)(0.50)(0.25).

SCHEDULE 4 Analysis of Return and Risk for Entire Portfolio

		0% inflation (probability 0.1)		3-5-7% inflation (probability 0.6)		5% inflation (probability 0.3)	
		IRR, %	Risk	IRR, %	Risk	IRR, %	Risk
Joint ventures	15%	5.4%	= 0.0081	15%	= 0.0225	20.1%	= 0.0302
Apartments (used)	20	5.6	= 0.0112	13	= 0.260	19.8	= 0.0396
Shopping centers	20	2.8	= 0.0056	21.5	= 0.0450	32.7	= 0.0654
Office buildings	20	5.5	= 0.0110	12.5	= 0.0250	19.5	= 0.0390
Long-term mortgages	15	4	= 0.006	4.5	= 0.0067	5	= 0.0025
Short-term C & D loans	10	5	= 0.005	6	= 0.006	7	= 0.007
	100%		0.0469		0.1292		0.1837
Weighted IRR, %		4.69		12.92		18.37	

$(4.69\%)(0.1) + (12.92\%)(0.6) + (18.37\%)(0.3) =$ expected return 13.73%

Standard deviation $= [(4.69 - 13.73\%)^2(0.1) + (12.92\% - 13.73\%)^2(0.6) + (18.37\% - 13.73)^2(0.3)]^{1/2} = 3.87\%$

	Risk analysis	
	Range	
Standard deviation, %	66%	95%
3.87%	17.60% → 9.86%	21.47% → 5.99%

REAL ESTATE IN THE
INVESTMENT PORTFOLIO

It is useful to distinguish between the prediction of future prospects and returns for specific types of investment assets, i.e., *investment analysis,* and the prediction of the magnitude and variability of returns from portfolios, i.e., *portfolio analysis.*

An investment portfolio represents the result of an investor's choices between a wide range of assets, including insurance policies, savings accounts, bonds, stocks, mortgages, home ownership, and equity interests in real estate, oil, mining, and other ventures. We must assume that investors are uncertain of the future but not completely ignorant, unless we are prepared to resolve portfolio decisions by coin tossing or crystal gazing.

Investors seek to maximize the overall return on their portfolios and to minimize the variance of the return or risk. These objectives involve an inherent conflict since we have already observed that in order to increase returns, investors must accept higher risks. Investors usually resolve this dilemma by specifying some minimum rate of return they are willing to accept; alternatively they may specify some maximum degree of variability in returns.

The first step in portfolio construction is the formulation of beliefs about the expected yields and possible variations in yields which the investor may expect from various classes of investments to be included in the portfolio. The investor may also express some specific preferences or constraints with respect to maximum or minimum proportions of each class of investment in the portfolio.

Statistical techniques have been developed which enable the investor to calculate the rates of return on various portfolio mixes and the associated variance and standard deviations associated with each different portfolio. The use of these techniques assumes that it is possible to predict with some degree of accuracy the expected future returns from each class of investment and the expected variability in that return.

This technique of portfolio selection is associated with the early work of Markowitz and was set forth in more operational terms by Sharpe.[1] The following application of this method of portfolio selection is based upon a nontechnical exposition and case example.[2]

Covariance between various segments of a portfolio is the key to effective portfolio diversification. Covariance is a statistical measure of the degree of dependence between random variables. The sign of the covariance measure

[1] William F. Sharpe, *Portfolio Theory and Capital Markets,* McGraw-Hill, New York, 1970.
[2] J. Fred Weston and William Beranek, "Programming Investment Portfolio Construction," *Financial Analysts Journal,* May 1955; reprinted in *CFA Readings in Financial Analysis,* Institute of Chartered Financial Analysts, New York, 1966, pp. 719–729.

cov(X,Y) reveals whether X (common-stock returns) and Y (real estate returns), for example, vary directly or inversely with each other. Diversification reduces investment risk so long as the correlation between returns from two or more investments is less than +1. Measurement of the variance and standard deviation of the returns from a portfolio requires the calculation of the standard deviations for each component of the portfolio, as well as the covariance between the various components. The formula for the covariance between two components, which provides the basis for calculation of portfolio variance, is[1]

$$cov(X,Y) = r_{XY}(\sigma_X \sigma_Y)$$

Assume that the bank's client investor described earlier in this chapter wishes to decide upon the division of his total portfolio between three classes of investments, a municipal bond fund, common stocks (Standard and Poor's 500 stocks), and a diversified real estate portfolio. The hypothetical investor wishes to maximize after-tax cash-flow returns on the total portfolio subject to the following constraints:

1. The minimum yield on the overall portfolio shall be at least 8 percent.

2. Not more than 25 percent of his portfolio or less than 15 percent shall be invested in municipal bonds.

3. No more than 50 percent of his portfolio shall be invested in real estate investments.

4. The expected standard deviation of the overall after-tax return on the portfolio shall not exceed one-half of the mean average return.

ESTIMATING RETURNS ON INVESTMENT

Municipal bond funds are offered currently in mid-1977 to yield a 5½ percent after-tax return to investors. The investor accepts this pro forma annual yield as a basis for his portfolio structuring. From the economic forecast prepared for the bank it is estimated that 5½ percent will represent a true annual yield on the municipal bond fund investment for 5-year holding with no variation over the period.

Studies by Fisher and Lorie[2] of after-tax returns on a portfolio made up of all stocks listed on the New York Stock Exchange from 1926 to 1962 revealed annual returns of 10.1 percent without reinvestment of dividends on a "cash-to-cash basis from 1946 to 1965 for investors with an assumed income of $50,000."

The study summarized in Table 2-2 estimated after-tax returns on com-

---

[1] Ibid., p. 723.

[2] Lawrence Fisher and James H. Lorie, "Rates of Return on Common Stock: The Year-by-Year Record, 1926–1965," *Journal of Business*, vol. 41, no. 3, July 1969, pp. 291–316.

mon stocks in a range between 5.7 and 7.9 percent during the decade from 1952 to 1962. This estimate was closely equivalent to the average annual return of 7.3 percent reported by Fisher and Lorie for 1926 to 1962.[1]

There is general agreement that common-stock returns have been substantially lower over the past decade than in earlier postwar decades. A study of the internal rates of return on the Standard and Poor's 500-stock average shown in Table 2-4 indicated an average before-tax return of 7.2 percent, assuming a single investment in the 500-stock average in 1960 held until December 1973 with no reinvestment or borrowing. Ibbotson and Sinquefield[2] estimated an annual before-tax rate of return on a weighted average of the Standard and Poor's 500 stocks at 8.5 percent from 1926 to 1974, 9.4 percent from 1946 to 1974, 4.2 percent from 1960 to 1974, and at only 1.4 percent from 1967 to 1974. This study revealed that common-stock returns averaged approximately 15 percent per annum before taxes during most years from 1946 to 1970.

Relying upon the historical record of common stock returns cited above and the conclusion of the bank's consultant that corporate profits would rise at an average compound rate of 10 percent per annum for the 5-year period ending in 1981, the investor forecasts that the common-stock sector of his portfolio should provide a before-tax return of approximately 16 percent per annum for the next 5 years with an after-tax return of approximately 11 percent for the same period. From analysis of the record of volatility in common-stock returns from 1967 to 1973 shown in Table 2-4 it is estimated that the common-stock returns would have an expected standard deviation of approximately 6.4 percent over the period.

Historical real estate equity yields were reviewed in Chap. 2. Table 2-2 showed estimated real estate equity yields on an after-tax basis at 12.1 percent for the decade from 1952 to 1962. Figure 2-4 showed an estimated range of after-tax cash flow returns of 8 to 11.4 percent on net leased investments. It was observed in Chap. 2 that net leased investments tend to sell on a lower yield basis than other properties and that estimated returns vary with the assumed income tax bracket of the investor and with assumptions about future resale prices. The returns shown in Table 2-4 were also based upon the assumption that income would remain constant over a 10-year holding period.

From the evidence examined in Chap. 2, the author estimated that after-tax returns on equity real estate investment were in a range between 10 and 15 percent for 1967 to 1976. The estimated yield on the diversified portfolio recommended in the case study earlier in this chapter was 13.73

---

[1] Ibid.

[2] Roger G. Ibbotson and Rex A. Sinquefield, "Stocks, Bonds, Bills, and Inflation: Simulations of the Future (1976–2000)," *Journal of Business*, vol. 49, no. 3, July 1976, pp. 11–47.

TABLE 10-11   Forecasts of After-Tax Returns, Variances, Covariances, and Correlation
Coefficients for Municipal Bond Fund, Common Stock, and Real Estate Equity Investment*

Type of investment	1977–1981 Estimated mean average after-tax return, %	Standard deviation, %	Variance	Correlation coefficient	Covariance measures
Municipal-bond fund	5.5%	0	0	r_{12} 0	0
Common stock (Standard and Poor's 500)	11.	6.4	0.4096	r_{13} 0	0
Real estate equities and mortgages	13.73	3.87	0.1497	r_{23} 0.51	12.63

* See text for sources of estimated returns and standard deviations; covariance measures calculated by the author.

percent, with an expected standard deviation of 3.87 percent. It will be recalled that this estimated yield was based upon economic forecasts of continued high economic growth for the 5 years from 1977 to 1981, with moderate inflation. These expected yields for real estate investments were accepted by the investor as the basis for his overall portfolio analysis which follows.

Following Markowitz and Sharpe, we can present the summary in Table 10-11 of the investor's beliefs concerning future investment returns, their expected standard deviations and variance, and the covariance between returns on the three classes of assets to be included in the portfolio.

The estimated future returns for municipal-bond fund, common stocks, and real estate shown in Table 10-11 represent judgmental forecasts based upon past experience and the economic forecast summarized earlier. Specific assumptions by individual investors concerning the future will of course vary with their judgments concerning future economic growth, interest rates, political developments, and investor psychology.

The assumptions concerning the expected variance in returns for each class of investment and the covariance between returns from the three segments of the portfolio represent judgmental estimates based upon limited empirical evidence. For these reasons, the conclusions that follow with respect to portfolio composition should be viewed as illustrative of the use of an analytical technique for a hypothetical investor under specific assumptions and criteria rather than as a guide to portfolio structure for investors generally.

It is not surprising to observe in Table 10-12 that our hypothetical investor can raise the overall yields on his portfolio by maximizing the proportion of total funds in real estate investment. Three portfolios which meet the

TABLE 10-12 Estimated After-Tax Yields on Three Hypothetical Portfolios, 1977–1981*

Type of investment	Portfolio, %		
	A	B	C
Municipal-bond fund	25 %	20 %	15 %
Standard and Poor's 500	50	40	35
Real estate investments	25	40	50
Estimated mean average after-tax return	10.3	11.0	11.5
Standard deviation of portfolio returns	5.27	3.28	2.49
Range:			
±1	5.03 to 15.57	7.72 to 14.28	9.01 to 13.99
±2	−0.24 to 20.84	4.44 to 17.56	6.52 to 16.48

* See Table 10-11 for standard deviations and covariance measures.

criteria established by our hypothetical investor are outlined in Table 10-12. Note that the portfolio returns are higher when the proportion of the total portfolio invested in real estate is raised to the 50 percent maximum percentage specified by the investor. Investment of the minimum percentage of 15 percent in the municipal-bond fund leaves a balance of 35 percent for investment in common stocks. Table 10-12 shows that the expected return is higher and the standard deviation is lower for portfolio C than for portfolio A or B. Portfolio C also meets the other criteria set by the investor, since the standard deviation is less than one-half the mean expected return, which exceeds the minimum specified of 8 percent, and the proportion of the portfolio in real estate investments does not exceed 50 percent of the total.

The portfolios shown in Table 10-12, resulting from trial-and-error calculations, represent only three of the set of possible portfolios meeting the criteria of our hypothetical investor. A graphic analytical technique has been devised which makes it possible to determine the combinations of any three classes of investment in a portfolio. This technique, which is too complex for presentation here, identifies a set of "efficient" portfolios from which the investor can make his choice, depending upon the amount of risk or variance he is prepared to accept on his returns.[1]

It is also possible to calculate the portfolio returns and variance for an infinitely large number of combinations of specific securities and real estate investments with the aid of the computer.[2]

The extension of the Markowitz portfolio-selection technique in such detail represents a major forecasting and computational task. The opera-

[1] See Weston and Beranek, op. cit.
[2] Described in Sharpe, op. cit.

tional usefulness of the technique depends entirely upon the reliability of the forecasts of returns and variance for the individual portfolio components. These limitations restrict the application of these techniques at the micro-investment decision level to institutional investors with large analytical staffs and computer capabilities.

SUMMARY

Real estate investment and marketing institutions are evolving and changing rapidly in response to increasing investor interest and the expanded flow of savings into real estate assets. The analytical techniques employed in real estate investment analysis have lagged far behind those used in securities analysis and portfolio theory. The art of selecting individual real estate investments will probably continue to be practiced successfully only by professional high-income investors seeking tax shelter, who are prepared to accept the substantial economic, financial, and political risks involved.

Unfortunately, the debacle of the REITs during the 1970s resulted in heavy losses and disillusionment among many public real estate investors. It can be hoped that the industry and its institutions will respond to the large public and institutional interest in real estate investment by accelerating professionalization of its personnel and upgrading resources to meet the new challenges of serving the real estate investment clientele.

Index